Americans in Egypt, 1770–1915

Americans in Egypt, 1770–1915

Explorers, Consuls, Travelers, Soldiers, Missionaries, Writers and Scientists

CASSANDRA VIVIAN

McFarland & Company, Inc., Publishers

Jefferson, North Carolina, and London

From time to time the reader will note the transcription of Arabic words
in a quoted extract are not the same as in the spellings adopted in the text. In fact
one quotation may vary a spelling from a second one. There have been attempts to
standardize Arabic word spellings in English but to date no single standard
has been agreed to. The index has taken note of the various ways
a word is spelled in the text and within the quoted passages.

LIBRARY OF CONGRESS CATALOGUING-IN-PUBLICATION DATA

Vivian, Cassandra.
Americans in Egypt, 1770–1915 : explorers, consuls, travelers,
soldiers, missionaries, writers and scientist / Cassandra Vivian.

p.   cm.
Includes bibliographical references and index.

ISBN 978-0-7864-6304-6
softcover : acid free paper ∞

1. Americans — Egypt — History — 19th century.
2. Americans — Egypt — Biography.   I. Title.
DT102.A2V59 2012   305.813'06209034 — dc23   2012024583

BRITISH LIBRARY CATALOGUING DATA ARE AVAILABLE

Front cover image: Travelers to the pyramids in the 19th century were
eager to have a photograph taken by a number of professional
photographers who awaited them near the Sphinx
(Library of Congress); sand and sky © 2012 Shutterstock

Manufactured in the United States of America

*McFarland & Company, Inc., Publishers
Box 611, Jefferson, North Carolina 28640
www.mcfarlandpub.com*

To my country, that it may find its way back...

Table of Contents

Acknowledgments

This has been a work of many years and to thank everyone who influenced its progress is almost impossible.

My heartfelt thanks to the early readers who encouraged me in this project: Richard Lobban, professor emeritus of anthropology and African studies at Rhode Island College and executive director of the Sudan Studies Association; Jason Thompson, professor of Middle East history and author of multiple books on Egypt.

In addition, John M. Adams, director emeritus of the Orange County (California) Public Library and a former member of the Board of Governors of the American Research Center in Egypt, who guided me through the complex world of Theodore M. Davis, whom he has been researching for years; S.J. Wolfe, senior cataloguer and serials specialist for the American Antiquarian Society and author of *Mummies in Nineteenth Century America,* who read my manuscript and taught me that I did not know the difference between pronouns; Sandra Gamal, former librarian at Cairo American College, for her friendship and support; the Association for the Study of Travelers in Egypt and the Near East (ASTENE), where for ten years I presented papers on many of the subjects in this book and received ample encouragement; Deborah Manley, co-founder of ASTENE, who read draft after draft of this book, giving a British perspective to the discussion and keeping me focused, and her sister Peta Ree, who likewise read drafts and then gave me the most important citation in regard to Francis Barthow; Russell McGuirk, who reviewed and commented on several chapters; Derek Welsby of SARS, who helped sort out the names of the rapids on the Nile in the Sudan; Yvonne Neville-Rolfe, also of ASTENE, for a wonderful weekend at her home in England where I read the letters of her ancestor Joseph Bonomi and the correspondence of George Gliddon; and a special thanks to Drs. Jochen and Gabriele Halof, who translated John Antes's letters from Bristol and portions of the Moravian journal from Herrenhut, Germany.

Permissions for photos: Thanks to The American University in Cairo Press for the map of Mamluk Cairo from Caroline Williams's *Islamic Monuments in Cairo.* To Doris Behrens-Abuseif for the map from her book *Azbakiyya and Its Environs from Azbak to Ismail 1476–1879.* To the Naval History Center for the images related to William Eaton. To the Presbyterian Historical Society of the Presbyterian Church for the portrait of Anna Young Thompson.

Permissions for journals, letters, and other unpublished material: the American Philosophical Society in Philadelphia for letters from John Antes and George Gliddon to various persons; the Moravian Archives in both Herrnhut, Germany, and London, England, for the right to translate a number of letters from John Antes to various persons and to translate portions of the Moravian journal written in Cairo for many years; the Maryland Historical Society for permission to refer to and use the *Journal from Cairo on to Wadi Halfa* by Mendes Cohen; the New-York Historical Society for a letter from Luther Bradish; the Academy of Natural Science of Philadelphia for an unpublished biography of George Gliddon; the Clements Library of the University of Michigan for letters from the Benjamin Brown Collection; the Sophia Smith Collection of Smith College for permission to quote from material about Charles Hale; the University of Virginia Library for permission to quote from the Papers of William Sydney Thayer; and the Presbyterian Historical Society for permission to use the *Diary of a Trip on the Ibis* by Anna Young Thompson.

Preface

American sources are mostly ignored when scholars study modern Egypt. The assumption was and is that Americans were either not in Egypt during the nineteenth century or they had nothing of importance to say. Neither reason is intellectually valid. My first realization that there was an interesting and understudied American experience in Egypt was when I lived there from the 1970s to the 1990s. No one talked about Americans or what role they played in the foreign presence in Egypt. For most of that time I worked at the The American University in Cairo Press: first in the English Department and later as the marketing manager of The American University in Cairo Press. So I mingled with contemporary scholars on a regular basis at work, in conferences, and at cocktail parties. The interesting discussions often referred to British exploitation, French cultural achievements, and German exploration, but as for Americans, the comments were often caustic about current American involvement in the Middle East. It became obvious the American presence in Egypt was an area plump for research.

Once my research got underway it became clear that the Americans were indeed in Egypt and they were there in great numbers. It is an entire field of study. The sheer volume of material by Americans on all aspects of Egyptian life made it necessary to focus on one area. I began at the beginning. The subject of this volume is Americans in Egypt from the earliest known reference through to the commencement of World War I. The world changed after the First World War, and so did America. The focus was still too broad to cover everything that needed to be mentioned, so I had to narrow my subject to a few personalities who would reflect the American attitude about Egypt mostly in the nineteenth century. To select those subjects I divided the Americans into genres: explorers, consuls, travelers, soldiers, missionaries, writers, and scientists.

What these Americans saw and how they interpreted it is what is important. This book informs. It does not analyze. That is left to others. In presenting the long-overlooked American voice it is not my obligation to present alternate points of view. Let the reader take what I have written and compare it, debate it, accept it, or reject it. My mission is to bring to the front what Americans saw, did, and thought while in Egypt. Their voices have been silent too long. The importance of the American observations in Egypt differs by topic. When a traveler talks of a tour along the Nile, his or her observations are valuable to see the condition of the monuments, the method of travel, the name of the hotel, and who was also on the Nile at that time. The weight of the voice rises when Americans were involved in historically significant events like the expedition to Sudan in 1820, the exploration of the Nile in Uganda in 1874, the expulsion of the Khedive Ismail in 1879, the establishment of the Mixed Courts, and the

Bombardment of Alexandria in 1882. The American viewpoint mostly supports Egypt against the Europeans who took control of the country. That is why there are so many lengthy quotes in the pages to follow. I have purposely chosen to use the exact words of the authors so there is no question as to their message. I am not saying everything the Americans did or saw or concluded is true. The Americans had their own bias. I am saying the voices recorded here are their point of view.

It becomes obvious why the American voice is important to any discussion about modern Egypt. Not so obvious is the error that has been introduced into history by not knowing what the Americas did and achieved in Egypt. Correcting those longstanding errors is also an important aspect of this book. Whenever I used an American source in my various books on Egypt I was often challenged. For example, I called the valley in the Western Desert where the fossils of the great whales were found, Wadi Zeuglodon. Zeuglodon was the name that the German scientist Georg Schweinfurth had given to the whales he discovered in the region in 1879. The name was based on the same species discovered and named in Alabama in the 1830s. While we were editing my book *The Western Desert of Egypt: An Explorer's Handbook,* the AUC editor questioned my use of Wadi Zeuglodon because a reputable English naturalist living in Egypt had never heard of it. He called the valley Wadi Hitan, the Arabic name that appeared on English maps of Egypt. I, of course, produced the appropriate quotes, and we moved on. The chapter on Charles Chaillé-Long will illustrate what a longstanding problem I had fallen prey to: the explorer's right to name a discovery. It has been an ongoing dispute between nations for centuries. I have had dozens and dozens of similar incidents over facts I drew from American sources that most Europeans, including experts in various fields, had never read.

The English-language history of the nineteenth century was written by British writers and historians. England was a country at the peak of its empire and, as with any nation, its citizens wrote history as viewed through its own needs and interests. Most of English-speaking America accepted the English version of international history as fact. But Egypt was a country coveted by many nations and they all created and recorded the history of events as they saw it. France, Russia, Italy, and Germany each have a plethora of literature about Egypt. Each tells a slightly different version of the various events that transpired through the tumultuous nineteenth century. America was the same. American archives are filled with dynamic and controversial opinions. The problem is too few have used them in modern research.

As mentioned, the Americans were witness to not only the daily lives of the Egyptians and foreigners in Egypt but to the major events that both glorified and demeaned the Egyptians and their way of life. The majority of Americans were primarily travelers, who not only recorded their impressions of Egyptian artifacts and wonders, but also witnessed events and noted who was there when. No matter the event, through the nineteenth century an American voice recorded the details. From the early explorers through the establishment of an American consular system, the arrival of American travelers, the pens of American writers, the proselytizing of American missionaries, and the discoveries of American scientists, the rich American experience in Egypt is recorded in thousands and thousands of government publications and personal books, journals, and letters published and unpublished. These men and women recorded their impressions through an American psyche and present a unique and surprising perspective.

Research into Americans in the nineteenth century paints a picture of an America of another time. It was a country following the mandate of George Washington: non-intervention. Although American leaders felt sympathetic to other colonial nations, they tried to not interfere. The United States and Egypt had many similarities in dealing with Europe. As France and England created the turmoil around the establishment of the Suez Canal, the United

States protested. When the Europeans pushed for the removal of the Khedive Ismail, the United States protested. When foreign powers established the mixed courts, the United States sided with Egypt. When England invaded Alexandria, the United States objected. Nineteenth-century America championed the Egyptians against British and French imperialism time and time again. The British and French, in turn, fought against American strides in Egypt, scoffed at American achievements, and censored the record of the American experience in Egypt. They succeeded. Even Americans do not study America in Egypt in the nineteenth century.

I researched this subject on three continents, in libraries, in historical societies, in personal papers, and on the Internet. Once I selected the individuals, I presented their involvement in Egypt at conferences, mainly at ASTENE, the Association for the Study of Travelers in Egypt and the Near East. Through them I connected with many experts in the field and learned of many sources. John Antes was my first topic. I found letters and journals, but they were in old German. Two ASTENE attendees, Drs. Jochen and Gabriele Hallof, worked with me. They went to Herrnhut, Germany, where the journals were located, acquired a microfilm copy for themselves and another for me, and translated some of the material for me to use in this book. In addition I found letters from John Antes in Bristol, England. Again, they were in German. Again, they were translated by Gabriele. Much of the Antes material is new material, in English for the first time. John Antes's clear voice on Egypt is finally heard, as is ample evidence of his heritage. I have but touched the surface of what is available in the Moravian archives in Herrnhut and Bristol.

In almost every chapter there is previously unpublished information that will change what we thought we knew about the person or the event: naval records, letters from the Huntingdon Library in California, and Thomas Jefferson's papers, revealed that William Eaton's persona was vastly exaggerated by a 1950s biographer; consular records from the National Archives prove that Francis Barthow remained in Egypt all of his life and founded an American family in Egypt; and a review of the events around the discovery of the source of the Nile tells us that we can no longer deny Charles Chaillé-Long his place in this saga.

All researchers owe gratitude to two pioneer books that gathered much of the American experience together in the past: David H. Finnie's *Pioneers East: The Early American Experience in the Middle East,* which was published by Harvard University Press in 1967; and John H. Wilson's *Signs and Wonders Upon Pharaoh,* published by the University of Chicago in 1964. Although they give us a strong foundation for exploring American sources, modern scholars cannot depend upon them for total accuracy. Research capabilities have become much more sophisticated since these pioneers delved into the history of Americans in Egypt. *Signs and Wonders* credits Mendes Cohen as "the first vessel on the Nile to fly the stars and stripes" in 1832. William Eaton had accomplished that deed in 1804. Both *Pioneers East* and *Signs and Wonders* give the honor of being the first known American in Egypt to John Ledyard. Not true. John Antes was in Egypt for twelve years before Ledyard arrived. Unfortunately this error has been perpetuated in an ever-growing number of new books.

The need is clear. We are at the dawn of a new century and as the years unfold, the anniversaries of these events (200 years old) will occur and newer publications will appear. While I have been researching, three already have. In 2005, *The Gates of Africa* (about the African Association), by Anthony Sattin; *American Traveler: The Life and Adventures of John Ledyard, the Man Who Dreamed of Walking the World,* by James Zug; and *The Pirate Coast: Thomas Jefferson, the First Marines, and the Secret Mission of 1805,* by Richard Zacks, were published. They are excellent. I cannot say the same for the History Channel's presentation of *The Battle of Tripoli* in 2004. It is fraught with errors. Samuel Edwards, in *Barbary General:*

The Life of William H. Eaton, exaggerates the story of William Eaton's journey and gives Eaton the air of Lawrence of Arabia, who fought in the Arabian Peninsula during World War I, more than a hundred years later. This type of mistake must not occur again. My text reexamines old material in the light of recent revisionism and introduces new material that leads to a fresh perspective of Americans in Egypt. It corrects the longstanding errors.

When Google Books became a reality my job became easier. Many of the hard-to-find texts located in libraries a fair distance from my home became available on Google. I was able to download them to my desktop. More important, they were searchable. The ability to search the book via keywords saved me enormous time and effort. This resource also means that scholars can no longer ignore the Americans because they cannot find the material. It is available and it is free. This is a bonanza to scholars.

I do not credit myself with discovering all the hidden information about Americans in Egypt. John Ledyard's grave has eluded me. I have not found any modern descendants of Francis Barthow in Alexandria. Determining how George Bethune English died is another failure. I was able to discover who was not Khalil Aga, but his true identity is still a mystery. Likewise, I know the Stone family lived near Muhammad Farid Street in Zamalek, but I did not find the exact villa where the drama in Fanny's diary took place. Hopefully, I have created the foundation upon which others will build.

The story of Americans in Egypt cannot be told in a single volume if it is expected to have any depth. There is just too much material and too many genres. The task of organizing the vast amount of material was long and difficult. Early on I decided to limit the research to the nineteenth century. That expanded into the eighteenth century with the inclusion of John Antes and John Ledyard. Further it expanded into the first decades of twentieth century when my publisher decided it was important to include Theodore M. Davis. As noted, I organized the text into seven major categories: explorers, consuls, travelers, soldiers, missionaries, and scientists, including archaeologists, Egyptologists, and paleontologists. Within each category there were hundreds of possibilities, so narrowing it further was again a time-consuming effort. I tried to pick two or three personalities for each genre. Sometimes the choice was obvious, like John Antes, the first known American in Egypt, but sometimes the choice was difficult, such as Charles Hale, an American consul general at mid-century. A more obvious choice for an American consul would have been Elbert Farman, an exceptionally astute observer and excellent writer. In fact, I had originally chosen him. But Farman is featured in no fewer than three chapters in the book, so his voice will be heard although he has not been selected to have a chapter unto himself. Once the choices were made I decided not to organize the book by genre, which would have been confusing because background about events would be out of order, but to organize the chapters chronologically. In that manner I could set the stage of events going on around my subjects, including the physical development of both Cairo and Alexandria, the improvements in communications, and the inroads of foreign powers into the government of Egypt.

As I read the material it became obvious that the original presence of each of the personalities in this book deserved to be heard. It is not my voice or my assessment that is important. What is important is what the people had to say and how they said it. Although the American presence in Egypt has been all but silent for nearly two centuries, as one reads these few Americans it becomes clear the voices are strong, plentiful, and beautifully articulated.

Introduction

If one knows anything about Egyptian history one is aware that foreigners have been visiting Egypt since the dawn of time. There are reports from all millennia telling us of the wonders of Egypt. They were written by monks, traders, explorers, invaders, and geographers in a myriad of languages. So visitors from the New World came very, very late to the Egyptian scene. The first Americans came by sea. Sailing ships from American ports were plying the Mediterranean Sea and Indian Ocean by the 1600s, well before the new country was born. Once the United States had a navy, the Americans, like every other nation, had the habit of "showing the flag": having their naval fleets visit ports not only as a courtesy, but to show their influence and strength. The Navy commanders became America's first diplomats, delivering messages to heads of state, observing the political and economic aspects of the country, and writing reports back to their superiors. Disgruntled sailors would take these opportunities to abandon ship and there may have been dozens of Americans in Egypt who left no trace.

But at the ebb of the eighteenth century a new breed of visitor would set foot in the Nile Valley, a breed that would explore, examine, dissect, and delve into ancient, medieval, and modern Egypt with an unending curiosity and an unbelievable intrusion into every aspect of Egyptian life. The new modern influx began when Napoleon invaded Egypt in 1798 and the Albanian mercenary Mohammad Ali united the country in 1805. For the first time in centuries, foreign experts were welcome in Egypt. It was a seminal moment, for the next 200 years would bring about incredible changes.

Europeans, encouraged by the French savants' *Description d'Égypte,* realized once again that Egypt was a rich plum at the crossroads of the world. The United States, although fearful of foreigners, looked to the Ottoman Empire, of which Egypt was a vassal, in the hopes of forming trade relations. Such ventures with the Ottomans were discussed by the Continental Congress as early as 1774, but the actual cementing of the relationship did not happen until the 1830s, over fifty years later.

The first American whom we can document in Egypt is John Antes. His voice is, perhaps, one of the strongest and most interesting of all the Americans. His observations of daily life in Cairo in the latter part of the eighteenth century, as the Mamluk rule was nearing its end, are as refreshing today as they were when they were first written. These views reflect the American spirit.

John Ledyard has received far less recognition than is his due when it comes to his achievements around the world, and more recognition than he deserves in relation to Egypt. He was in Egypt for three months. His mission in North Africa was to cross the continent east to west to look for the source of the Niger River. He was to begin his quest in Cairo when he died.

William Eaton was an American soldier, diplomat, and adventurer who came to Egypt in 1804 with the blessing of President Thomas Jefferson. His task was to find the Libyan exile Hamet Karamanli, cross the northern coast of the Libyan Desert, attack Derna, and set Karamanli on the throne of Tripoli. Where the British agents in Egypt were most cooperative, the French agent, Mr. Drovetti, was extremely uncooperative. He pulled America into the intrigues of Western powers in Egypt.

Among the first American expatriates to settle in Egypt was Francis Barthow. There is evidence that Barthow, a sea captain trading in the Red Sea, was in Egypt as early as 1805, maybe earlier. By 1813, he spoke fluent Arabic, had set up housekeeping in Alexandria, and was guiding foreigners up the Nile. Barthow became an agent of the Greek antiquities collector Anastasi and aided Henry Salt, the British agent in Cairo, in the discovery, capture, and sale of Egyptian antiquities. Francis Barthow's son, Victor Barthow, became American consul in Cairo in the 1870s. As far as is known, the descendants of Francis Barthow still reside in Egypt.

George Bethune English resigned a commission in the U.S. Navy while in Alexandria, Egypt. With the help of the British Consul Henry Salt, English was appointed Commander of Artillery for the Egyptian Army, and with his fluent Arabic, was able to travel up the Nile as far as Sennar, an amazing journey. He traveled with two other Americans, Khalil Aga and Achmed Aga, and recorded his journey in a book published in England and the United States.

Once American diplomatic relations were established with the Ottoman Porte, a consul was named to create and protect American interests in Egypt, a vassal to Constantinople. John Gliddon, an Englishman, was given that post. His son George Robbins Gliddon was appointed vice-consul, serving in Cairo. For a number of years the Gliddon family tried to build commercial ventures between the two countries and catered to the few Americans who were traveling in Egypt.

Among the travelers the Gliddons serviced were Richard and Sarah Rogers Haight of New York. Sarah wrote one of the first American guidebooks and is perhaps the first American woman to publish an account of her travels to Egypt. George Gliddon sent the couple south in his own boat and arranged their entire tour. Their journey forms the core of Sarah's book and reflects the typical tour on the Nile in the 1830s. Back in America, the Haights subsidized George Gliddon's work in the United States.

Bayard Taylor was a master craftsman. No one told the story of the adventures on the Nile as well as Taylor did. He began in Alexandria and went south nearly two thousand miles to beyond Khartoum. He wanted to go further, but time, conditions, and the river stopped him. Taylor was one of America's best travel writers. No one quotes him. Yet, his descriptions are highly quotable.

Charles Hale, as the title of his chapter suggests, is an enigma. He came from a distinguished American family, yet he seems to have been less a gentleman than the remainder of his family. While in Egypt he accomplished many things, including writing the guidelines for the consular courts and the capture of one of Abraham Lincoln's assassins. But he also became embroiled in shady and illegal dealings surrounding the protégé system.

Charles Chaillé-Long was an arrogant, flamboyant American hero. His adventures in Egypt spanned over thirty years and in each year he was involved in interesting, dangerous adventures. From Uganda, where he discovered a lake and the link to the river, to Alexandria, where he helped Americans during the bombardment of 1882, he was at the forefront of events. He told the world all about it in a number of books and never stopped lamenting that the world did not give him his due. He was right.

Ulysses S. Grant arrived in Egypt during his tour of the world. He was accompanied by a number of travelers, including newspapermen who reported his progress to American audiences. He was treated as the King of America and received every possible service while he traveled on the Nile. His every move in the valley of the Nile appears in a bevy of books, some excellent studies of life along the river.

Fanny Stone was not an American soldier, but her father was Charles Pomeroy Stone, head of the Egyptian Army for many years. When the British bombarded Alexandria in 1882, Fanny, back in Cairo with her mother and sisters, kept a diary of events. It is a most compelling account of what was happening to this American family during that trying time.

Anna Young Thompson was an American missionary who devoted her entire life to the Egyptian people. She arrived in Egypt as a young woman, and she died and was buried there in her old age. In between she was a moving force in missionary schools and fought for the rights of women, both American missionary women and Egyptian women, all her life. I have chosen a specific incident in Anna's life for this book. It sums up not only her personality, but her integrity and determination.

Walter Granger came by accident to this book. I intended to do Henry Fairfield Osborn, but discovered in my research that the heart and soul of the expedition of the American Museum of Natural History to Egypt was not Osborn, although he created the project, but Granger, who implemented the plan. Granger's diary of the expedition is filled with interesting observations on yet another aspect of the wonders of Egypt: the prehistoric desert fossils and artifacts.

Theodore M. Davis was the most elusive of subjects. Bits and pieces of his life are available, but not easy to find. Davis has received too much criticism and not enough praise. Although a scoundrel when it came to acquiring his fortune in America, his work in Egypt advanced our knowledge of the ancient civilization. His work in the Valley of the Kings was prolific and rewarding.

I make no excuses for the Americans. If the American voice creates controversy, good. If it pushes people to compare, good. If it distorts, let us hear about it. If it brings about a better truth, that is the best thing that could happen. For the truth of what happened in Egypt in the nineteenth century is found by comparing all the voices from all the languages, including the Egyptian voice. We are just beginning to do that, and this book will provide references for scholars who are revisiting these events.

Set your heart on being a scribe, for a book is of greater value than a house, than the tombs in the west. It is more beautiful than a castle, or than a sculptured slab in a temple.

— anonymous ancient Egyptian

1

John Antes: A Forgotten American Voice (Missionary, 1770)

It is difficult to understand how Egyptologists and other scholars fail to recognize John Antes as an American in Egypt. Yet, consistently, in past and newly published literature, he is not credited as the earliest known American in Egypt. In fact, he is not recognized as an American at all. He was not an archaeologist. He was not an Egyptologist. But he was an American, and through his books, journals, and letters, during his twelve-year sojourn in Egypt, he contributed significantly to the West's understanding of the valley of the Nile.

Antes did not help us when, in his book published in 1800, he claimed, "I consider myself an Englishman...."[1] In contradiction, he called himself an *Americano* when he wrote a violin trio while he was in Egypt (*Tre Trii per due Violini e Violoncello, Obligato, Dedicati a Sue Excellenza il Sig G J de Heidenstam, Ambassatore de Sa Maj il Ri de Suede a Constantinopel, Composti a Grand Cairo dal Sig Giovanni A T S Dilletante Americano. Op. 3.)* and six complete *Quartettos.*[2] In writing a letter to Benjamin Franklin, in his poor writing and spelling, he said, "If I could here be of any Service to my Mother Country or to you in Particular I should always embrace every Opportunity with the greatest Plassure"; "May God grand soon Peace to the Satisfaction of all to our Mother Country, for wich I have still the greatest Regard, and wish well to evry Individual of it from the bottom of my heart"; and "Pray excuse the Trouble I give you with my long Letter and bad Language. Be assured that it comes from a cordial and sincere American Heart."[3] This letter is ample evidence that John Antes considered himself American.

John Antes was born on March 24, 1740, in Frederick Township, Pennsylvania colony. He was, in fact, a native-born American, and a gifted American. As a craftsman, John Antes shaped handmade violins and cellos which musical scholars credit as the first such instruments in America. As a composer he created music for his instruments, noted as the first such music composed in America. As a writer he described his mission and observations in copious diaries, extensive missionary journals, and several books in which, as we shall see, he identified himself as an American. Antes was as intelligent as he was logical, and as observant as he was studious. His combined abilities created an informative mosaic of his adventures in Egypt before the arrival of Napoleon and his army.[4] Any country should be proud to claim him. We may find another American who was in Egypt prior to Antes, but it is doubtful he stayed as long as Antes did, wrote as profusely about it, or presented such an American persona in the valley of the Nile.

Antes was the eighth child of what would become a distinguished American family. His father, Johann Heinrich Antes (1701–1755), was descended from the noble German von Blume family, which had lost its title after years of unrest in the Rhineland region of Germany. Heinrich emigrated to America in 1720. Twenty-one years later, in 1741, the Moravian Brethren came to Pennsylvania to establish a religious colony. John Antes opened a carpenter shop in Bethlehem, Pennsylvania, in 1762. There he helped supply the Moravian homes with stools, chairs, cabinets, and his famous musical instruments. From the fine Pennsylvania hardwoods, John Antes slowly and painstakingly carved, planed, and fitted delicate violins, then violas, and ultimately cellos and harpsichords. These instruments are believed to be the first of their kind crafted in America and he is recognized as the first American to do this.[5]

In 1764, when he was 24 years old, John Antes left Pennsylvania for Herrnhut, Germany, to train as a missionary. While in Germany, in addition to preparing to become a missionary, Antes learned a new trade: clockmaking. It would serve him well in Cairo. On January 13, 1770, after months of religious preparation, John Antes set sail for Egypt as a member of the Moravian Brethren of Herrnhut, Germany, one of the first Western Christian missionary sects in Egypt.

Egypt in the 1700s

Egypt at the end of the eighteenth century was not the great commercial empire it had once been. Yet the great *wakalas* (market houses) were still full of merchandise and the pungent aromas of coffee and spices still filled the air. Although the apogee of Islamic art and architecture had passed, its results still graced the community in the form of elegant homes, great mosques, spectacular mausoleums, and working *madressas* (schools). Although it was still a vassal to the Ottoman Empire, Cairo's rulers fought to gain their independence. The bazaars of Cairo still thrived. The silk merchants' bazaar displayed rich damasks, precious brocades, soft and elegant silks. In *al-Sukkariyyah*, Sugar Street, exotic pastries, candies, nougats, and sweet-coated nuts tempted the palate. Cairo was an exciting mosaic.

The Cairenes lived in a Cairo that had expanded beyond the walled city the tenth century Fatimid rulers built on the plains and marshes east of the Nile. To the southeast, perched upon the Mokattam Hills, was Sala-al-din's enormous eleventh-century Citadel. The Turkish-appointed rulers, who lived in the Citadel, came in and out of power so frequently that most history books do not list them. They lived in isolation from the Mamluks, former slave rulers, whom they had conquered in 1517. On the plain below the Citadel a *suq* and camel market filled the square, while the latticed-windowed, courtyarded mansions of the Mamluk Beys exited the northern edge of the square along the Darb al-Ahmar. That road fell down the gentle slope to the southern gate of the Fatimid city (Bab Zuwayla).

The banner-hung streets of Cairo bustled with a cacophony of sounds and smells. Donkeys, camels, and horses filled the narrow passages, pushing and carrying men, and sometimes women, dressed in a variety of Middle Eastern garbs, to bathhouses, markets, mosques, and churches. Street vendors sold *fuul* beans, sweetmeats, and fresh cool licorice drinks. One street held the coppersmith shops, another the glass blowers, a third the gold merchants. There was an entire street devoted to musical instruments which John Antes surely patronized. Scribes, like their Pharaonic ancestors, sat cross-legged in corners ready to write letters or other documents for anyone who asked and paid them. Bookbinders handcrafted fine hard-bound books. Muezzins sang the call to prayer from hundreds of minarets five times a day.

Opposite: **Map of Mamluk Cairo from *Islamic Monuments in Cairo* by Caroline Williams (courtesy The American University in Cairo Press).**

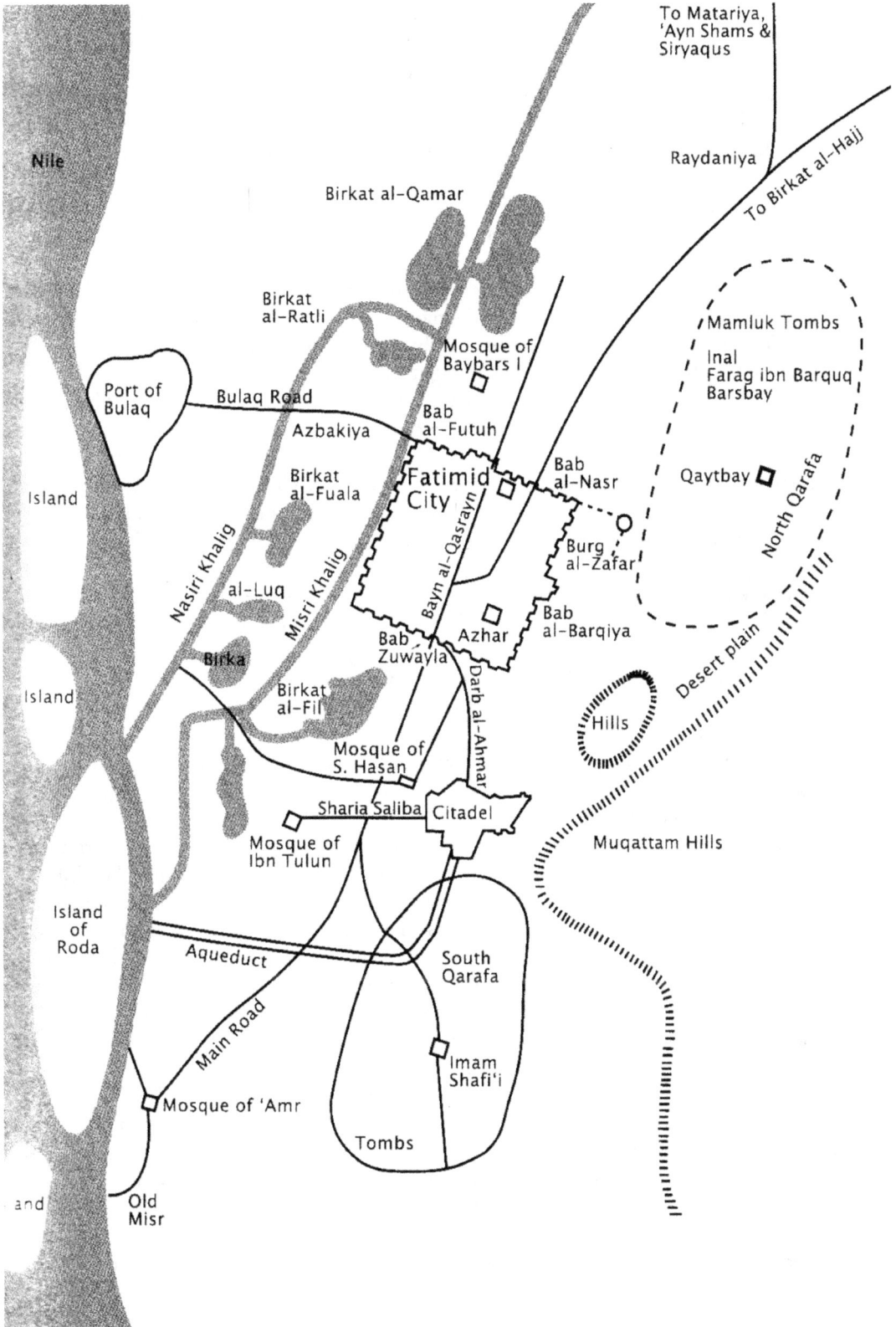

Nile

Birkat al-Qamar

Birkat al-Ratli

To Matariya, 'Ayn Shams & Siryaqus

Raydaniya

To Birkat al-Hajj

Mosque of Baybars I

Port of Bulaq

Bulaq Road

Azbakiya

Bab al-Futuh

Mamluk Tombs

Inal
Farag ibn Barquq
Barsbay

Island

Birkat al-Fuala

Fatimid City

Bab al-Nasr

Qaytbay

North Qarafa

Nasiri Khalig

al-Luq

Misri Khalig

Bayn al-Qasrayn

Burg al-Zafar

Birka

Island

Birkat al-Fil

Azhar

Bab al-Barqiya

Desert plain

Bab Zuwayla

Darb al-Ahmar

Hills

Mosque of S. Hasan

Sharia Saliba   Citadel

Island of Roda

Mosque of Ibn Tulun

Muqattam Hills

Aqueduct

South Qarafa

Main Road

Imam Shafi'i

Mosque of 'Amr

and

Old Misr

Tombs

To the west of the city were several canals and a number of lakes. On festive evenings the lakes were festooned with magic lanterns of many colors. Colorful boats lazily floated by. Music filled the air. This area was where the foreigners, the "Franks," lived. Further southwest was Bulaq, Cairo's river port. It stood along the eastern bank of the Nile separated by a few miles from the city it served. Its shoreline buzzed with cargo being loaded and unloaded to travel up the Nile into Africa or down the river to Alexandria and the Mediterranean. From most of the walls of the city the ancient pyramids were visible across the Nile in far-off Giza, accessible over a cultivated plain.

The Egyptian political climate was undergoing tremendous change when John Antes arrived. In 1760, the Mamluk Ali Bey al Kabir overthrew the Ottoman ruler in Egypt and reinstated the Mamluk regime, whose system had managed to survive through more than two hundred years of oppression. It had been the most unusual power system the world had ever devised. The word *mamluk* means *slave,* and that is what these rulers were. As young men they were sold into "white" slavery and brought to Egypt to be trained as warriors and to enjoy lives of privilege and command. There were two types of Mamluks in Egypt. The young Turkish slaves from near the Caspian Sea were called *Bahri,* meaning *from the sea,* for their original barracks were on Roda Island in the Nile. They established Mamluk rule in 1250. The rival Mamluks, the *Burgi,* meaning *from the tower,* were Circassian and Georgian slaves who ruled from their enclave at the Citadel. They took power from the *Bahri* in 1382. Lacking any type of system of succession, or a common language for many did not speak Arabic, few Mamluk reigns lasted longer than three generations. Power was not passed on. It was seized. That left a weak central government — weak enough in 1517 for the Ottomans to sweep into Egypt and take power, but not weak enough to dissolve Mamluk power completely. In fact, the Porte rulers used the Mamluks to keep peace in Egypt. Outlasting their enemies, it was the Mamluks who faced Napoleon when he invaded Egypt. Ruling almost three hundred years, these men left their mark on the city as Islamic art reached its zenith during their reign. When John Antes walked the streets of Cairo, he could thank them for the magnificent architecture and the amazing arts in metalwork, ceramics, intricate inland woods, marble arabesque domes and minarets created during Mamluk reign. Surely his fine carpenter's hand was influenced by what he saw.

A very powerful and interesting Mamluk, Ali Bey al Kabir won the reins of government, conquered his fellow Mamluks, and tried to orchestrate the Ottoman collapse. He did not succeed. Despite the turbulence of his short reign, Ali Bey made a number of dynamic moves which set him apart from his predecessors. First, he stopped paying tribute to the Ottoman Empire in Constantinople in an attempt to gain independence for Egypt. Then he went to war with Syria in order to expand Egyptian territory. He increased trade with Europe, trying to develop Egypt's interests in the Mediterranean, and he tried to open Suez to trade on the Red Sea. He looked West and brought European experts to Egypt. These were stunning maneuvers. In order to accomplish them, Ali Bey al Kabir extorted exorbitant taxes from merchants, villages, Christians, customs officials, and Copts (who were considered separate from other Christians).[6] Ali Bey al Kabir lost power for the last time in 1772 to Muhammad Bey Abu adh Dhahab, but the programs he had initiated continued under his successor. These policies would be continued by Mohammad Ali and his dynasty in years to come. Egypt was being primed to enter the Mediterranean world.

John Antes lived in Egypt during this interesting and important time. He not only recorded many of the events related to the rulers in letters he wrote home to friends and relatives, but he assessed their importance.

The Moravians in Egypt

Founded in the fifteenth century and transformed in the eighteenth, the Moravian faith, defined as Protestant ecumenical evangelicals, had established a mission in Cairo by 1752. The Moravians planned to move south into Abyssinia looking for converts to Christianity — an ambition that was doomed to failure. The mission was supervised by a physician named Friedrich Wilhelm Hocker. He learned the Arabic language, made an effort to establish a relationship with the Patriarch of the Copts, and was preparing to go to Abyssinia when the Ottoman ruler died and Cairo became unstable. Hocker sailed back to Europe in 1755.[7] Returning the following year, accompanied by George Pilder, Hocker started the mission to Abyssinia again. Shipwreck put an end to this second attempt. Pilder returned to Europe in 1759. By 1761 Hocker joined him.[8] He would return one more time.

Hocker's medical skills made him popular not only among the Copts, Greeks, and foreigners, but among the ruling class as well.[9] He served as physician to Ali Bey. In the chaotic world of Egyptian politics of the day, when Ali Bey fell from power, the Moravians, because Hocker treated him, were objects of plunder.

On his third tour of duty in 1769, Hocker was joined by brethren Johanna Heinrich Danke and John Antes. Antes's journey to Egypt, like everything else connected with his mission, was not easy. He fell ill in Cyprus, and while trying to get to Limasol to board the boat for Egypt, he was robbed. Without funds, he had to walk through the rain across the island and became sick again. Despite these difficulties, he journeyed on to Alexandria, Egypt's Mediterranean port. In a method that would be repeated by travelers for much of the next century, Antes had to find passage from Alexandria to Rosetta, where he would board another vessel for Cairo. Pale and frail, Antes found the journey a horrific struggle. When he finally procured a boat to Cairo, instead of the customary four- to six-day journey, John Antes spent eighteen damp, miserable days on the Nile. He described the journey in detail in his book *Observations on the Manners and Customs of the Egyptians:*

> My Janissary had, in order to save something, embarked in a very old vessel, which was far from watertight over head; the heavy rain, therefore, penetrated every where, so that I had not one one spot where I could sit dry, though under cover; my bed soon began to moulder under me, till at last I contrived to suspend it with a cord, so that the penetrating water could run off underneath, which was of some service. My guide had provided sufficient, and very good victuals, for a journey of five or six days, such as bread, fowls, rice, &c.; but as it lasted so long, all the bread by degrees grew mouldy, and the fowls were consumed....We frequently lay to at a paltry village, or at anchor in the middle of the river for four, five, or six days together, and no offer could make them exert themselves; they continually exclaimed: Min Allah! Mukkader! &c. It is from God! It is so written in the Book of Fate &c.... At last we arrived before Bulac ... [62–63].

The Moravians lived in the European quarter of Cairo, the *Harat al-Afranj,* Alley of the Franks (or foreigners), outside the western walls of the medieval city. The district had been created for the foreign community about a hundred years earlier and stood along the *Khalig,* a canal that cut through the heart of the new area. There, for the next decades, John Antes and the Moravians intermingled with and were involved in the daily events of the city. Day by day John Antes recorded those events in the official diary that was sent back to the Moravian center in Herrnhut, Germany.[10] The entries contain such brief notations as:

> March 13: looking for a house to live in.
> March 14: bought wood to deal with joiner's work.

March 15: medical visit of an Arabian Bey.
March 16: rain at Cairo.
March 17: continuation of the joiner's work of John Antes.
March 18: looking for a house to live in.
March 20: Medical visits.
March 21: unsuccessful attempt to visit the Greek patriarch at Cairo.
March 22: finished first joiner's work at Cairo.
March 27: visit the French consul, the army of Ruler of Cairo goes to Upper
Egypt to fight against Sheikh Hamaam.[11]

This diary is a most important source for information about daily life in Cairo as seen by the Moravians.

Antes arrived in Egypt as plague was developing in Alexandria, and he lived through two additional plagues while he was in Cairo, one in 1771 and another in 1781. He studied the disease intently. The plague was not only a medieval phenomenon. The ancient Egyptians feared it as well, and to avoid it, each spring the people would go to Sinai to escape. In the Middle Ages huge pandemics erupted, killing as much as 50 percent of the populations of Asia, North Africa, and Europe. Keen to unravel the mysteries of this terror, Antes came to the conclusion that Egypt, contrary to what most of Europe supposed, was not the mother of the plague. Antes believed a quarantine established in the maritime towns would rid not only Egypt, but most of Europe from the dreaded pandemic (41). He was not wrong.

According to Antes, everyone had different methods for avoiding the plague, including the Friars de Propaganda Fide. There were two Latin religious orders in Cairo at this time, the Friars de Propaganda Fide and the Padres de Terra Santa. The Friars and the Venetian doctor at Cairo believed they could keep the plague away by drinking excessive amounts of brandy, or so reported Antes. Other Europeans in the city, including Antes and his brothers, locked themselves within their homes until the threat was over.

> The usual way of doing this among the Europeans is, to make a partition of boards at the inside of their house door. In this partition a small door is fixed to receive the necessary provisions. This little door is kept constantly locked, in order to prevent careless servants from taking any thing in secretly. Before this door, on the inside, a tub of water is placed, into which the servant, who is kept without, puts all such victuals as will bear water, out of which they are taken on the inside with an iron hook. But bread, rice, coffee, or any such dry article, are found not to convey the infection, and may, therefore, be taken in with safety from a board upon which the servants hand them in. Such things may also be drawn up through a window, by a rope formed of the filaments of the date tree, and a basket made of its leaves. But any thing of woolens, cotton, linen, silk, and the like, must by no means be taken in during the time of quarantine [34].

When the city was fairly healthy, both Antes and Hocker earned a good living. Antes reported that Armenians, Greeks, Turks, an Irishman, and a Frenchman were all clockmakers in Cairo, but he considered their work inferior to his own. He wrote about his work often to his friends in England, asking for equipment, and telling them the types of clocks he was making: a cylinder clock for the Greek patriarch,[12] and another for the Swedish Ambassador to Constantinople.[13] One of his biggest and most impressive orders was three clocks he made for Mohammad Bey, the ruler of Egypt. "Concerning my clockmaker work," he reported, "I have found much to do, especially now I got 3 pieces of work for Mohammad Bey, I have much to do with them. It is a kind of clock, but serves only to start three roses of diamonds on a belt of women, richly adorned with precious stones. A real Turkish finery."[14] Unquestionably this project was a series of master locks for a diamond-encrusted chastity belt; the clock mechanism unlocked the belt.

As the Moravians began to spread their religious philosophy, they established a foothold in Behnesse, a Coptic village four days south of Cairo in Upper Egypt. The *Umda* (mayor) of the village, Michael Baschara, permitted them to have a house there. The Moravians would travel to villages in the area talking to the people and hoping for converts from Coptic Christianity to Protestant Christianity, in the same manner as the American Protestant missionaries would do in the nineteenth century. In 1772, just after the plague, Brother Danke returned from there and died in Cairo.[15] Antes took over his responsibilities and sailed for Upper Egypt. He stayed there for six weeks. Neither Danke nor Antes were very successful. In fact, in 1780, near the end of his tenure in Egypt, Antes admitted, "Brother Winiger is now about one month in Behnesse; the poor Copts there have gone back to sleep almost completely during his, this time too long, stay here. And often he will have a hard time among them; indeed...."[16]

Antes's Observations

Antes's natural curiosity made him a keen observer. He loved to tour around the city and nearby countryside. As he worked and moved about Cairo, Antes developed strong and interesting opinions about the community he called "home." He seemed not to hold the negative prejudices of some Western writers. He admitted that some Cairenes were "naturally inclined to wickedness," but on the whole found them calm, friendly, clean, and religious. He did not find the city as filthy as other foreigners described it. He thought the cities of Europe were far dirtier (38).

Nor did he feel that all Muslims hated all Christians. His opinions were fresh and refreshing. John Antes decided rather early in his stay in Egypt that Westerners who came briefly into the country did not understand Egypt at all and returned home with false impressions, not relating a true picture of the country or its inhabitants. The main explanation for their failure was that most Europeans did not speak Arabic and thus did not have access to most native inhabitants. So they asked other Europeans, or indigenous Greeks, for information about Egypt and the Egyptians — and got wrong information. Antes had found in the eighteenth century what people in the nineteenth and twentieth centuries rarely understood: the observations and understandings of the West cannot be placed on the culture of the East. An interesting example of Antes's knowledge was his observation about the claim that Christians were forbidden to ride on horses (a legend which continues to this day) in Cairo. He pointed out it simply was not true and provided a logical explanation in a letter to Benjamin LaTrobe in August of 1771:

> What you have heard about the Christians having obtained leave to ride on horses is without any foundation. There is a misapprehension in this whole affair. When you are truly informed of the circumstances, you will easily understand the reason for this law. Necessity has been the Parent of it, for the streets of this city are so narrow, that the broadest of them are not broader than Fetter Lane [London], and moreover they are not paved, which is easier for the camels and asses; The streets are always very full of people; therefore if everyone who hoped had leave to ride on horses, there would be no possibility of walking the streets, and especially as many streets are so narrow that not above 2 or 3 persons can walk abreast. The narrowness of the streets is extremely beneficial, on account of the great heat, and for this reason many streets are closed at the top, except a few holes which are left to admit the light; everyone is obliged to sprinkle water several times a day before his house to lay the dust, this and

the dry air here are the reasons that the streets of Cairo are by far not so dirty and stinking as most of the streets in London. For the above reason not all the Turks are permitted to ride on horseback, yea none but the great, and those in office and such who have a special license for it. On the other hand both Christians and Turks may ride as much as they please on horseback in the country and also in other cities, such as Rosetta. I should always prefer, for a short journey, one of these asses for they are much easier, and some of the asses are very large. Do not trust the newspapers in future when they tell you such things. I will send you always the first and most secure news if a peculiar changing happens.[17]

The horse and ass idea was but one of dozens and dozens of examples of misinformation sent back to the West. Antes was convinced that most travelers also gave the Western world a poor interpretation of life in Egypt. He did not agree with two of the prominent observers that scholars still rely on today: Savary and Volney. Antes noted Savary described Upper Egypt but was never there. Volney did not speak Arabic. He felt Pococke, Norden, and Niebuhr provided more accurate information (4–5).[18]

Antes and Ali Bey

A few years after his arrival in Egypt, John Antes saw Ali Bey take power. On September 8, 1770, he wrote a lengthy letter to Benjamin LaTrobe outlining the events as he understood them. The letter, newly translated, sheds light on the character of Ali Bey, the happenings in Cairo, and, most important to Antes, the fate of Franks and Christians under Ali Bey's reign.

> ... since the Christians who suffered much in all Turkish provinces now, have here, and especially the Franks, much more freedom than before, because Ali Bey is not against but rather good to the Christians. His regime is generally the best among the Barbarians. He listens to the lowest people and gives them their rights; but on the Jews he is not very well disposed. His distinguished services are done by Christians acting as tax collector, chief cashiers, and such like.
>
> The Russians in Archipelago, which, we were told, have captured Senodos and Lemnos near the Hellespont, have recently stopped an Alexandrian ship. After they inquired surely that they were all Alexandrinians, the Russians let the ship and its cargo go saying, that they shall go in peace because they are under the command of the good man Ali Bey. When the news of the total defeat of the Turkish armada reached Alexandria and all Alexandrians believed their commerce would be blocked, the mob wanted to rebel and kill all Franks, who were able to trade always freely. In Rosetta they had in mind to do the same not only against the Franks but also against all the other Christians. The commander of the castle in Alexandria followed the mob, the Sitar on the other hand, who headed the whole town, reported it to Ali Bey who sent troops immediately, deposed the commander, brought him over here. After a short interrogation he was brought to Boukir and drowned....[19]

The plague blocked mail for some time, but in an August 15, 1771, letter to the Rev. Benjamin LaTrobe, Antes continued his explanation of political events in Cairo:

> Ali Bey has not as yet declared himself Sultan, and what your newspapers have placed upon that head, is entirely false. Last autumn he sent a part of his troops to Syria, and reinforced them this spring. They had all possible success, and having defeated 4 Bashawes who opposed their advances, they went so far as to take Damascus, on account of which there was great rejoicings here. Ali Bey gave immediate Orders to his Generalissimo to proceed farther and take Aleppo, which might have been done without much difficulty, and at that time it was much talked of that he

would be proclaimed Sultan. But the Generalissimo put a stop to it. He went (it is said) unwillingly to Damascus. It is supposed that he thought the intention of sending him thither was that he might be absent from Cairo. For this reason he opposed the intentions of Ali Bey. He made a treaty with the People of Damascus which they agreed that they would not admit their Bashaw into the city, and then he led the army back to Cairo. Ali Bey did not find it wise to show his displeasure as the Generalissimo had the army with him, and since that time all is quiet....[20]

John Antes wrote several letters to different friends about the events surrounding the new ruler. He called Ali Bey's activities a great revolution and watched as the city began to prepare for an expedition against Syria. Ali Bey's brother-in-law, General Mohamed Bey (for whom Antes created the chastity belt), was against the invasion and revolted against him. Translated from the German for the first time, these letters and other comments found in the Herrnhut diaries offer a view of life in Cairo and Egypt in the eighteenth century that we have not seen before.

Antes and James Bruce

The Scottish explorer James Bruce (1730–1794) returned to Cairo from his now famous journey into Africa as the political environment in Egypt was stabilizing a bit. John Antes formed a great friendship with Bruce, who had been in Abyssinia for four years. He had sent a number of letters to Cairo, and since the Moravians' main purpose in Africa was to establish a mission in Abyssinia, Antes was anxious to meet him. The letters stopped coming, and rumors began to spread that Bruce had been murdered on his return journey.[21] However, Bruce survived and eventually arrived in Cairo on January 15, 1773. He took up residence with Mr. Rose, a French merchant, whose house was located in the same area of the city as the Moravians. For three months Antes and Bruce seem to have conversed daily. Antes came to admire Bruce and also trusted his observations. In fact, based on Bruce's conclusions, Antes determined that a missionary venture to Abyssinia was not a wise move for the Moravians.

According to Antes, Bruce found few redeeming characteristics among the natives in Abyssinia. Murder was common and often went unpunished. There were no factories. The only work which seemed to exist was in the army. Anyone who planted crops had no way of protecting the harvest from vandals. It was all very barbaric with few structured institutions such as marriage. Antes was horrified at the lack of traditions and the poor value placed upon women. He often questioned Bruce on that point. The Moravians were eager for details as they wished to journey there themselves. Bruce told Antes who told LaTrobe in one of his many letters:

> Their highest profession is war. For this they use guns with fuses. Powder the women are making; their bullets are from iron. The guns they get from the Turks, the lances they make themselves. The country is very fertile and you dont need to watch for a right moment to seed, because it ripens so often. But when somebody has sown something and another comes and lets his horses eat it, he cannot go to court, but he can kill him. This disorder causes, all to be more expensive than here. They do not have coins, instead of them they make use of a kind of rock salt, coming from the country of the Galls. There should be thousands of Jews in the country, who design themselves as exiled; according to his opinion they have come there very early, if not soon after Moses but at the time of Salomo; they are white as the Royal family. About religion you dare not tell too much, if you do not want to be stoned. Polygamy is also very common. In the house of the king is a priest who has about

200. And the most incomprehensible is, Mr. Bruce assures me, that he has never seen
a real marriage; when a man comes into a house and he sees a woman who likes him,
it is up to him to do with her whatever he wants, yeah, she offers herself for that, as
a matter of politeness. I have questioned him about this point many times and he
has assured me always the same. I asked him, if there is no indication, that it will
quiet down in the country with the time, but he said, that it is to expect the exact
opposite. I asked him then: If somebody ignores all these difficulties and wants to go
there, how can he scrape through there; are they not curious to have arts and profes-
sions? But he said, that with clocks and something similar nothing can be gained
there. The only one, which perhaps could work would be above all a doctor and a
rough painter of portraits to paint their saints and similar things and at a pinch a
carpenter, who can make all kinds of products made from wood like boats and something similar....[22]

Antes was anxious for Bruce to publish his account of his journey. Once Bruce returned
to Scotland, it took him some time to write the account that Antes eagerly awaited. When it
was finally published in 1790, well after Antes left Egypt, it became shrouded in controversy.
Bruce had enemies in high places and they were not willing to give him credit for much that
he had discovered. Antes found himself defending his friend. He criticized Bruce's detractors
both in his book and more extensively in an article he wrote for *Spirit of the Foreign Magazine*
in 1811. Antes went through Bruce's book very carefully and made extensive notes that he
intended to send to Bruce for a second edition. But Bruce died in 1794 before Antes could
send his comments. The notes have never surfaced, but Antes wrote in his book:

> There is no doubt at all of Mr. Bruce having been at the source of the Nile; but I
> cannot approve of his laying so very great stress upon this particular, and his signifying
> as much as if he was the first European that ever had been there. P. J. Lobo's description
> is very well known, and differs little in the main points from Mr. Bruce's. Besides this,
> I wish there did not appear so much egotism through the whole performance, that he
> had been a little more accurate in mentioning distances, bearings and names, and that
> he had not coloured every thing so very high, which may incline readers to scruple the
> whole. I selected many errors and contradictions of this kind, and intended to send
> them to him, because he had mentioned to me an intention to publish his travels again
> with additions and amendments, when I heard that he was no more [19].

It is in the magazine article written in 1811, well after his time in Cairo, that the negative
remarks against Bruce were criticized at length by Antes. He was concerned about the observations of Henry Salt and Lord Valentia (George Annesley, the 2nd Earl of Mountnorris,
1770–1844)[23] in the publication of their books: Valentia's *Voyages and Travels to India, Ceylon,
the Red Sea, Abyssinia and Egypt,* and Salt's *Account of a Voyage to Abyssinia, and Travels into
the Interior of that country in the years 1809 and 1810.* Both books were very influential. Henry
Salt was an important figure in Anglo-Egyptian history in the 19th century. In 1816, Salt
became the British consul general in Egypt and served in that position for many years. In
addition to assisting British travelers on the Nile and seeing to other consular duties, he was
very active in removing many artifacts from the Nile Valley and hired a host of foreigners for
the task, including the famous Italian Giovanni Belzoni.

Prior to Salt's residence in Egypt, the two gentlemen made a journey in 1802–06 to the
East, where they collected natural specimens and antiquities. It was on this journey that Valentia
met another early American in Egypt, Red Sea captain Francis Barthow. Both were unkind in
their comments concerning Bruce. Because of his many discussions with Bruce, Antes noted:

> I therefore had sufficient opportunity to investigate his character; which I do not
> conceive was such as would allow of his advancing an unfounded falsehood. He had,

moreover, too much good sense not to know, that in process of time, he might be detected by some future traveler; and besides that, his Greek servant, Michael, who followed him in all his travels, whom I knew for at least ten years afterwards, and with whom I had dealings in a mercantile way, might have contradicted any thing which was absolutely false.[24]

Antes wrote, "Mr. Salt entered on his journey with a mind prejudiced against Mr. Bruce, and determined to find fault with him." Antes continued:

> Thus Mr. Salt was told that Mr. Bruce had never been in any battle; that the battle of Serbraxos was fought two years before he entered Abyssinia; that Mr. Bruce never had any office; nor was any territory given to him. Now, with regard to the first particular, I think I can bring a positive proof to the contrary. Mr. Bruce repeatedly showed me a wound in his arm by a spear, received in one of the battles at Serbraxos; and it was still troublesome, from not having been rightly cured; it even sometimes opened again and discharged matter. With regard to the other assertions, I have no other evidence than the statements of Mr. B. These, however, I think, are entitled to more credit, than the loose hints partly gathered, and partly forced out, from some of the natives.[25]

Antes pointed out that the time that had passed between the two visits, Bruce's in 1768–1773 and Salt's in 1805, a lapse of nearly 30 years, made a disparity both in the memory of the people in Abyssinia and the advantages Salt's expedition had over Bruce's second expedition.

Antes could not confirm some of the other contradictions of Bruce by Salt and Valentia, such as whether "the Abyssinians cut raw flesh stripped from the living animal." Bruce said they did. Salt said they did not. He could, however, dispute the assertion, "He [Bruce] did not well understand Amharick, or Tigre, and did not speak much more Arabick than I [Salt] do." Antes had heard Bruce speak Amharic on more than one occasion:

> Now with regard to Amharick, I heard him speak it, in the house of Mr. Ini, with a very respectable Armenian, who had known him in Abyssinia, from whence he was just returned. This Armenian said that he spoke Amharick "very well." With respect to Arabick, I myself was able to judge. He spoke it fluently, though in the Mecca dialect; which differs in a few instances from that spoken at Cairo....[26]

According to Antes, one of the people upon whom Salt relied for his information was longtime Venetian merchant and diplomat Carlo Rosetti (Rossetti). Rossetti had a long association with Egypt. After becoming the consul general for Austria and Russia he became friends with Ali Bey al Kabir and wielded great power, becoming the exclusive merchant for the herb *cassia-senna,* a monopoly he passed on to his nephews upon his death.[27] John Antes did not like Rossetti. He called him a "lucky adventurer," and disputed his information on a number of points, dismissing him as a poor source of information about Bruce. In the end, Antes raised enough points for one to reconsider what Valentia and Salt had to say about his friend. It is doubtful that much of what John Antes had to say about James Bruce saw the light of day in England.

Antes and His Music in Cairo

Antes does not mention his music much in his known letters; yet we know that throughout his life John Antes continued his musical interest. He developed a mechanical page-turner, a new type of violin peg, a piano hammer, and experimented with building organs. He wrote at least 59 hymn tunes, 41 anthems, and 13 chorales. When in Egypt he created at least two sets of music, a violin trio (*Tre Trii per due Violini e Violoncello, Obligato, Dedicati a Sue Excellenza il Sig G J de Heidenstam, Ambassatore de Sa Maj il Ri de Suede a Constantinopel, Composti a Grand Cairo dal Sig Giovanni A T S Dilletante Americano. Op. 3.*) and six complete *Quartettos*. The former, published in London in the 1790s by John Bland at No. 45 Holborn, is the earliest known chamber music written by an American (yet another example to prove that John Antes considered himself an American).[28] The two original copies of this work are found at Salem, North Carolina, *Collegium Musicium* and the Eastman School of Music. The *Quartettos* were sent to two people, the Marquis de Hauteford for the Harmonical Society of Bengal and Benjamin Franklin. Neither copy has ever been found.

John Antes had a small association with Franklin. His love of music led him to visit Franklin in Philadelphia in 1763. Later, on his way to Germany in 1769, he stopped in London in August and attempted to visit Franklin once again, but Franklin was in Paris at the time. Sending Franklin the music is the only other known correspondence.

> Sir,
>
> You may perhaps still remember a young Man wich in the Year 1763 amused himself with making Musicall Instruments such as Harpsicords Violins etc. whome Curiosity and Desire of Learning once led to your House at Philadelphia, without anything to introduce him but a little American Cordiality. This Man am I. The noble and generous Treatment I received of you that Time, when I have been an intire Stranger to you has all this many Years left a deep Sense of Gratidute, and the highest Opinion of your kind and obliging Caracter in my Heart. And this is the only Motive wich induce me to send you with the Present a Copy of six Quartetto's wich I have lately compossed in my lessure hours for my Frind the Marquis de Hauteford, to make use of at the Harmonical Society of Bengal, where he has last year an Intention to go, if the present War had not make him change his Ressolution. I am very sensible that in Paris you are not in Want of good and much superior Music to what my poor Talents may afor'd, But poor as the may be, The Composition of a Countryman, and the Manner in wich the are given, as a mere Sign of sincere Gratidute, will perhaps make them agreeable. And if after a fair Trial, by able Performers such as play wich good Expression and Taste, the should still be so lucky to afor'd you some Amussement, I should certainly be extremely happy. I acknowledge I don't make Profession of Music, and all I know of I picked up here and there by good Frinds, Therefore I should not be surprised if great Master, should find Faults here and there.
>
> Since I left America, wich had been in the Year 64, I employed all my Talents to Mechanic, and chiefly to the Watchmaking Branch, in wich I have been pretty lucky, so that I did something above the common Way.
>
> Being in London in August 69, I took the Liberty to call at your Lodgings, but have not been so fortunate to see you as you had just made a Trip to Paris. Most of my Time since that I have spent here in Egypt, where the United Brethren, to wich Society I belong, have a Missionary Post, tho observe what good may be done for the Furtherance of the Gospel in this Country and Abissiny.
>
> If I could here be of any Service to my Mother Country or to you in Particular I should always embrace every Opportunity with the greatest Plassure. I will not begin wich any Discription of things concerning this Country, well knowing that Paris is not in Want of better than ever I could afor'd. But any particular Question put to me I should always answer with Plessure according to my Abilities. One Circumstance however will perhaps not be disagreeable to mention that after a few Days southerly Wind, the Heat has been so excessive in the Night between 6th of June to the 7th that the Thermometre of Reaumur rose at 11 o Clock the Night to the 36th Degree,

wich is a very extraordinary Thing, the greatest heat in the middle of the Day is in Somer commonly no more but between 25 to 30. Many People died verry sudden that Night and the following Day, but thank God it did not last long.

May God grand soon Peace to the Satisfaction of all to our Mother Country, for wich I have still the greatest Regard, and wish well to evry Individual of it from the bottom of my heart....[29]

Antes in Trouble

It was probably inevitable that in twelve years John Antes would eventually fall foul of one menacing group or another on the Cairo streets. On November 15, 1779, he felt the full wrath of the Mamluk Osman Bey. Antes was in the habit of walking in the fields on the outskirts of the city where he could enjoy the quiet of sitting under a tree, much as he had done in his childhood home in Pennsylvania. He often had a gun, or fowling piece, with him. There were a profusion of ducks, geese, and quail on the canals surrounding the city, surely welcome additions to the Moravian table! Antes was careful to avoid the Turkish and Mamluk parties who roamed the countryside outside the walls of Cairo because he knew that they would "find some pretext or other for extorting money, from Europeans especially, whom they always suspect of being rich" (116–127 ff).

On that November day, as he was walking with the secretary of the Venetian consul, two of Osman Bey's Mamluks "came full gallop toward us, with drawn swords in their hands." They stripped Antes and his companion and demanded "one hundred *machbul* or Turkish *schechines,* each in value about seven shillings and six-pence." Antes said he did not have such a sum on him. In fact, he gave up his purse, which contained only 25 shillings. They threw it back at him and demanded gold. Antes told them to follow him home and he would give them some gold. But the thieves could not leave their posts and cursed Antes as more villains joined them. They decided to send Antes home for his gold while detaining his friend with the threat of cutting off his head. This was too much for Antes's companion, who began to cry. Antes decided he could not leave his friend and offered to be the hostage instead. It was of no consequence to the thieves which of their captives remained behind, but as a parting insult they took the Venetian's clothing, forcing the poor man "to go naked into the town."

Osman Bey became aware of the situation and ordered Antes before him. Antes took it upon himself to plead with the Bey for reason, saying, "I am under your protection." He knew this often was met with the response, "You are welcome." But not this time. Instead Osman Bey accused him of being a thief as only thieves would be outside the gates of the city at night. Antes tried to explain, but to no avail, and the Bey ordered Antes taken to "a castle," one of the Bey's palaces.

And so the abuse began. He was kicked, spat upon, roped like a calf, and dragged. He was told, "Give the guard money and he will let you go." Antes dredged up his purse once again. The guard took it. But he continued the walk to the castle and was chained in a cell. It was not long before he was taken before the Bey and given the *bastinado.* Antes wrote:

> Upon entering, I found a small neat Persian carpet spread for me, which was in fact a piece of civility, for the common people, when about to receive the *bastinado,* are thrown on the ground. The Bey again asked me, who I was:
> "An Englishman."
> "What is your business?"
> "I live by what God sends (an usual Arabian phrase)."

The *bastinado* was a method of punishment involving beating the subject on the bottom of the feet. It was used for all types of infractions.

He then said, "throw him down": when I asked what I had done. "How, you dog," answered he "dare you ask what you have done? Throw him down."

The servant then threw me upon my belly, the usual position upon such occasions, that when the legs are raised up, the soles of the feet may be made horizontal. They then brought a strong staff about six feet long, with a piece of an iron chain fixed to it with both ends; this chain they throw round both feet above the ancles, and then twist them together, and two fellows on each side, provided with what they call a corbage, hold up the soles of the feet by means of the stick, and so wait for their master's orders. When they had placed me in this position, an officer came and whispered into my ear, do not suffer yourself to be beaten, give him a thousand dollars and he will let you go. I reflected, that should I now offer any thing, he would probably send one of his men with me to receive it; that then I should be obliged to open my strong chest in which I kept not only my own, but a great deal of money belonging to others, which I had in trust, having received it in payment for goods sold for other merchants. The whole of this would in all probability have been taken away at the same time; and as I could not think of involving others in my misfortunes, I said, *mafish!* That is, no money! Upon which he immediately ordered them to begin, which they did, at first however moderately. But I at once gave myself up for lost, well knowing that my life only depended upon the caprice of a brute in human shape; and having heard and seen so many examples of unrelenting cruelty, I could not expect to fare better than others had done before me.

And he didn't. They beat him. They again asked for money. He offered a blunderbuss. The Bey snorted, "'*Ettrup il kelp!*' Beat the dog!!" And they did. Antes continued, "At first the pain was excruciating, but after some time my feeling grew numb, and it was like beating a bag of wool." They stopped and sent him back to his cell. He was forced to walk the distance on his pathetically injured feet. His reprieve lasted only a half hour. He was ordered back in front of the Bey. Up he walked on his tortured feet, but one of the servants had pity and carried him "till I was near the door."

Now a new game was afoot. When Antes entered the door it was as if he were interrupting the Bey and an officer. The officer said that Antes was his good friend, the "best man in all Cairo" to which the Bey said, "There take him, I give him to you, and if he has lost any thing, see to get it him again." Antes was carried to the lodgings of the officer where he was offered food, a bed, and a Cashmere shawl. His feet were anointed and tied with rags. In the morning he was taken to the Master of the Customs, whom Antes knew. "I only begged him to settle for me with my new friend; for I well knew that the whole farce was meant to play a little money into the hands of this officer, ... I found it had cost me about 20l. [20 pounds] in presents to the servants, and my *soi-disant* deliverer."

Antes was finally taken home, where his servant carried him upstairs. That ended his experience with Osman Bey and his men. He remained in bed for six weeks, then moved to crutches, and for "three years my feet and ancles were very much swelled, the latter having been severely hurt by the twisting chain, so that even now, after twenty years, they are apt to swell upon strong exertion."

> But though there are such villains among the Beys and Mamelucks, and one may even safely say that the major part is of that description; yet, during my long stay among them, I found several, both Mamelucks and Turks, of strictly honest principles, and of benevolent dispositions, who were not only good-natured, but faithful to their conviction in regard to right and wrong. Some of these became my sincere friends; but I have almost invariably observed, that those who came to me with the most friendly faces, had commonly some design to cheat or to make some advantage of me. Those, on the other hand, who looked stern and suspicious at the first interview, when they found I was not that designing villain which prejudice had taught them to think me, very often became my best friends, and some of them I would have entrusted with any thing of value without the least fear of being imposed upon.
>
> Upon the whole, I am not so blinded by the ill-treatment I have received from some of them as to condemn them indiscriminately. I am fully persuaded, that many of them would naturally be benevolent and well-disposed, if superstition in some, and prejudice chiefly arising from thence in others, did not give them a different bias [127].

Nor did he try to avenge himself on Osman Bey. He felt, "Had I complained to them [Ibrahim and Murad Bey], and accompanied my complaint with a present of from twenty to fifty thousand dollars (for a smaller sum would not have answered) they might perhaps have gone so far as to have banished Osman Bey from Cairo; but they would, probably, in a few months have recalled him ... [125]. Then Osman would have taken his revenge on the Moravians.

John Antes never recovered from his beating. He stayed in Cairo for only two more years, but his feet and ankles always bothered him. It was during his convalescence that he wrote the letter to Benjamin Franklin, then in France. He was replaced in Cairo in 1781, and by May 20, 1782, he was in Herrnhut, Germany. He never returned to America and retired to England, where he wed Susanna Crabtree. He moved to Bristol in 1808, where he died on December 11, 1811, and was buried in a Moravian cemetery (since destroyed).[30]

2

John Ledyard: The Man Who Walked the World (Explorer, 1788)

John Ledyard was an American explorer. He ranked among American adventurers such as Christopher Gist, who blazed the trail over the Allegheny Mountains; Daniel Boone, who opened Kentucky; and Lewis and Clark, who explored the continent to the Pacific Ocean. Whereas these legends walked the American continent, John Ledyard walked the world. As far as is known, Ledyard was the first person from the United States in Hawaii, the first in Alaska, the first to cross the Pacific Ocean, and the first in China, Russia, and Siberia. Some say he was the first American in Egypt, and, had he lived, he would have been the first African Association explorer to cross the Sahara Desert east to west. He was a keen observer of human manners and customs from the forest peoples of the Americas to the inhabitants of the steppes of Mother Russia. Ledyard brought a world of wisdom to Africa where he could have made important observations about how the world was so similar, yet so different.

John Ledyard was born in 1751 in Groton, Connecticut, to sea captain John Ledyard and his wife Abigail Hempstead Ledyard. In 1772, hoping to become a minister to the American Indians, he entered Dartmouth College. Shortly thereafter, the college, whose president was a friend of the family, sent him in quest of students among the Iroquois Nations, a consortium of North American Indian tribes in the northeastern United States and Canada. He stayed in the wilderness with the Indians long enough to learn their ways and know that servicing their souls was not what he wanted to do. He only returned to college long enough to leave it in grand style. Taking what he had learned from the tribes of the forest, Ledyard felled a lofty pine, built a 50-foot long, 3-foot wide dugout canoe, and, comforted by a bear skin, paddled 140 miles down the Connecticut River into the rest of his life.

Ledyard penned his own portrait of his character. As he was preparing to travel to Egypt he noted, "I am alone in everything, and in most things so, because nobody has been accustomed to think and act in traveling matters as I do."[1] Later he continued, "I am accustomed to hardships. I have known both hunger and nakedness to the utmost extremity of human suffering. I have known what it is to have food given me as charity to a madman; and I have at times been obliged to shelter myself under the miseries of that character, to avoid a heavier calamity."[2] He was well aware that he did not live the life of an ordinary man. "My distresses have been greater than I have ever owned, or ever will own to any man. Such evils are terrible to bear; but they never yet had power to turn me from my purpose."[3] John Ledyard was an eccentric loner who was fated to never quite complete a mission, never taste the true victory of success, but who accomplished incredible feats on his way to defeat.

His grand adventures began by taking a ship to Gibraltar, through to the Mediterranean, and along the Barbary Coast of North Africa. True to the vagabond he was becoming, Ledyard saw an opportunity to travel even further into the exotic and enlisted in the British Army. In 1776, while his country was becoming an independent nation, he was a corporal with the famous Captain Cook on Cook's third and last voyage: an expedition to find a Northwest Passage, a channel linking the two great oceans for a northern and easier route from Europe to China. If found, the Northwest Passage would have a profound influence on world trade, as it would eliminate the long journey around Africa or South America, and diminish Ottoman and Middle Eastern power over Far East goods. A shorter route to the Orient is what Christopher Columbus was trying to find in 1492 when he bumped into the Americas. Henry Hudson went looking for a Northwest Passage from the northeastern edge of North America in 1607. Hudson operated under the monopoly of the Muscovy Trading Company, the first of the English joint-stock trading companies (1555) that created the Age of Discovery by sending ships around the world looking for trade routes. Failing, Hudson attempted again in 1609 for another trading company, the Dutch East India Company. Almost two centuries later, the passage was still a consuming quest.

Ledyard's four-year journey with the Cook expedition was spectacular. Two ships, the *Discovery* and the *Resolution* (with Ledyard on board) went from Cape Town, South Africa, to Tasmania, Australia, and on to New Zealand and across the Pacific Ocean to Tahiti, where they remained for some time. Outward bound from Tahiti, the expedition discovered what Cook called the Sandwich Islands (Hawaiian Islands). After restocking the ships, Cook headed north up the edge of the North American continent, mapping and exploring the Pacific coast of North America while looking for the channel which would lead to the Atlantic Ocean. They reached the Bering Strait before abandoning their quest and retraced their steps south to the Sandwich Islands, where Cook was murdered.[4]

Ledyard's journey with Captain Cook presented one more idea to him: trade with China around what would come to be known as the Pacific Rim. While on the Cook journey the crew had sold furs in Canton, China, for rich profits, and the idea of a fur trade emanating from the west coast of the American continent was born. Ledyard believed that was where the Northwest Passage lay, not to the north of the continent as Henry Hudson assumed, but through the river systems of America. Unfortunately, it was unexplored territory. John Ledyard peddled his idea in Philadelphia, where he found Robert Morris, a member of the Continental Congress, a signatory to the Declaration of Independence, and superintendent of finance for fledgling America. Morris, perhaps the wealthiest merchant in America, was interested in Ledyard's plan and agreed to finance the venture. With additional assistance the partners worked for over a year to put the plan into effect. A good idea is only as good as the people who manage it. In this instance Morris and Ledyard had chosen men who fought among themselves, were distrustful of each other, and in the end abandoned Ledyard and Morris to launch two ships of their own: the *Empress of China* without Ledyard, and the *Columbia*, without Ledyard and Morris. The *Empress* was the first American ship in Canton and founded the American China Trade, and the *Columbia* entered what would become the lucrative fur trade. Both missions were legendary. John Ledyard, the man with the idea, received nothing for his efforts.

Morris ended in debtor's prison while a disappointed and disillusioned John Ledyard went on to Europe and tried to convince America's envoy Thomas Jefferson and Captain John Paul Jones of his project. For a while it looked as if Jones would invest, but once again, the project was abandoned. The only good thing to come out of it was a friendship with Thomas Jefferson. Jefferson was anxious to explore further west from the American states, which at that time did not exist west of the Mississippi River. He, too, felt the Northwest Passage could be found through the American river system. When Jefferson met Ledyard in Paris in 1786, he was impressed:

> In 1786, while at Paris, I became acquainted with John Ledyard, of Connecticut, a man of genius, of some science, and of fearless courage and enterprise. He had accompanied Captain Cook in his voyage to the Pacific, had distinguished himself on several occasions by an unrivalled intrepidity, and published an account of that voyage with details unfavorable to Cook's deportment towards the savages, and lessening our regrets at his fate. Ledyard had come to Paris in the hope of forming a company to engage in the fur trade of the Western coast of America. He was disappointed in this, and being out of business, and of a roaming, restless character, I suggested to him the enterprise of exploring the western part of our continent by passing through St. Petersburg to Kamschatka, and procuring a passage thence in some of the Russian vessels to Nootka Sound, whence he might make his way across the continent to the United States; and I undertook to have the permission of the Empress of Russia solicited.[5]

Jefferson thought he had found the perfect explorer for his mission and encouraged Ledyard to consider a scheme to travel east to west from Russia to America. To accomplish this mission Jefferson contacted the Empress of Russia to ask for permission for Ledyard to enter Russia.[6] The formidable Catherine the Great did not cooperate. She refused to offer the permission partly in fear that Ledyard was a spy for the United States. Despite this defeat, Ledyard, showing the intelligence and fearless courage that Jefferson saw in him, persisted.

Ledyard and Joseph Banks

It was at this point that John Ledyard met Joseph Banks (1743–1820) the wealthy, highly influential, philanthropic botanist who would become his patron and determine his fate. Banks was one of the founders of the African Association and a friend of Thomas Jefferson.[7] It was the Enlightenment, and Joseph Banks used his influence and his wealth to *enlighten* England through science and exploration. Banks's family wealth allowed him to support scientists and scholars on worldwide expeditions, especially botanists, and his name was associated with leading ventures including all Cook's journeys and the ill-fated trip of the HMS *Bounty*. As Ledyard had accompanied the third Cook expedition, Banks had accompanied, financed, and encouraged the first Cook adventure into the South Pacific aboard the *Endeavour*.

John Ledyard could not have found a better patron. When Banks discovered that Ledyard was looking for someone to help finance his trip to Russia, he felt that it was a worthy mission and decided to sponsor him. By 1786, with Banks's money in his pocket, Ledyard set out to reach the American west via Russia. From Paris, Ledyard crossed to Ostend in Belgium and then proceeded north along the European coast to Denmark and on to Stockholm. By then it was winter and very cold. Ledyard hoped the Gulph of Bothnia between Sweden and Russia would be covered with ice and he could walk about 100 miles to cross it. When he reached the middle it was not frozen. He had to retrace his steps and travel through Scandinavia around the northern perimeter of the Gulph.[8] Against incredible odds, and weather that would kill any human being, John Ledyard succeeded in reaching St. Petersburg. He was without funds. His shoes were gone. His stockings were rags. But John Ledyard was in Russia. Despite his pathetic, ragged appearance, he was invited to dine with the Portuguese ambassador. Over a hot meal, he begged twenty pounds on the account of Sir Joseph Banks, confessing he had no right to ask. But £20 he got.

Then he continued across Russia. By February of 1787, he had traveled thousands of miles in horrific weather and it looked as if he would finish his challenging journey. Then his venture came to an abrupt halt. He was arrested at the instructions of Catherine the Great and ordered out of the country. He had traveled 7,000 miles in seventeen months. Ledyard's trip across Russia was an incredible accomplishment. Yet, it brought no glory, no victory, no satisfaction to John Ledyard. Forbidden to reach the American continent, the shorter distance, Ledyard had to retrace his steps, the longer distance. By the time he reached Koningsberg in Prussia he was in dire straits. He had no money, again! With another loan on Banks's name, Ledyard went back to London.

The African Association

Banks did not abandon the American. He introduced Ledyard to the African Association, which had been established while Ledyard was on his Russian trek (June 9, 1788). It would make an important mark on western exploration. Twelve distinguished men formed the African Association. Its mission was to explore Africa, the "dark continent."[9] Among the many goals of the African Association was the abolition of the slave trade, which was carried out along many of the North African trade routes. A second objective was to investigate the geography and natural history of Africa, which included the discovery of the paths of the trade routes. One of the major considerations of the African Association was to find markets for the products of Britain's growing Industrial Revolution, which, of course, would travel over the trade routes. With the American colonies lost, Britain needed new outlets for her products to keep the populace working and the economy thriving (the heart of the Imperialist theory). There was an additional consideration. Britain had too many prisoners and no place to send them, so they were looking for a penal colony, and as the ancient Egyptians and the Romans had done in antiquity, the British looked to the North African deserts.[10]

For Europe, Africa was the elusive unknown. Travelers from Herodotus to Volney spoke of it. As early as the tenth century, Venetian traders went to Cairo. By the fourteenth century Portuguese traders had reached West Africa. In the sixteenth century the Moorish traveler Leo Africanus wrote of many of the North African sites including Timbuktu. Yet, except for coastal regions, Africa remained mostly uncharted by Europeans. The source of the fabled Nile and the twisting Niger, the extent of the desert wilderness (named the Sahara by the French), the number and direction of the trade routes, the fabled city of Timbuktu, were all still shrouded in secrecy when John Ledyard arrived in Egypt. All of these mysteries were not only enhanced with promises of gold, ivory, and other treasures, but each had a connection to Egypt, which sat at the northeastern edge of the continent at the "crossroads of the world." Egypt promised access: access not only to the trade routes of Africa but to the shorter passages to the Far East. Then there was Egypt itself. Few of its wonders were known. Europeans were hungry to explore the splendors of Egypt. The door was opening, the centuries of Egyptophilia and Egyptomania lay ahead, and John Ledyard was one of the first foreign explorers to walk through the door.

Here, at last, was a financed adventure. John Ledyard became the first explorer on the first mission of the African Association: the quest to discover the source of the Niger River. Three weeks after the Association was formally founded, they sent Ledyard to Egypt. Their written instructions announced:

> That the Committee do require from Mr. Ledyard that he shall proceed, with all possible dispatch, by the way of Marseilles and Cairo to Mecca; that from thence (unless insuperable difficulties shall occur) he shall cross the Red Sea, and taking the

route of Nubia, shall traverse the Continent of Africa, as nearly as possible in the direction of the Niger, with which River, and with the Towns and Countries on its borders, he shall endeavour to make himself acquainted — and that he shall return to Britain by the way of any of the European Settlements on the Western Coast. But that if the above mentioned Plan should be found altogether impracticable, he shall proceed to the discovery of the Interior parts of Africa, by the route which may appear to him the best suited to the purpose.[11]

On June 30, 1788, John Ledyard left London. In Paris he again met Thomas Jefferson and promised that he would return to his American exploration once he came back from Africa.

Ledyard in Egypt

John Ledyard arrived in Alexandria on August 19, 1788. It is disappointing that Ledyard, the world traveler, the keen observer, the astute deductor, did not have the opportunity of an extended stay, as had his American predecessor John Antes. In twelve years Antes truly saw Egypt. John Ledyard's short three months led him to see most of Egypt as many traveler/authors did: through flawed eyes. Had he read or talked to John Antes, who resided in England when Ledyard was there, he may have had a different perspective. Perhaps he expected too much from the fabled nation. Perhaps his disappointments in the fur trade and the trek across Russia had made him bitter. In Egypt, he was a harsh and misguided critic. John Ledyard did not see in the mighty Nile River what so many before and after him saw. "What eyes do travelers see with?" he wrote to Thomas Jefferson on his first viewing of the river. "Are they fools or rogues? For Heaven's sake, hear the plain truth about it." He ridiculed the size of the river, comparing it to the Connecticut River back home. "This," he mocked,

> is the mighty, the sovereign of rivers, the vast Nile, that has been metamorphosed into one of the wonders of the world....
> You have heard and read, too, much of its inundations. If the thousands of large and small canals from it, and the thousands of men and machines employed to trans-fer by artificial means the water of the Nile to the meadows on its banks, if this be the inundation that is meant, it is true; any other is false. It is not an inundating river. I came up the river from the fifteenth to the twentieth of August, and about the thirtieth the water will be at the height of the freshet. When I left the river, its banks were four, five, and six feet, above the water. And here in town I am told they expect the Nile to be only one or two feet higher at the most. This is a proof, if any were wanted, that the river does not overflow its banks.[12]

Surely had he had the opportunity to travel further up the river he would have seen this river was worthy of its fame. He would have understood that indeed there was an inundation and it was phenomenal: for over a thousand miles the water spread through the breadth of the valley from mountain edge to mountain edge. Villages were turned into islands in a vast lake, causing villagers to abandon their donkeys and camels for small boats that maneuvered between the tops of palm trees. He was in the Delta of the Nile in August. The typical Nile flood began at Khartoum in July and wended its way north through August, crested in September, and began to recede in October. The further north the more delayed the flood. Of course the inundation varied from year to year. Had Ledyard arrived in 1780 he would have seen a spec-tacular flood.

Reaching Cairo, Ledyard made his way on his "Christian donkey" to the Venetian Consul, Carlo Rossetti, who was also the charge d'affaires for the British, the same Rossetti family known and disliked by John Antes. Ledyard was upset when the consul did not offer to house him.[13] Instead, as with other travelers, Ledyard was housed by Christian monks. Rossetti redeemed himself by arranging an introduction to the Aga Mahommed, the confidential minister of Ismail (one of the current four ruling beys). Ledyard was seeking and received letters from the ruler, which would provide him introductions and safe passage on his journey. He was not impressed with Aga Mahommed's appearance, nor his intellect. Nor did he realize that the rulers, the Turks, and the Egyptians were not the same people. "Is it not curious, that the Egyptians (for I speak of the natives of the country, as well as of him, when I make the observation) are still such dupes to the arts of sorcery? Was it the same people who built the pyramids?"[14] The Egyptians had not ruled their own country since the days of the Pharaohs. Arabs and Turks had dominated them, dictated their art, governed their laws, and made them subservient for centuries. Two centuries after Ledyard penned the question scholars are still speculating if the modern Egyptians are descendants of the ancient Egyptians.

Having read the recent travelers on Egypt, Ledyard felt he was now in a position to dispute them, and that he did:

You have the travels of Savary in this country. Burn them. Without entering into a discussion, that would be too long for a letter, I cannot tell you why I think most historians have written more to satisfy Themselves,

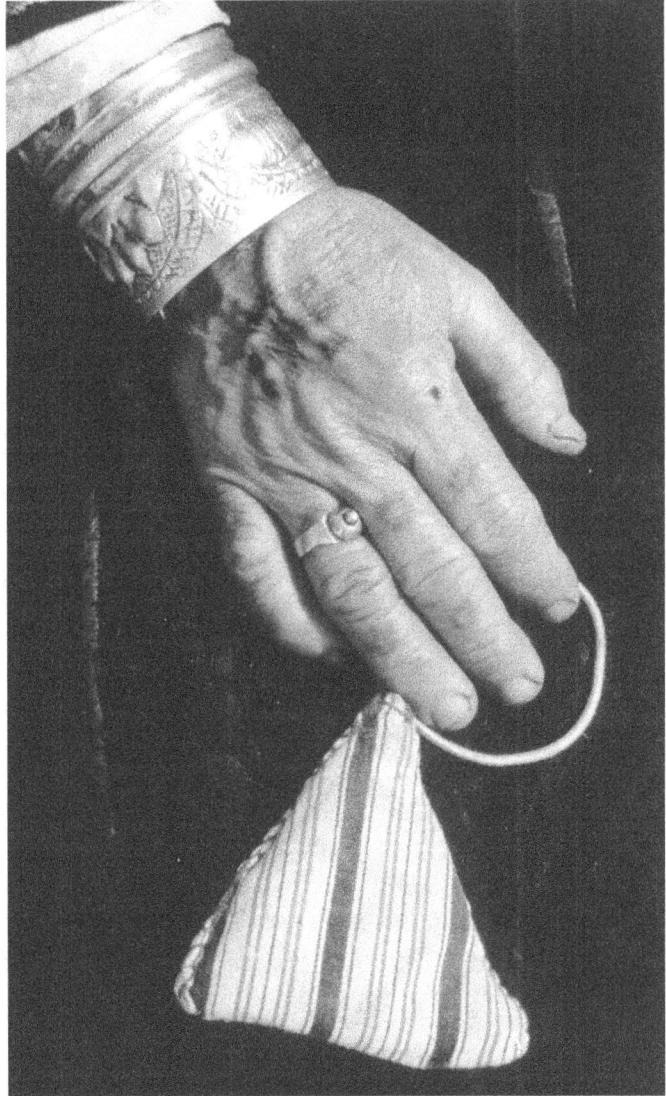

Hand of a woman from Bahariya Oasis in the Western Desert of Egypt. Tattooing was still used as adornment and healing as late as 1978 when this photograph was taken. Each tattoo had a meaning or use. Three dots at the edge of the eye protected the eye against disease. A tattoo of a tree on the chin symbolized fertility. The tattoos on the hand guarded against rheumatism. (Author's photo: Cassandra Vivian Collection in the Carnegie Museum of Natural History.)

than to benefit others. I am certainly very angry with those, who have written of the countries where I have traveled, and of this particularly. They have all more or less deceived me. In some cases perhaps it is difficult to determine, which does the most mischief, the self-love of the historian, or the curiosity of the reader; but both together have led us into errors, that it is now too late to rectify. You will think my

head is turned, to write you such a letter from Egypt; but the reason is, I do not
intend it shall be returned.[15]

Ledyard's fellow Egyptian traveler John Antes, as we have seen in the previous chapter, had
the same observation about travelers and their views on Egypt. It would not be the last time
this was an issue for Ledyard.

Just as he had done in other countries throughout his travels, John Ledyard began to
observe the manners and customs of the Egyptians, and because of his extensive travels he
was able to provide more positive comments and interesting comparisons with the peoples of
other lands. "I have seen a small mummy; it has what I call wampum-work on it,"[16] he said,
remembering his days among the American Indians. "The women dress their hair behind,
exactly in the same manner in which the women of the Kalmuk Tartars dress theirs,"[17] he
wrote a few pages later. He had had his hands tattooed by the natives of the Society Islands
(Tahiti and Mo'orea), and now he commented on Egyptian tattooing and found the idea of
patterns on the chin similar to the practice of the Indian women in the northwestern United
States. The use of henna he compared to the Chinese and northern Tartars. The type of veils
used by Egyptian women he found similar to the priests at Otaheite (Tahiti) and people on
the Sandwich Islands (Hawaii). He was truly amazed at the Egyptian "Ferris wheel," which
he had also seen in Russia. Then there was the music:

> Their music is instrumental, consisting of a drum and pipe, both of which resemble
> those two instruments in the South Seas. The drum is exactly like the Otaheite drum;
> the pipe is made of cane, and consists of a long and short tube joined; the music
> resembles very much the bagpipe, and is pleasant. All their music is concluded, if not
> accompanied, by the clapping of hands. I think it singular that the women here make
> a noise with their mouths like frogs, and that this frog music is always made at wed-
> dings, and I believe, on all other occasions of merriment where there are women.[18]

There is no doubt that Ledyard was observing the panorama of scenes on the streets of
Cairo. He could not miss the variety of Bedouins in flowing robes, Syrians in baggy pants
and braided vests, Persians wearing high mitre-like hats, Mamluks, Turks, Copts, Mongols,
and Jews, each dressed in their own attire, each following their own traditions. He could not
have been insulated from the Janissaries, the veiled women, the watercarriers, and even the
prostitutes who roamed the streets. He must have seen the marriage and funeral processions,
the victory parades, the processions of important personages, and the caravans wending their
way to the bazaars of the city. Cairo was still the city of *The Thousand and One Nights*.

Ledyard and the Caravan Routes

Of the few observations left to us, John Ledyard's remarks about the caravan routes have
proved to be the most important information he recorded in his now-lost journal. As he
settled into life in Cairo and began to plan the crossing of the African continent from east to
west to find the source of the Niger River, he turned to what he could do best: find his way
over the unknown. Where in Russia he had traveled through some of the coldest places on
earth, in Africa he intended to cross the Sahara Desert, the hottest place on earth.

From antiquity the African nations knew and used a number of north/south and east/west
trade routes across the northern portion of the continent. Rome knew them, conquered some
of them, and built fortresses along others. The Africans continued to trade along them, bringing
the riches of Africa to the northern shores of the continent, where European merchants laden
with cloth, sugar, brass, horses, and books traded for gold, ivory, and slaves and transported
the goods across the Mediterranean. These were the routes John Ledyard needed to find.

North African trade routes with their Western names. From west to east: Taghaza Road from Timbuktu in the south to the Atlas Mountains in the north; Ghadames-Air-Kano Road from Niger to Tunis; Garamantian Road from the Niger River to modern day Fezzan and Tripoli; Fezzan-Kawan Road, from Chad to Murzuk in Libya and east through Benghazi along the North African coast to Alexandria; Tripoli-Benghazi-Waidai Road, known as the Sanusi Road; and the famous Darb-al-Arbain, the Road of the Forty, from Sudan to Middle Egypt (from *The Western Desert of Egypt* by Cassandra Vivian. Courtesy The American University in Cairo Press).

These routes were linked to such fabled cities as Sijilmasa, Djenne, and Timbuktu, all rich centers of gold, salt, and slaves; Tripoli, Gao, and Kano, where the road carried south Venetian glass beads, paper, mirrors, needles, sugar, and tea, while transporting north Kano cloth, kola nuts, salt, and natron. The West knew of the cities and what they traded, but their locations and routes that led to them were guarded and secret. Europe was about to conquer them, take over the trade, and colonize Africa. John Ledyard stood at the vanguard of this long and imperialistic journey.

By October 14, 1788, John Ledyard's quest took him to the heart of the Fatimid city (the original gated city of Cairo)—to the places where the desert caravans deposited their wares and the black slave markets were found: the three *Wakalat al-Gallaba*, Inns of the Traveling Merchants. All three of these buildings were at the northern portion of the Qasaba, the main street that dissected the Fatimid City between the northern gate, Bab al Futuh, and the southern gate, Bab Zuwayla (see map on page 9).[19] There were dozens of such buildings in Cairo. They were the heart of trade in this trading city. Dozens existed including the *Wakala of Nafisa El-Bayda*[20] that to this day continues to sell wax candles, and the *Khan Khalili*, where gold and silversmiths still live and work.

> I went to-day to the market-place, where they vend the black slaves, that come
> from towards the interior parts of Africa. There were two hundred of them together,
> dressed and ornamented as in their country. The appearance of a savage in every
> region is almost the same. There were very few men among them; this indicates that
> they are prisoners of war.[21]

Ledyard was wrong about the reason for the lack of men among the slaves. Many men were kidnapped from their villages, or committed to enslavement because they were criminals, or given to slavers in payment of family debts, and sent north. They resisted. They refused to eat. They tried to run away. They did not survive the journey and their bodies were left in the desert. Women and children survived because they were submissive, more accepting of their fate, easier to handle.

Ledyard was correct about the routes. He concluded there were two main north-south routes from Egypt: Darfoor and Sennaar. "This caravan, which I call the Darfoor caravan, is not very rich," he commented. "The Sennaar is the rich caravan."[22] In fact, since the 1500s these two caravan routes vied with each other for dominance of the trade. In safe times the Sennar route, closer to the Nile and composed of several trails, flourished. When times were tough, when pirates dominated the Nile valley, or greedy officials demanded too many taxes too often, the Darfur caravan, swinging west through Kharga Oasis, grew in fame. The latter route was the *Darb al-Arbain* and became one of the most fabled trade routes in all of Africa. Covering 1,082 miles, it began at Kobbe in Darfur province, where the slaves were gathered and held, and made its way north from waterhole to waterhole through very inhospitable terrain. From the earliest times it entered Kharga Oasis, west of Luxor, at two customs points, Maks Qibli and Maks Bahri, where taxes were assessed, and then continued north under the watchful eyes of Persian and Roman fortresses to the Nile Valley at Asyut in middle Egypt. There the goods were rested, sorted, and passed on to Cairo via the river. By Ledyard's time two major caravans were expected in Cairo each year, each consisting of tens of thousands of people.

The Cairene merchants who controlled these caravans and sold their goods in the *wakalas* in Cairo were mostly Upper Egyptians. It was to them that Ledyard was to direct many of his questions. Ledyard thought it curious that no Westerner had traveled the caravan routes. This was another error. In fact, a number of Europeans had. If Ledyard had made the journey south, he would not have been the first, but he would have been the first known American.[23] The Americans George Bethune English, Khalil Aga, and Achmed Aga, would take that honor in 1820–21.

By mid–October Ledyard was a regular visitor at the caravan haunts, picking up information almost daily. It did not always go well, as he recorded on October 16: "I have renewed my visit today, and passed it more agreeable than yesterday; for yesterday I was rudely treated. The Franks are prohibited to purchase slaves, and therefore the Turkes do not like to see them in the market."[24] After spending considerable time among the traders and asking a myriad of questions, Ledyard felt that he had a good idea of where he was going, what the route was like, and what he would find when he got there. He was satisfied. He also knew the currency to use to get what he wanted: Venetian beads. Made of glass in various shapes and colors, the beads were used in place of coins on many of the caravans. Ledyard wrote in his journal:

> ... having observed yesterday among the ornaments of the Negroes a variety of
> beads, and wanting to know from what country they came, I requested Mr. Rosetti,
> previously to my second visit, to shew me from his store samples of Venetian beads.
> He shewed me samples of fifteen hundred different kinds: after this I set out....
> The beads they are ornamented with are Venetian; and they have some Venetian

brass medals, which the Venetians made for trade. The beads are worked wampum-wise. I know not where they got the marine shells they worked among their beads....[25]

Having yet to enter the African desert, Ledyard was unaware of the desert snails that subsist in areas that received morning mists, or the billions of fossilized shells deposited in the desert by receding ancient seas. The trail itself was his main focus. He not only heard of a number of the trade routes of North Africa, but, and most important, *he understood and recorded the secret of their names. This is John Ledyard's most important achievement!* "A caravan goes from here [Cairo] to Fezzan [west in Libya], which they call a journey of fifty days; and from Fezzan to Tombuctou, which they call a journey of ninety days."[26] The Arabic names for such roads would have been the *Darb al-Khamseen* (Fifty Day Road) and the *Darb al-Tissaein* (Ninety Day Road), just as the Darfur caravan would be and is called the *Darb al-Arbain,* the Forty Day Road. He was also observant enough to understand why such names were used: they helped calculate not only time, but distances too, and by merely saying the name a person distributed a lot of information. Ledyard concluded, "The caravans travel about twenty miles a day, which makes the distance on the road from here to Fezzan one thousand miles; and from Fezzan to Tombuctou, one thousand eight hundred miles."[27] These were not shocking distances to a man who had traveled over 7,000 miles through frozen Russia. Instead, and most important, they were a road map of North Africa.

Did he record more details about the origins of these names in his journal? Did the African Association realize the importance of the information he provided? If they did it was not something they wanted to share with the world. The French, the English, and the Germans were competing for control of the continent. This knowledge gave the African Association and its explorers an edge in the European incursion into Africa in the nineteenth century. Therefore, John Ledyard was never celebrated as the source of this detailed and important information. Hopefully African Association explorers made their way over these roads with Ledyard's knowledge as a guide. We say hopefully because a century and a half later, travelers and scholars were still speculating what the words *Darb al Arbain* actually meant, and no one was speaking of a *Darb al-Khamseen* (Fifty Day Road) or a *Darb al-Tamanein* (Twenty Day Road). The modern desert explorers agreed that *Darb al Arbain* meant Forty Day Road or Road of the Forty, but forty what? Among the speculators was one of Britain's top desert map-makers from the 1940s: George Murray, head of the Geological Survey of Egypt from 1932 to 1948. In his book *Dare Me to the Desert* Murray concluded that it could not take forty days to go from Kobbe in Sudan to Asyut in Egypt so the meaning of the name was that the prophet Mohammed and his forty men traveled this route.

In 1788 John Ledyard mused:

> I wonder why travellers to Cairo have not visited these slave markets, and conversed with the Jelabs, or traveling merchants of these caravans: both are certainly sources of great information. The eighth part of the money expended on other accounts, might here answer some good solid purpose. For my part, I have not expended a crown, and I have a better idea of the people of Africa, of its trade, of the position of places, the nature of the country, manner of traveling, etc. than ever I had by any other means; and, I believe better than any other means would afford me.[28]

The failure to ask questions was one of the basic flaws in the Western understanding of the East. If a question were asked, it was never asked of the right source. John Antes saw this as a problem and chastised his readers. European countries assumed the African states were too backward to have kept records. They were wrong. They never looked for them. They never read them. They never profited by them. "Franks" believed that no records were kept of the caravans and trade in general, therefore no information of any importance could be gained by investigating indigenous records. This, like the misconceptions concerning the riding of the donkey and the horse, was another fallacy. Trade documents, contracts, and other agreements covering over a thousand years could be found in Cairo records in a variety of places. Today these long-ignored materials are being consulted by enlightened scholars and will revise Cairene, Egyptian, and Middle Eastern history in the medieval era and beyond. Nelly Hanna in *Making Big Money in 1600: The Life and Times of Isma'il Abu Taqiyya, Egyptian Merchant,* pointed out, "Historians have so often stated that Middle Eastern merchants have not left us with any commercial papers.... So much of the commercial history of the Middle East has been written on the basis of European sources — consular reports, company correspondences, and travelers' accounts — that certain biases, such as an overemphasis of the importance of trading relations with Europe during this period, cannot be avoided."[29] Hanna found her indigenous trade documents in the court records. "The documents in these archives [15 courts of Cairo] are not only very detailed but also very varied, providing us with information about different kinds of dealings and transactions — sales on credit, loans, and partnerships ... we can piece together the trading patterns and commercial techniques of this period, and, crucial for a period undergoing transformations, the adaptability of these patterns and techniques to changing conditions."[30] John Ledyard, despite his many wrong conclusions, also saw the folly of relying on Westerners to explain the East.

Ultimately Ledyard contracted to go to the Sudan[31] with the caravan from Sennar. It would run along the Nile and be a journey that three Americans would perform two decades later as part of the Egyptian Expeditionary Force of 1820. "The merchant here who contracts to convey me to Sennar, is Procurer at Cairo to the King of Sennar; this is a good circumstance, and one I knew not of till today [Oct. 25, 1788]." Although anxious to begin, he was still in Cairo in November and restless to get underway. On November 15 he wrote a letter to his friend Thomas Jefferson.[32] It was his third letter, one for each month Ledyard was in Egypt. He said, "I am doing up my baggage — and most curious baggage it is — for my journey; and that I leave Cairo in 2 or 3 days."[33]

The letter to Jefferson was the last Ledyard was to write. He discloses his route: "I travel from here SW about three hundred leagues to a Black King: there my present conductors leave me to my fate — beyond, I suppose I go alone. I expect to cut the continent across between the parallels of 12 and 20 degrees of N Lat. I shall, if possible, write you from the kingdom of this black gentleman."[34] But he never got there.

Death of Ledyard

John Ledyard died in Cairo. The African Association minutes report his mortal illness was an attack of a "bilious complaint," so he took vitriolic acid. In other words, John Ledyard was in gastric distress and took a sulfur drug — too much of it. He had violent and burning pains that the best medical skills in Cairo could not help. The drug also contained sulfuric acid, which, if he took too much, could have burned up his stomach. He died January 10, 1789. He was only 38 years old.

Jefferson did not want to believe his friend was dead. He wrote to Thomas Paine, the American Patriot, author of *Common Sense,* in May of 1789 that he had just received Ledyard's last letter: "This seems to contradict the story of his having died at Cairo in January; as he was then probably in the interior parts of Africa. If Sr. Joseph Banks has no news from him later than the letter of September. It may do him pleasure if you will communicate the above. If he or any other person knows whether there is any foundation for the story of his death, I will thank you to be informed of it."[35]

Thomas Paine's response was not written until June 17, 1789, and he wrote again the following day, for he received a letter from Banks on the former date and had more information to convey to Jefferson. In the second letter Paine told Jefferson that Mr. Beaufoy of the African Association received a letter from Mr. George Baldwin, the British consul at Cairo:

> That a day was fixed for Mr. Ledyard's departure as he was prepared and seemed anxious to set off, but bad weather or other causes occasioned delay as happens to most caravans. Mr. Ledyard took offence at the delay and threw himself into a violent rage with his conductors which deranged something in his system that he thought to cure by an emetic, but he took the dose so strong as at the first or second effort of its operations to break a blood vessel. In three days he was suffocated and died.
> This Account is confirmed by a letter from Rosetti, the Venetian Resident at Cairo, to Mr. Hunter, an English Merchant who had lived in great intimacy with Mr. Ledyard from the time of their travelling together from Alexandria to Cairo to that of Mr. Hunter's departure for England.[36]

Jefferson resigned himself to the fact that Ledyard was dead.

It was left to Lewis and Clark to explore northwestern America. Their expedition west to the Pacific fulfilled not only Ledyard's dream but a 200-year-old quest. Jefferson as early as 1788–89 wrote to two friends that Ledyard "has promised me to go to America and penetrate from Kentucky to the western side of the continent."[37] In the introduction to the *Memoir* of Meriwether Lewis, Jefferson acknowledged Ledyard's role by saying that when Ledyard died: "Thus failed the first attempt to explore the western part of our northern continent."[38]

Jefferson remembered his vagabond friend. As for how John Ledyard perceived himself we do not know. All his dreams were unrealized. The fur trade went on without him. The Russian connection to the American continent remained undiscovered by the Americans. The road across Africa to the Niger, if it existed at all, was as much a mystery to the West as it had been before he arrived. The walk to the west coast of the Americas would remain a promise unfulfilled. To add to the misery of John Ledyard, his journal, in the hands of the African Association and later the Royal Geographical Society, is lost. And so is his grave.

John Ledyard's Grave

John Ledyard was buried in Cairo. Today we do not know where. The famous Swiss explorer John Burckhardt, who died in Cairo a few decades later in 1817, was buried near the northern gates to the city, but Burckhardt had converted to Islam and was interred in a Muslim cemetery. John Ledyard could not be buried there. Coptic Christians were buried on desert land near Old Cairo, east of the Nile and south of the medieval city. Nearly half a century after his death, the Khedive Ismail (1863–1879) set aside desert wasteland for the burial of "Franks" in that same area and a number of foreign cemeteries were established. Logically John Ledyard was buried in the same region.

As late as 1842 the site of Ledyard's grave was known. In a *New World* magazine review of James Ewing Cooley's book *The American in Egypt,* which was reprinted in its entirety in George Gliddon's *Appendix to The American in Egypt,* written in 1842, there is an interesting if incomprehensible note about Ledyard's grave. While chastising Cooley for misrepresenting the American David Bushnell, the reviewer remarked on Bushnell's kindnesses and his philanthropy, which "shed so bright a luster over the tomb of Ledyard."[39] This could be interpreted to mean that Gliddon and his contemporaries knew where Ledyard was buried.

Sometime in that decade Jared Sparks made an attempt to erect an obelisk to John

Ledyard in Cairo. Sparks was the editor of the *North American Review* and soon to be president of Harvard University. He wrote the first published biography of Ledyard. John Ledyard's cousin Isaac Ledyard and Isaac's brother-in-law Phillip Freneau, the noted American poet, had planned a biography, but after much publicity and a number of subscription drives, it never materialized. Jared Sparks took up the challenge and after ten years of research published *The Life of John Ledyard.*[40] The obelisk never rose.

On a visit to Egypt in 1857, William Cowper Prime, New York lawyer and American traveler, mentioned his efforts to find Ledyard's grave in his book *Boat Life in Egypt and Nubia,* but extended his comments considerably in a feature article in the *New York Times* in July of 1857.[41] Prime had more than a passing interest in John Ledyard. They were distantly related. The family relationship went back three generations. Prime had read Ledyard's letters to his mother and they had inspired him to travel and explore. So he really wanted to honor the man he considered not only a friend, but part of his family. The fact that Prime was privy to family papers and discourse provided a very important clue as to Ledyard's grave, "that he lay in one of the convents, then the only places in which Christian strangers found shelter, and finally died, alone or attended only by unknown priests."[42] There were other Americans laid to rest in the Christian convents of Alexandria and Cairo. Sixteen years earlier John Antes's Brother Danke was placed in the Coptic Church of Saint George, called Mari Girgis in Old Cairo, and Levi Parsons, the American missionary, would be buried in Alexandria at the Greek Convent a few decades after Ledyard died. The American consul, European and British merchants, and Christian religious figures accompanied Parsons to his grave.[43] John Ledyard probably had a similar funeral. Surely he was not placed in an anonymous desert grave without any ceremony.

Prime began his search in the "Latin Convent." This would be the residence of either the Friars de Propaganda Fide or the Padres de Terra Santa. He inquired and found "there were no books, no records, of the old men, no one who could furnish any information on any subject later than eighteen hundred years ago."[44] Next he went to the Armenian church "which stands in a cemetery about a mile from the city."[45] No luck there either. "The attendant was an old man, but he never heard of an American having died there, and there were no books nor records — nothing whatever." Passing the English Cemetery, Prime stepped inside: "Tempted by the open gate of the English Cemetery, we pulled up the donkeys at its entrance, and entered the enclosure. It is a beautifully-arranged, garden-like spot, luxuriant with flowers and trees of a hundred kinds, from all parts of the world. There was one stone over the grave of an American gentleman, who died here two or three years ago.... Edward Irving Bigelow was the name."[46]

Next Prime went to the Greek Church near Old Cairo. Old Cairo is also known by the ancient name of Babylon and is where the Romans built a fortress centuries earlier. Around it grew a city inhabited by the Copts after the Council of Chalcedon in 451 (see Chapter 13). They came to escape religious controversy with other Christians. In 641, the Arabs invaded Egypt and founded Fustat in the same area, building the Mosque of Amr there. In 969, when the Fatimids conquered Egypt from the east, they built the new city of Cairo to the north. Fustat and Old Cairo reverted back to Christian strongholds. The ancient churches and Christian cemeteries continued to grow through the nineteenth century and many Christian cemeteries are found in the area today, including the European cemeteries of Austria, France, England, as well as the American cemetery. Prime's description illustrated not only his journey but the environment of Old Cairo in 1857.

Prime and his companions were at the Church of Saint George at Babylon in Old Cairo. Here Prime ran into bureaucracy. The attendant would not tell him anything. When asked to bring a book, he complied. But what he brought were old manuscripts, not old records. It was not an ingenuous act. Western travelers had been asking for and buying ancient manuscripts from the ancient churches of Egypt for a long time. Prime, however, was frustrated. He called the man stupid, one hopes not to his face, but in a letter to the *New York Times*. Prime gave up and asked the location of another church: "The one we particularly wished to find is the oldest, and is said to cover a grotto in which Mary and Joseph, with the infant Savior, rested and lived while in Egypt." But the man would not help him: "Here stupidity vanished and deceit and lying took its place." The man told him there was no such church: "Joseph and Mary never were in Cairo." They left the man, found the girl who had been acting as their guide again, and she, in fact, took them to the church they were looking for: the Church of St. Sergius.

> My search was in vain.... No one remembered him — none of the old men had any recollection of his death — no books remain to speak of him — no record was made, or if made, none was kept of that period — and I believe I may consider it settled that the grave of Ledyard will never be found....
> But somewhere here I think the tired traveler found repose, and I trust I will find it undisturbed. It were better to sleep thus, with all the old dead of four thousand years, than to sleep in a bought grave at the mercy of a Greek Christian. To him it was terrible to die thus. To no man did death ever come with more of terror. But I doubt not that when his stout soul fully realized the presence of the dread angel, he thought that, after all, next to the church-yard at his home, where his mother's eye would look in his grave till she slept by his side, this sleep in the sands of the Arabian desert, on the banks of the lordly Nile, was what he would have chosen who had seen all the world to choose from.[47]

There should be Arabic records of the death and burial of John Ledyard. Hopefully someone, after 200 years, will try to find them. Once the records and the grave are found, modern medicine can tell how John Ledyard died.

Five years after John Ledyard told the African Association about the trade routes to Darfur and Sennar, the English traveler W.G. Browne traveled both of them. Starting along the route to Sennar, Browne was detoured by a war, crossed the desert to Kharga Oasis, and continued down the route to Darfur, the *Darb al-Arbain,* to Kobbe and on to Sennar. To him goes the credit of Ledyard's journey. As for the Niger, Mungo Park of Scotland discovered the route of the Niger River for the African Association in 1798, ten years after Ledyard made his attempt. The English explorers William Lucas and Major Houghton and the German Frederic Horneman, all sent out by the African Association, failed.

Park died in 1805 while attempting to trace the river's source and find the mythical Timbuktu. African-American Robert Adams from New York was shipwrecked off the coast of West Africa five years later in 1810.[48] He was taken in chains to the city of Timbuktu, where he stayed for several months as a slave. He was the first Westerner since the traveler Leo Africanus in 1550 to write about the city. Adams's story about the exotic city, published in England as *The Narrative of Robert Adams* in 1816, was dismissed as fiction. As the following chapters will show, Americans were often denied credit for their discoveries in Africa. George Bethune English, the American who accompanied Egypt's army deep into Africa in 1820–1, held a different view: "The honour of the discovery of Tombuctoo also, in my opinion, belongs to the United States. As I have understood that some doubts have been insinuated in this country [England] as to the truth of Adams' *Narrative,* I would beg leave to oppose to such doubts the opinion of Sheck Ibrahim [John Lewis Burckhardt] who was unquestionably the man best qualified to give a sound judgment on this subject...."[49] Not believing Adams, the African Association continued its search. Gordon Laing went looking for Timbuktu in August of 1826, but died on his return journey to England. Hugh Clapperton, looking for the city at the same time as Laing, never reached it. The man credited with the rediscovery of Timbuktu is the Frenchman Rene Caillié, who arrived there around 1826, sixteen years and a lot of tragedy since Adams was there. He, too, was accused of lying until Henrick Barth, the German explorer, verified his claim nearly 30 years later.

In his last letter to Thomas Jefferson, John Ledyard wrote, "...do not forget me in the interval of time.... I shall not forget you; indeed, it will be a consolation to think of you in my last moments. Be happy."[50]

3

William Eaton: To the Shores of Tripoli (Soldier, 1804–1805)

The first official American military mission on foreign soil landed in Alexandria, Egypt, on November 26, 1804, sixteen years after the African Association sent John Ledyard to Cairo.[1] The unusual, difficult, and nearly disastrous mission really began among the Barbary States of North Africa eight years before in 1796. After the American Revolution, the states of Algeria, Tunis, and Tripoli were causing serious problems for American merchants and naval vessels in the Mediterranean. For nearly a century, they had been extorting ransoms from foreign vessels along what became known as the Barbary Coast. As long as the United States was a colony of the British Empire, the power of the British fleet protected American vessels. Once independence was won, that was no longer the case. The high seas, be it in the West Indies or the Mediterranean, became a nightmare for America. Because of this, the American government, which had dismantled its navy after the Revolutionary War, found it necessary to rebuild a navy to protect its merchant ships in the Mediterranean and around the world. The Americans signed the Treaty of Peace and Friendship at Tripoli November 4, 1796.[2] But North Africa was only one of their problems.

These were turbulent times on the high seas. Britain and France were at war. Western nations fought each other to open trade in exotic places like the West Indies, the Red Sea, and the Orient. A new nation was easy prey, or so it was believed. The United States created a special department, the Department of Captures by the Belligerent Powers, to record incidents against American ships and to try to solve the problem. The French and English were just as apt to attack an American ship as were the Spanish or the Barbary States. The French were so aggressive in their attacks on American ships in the West Indies and the Mediterranean that dozens of American vessels were captured and hundreds of Americans languished in French prisons. Between 1797 and 1798 the *Naval Documents related to the Quasi-War between the United States and France* listed account after account of French violations against Americans.[3] It reached such a crisis that a "quasi" war was declared between the two countries.

> The depredations of French cruisers and privateers had been so great that on the 2d of March, 1794, Edmund Randolph charged France with flagrant violations of the treaty, and a list of thirty-eight American vessels carried into French ports by French cruisers and privateers was given. It was not until several years later that Congress gave up all hope of adjusting the difficulty, but on the 4th of May, 1798, the construction of galleys and several small vessels was ordered, and on the 28th of the same

ROUTE OF WILLIAM EATON'S ARMY
FROM ALEXANDRIA TO DERNA
8 MARCH TO 25 APRIL, 1805

month our cruisers were authorized to capture any French vessel that might be found near the coast preying upon American commerce. On the 7th of July, 1798, all treaties with France were abrogated, and American cruisers were ordered to capture French vessels when found within the limits, and two days afterward they were permitted to attack them wherever found....[4]

The English were more cagey. English ships of the line fell upon American ships trading with French colonies in the West Indies. Yet, when called upon for aid against Spanish ships in the Mediterranean, the English assisted the Americans. To make it even more complicated, the English supported and encouraged the Barbary States to attack and capture American vessels in the Mediterranean.

> England's aim was to secure a monopoly of the carrying trade and commerce of the world, and in furtherance of this purpose she encouraged the pirates of the Mediterranean, so that, with the aid of her fleet and by paying them a small tribute, her commerce was unmolested while that of weaker maritime nations was constantly harassed. By acknowledging the independence of the United States, England admitted a dangerous competitor to this trade, and in a few years American shipping reached a million tons. The means Great Britain took to cut off this competitor is seen in the following extract from a speech made by Lord Sheffield in Parliament in 1784: "It is not probable that the American States will have a very free trade in the Mediterranean. It will not be to the interest of any of the great maritime powers to protect them from the Barbary States. If they know their interests, they will not encourage the Americans to be carriers. That the Barbary States are advantageous to maritime powers is certain. If they are suppressed, the little States of Italy would have much more of the carrying trade."[5]

Of course relations between the world's countries and events on the high seas were far more convoluted than explained here. The point of these incidents is that harassment of ships by foreign nations, be they Barbary, European, or American, was the norm, not the exception. It was also the norm for non–European nations mostly in the Near and Far East to make outrageous demands on Europeans wishing to inaugurate trade. Here, too, the Barbary States' humiliating and humbling demands followed an established international pattern. When the Dutch attempted to trade with Japan they met with many degradations. Their "chief agent, journeyed to Yeddo to offer gifts ... 'creeping forward on his hands and feet, and falling on his knees, bowed his head to the ground, and retired again in absolute silence, crawling exactly like a crab....'"[6]

Of course, the Barbary demands were no less outrageous. At first, in the same manner as all the other nations, the United States had agreed to pay tribute in order to continue to trade in the Mediterranean. In the original agreement:

> The United States were to pay for the friendship and forbearance of Tunis one hundred and seven thousand dollars in money, jewels, and naval stores. Tunisian cargoes were to be admitted into American ports on payment of three per cent; the same duty to be levied at Tunis on American shipments. If the Bey saluted an American man-of-war, he was to receive a barrel of powder for every gun fired. And he reserved the right of taking any American ship that might be in his harbor into his service to carry despatches or a cargo to any port in the Mediterranean.[7]

Opposite: **Map of trek across desert (Dudley W. Knox,** *Naval Documents Related to the U.S. Wars with the Barbary Powers,* **Volume V:** *Naval Operations Including Diplomatic Background from September 7, 1804 through April 1805.* **Washington, D.C.: Government Printing Office, 1944).**

By trying to save its own ships from confiscation within this system, the fledgling United States with nothing much to lose and a lot to gain, took the first strides that ultimately freed the seas.

Jefferson believed this. He wrote to Judge John Tyler on March 29, 1805, while the American marines were still crossing the Western Desert: "There is reason to believe the example we have set begins already to work on the dispositions of the powers of Europe to emancipate themselves from that degrading yoke. Should we produce such a revolution there, we shall be ably regarded for what we have done."[8] It was a long and complicated process, but it began when the demands of the Treaty of Peace and Friendship between the United States and Tripoli arrived in Philadelphia (then the U.S. capital) and the American Congress refused to provide such booty. A year later, in 1797, President John Adams appointed a feisty New Englander named William Eaton as the first United States consular agent to Tunis with the mandate to deal with the matter of the tribute. When the Bey of Tunis demanded his tribute, Eaton explained that the Senate demanded changes to the content before they would ratify the treaty.

The United States had caved in to most of the demands, for now. They did not, however, want to pay the jewels. The Bey was outraged. He had abandoned the request for a frigate, but brought it back to the table and now insisted on the jewels and the frigate. The United States ordered the jewels in London, where they were cheaper than in the United States. All of this took another year. While awaiting the jewels, the Bey continued making intermittent demands. When there was a fire at the palace the Bey called upon Eaton and the United States to give him "ten thousand stand of arms," which Eaton refused. The Bey insisted and threatened to send the request directly to Washington. Eaton wanted to know if the demands would ever end. The Bey replied that demands on Christian nations would never be over.

Tripoli was controlled by two brothers of a longstanding ruling family: Yusef and Hamet Karamanli. The younger, Yusef, had thrown the legitimate ruler, Hamet, out of the country. The latter ended up in Egypt (as almost every exile throughout history managed to do). Yusef made every attempt to humiliate the American consul, James Cathcart. Finally, in May of 1801, he declared war on the United States and Cathcart joined Eaton in Tunis. Eaton was against paying any type of ransom or tribute. After several years of humiliation he came to the conclusion that what was needed in Barbary was force. He believed as long as the United States and other nations capitulated to the outrageous demands of the Barbary rulers, merchant ships would continue to be attacked, their goods confiscated, and their crews sold into slavery. In a report to Secretary of State James Madison he chastised his government for not acting forcefully. Eaton and Cathcart devised a plan to restore Hamet to power by launching a land attack against Derna, a small town in Eastern Tripoli situated between the Gebel al Akhdar (Green Mountain) and the Mediterranean Sea. Eaton went back to the United States to win the approval of President Thomas Jefferson. Jefferson and Secretary of State James Madison were agitated by the treatment of American diplomats by the Barbary rulers, but they hesitated to take up arms.

All the tension culminated in 1803 with the USS *Philadelphia* incident. The frigate *Philadelphia* and the schooner *Vixen* had been sent to Tripoli. Their mission, under the Mediterranean commander Commodore Edward Preble, was to blockade the Tripoli port to try to end the war recently declared on the United States by Tripoli. The *Philadelphia,* in pursuit of an enemy vessel, hit the uncharted Kaliusa Reef and went aground. When Tripolitan vessels began to approach the American ship, its captain, William Bainbridge, lowered the flag in capitulation without a shot being fired (in a hearing after the incident he was acquitted of all charges, but history has judged him otherwise).[9] The ship, which dislodged itself from the reef, its 27 officers, and 270 tars were taken to the port at Tripoli, and an enormous and embarrassing ransom was demanded. In mid–February 1804, 74 men under the leadership of Stephen Decatur, a naval lieutenant attached to the Mediterranean fleet, crept into the harbor and set the *Philadelphia* on fire, winning back some American prestige (and a captaincy for Decatur). Yet the men remained prisoners.

After the *Philadelphia* incident, Jefferson agreed to Eaton's plan and appointed him United States Navy agent for the Barbary States. James Madison allotted $20,000 for the mission. Operations were under the control of Commodore Samuel Barron, the ailing and inert head of the Mediterranean Fleet. The finances were to be controlled by the newly appointed consul general Tobias Lear, a former personal secretary to George Washington. These two men did not appreciate the personality or exploits of William Eaton. Barron delayed Eaton's mission, but in the end provided some finances for Eaton. Lear would not use a penny of the finances to aid Eaton. Under these conditions, the tiny American ship *Argus,* commanded by Lieutenant Isaac Hull, pulled into the bay of Alexandria on November 26, 1804. William Eaton and a detachment of U.S. Marines were on board.

Egypt in 1804

Much had happened since Antes and Ledyard lived in Cairo a few decades earlier. With the British and French at war, Napoleon Bonaparte had struck another blow at the English. He had invaded Egypt. Knowing a cut in the short landmass between the Mediterranean and the Red Sea could bring victory to France in the battle that had been devastating world shipping in the past decade, Napoleon aimed the 400 ships and the 38,000 men of the *Armée d'Orient* south in May of 1798. They crossed the sea, and in June arrived in Abu Qir Bay to disgorge both fighters and scholars in an unprecedented offensive. Nothing could stop the invasion. Napoleon brought guns and cannon to Egypt, which outclassed the medieval arms of the Egyptian army. But he also brought 167 scholars: the *Commission des Sciences et des Arts.* By July 1 the French had defeated Alexandria and pushed on to Cairo. By mid–July the army stood before the Mamluk army assembled at Imbaba, a small area then located south of Cairo on the west bank of the Nile. Dubbed the Battle of the Pyramids, their encounter was fought July 21 and by July 23–24, Napoleon entered the walled and gated city of Cairo.

It did not take Napoleon long to launch changes in Egypt. French law, French courts, and French financial methods were introduced. Hospitals and school were built. A printing press called the *Imprimerie Nationale du Caire* was created. A new quarantine system was developed. Probably the most interesting event was extending landownership to the peasants, something which gave them a chance at new lives. Then construction began carving wide, straight boulevards through the twisting narrow neighborhoods of Cairo. These events affected life on the streets. For centuries foreigners had been segregated in Cairo. Now the French soldiers in form-fitting pants roamed freely through the city. European taverns began to appear on the newly carved boulevards. The soldiers got drunk and flirted with Eastern women. It was a shocking change in the city.

While Napoleon was westernizing the government, French scientists, engineers, geographers, writers, and economists were recording ancient and modern Egypt. They covered every topic: from the antiquities, the flora and fauna, the flow of the Nile, the social composition, the law, the language, the religions, to the ethnographic customs, dress, music, and art. On August 22, 1798, a month after arriving in Cairo, Napoleon established the *Institut d'Égypte.* Papers related to the discoveries underway in Egypt were presented every five days by the thirty-seven members. The savants radiated into all areas of the country. They studied birds in the Delta, observed the fish in the Nile, mapped the country, measured, copied, and recorded temples and their contents. In July 1799 a letter was read at the *Institut* reporting a black basalt stone covered with inscriptions had been found in Rosetta. Of course, this became known as the Rosetta Stone, the key that would one day unravel the mysteries of the hieroglyphics. It was a seminal moment in the thousands of years of life in Cairo.

But Napoleon's time in Egypt was short. England could not allow the French to claim Egypt. Rear Admiral Horatio Nelson was promptly sent to Egypt at the head of the English fleet. He found the French ships in the harbor of Abu Qir Bay and destroyed most of them. Known as the Battle of the Nile, or the Battle of Abu Qir Bay, the events on August 1–2, 1798, stranded Napoleon and his men in Egypt. The Ottoman leaders in Constantinople could not stand by and allow the French and English to take their most important possession. They landed their army at Abu Qir in an attempt to throw the French out of the country. That battle with the French took place July 25, 1799. The French routed the Turks. By August 23, 1799, Napoleon was out of Egypt, leaving his army and his savants behind, where they remained for several more years.

In 1801 there was a joint invasion by the British at Abu Qir, the Ottoman overland via Syria, and British India via Quseir on the Red Sea. Yet another battle took place at Abu Qir. In June the French capitulated and began to leave Egypt. The military battles were over, but the battle for the documents and antiquities that the French had researched and planned to take to France had just begun. As part of their victory, the British intended to take all of the French research material to England. The French scientists said no. In the end the French took most of their booty, but the British took the Rosetta Stone and a few other special antiquities. The French collection became the base upon which the *Description d'Égypte* was created. The first of the twenty folio volumes would not appear until 1809. Its publication created the first era of Egyptomania in the West.

When William Eaton and his Americans landed at Alexandria, the British were still in Egypt. They would not leave until 1807 at the insistence of Mohammad Ali. What Eaton saw was an Ottoman leadership under siege from a number of internal forces. Kusruf Pasha had just begun his short reign as the Turkish Viceroy in Cairo. Muhammad al-Alfi Bey was waiting in Minya with his Mamluk army for his opportunity to strike. Rival Mamluk leaders were spread throughout the country. Albanian Arnouts from the Balkans were roaming the river banks, attacking villages for food and water. Nomadic desert Bedouins seized the opportunity to raid accessible villages along the Nile that no longer had the protection of a central government. Mohammad Ali, whose dynasty would modernize and rule Egypt for the next century, was just beginning his ascent towards control of Egypt. The remaining French and British were competing with each other for dominant positions in the country that sat at the crossroads of the world. European soldiers of fortune, many of them deserters from various armies, found Egypt a good place to "hide out." Egypt was in chaos.

The Men of the Mission

The American expedition consisted of at least twelve marines and sailors. The 5'8," fair-skinned, blue-eyed William Eaton (1764–1811) was a headstrong, eccentric New Englander, the son of a poor farmer in Connecticut. He became a soldier in the Revolutionary War at the age of sixteen, attended Dartmouth College, and then pursued a law career. For a time he clerked for the General Assembly of Connecticut, then in 1792 he joined General Mad Anthony Wayne on a mission against Indians in the region of Ohio. Called the Legion of the United States, Wayne's army had been established by George Washington. Eaton was one of his officers, as was William Clark who, in 1803, would be one of the leaders of the Lewis and Clark expedition that fulfilled John Ledyard's dream and found the Northwest Passage to the Pacific Ocean via an overland route. Wayne and his men defeated the Indians at the Battle of Fallen Timbers. This experience steeled Eaton to suffer a tough military mission.

William Eaton was a flawed man. Throughout his career his temperament often led him into unfortunate situations. When he was in the Ohio wilderness in 1793 he was court-martialed because of an altercation with his superior.[10] He left Tunis under yet another cloud. Without authorization he paid $22,000 in government funds to free a young European girl from slavery. The Secretary of the Treasury insisted Eaton reimburse the fee, which grew to over $44,000 once Thomas Jefferson discovered Eaton had used his own ship the *Gloria* for naval matters. He was nearly sent home in disgrace, but the *Philadelphia* incident occurred and saved his career. His plan received new life. By Thomas Jefferson's petition and Congress's approval, William Eaton led the first American covert mission to attempt to overthrow a foreign power.

The Marine lieutenant on the mission was a Freemason named Presley Neville O'Bannon (1776–1850). O'Bannon, born in Virginia, became a second lieutenant in the U.S. Marine Corps on January 18, 1801. His first mission to the Mediterranean was aboard the *Adams* in 1802. Upon returning to the United States he served at the Marine Barracks in Washington, D.C. Returning to the Mediterranean in 1804 he first served on the USS *President,* then the USS *Constitution,* and finally the USS *Argus.* The sergeant was Arthur Campbell. The privates were Bernard O'Brian, David Thomas, James Owens, John Whitten, Edward Stewart, and an unnamed marine.[11] (Whitten and Stewart were to die at Derna.) There were three midshipmen. One of them, Pascal Paoli Peck of Providence, Rhode Island, provided an account of his trek across North Africa in a letter to a friend written at Malta on July 4, 1805.[12] It became part of the official naval record. At Bomba, Peck left the ground expedition and boarded the American ship *Argus,* and was replaced by midshipman George Washington Mann. Mann became one of the heroes of Derna.[13]

Of the Europeans in the expedition, there were two Farquhars, a father and son. In the official naval record, all the references to Farquhar are indexed under a single name, Richard. This is an error. In fact, there were two men: Richard and his son Percival. The first encounter with Richard was when he contacted Thomas Jefferson by letter in 1804 hoping to become the American liaison with Hamet Karamanli. Eaton met Richard in Malta and the Scotsman sailed to Egypt aboard the *Argus.*[14] It is assumed that Percival was with his father at that time. What is clear is that Percival was on the desert journey, where he stood shoulder to shoulder with Eaton through the long ordeal of desert travel.[15] Richard was long gone before the desert crossing began.[16] On April 17, while Eaton was at Bomba, trying to unload provisions, Richard was in Syracuse, where he addressed a letter to Samuel Barron, commander of the American Mediterranean fleet, saying, "I sailed from Alexandria on 13 March."[17] On that date, Eaton was between modern Alamein and Mersa Matruh.[18] These incidents provide enough evidence to prove Richard Farquhar did not cross the desert with the Eaton expedition, as some sources maintain. It was Percival Farquhar who was on the desert journey.[19]

A trusted European ally was the Italian doctor, Francisco Mendrici, a friend from Tunis where Eaton had been the American consul. According to Eaton, Mendrici was forced to leave Tunis "for possessing dispositions congenial to the interest of the Bey's wife."[20] In Egypt, Mendrici served as doctor to the Egyptian Viceroy (and later to the British Consul General Ernesto Missett). Mendrici accompanied Eaton on his tasks in the Nile Valley and kept a lookout for foreign intrigue against the Americans. He was not on the desert journey. He was more useful to Eaton in the Nile Valley, where he could keep an eye on the French Consul.

Eaton so admired Mendrici's abilities that he appointed him "Agent of the United States in Grand Cairo and its dependencies until pleasure of the President shall be expressed on the subject." Eaton confirmed this appointment in a letter to the Secretary of the Navy on the same day, December 13, 1804.[21] That act made Mendrici the United States' first commercial representative in Cairo. Eaton overstepped his authority here, for Egypt was subject to Constantinople and any trade or agency had to be negotiated through the Porte.

Eaton's next choice was a mysterious man of many names, Eugene Leitensdorfer, a five-foot-nine, dark-haired, brown-eyed Tyrolean, whom Eaton employed in Cairo on December 21, 1804.[22] As he told Eaton, he was not born Leitensdorfer, but Gervasio Santuari, near Trentino (in modern Italy) in 1772, and under that name joined the Austrian army. At the time he met Eaton he was the "chief of staff and director of artillery to the Turkish army in Egypt." He was to serve as Eaton's adjutant and Inspector general. Obviously, Leitensdorfer was a survivor. Of all the men on the expedition, including Eaton, Leitensdorfer fared the best in later years, when he won a pension from the American government and established himself along the Mississippi River.[23]

The exact number of the remaining participants in the expedition is not clear. Additional mercenaries included Selim the Janissary (an Ottoman soldier), who had been an officer in the Turkish army and commanded 25 cannoniers on the journey.[24] There were 38 to 50 Greeks, 500 to 700 Tripolitan Arabs, 50 to 100 Egyptians, 90 men belonging to Hamet Karamanli of the ruling family of Tripoli, and a party of Arab cavalry under sheikhs el Taiib and Mahamet. To carry the supplies Eaton hired "one hundred and seven camels and a few asses."[25] The army would grow as it moved across North Africa, picking up Bedouins and their families eager to return to Tripoli.

Gathering the Army

Amid all the turmoil following the French/English invasion, William Eaton had to find the exiled ruler of Tripoli, Hamet Karamanli. Karamanli had rejected the aid of Kusruf Pasha and placed his fate with the rebellious Mamluk army of Elfi Bey, which was to the south of Cairo in the city of Minya. Reaching Hamet was a formidable task in a country near anarchy. Eaton and some members of his party left Alexandria and set sail up the Nile for Cairo, about 100 miles further south.[26] He ordered the American flag to be hoisted on the Nile. This is a significant event, for it was probably the first time the American flag flew on the Nile. Eaton's journal and the official naval records of the trip are clear on this event:

> Rosetta 2[d] Dec 1804
> ... Yesterday Morning we displayed the flag of the United States upon our Gume [Germe or Jerm], and about One O.Clock P.M. entered the Nile several miles below Rosetta....[27]

and again:

> Wednesday, 5 December 1804
> Wind contrary, went ashore: inhabitants oppressed and miserable. At 11, A. M. made sail. The British flag displayed on Capt. Vincent's vessel; that of the United States on ours.[28]

Finding Hamet was acerbated from an unexpected source: the formidable and capable hands of the French agent in Egypt, Bernardino Drovetti. Drovetti is undoubtedly one of the most important European figures in Egypt. Piedmontese by birth and a lawyer by profession, he was French consul in Egypt for over thirty years. He arrived in Egypt in 1803 and in addition to his consular duties was involved in archaeology and exploration. Drovetti, more than any other foreigner, aided Mohammad Ali in securing power in Egypt and influenced the direction of modern Egypt for the next decades. For a third of a century, Drovetti was a key player in the fate of Egypt. When the Americans arrived in Egypt in 1804, Drovetti was at the beginning of his influence and power. Just as England and France did not want the Americans in the Mediterranean, Drovetti did not want them in Egypt. He underestimated William Eaton and his stubborn New England persistence. When Eaton attempted to make an appointment with the Viceroy to get permission to go in quest of Hamet, Drovetti tried to convince the Viceroy it was not in Egypt's interest to grant the Americans an audience. Eaton wrote to Commander Edward Preble on January 25, 1805, that Drovetti

> had insinuated that we were British spies in American masks; and that our pretext of friendship for Hamet Bashaw aimed at nothing but an intercourse with the Mamluks, who are suspected of being in British subsidy.... I am yet totally at a loss to account for this strange conduct of Mr. Drovitte — as I am equally so at the indignity of our flag being refused by that of the French throughout this Country, those marks of civility never refused to a foreign flag, in ordinary cases, and which we receive from every other Nation represented here; except that, informed of our Object, and pursuing the same line of conduct with his colleague at Tripoli he thought by these means, to defeat that Object.[29]

It is apparent from naval correspondence that the Americans believed the French had also interfered with diplomatic affairs in Tripoli. Captain Edward Preble, in a letter to Robert Livingston on December 15, 1804, stated, "It is my opinion that we should long since have been at Peace with Tripoli if the French Consul there had not interfered. It is for the Interest of his Nation to keep us at War with that Regency...."[30]

The French were just one of the problems for the Americans on the Nile. Eaton was in a politically sensitive position. Hamet was with the Mamluk Army, which meant the dethroned ruler had taken a stand against the Ottoman Empire, yet Eaton had to persuade the Viceroy, a representative of the Ottoman Empire, to allow Hamet free passage through Egypt. Through the aid of Dr. Mendrici, an audience was granted, and Eaton, as many foreigners before and after, paraded up the avenue to the Citadel and marveled at a royal audience with a ruler of Egypt.

Despite Drovetti's intrigues and Hamet's alliance with the Mamluks, Eaton obtained the Viceroy's letter of amnesty and passport of safe conduct for Hamet. It would be assumed that it was not within Turkish interest to allow the Americans to form an alliance with Tripoli, but, as will be determined, the Viceroy was eager for Eaton to succeed.

Finding Hamet

Eaton's attempts to get messages through to Hamet in Minya were unsuccessful. As events unfolded it became clear that the Mamluk beys, at Drovetti's instigation, were not passing the messages through. Drovetti's actions made the American mission very uneasy. Eaton's colleagues were restless and wanted to leave Egypt. As early as January 5, 1805, Captain Hull, still aboard the *Argus* in Alexandria harbor, was anxious to depart. He felt the mission was taking too long and the attempts at sabotage by the French were diverting them from their task.[31]

Nevertheless, that same month, January 1805, Eaton heard from Hamet. They agreed to meet, but Hamet was distrustful of the Viceroy, and although he first agreed to meet Eaton in Behera in the Nile Delta, he changed his mind and asked to meet Eaton further south in the oasis of the Fayoum to the west of the Nile. Despite all the dangers and the pressures from his fellow officers, Eaton, accompanied by Eugene Leitensdorfer, Lieutenant Blake, George W. Mann, and twenty-three additional men, and perhaps flying the American flag at the head of their column, left Alexandria and advanced toward the Fayoum oasis.

If Eaton did march behind the flag, this was the second time the American flag was unfurled by the expedition. More than one American source has claimed that Mendes Cohen, one of the United States' first antiquities collectors, as late as 1832, was the first American to fly the American flag in Egypt. Their information came from the journals of Mendes Cohen, who himself believed he was the first to fly the flag on the Nile.[32] Obviously he was incorrect. In addition, almost every military reference to these events claims that after the victory at Derna, Presley Neville O'Bannon raised the American flag for the first time on foreign soil. This belief may have come from the Senate Resolution of March 18, 1806, which stated that the mission had "courageously marched through the Libyan desert, defeated the Tripolitan army near Derne, and took that city of the twenty seventh day of April, eighteen hundred and five, and for the first time spread the American eagle in Africa, on the ramparts of a Tripolitan fort, and thereby contributed to release three hundred American prisoners from bondage in Tripoli."[33] O'Bannon was late by a few months. His commander had done it before him along the Nile.

Eaton and his party never made it to the Fayoum. They were arrested by the Kercheif of Damanhour's 500 Ottoman troops somewhere in the Nile Delta well north of Cairo. Once more Eaton suspected Bernardino Drovetti, and he wrote in his journal: "But this suspicious circumstance was strengthened and aggravated by the insinuation gone out from the French Consul that we came into this country with secret views hostile to the Turks."[34]

Eaton knew he was in serious trouble. In a simple, straightforward manner, he explained to the Kercheif what he wanted to do in Egypt. The Kercheif in turn called in an Arab of the "Ou ad Allis" (the Awlad Ali Bedouins) and asked him about Hamet. The Arab confirmed Eaton's story, adding that he knew 20,000 Barbary Arabs were willing to follow Eaton to Tripoli. He also pledged to bring Hamet to Eaton within ten days. The Kercheif was reluctant to let this happen, so Eaton offered to stay with him as his guest until Hamet arrived.

Samuel Edwards, in his biography of Eaton published in the 1960s, exaggerated the story of William Eaton's journey considerably, tainting much of the research after that date. At this point, Edwards stated that Eaton was placed in a dirty Turkish jail in Damanhour. He credited Eli Danielson, Eaton's stepson, with describing "the interior of a Turkish prison to you, or to convey some idea of the existence one is forced to endure there. The stench is beyond imagination, there are vermin and rodents everywhere, the slops one is fed are unpalatable...."[35] This was not true. On the contrary, Eaton reported his accommodations were, in fact, satisfactory and his jailers quite cordial: "We left him and retired to a handsome pavilion prepared for the purpose; took refreshments he had ordered to be in readiness; and the next morning returned, with an additional escort from his camp, to this place; where we found handsome lodgings in Turkish stile prepared for us."[36]

Edwards did not end his exaggeration with the jail accommodations. He further enhanced his description by giving Eaton the air of Lawrence of Arabia, who fought in the Arabian Peninsula during World War I, more than a hundred years later. In fact, the cover of his book heralded "the amazing account of a flamboyant hero who was truly America's 'Lawrence of Arabia.'" Edwards claimed Eaton was an Arabic-speaking, robe-flowing, scimitar-wielding hero. This, of course, was pure romanticism. There were similarities between the situations of the two men. They both crossed an unknown desert under difficult circumstances. They both dealt with an army of mixed origins and therefore with complicated problems. They were both successful, and in the end their successes were destroyed by their own country, amounting to what each considered a personal betrayal. Eaton, who made his journey a hundred years before Lawrence, was eccentric, headstrong, and erratic; so was Lawrence. But there the similarities end.

No, Eaton did not go native, as Edwards suggested. Where Edwards claimed, "He astonished the sentries assigned to stand watch over him by speaking fluent Arabic,"[37] in truth, Eaton's Arabic was not good enough and he used an interpreter on this journey. Leitensdorfer, whom, as we have noted, was one of Eaton's trusted soldiers, supported this fact a few years later in his petition to the United States Senate and House of Representatives when he spoke of Eaton, "Without a knowledge of the language and without any means of influence he [Eaton] must have found insuperable difficulties in every attempt to accomplish his object."[38] The fact that his Arabic was not fluent was also supported by Eaton himself, for in his diary he reported he spoke French and the court interpreter translated into Arabic: "And, through the intervention of my friend Doctor Mendrici who has great influence at court, and of the Viceroy's chief interpreter, whom we have gained, there is no doubt of obtaining his permission...."[39] Then again, "A woman offered her daughter to my interpreter for a sack of it [rice];"[40] and, "The Bashaw with twelve horsemen and my interpreter returned to the castle,"[41] further confirming he had someone helping him with the language. Nor did Eaton don Arab dress as

General Eaton and Hamet Bashaw on the March to Derne, circa 1805. From a woodcut in *Life and Times* (Winnigerodet), page 80, date unknown (NHHC Photograph Collection, NH 56755. Courtesy of the Naval History and Heritage Command).

did Lawrence. Edwards wrote, "Most of the Americans were stunned, but William, who changed into Arab attire, seemed completely at home."[42] And again, "Naval Agent Eaton no longer dressed in Western attire, but was seen everywhere in Alexandria wearing flowing Arab robes."[43] Edwards even dressed O'Bannon as an Arab: "O'Bannon went out every day in flowing Arab robes, a pair of pistols and his superbly fashioned scimitar in his belt."[44] It is simply not true. To wear foreign clothes as a disguise for a specific mission is a possibility, but William Eaton, a military man who gave himself a general's title, would not don Arab dress as an affectation. The requirement that all foreigners wear Arabic dress in Egypt was destroyed by the French army, and the military men of England and France all wore their uniforms in Egypt at this time. For the Americans not to wear their uniforms would diminish the American cause in foreign eyes. There are a number of references within Eaton's journal that provide evidence that Eaton wore the American military uniform throughout his journey. Eaton recorded in his journal while on the desert trek, "They laughed at the oddity of our dress; gazed at our polished arms with astonishment; at the same time they observed the greatest deference towards such of us as born any distinctive marks of office."[45] And again on March 30, nearly a month after they began their desert trek and three months after the *Argus* landed in Egypt, both his dress and his language are verified by a single entry: "Curiosity brought every Arab about me who belonged to the tribe. They examined the lace of my hat, epaulettes, buttons, spurs, and mounting of my arms. These they took to be all gold and silver. They were astonished that God should permit people to possess such riches who followed the religion of the devil! My interpreter explained that the religion of the Americans...."[46] In addition, the naval art of the day depicting the battle showed Eaton in American military dress (see image on previous page). Finally and definitively, in a letter to William Ray, captive from the *Philadelphia* and author of *Horrors of Slavery,* William Eaton remarked that he "didn't take his uniform off for the next ninety-five days except to change his linen."[47] Nothing can be more clear. Unfortunately, Edwards's book has caused considerable damage to the facts of the amazing trek across the Western Desert. His disservice denigrates the heroic efforts that were true.[48]

Once Hamet arrived at Damanhour, Eaton received permission to continue his journey. Eaton prepared to move to Alexandria as the first stage of his desert crossing. However, Drovetti's interference in the American mission was not over. He had Eaton's party stopped again at the place where in 1801 the British had cut the dyke between the freshwater Lake Mareotis and the saltwater Mediterranean between Damanhour and Alexandria.[49] The American party was told by the governor of Alexandria that Hamet could not enter the city. Instead of proceeding to Alexandria with Eaton, Hamet went to a location in the desert that Eaton called Arab's Tower. That was Borg el Arab.[50]

In a letter to the Secretary of the Navy dated February 13, 1805, where he recounted the same events, Eaton added, "This comes from the French Consul ... [who] excuses himself for this intrigue, by saying his zeal for the interest of the Emperor, will justify his conduct and save him from reproach."[51] Drovetti would not desist. Eaton went on to Alexandria without Hamet. Hamet went off into the desert to the Arab's Tower.

The reason Drovetti failed to stop Eaton or to influence the Viceroy against the Americans was simple. The Viceroy wanted Eaton to take Hamet and the Bedouin tribe known as the Awlad Ali out of Egypt. So did the Ottoman Porte, who, despite the bedlam in its empire, still managed to hold Egypt under its control. The Viceroy sent a letter to Hamet Karamanli sometime around February 8, 1805:

> ... arrange to bring them [Awlad Ali] under you by strategy and perhaps you will need troops to go into Barbary; friend, it is necessary to bring them all under you immediately and take them there [where you are]; this [is] a very great and important

service, and you will be recognized by us, and render great service to the Sublime Porte, [and] for this [you will] obtain the greatest honors imaginable, and I shall do my best for you; I have also written to your said friend, the General; in short, do not fail in this particular because it is a very great service for the Sublime Porte, when this service is terminated you will obtain many "inconsiderable" honors if you bring [the Awlad Ali with you; this is the only service [we shall ask of you]; do it. I salute you.[52]

So it was in the interest of the Porte that Hamet leave Egypt and take the Awlad Ali with him. It made sense, as there would be one less problem in the complicated politics of Egypt at that time. Eaton's plan was to move ahead with the blessing of the rulers.

The Treaty and March

During these hectic days, William Eaton prepared a treaty between the United States of America and Hamet Karamanli of Tripoli. There were fourteen provisions, plus a secret provision between Eaton and Hamet. The United States was to provide the means and process of restoring Hamet to the throne. In return, Hamet was to release all American prisoners in Tripoli, which included the men of the *Philadelphia*. To pay for the expedition, Hamet was to cede to the United States the tributes paid to Tripoli by Denmark, Sweden, and Bavaria. The treaty also called for an expedition against Tripoli. The final, and secret, article demanded that once Hamet regained his power he would turn over to the United States "the Usurper Joseph Bashaw together with his family and Chief Admiral called Mamad [Murad] Rais, alias Peter Lisle," who would be held as hostages by the United States to be sure the treaty was upheld.[53]

Eaton's decision to lead the expedition outraged the American consul to Algiers and the naval officials in the Mediterranean, who withheld some of his funds in protest. The question as to whether Eaton had the authority to create and sign such a treaty on behalf of the United States was so contentious it was debated in the United States Senate and House of Representatives once Eaton returned to the United States in late 1805. In the end, Jefferson ratified it.

The trek west across North Africa from Borg el Arab where the treaty was signed, to Derna (in modern Libya) where the decisive battle was fought, is the stuff of legend and tragedy. The northern coast was mostly deserted when Eaton make the long, difficult journey over its sands. It had been deserted for most of known history. It is also almost featureless. There are no mountains. There are no rivers, streams, or brooks. There are a few Greek, Roman, and Arab ruins. The sea is to the north. To the south, with the exception of a few rises, all is flat (see map on page 41).

This was mostly unknown, uninhabited, and uncharted territory for foreigners. Like the interior of the Libyan Desert to which it is prelude, the northern coast that stretches between modern Libya and Egypt was as mysterious to William Eaton as it had been in antiquity, when the region was thought to be the home of demons, sirens, and Gorgons. Like the heroes of old, General William Eaton and his army stepped off into desert history when he crossed the Libyan Desert.

In his journal, Eaton seldom provided a name for a site, but rather presented a descriptive image: "[Saw] vestiges of ancient fortifications and raised and encamped upon the dividing ridge between Egypt and Tripoli, near a cistern of excellent water"; or "in a ravine, at the head of which we found rain water, preserved in natural reservoirs excavated in the rocks by the cascades of water during the winter rains"; or "a castle called by the Arabs Masroscah." There are dozens and dozens of such descriptions which Eaton used to help describe his locations, but although his descriptions are clear, in most instances they do not help to locate many of his camps on a modern map.

The Bedouins had one set of names for landmarks, the old maps a second, or third, or fourth name. The Greeks had their names, the Romans theirs, the Arabs theirs. Known history in the area reaches back more than 5,000 years; a single site may have had ten different names over those fifty centuries. Mersa Matruh alone has been the Ammonia of the Greeks, the Paraetonium of the Romans, the Baratun, Portalberton, and Porto Alberto of the Middle Ages and Renaissance, and the Bareton of the eighteenth and nineteenth centuries.[54] So all along the coast, Eaton had trouble estimating distances and duration, and scholars have trouble identifying Eaton's route. Only a few of Eaton's sites can be identified with certainty: Mersa Matruh, al-Shammas, Sollum, and perhaps Suani Samaluth in Egypt are obvious, and so is Bomba in Tripoli, the rest are mostly speculation.

The expedition was plagued by a lack of resources. Eaton never had enough money for the expedition. Eaton's Arab troops complained frequently about the lack of food, and they had a legitimate complaint. Eaton placed most of the blame on Richard Farquhar, whom he said misused his funds and absconded with the supplies. This was probably only part of the truth, for Eaton appeared to have cut corners as well. Halfway through the journey, Midshipman Pascal Paoli Peck exclaimed their only provisions were "a handful of rice and two biscuits a day,"[55] showing that the expedition was nowhere near English standards.

It was not that provisions were unavailable once the expedition was underway. At Mersa Matruh, just as the supplies became a major crisis, a local sheikh could provide cattle, sheep, goats, fowl, butter in skins, dates, and milk. A few days later, the army encountered 3,000 to 4,000 Awlad Ali, and the Bedouins had considerable provisions for sale, including gazelle and ostrich.[56] Eaton had no money to buy them. This lack of resources led to mistrust. Ultimately, if it had not been for the wise council of Dr. Mendrici prior to the beginning of the expedition, the men all would have perished. In a letter dated March 6, 1805, Mendrici had suggested that Briggs Brothers of Alexandria, who underwrote most of Eaton's supplies, outfit a ship to meet the expedition at Bomba. This was done at Briggs's expense. It would save their lives.

Water was a persistent problem for this desert army. The expedition was totally dependent on known wells, and if the Romans had not carved cisterns out of the limestone centuries earlier, Eaton's army would have perished, for these reservoirs produced the best tasting and the most abundant water. Eaton relied on the Arabs and their knowledge of the Libyan Desert to find the water. And they did. Time after time Eaton was led to a well. But there was simply not enough water to satisfy such a large force. Thirst was always with them. No one had anticipated that the Arabs and Egyptians could go so much longer without water than the Americans. On the first night, Peck reported he went to bed "for the first time in my life almost dead with thirst."[57] And the 450-mile journey had just begun. Peck continued, "We were very frequently 24 hours without water, and once 47 hours without a drop. Our horses were sometimes three days without, and for the last 20 days had nothing to eat except what they picked out of the sand."[58] Once two dead bodies were floating at the bottom of the shaft, and at another time the crush was so great a horse fell into the water. In both instances, the men and animals were so thirsty they drank anyway.

In fairness to Eaton, the journey took much longer than he anticipated, a fact that Eaton attributed to a man named Sheikh el Taiib. Whether it was due to the Sheikh, or language problems, or differences in interpretation by Eastern and Western minds, or even the long arm of Drovetti, the protraction of the trek is a mystery. On March 18, at Mersa Matruh, the army had been traveling through the desert for about ten days and should have been near their destination. In fact, they had not covered half the distance. Yet they were out of money, and nearly out of supplies. El Taiib maintained that Matruh was as far as he had agreed to go, thus he had delivered Eaton in the estimated time. The Bedouin concurred that they were finished at this place and were complaining that they had not been paid. Obviously there had been a grievous misunderstanding that could have caused the death of the expedition. Eaton passed the hat among the non–Arabs and collected $673.00. Once the Bedouins had been paid, all but forty camels and their riders went back to Borg el Arab, their task, according to them, finished. The remainder refused to budge from Matruh without news from Bomba about provisions, for they did not want to continue the journey at their peril.[59] Since the first half of the journey had suffered from a lack of provisions, that request was legitimate.

Eaton claimed El Taiib acerbated the problems, for he repeatedly delayed, disjointed, and defrauded the desert odyssey. In truth, three different worlds collided within this army: the foreigners (Americans and Europeans), the Libyans (Hamet and the Awlad Ali), and the local people (indigenous Bedouins and Egyptians — the latter could be considered a fourth). It was not an easy mix. The bickering and distrust began immediately. For example, on March 9 the camel and horse owners wanted to be paid in advance. At the center of the controversy was Sheikh el Taiib. Eaton thought that El Taiib had generated distrust among the Egyptian Bedouins and they were worried the Christians would not pay them. They probably also feared that El Taiib would pocket the money for himself and after a hard year's work they would end up with nothing. Eaton's answer was to pretend he was about to abandon the mission. He ordered his men to arms. It settled everyone down for a while, especially El Taiib.

Eaton, who assumed Bomba was a village, said he would send a courier for news of the fleet. Then he ordered all rations stopped. He considered the crisis serious enough that he was ready to separate his men from the army and put them in a secure place while awaiting a rescue mission.[60]

By now there was so much distrust that nothing short of a miracle could keep the various groups together. March 26 proved to be a most difficult day. First the courier from Derna arrived. He frightened the Arabs by claiming Hamet's brother Yusef had a large cavalry headed for Derna. Hamet hesitated. The camel drivers left. All wanted to return to Egypt, this time by heading south to the Fayoum, the large oasis to the west of the Nile which was accessible through the desert tracks. Once again Eaton stopped doling out rations. He would not provide any food until the caravan returned and the march continued. Sheikh el Taiib would go no further.

On the 27th, El Taiib gathered some of the Awlad Ali around him and once again started for Egypt. Hamet asked Eaton to go get him. Eaton refused. Hamet was worried that El Taiib would join the enemy. Eaton then ordered a march. El Taiib sent a messenger. He was headed for Behara. Then he sent another messenger. He would rejoin the group if they halted. They halted. He came into camp. When the march continued on March 30, the column had become segregated: Christians in the front and Arabs in the rear. El Taiib and Sheikh Mahamet began to argue over the considerable sum of $1500, which Eaton had paid El Taiib at the beginning of the journey. El Taiib had been told to distribute it equally. He did not. The argument drew the caravan to another halt as three other sheiks joined Mahamet and began to return to the east. Hamet implored Eaton to stop moving ahead. Eaton agreed to return three miles to camp at a water hole. Eaton calculated that these three sheikhs were vital to their cause.

On April 8, just west of Sollum, an outpost along the modern border of Egypt, with only four days' rations left, Eaton feared the Arabs would try to take what little provisions remained. It was the most formidable of all the encounters between the opposing forces in the army. He wrote:

> At 3 P.M. the Bashaw, compelled by his Arab host, struck his tent, ordered his bag-
> gage packed, mounted, and took up a march for Faiume by the mountain. I waited
> without emotion the result of this movement; not chusing to betray a concern for
> ourselves. Discovering however an intention in the Arabs to seize our provisions, I
> beat to arms. My Christians formed a line in front of the magazine tent. Each party
> held an opposite position the space of an hour. The Bashaw prevailed on the Arabs to
> return; they dismounted; and he pitched his tent. Supposing the tumult tranquilised,
> I ordered the troops to pass the manual exercise, according to our daily practice. In
> an instant the Arabs took an alarm; remounted, and explained, "The Christians are
> preparing to fire on us!" The Bashaw mounted and put himself at their head, appar-
> ently impressed with the same apprehension. A body of about two hundred advanced
> in full charge upon our people, who stood their ground motionless. The enemy
> withdrew at as mall [sic; a small] distance, singled out the officers, and, with delib-
> erat aim, cried —fire! Some of the Bashaw's officers, exclaimed, "For God's sake do
> not fire! The Christians are our friends." Mr. O'Bannon, Mr. Peck, and young Far-
> quhar, stood firmly by me Selem Aga, (Capts of Canoniers,) his Lieutenants and the
> two Greek officers, remained steadfast at their posts. The other were agitated, and in
> fact abandoned us. I advanced towards the Bashaw and cautioned him against giving
> countenance to a desperate act. At once a column of musket were aimed at my
> breast. The Bashaw was distracted. A universal clamor drowned my voice. I waved
> my hand as a signal for attention. At this critical moment some of the Bashaw's
> officers and sundry Arab chiefs rode between us with drawn sabres and repelled the
> mutineers. I reproached the Bashaw for his rashness, or rather weakness. His Cas-
> nadar asked him if he was in his senses. The Bashaw struck him with his naked
> sabre. The fracas had nearly resumed its rage, when I took the Bashaw by the arm;
> led him from the croud, and asked him if he knew his own interests and his friends![61]

Everything seemed to be conspiring against the expedition. The heat, lack of food, and
distrust all took a terrible toll on the men. The caravan had grown to almost 1200 people, as
they continued to pick up Awlad Ali families from Mersa Matruh to Bomba. Hamet now
believed that he was being used by the Americans to make peace with his brother. He was
not wrong. Eaton did not know it, but Tobias Lear, United States consul general to Algiers,
was discussing peace terms with Yusef.

The tattered and starving army arrived at Bomba on April 15, 1805. There was no way
to keep them together without a miracle. That miracle was to be the arrival of the Briggs's
supply ship, which had set sail from Alexandria when the desert trek began. It had to be in
the harbor. It was not. Nor was there a village at Bomba as Eaton had supposed. The stores
could not to be replenished. The split was final. The Arabs prepared to leave the next morning.
On April 16, just as the Arabs were mounting to return to Egypt, the *Argus* sailed into the
bay and the ordeal in the desert was over. The American army of Hamet Basha was fed and
rested. Spirits were restored. They marched on to capture Derna with ease, built a fort, and
awaited instructions from the fleet commander.

But their glorious victory was short-lived. Eaton's achievements would be neutralized.
The instructions came quickly and painfully. The Americans had negotiated a peace with
Yusef Karamanli.

The Betrayal

William Eaton was not only shocked that his country would negotiate with the Bey of
Tripoli while he and his men were winning an honorable victory, but was appalled that Tobias
Lear agreed to pay a ransom for the captives of the *Philadelphia*. The Americans had bungled
their first international confrontation. Eaton wrote a five-point memorandum in June 1805

pointing out how, step by step, he had the assurance of everyone from the president of the United States to the commodore in the Mediterranean that no ransom would be paid.

The betrayal of Eaton and his army boded poorly for America. In North Africa it also had long-term consequences, for Hamet's fears had come true: the Christian country had betrayed him. No provisions were made for him and his men despite continuous promises that he would be reinstated. In the original instructions to Isaac Hull and William Eaton on September 15, 1804, Captain Samuel Barron promised to "take the most effectual measures with the forces under my Command for co-operation with him [Hamet] against the usurper, his brother; and for re-establishing him in the regency of Tripoli...."[62] Eaton had been adamant throughout the lengthy mission that no ransom should be paid. On January 8, 1805, in a letter to Isaac Hull from Cairo he stated, "If we surmount these perils, we shall have carried a point, and gained an object, if we fail of success you will do us the justice to believe us Marty[r]s to a cause in which we feel the honour and interest of our Country deeply involved— Release of our Prisoners without Ransom, and peace without the disgraceful condition of Tribute."[63] In a letter to Samuel Barron on February 14, 1805, he again stated, "He [Hamet] engages also to release to you, without Ransom, Captain Bainbridge the officers, and all American prisoners who may be in captivity at Tripoli...." Eaton, Hamet, and the Americans eventually slunk out of the harbor of Tripoli in disgrace, leaving behind the Bedouins, the loyal soldiers of Hamet's army, and the cannoniers who had recently signed a pledge to Eaton. Eaton could not be consoled. He had supported Hamet from 1801 with his own money. He would not let the matter rest. The strong will and arrogance that had enabled him to accomplish the near-impossible in his journey through Egypt, now drove him to vindicate himself and, to his way of thinking, America's honor.

In the end William Eaton's eccentricities and anger made too many enemies. It did not help that he became embroiled in the trial of Aaron Burr. After a few years in politics in Massachusetts, his career was over. He went home, drank too much, became rheumatic and gouty, and died too young on June 1, 1811, at his home at Brimfield.

4

Francis Barthow: American Dragoman in Egypt (Explorer, c. 1804–1840)

One of the most elusive Americans in Egypt was a man named Francis Barthow (variously spelled Barthou, Barthoro, Bartou, Bartheau, Barthoe, Barton).[1] Barthow did not leave many public documents, nor did he write a book. Even his nationality was open to question. Fellow explorer Giovanni Finati, an Italian from Ferrara, said that Barthow was French and born in Santo Domingo.[2] This is possible, for Barthow was a man of the sea and the American shipping ports traded in the West Indies. The truth, however, according to his son Victor Barthow, is that Francis Barthow was the son of Peter Barthow and Mary Sprung Barthow of Belleview (not Bellview or Bellesview), Chautauqua County, New York.[3]

Barthow's family claimed he was originally a naval officer in the United States Navy, but the United States Naval History Center has no documentation for such a person.[4] Although the date he first arrived in Egypt is not clear, evidence shows Francis Barthow arrived earlier than fellow American William Eaton in 1804 and stayed until he died around 1840: over 35 years. He may not have been a naval officer, but he was a Red Sea ship captain, as reported by William Eaton, Lord Valentia, and John Lewis Burckhardt; a dragoman, as told by Thomas Legh and William John Bankes; an antiquarian, as related by Bernardino Drovetti and Giovanni Anastasi; and a European baker, a prominent member of the foreign community in Egypt, and a family man, as reported by his son, Victor Barthow.

More on Egypt from 1804

Francis Barthow could not have entered Egypt at a more volatile time. The English, not willing for the French to control Egypt, challenged the French at the Battle of the Nile. They sank Napoleon's fleet, including his flagship, stranding the French army in Egypt. The country went to chaos. Mohammad Ali seized power in 1805 while William Eaton was on his march across the North African coast and Barthow was trading in the Red Sea. The Albanian would found a dynasty and begin the long process of stabilizing the country. It was the first secure government in Egypt for many decades. The greatest threat to his reign was the Mamluks, slave soldiers who still held considerable power in Egypt. The situation was so dire that in 1806, Lord Valentia, passing through Egypt after an extended journey, could not visit the pyramids even with an armed guard because it was rumored that the Mamluk Elfi Bey and 10,000 of his soldiers were in the region.[5] By 1811, Mohammad Ali rid himself of the main threat. He killed most of the Mamluks when he invited them to a conciliatory feast and then trapped them within a narrow passage in the Citadel and massacred them. His son chased the remainder deep into Nubia and beyond the first Nile cataracts into Dongola at the edge of the great bend of the Nile. The amazing and long-lived slave/ruler empire, begun in 1250, was finally at an end.

Finally, Mohammad Ali looked West to Europe and welcomed foreign experts and ideas. He slowly drew the country that sat at the crossroads of the world into the modern world of trade and commerce. It would be the beginning of industrialization, but also of Westernization, the very thing centuries of rulers in Egypt had guarded against. Keeping many of Napoleon's innovations in place, over the next forty years Mohammad Ali stabilized the country, expanded trade, increased agricultural production and exports, changed land ownership laws, developed raw materials, built factories, explored the deserts and the upper Nile, invaded his neighbors, and welcomed Europeans to Egypt. In fact, he created modern Egypt.

Barthow at the Red Sea

From the tenth century the eastern seas belonged to the great seagoing nations of the Arabs. Their sailing ships, called *dhows,* dominated the trades, bringing Chinese porcelain and spices from the Far East to the Red Sea ports where, in places such as Jedda in Arabia, they were bartered for the Western commodities of rum and munitions. The goods were then transported across the Red Sea to Suez and overland via caravan to the emporiums, the great *wakalas,* of Cairo. This monopoly of the seas and of oriental goods motivated European powers to find a safe and sure route to the Far East. It led to the Spanish discovery of the West Indies and the Americas in the late 1400s and to the Portuguese discovery of the routes around Africa to the East Indies and beyond.

In the late seventeenth century the battle for trade, power, and command of the world's waters was still being waged. All seagoing nations participated and still bear the consequences such turbulent times spawned. Sailing ships from American ports shared in these trades, often as privateers and pirates. The American ports of Boston, Salem, and New York prospered. For the small but growing port of New York the trade became known as the Red Sea Trade. Ships would leave New York harbor with full cargos of munitions and kegs of whiskey, and return from the Red Sea with spices, gemstones, gold, and coffee.[6] In some instances, in the same manner as all other nations, the American captains and their crews preyed on ships of other nations in order to acquire their return cargos. As the trade grew, New York merchants devised a plan to have a ship in the Red Sea pillaging, and a second ship taking the booty to America. They earned outrageous profits: rum bought at two shillings a gallon was sold for £3 in Madagascar; Madeira wine bought at £19, sold for £300. One ship's profits for a single voyage could be £30,000.[7]

By the late eighteenth century the dangers of the high seas were reaching a crisis. Every ship on the waters, regardless of its nationality, was not only a plunderer, but was a prey for plunder as well. America had to defend itself. It was not easy, for France and England were naturally not willing to let American traders take business away from them. Both nations seized American ships and held American men in their jails awaiting ransom. When America tried to trade in the Mediterranean, seizures increased. There, in addition to the Europeans, and as noted in the previous chapter, were the countries of the Barbary. With French and English blessing, the Barbary States harassed American ships. So in 1785, when Captain Isaac Stevens and five men aboard the schooner *Maria* became the first American captives of Barbary pirates in the Mediterranean, it was business as usual on the high seas. This event, however,

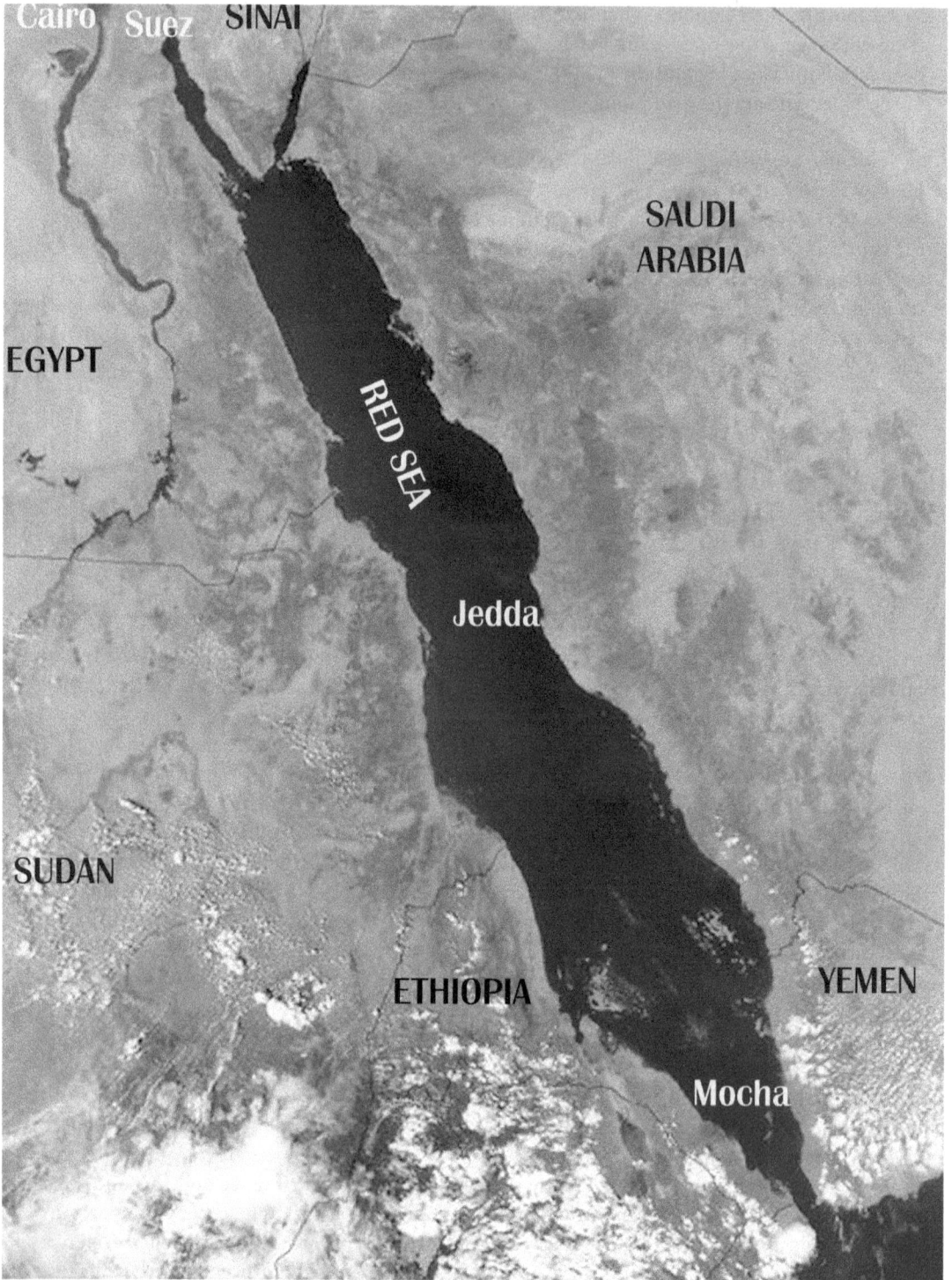

Red Sea Map (adapted from NASA's MODIS satellite image; satellite map with added names).

led to the formation of the American Navy.[8] It was the Americans, through a series of events over a period of years, who brought an end to high ransoms and piracy on the high seas. Francis Barthow was part of this exciting and interesting time.

Francis Barthow and the Red Sea

William Eaton, the American diplomat who took an army across the Western Desert to Derna in Tripoli, may have encountered Francis Barthow as he was gathering supplies and men in the Nile Valley. This connection was brief and not person to person, but the event was recorded in the official naval records of the day. The owner of the ship *Vegliere* approached Eaton on January 7, 1805, and asked him to provide an American passport for his ship so he could run the Suez-Jedda-Mocha circuit through the Red Sea. The ship was captained by a man named Barthoro and manned by European sailors.[9] Was Barthoro in fact Francis Barthow? Most likely.

The circuit between the three ports of Mocha, Jedda, and Suez was an ancient one predominantly used to trade within the northern section of the 1,200-mile-long Red Sea. The Red Sea is a deep sea dominated by the great rift that runs through the Near East, cuts through the Gulf of Aqaba to the east of Sinai, continues down the middle of the Red Sea, and hits land in Kenya in East Africa. But the sea's depth was not the dominating feature for trade. It was the weather. The winds blew from the north. So sailing ships had a difficult time returning to northern ports such as Suez. They had to be small enough to keep close to the coast where the land affected the wind patterns. The ancient Egyptians solved this problem by placing most of their ports like Quseir and Bernice well to the south.

The monsoon season along the Indian Ocean also affected the Red Sea, at least the southern portion below Jedda. These southern winds blew from October to March, but only as far north as Jedda. So Indian trading vessels sailed north as far as Jedda, while Egyptian ships, used to transport the merchandise on to Suez, sailed as far south as Jedda. Add to that the yearly pilgrimage to Mecca and Medina when thousands of Muslims arrived at Jedda for the month-long religious pilgrimage from both the eastern and western Muslim nations, and it is clear why Jedda became the most important port on the Red Sea.

Jedda was everything Suez was not. Jedda was a thriving community; Suez, at the northern end of the Gulf of Suez, lacked fresh water and could not sustain a large population. Jedda had an active harbor where ships daily loaded and unloaded cargo for transport to all parts of the region. Suez's port was only active periodically. Caravans from Cairo carried exports to Suez, where they were loaded on ships for Jedda. Those very same ships had just disgorged at Suez the wares from the Far East destined to be uploaded by those very caravans to cross the desert to Cairo. As caravans from Cairo arrived or departed, or during the pilgrimage season, the town bustled. At those times, surrounding Bedouins would come to sell everything from cheese to woven carpets to the pilgrims. Then Suez would settle back into the frontier town it was.

The third city of the Red Sea triangle was the Yemeni city of Mocha, at the entrance to the Red Sea just north of the strait called the *Bab el Mandeb,* Gate of Tears. Mocha was coffee. Coffee was Arabia's most important commodity and for over 200 years Cairo owned the world's sole monopoly on coffee. Mocha had a treacherous harbor filled with shifting sandbars which made navigation difficult. So close to the oceans, it was where most American ships picked up their cargo. Few Americans entered the Red Sea beyond Mocha. Francis Barthow did.

Lord Valentia and Barthow

In 1805, when Barthow was at the Red Sea, so were the English travelers Henry Salt and Lord Valentia, and so were dozens of American ships. Valentia reported on their activities.[10] Valentia's travels in India, Ceylon, the Red Sea, Abyssinia, and Egypt took him into the Red Sea on several occasions. In every instance he found American ships looking for cargo. There were so many Americans in the Red Sea during that season that the merchants in Mocha began to raise their prices. Eager for cargo, the Americans bid against each other. A 350-pound bale of Mocha coffee was raised from $40 to $50 a bale. Added to that were duty, packing, and shipping totaling 12 percent; insurance at 10 percent; interest on loans at 6 percent; loss of weight and damages at 10 percent; landing expenses at 1 percent; and duty in America at 4 percent.[11] Despite all the additions, the final rate was far less than it cost the East India Company to take the coffee overland via Suez and Alexandria to Europe. So the Americans could undersell the English in the Mediterranean.

While Valentia was in port, a brig sailed into the harbor from Suez. It was captained by a man Valentia calls Barton.[12] This was the summer of 1805. Valentia spoke of Barton again a month later when a seaman named Burns, who had jumped ship and converted to Islam, wanted to leave Mocha. Valentia contacted Captain Barton and he willingly took the man aboard.[13] In Valentia's third volume, when he entered the Red Sea in January of 1806 on a continuation of his journey, he wrote of another captain whom he called Bartou. It becomes obvious from reading the events surrounding this man that Barton and Bartou are the same person. The most telling fact that proves that Bartou and Barton were the same person is related to a number of letters given to him by Valentia. In the summer of 1805, when Barton sailed from Mocha to Jedda he took with him the letters written by Valentia to his friends in England and to British Consul General Major Missett in Cairo.[14] When Valentia met Bartou in Suez the following January, he was informed that his letters were delivered. I have concluded this captain was Francis Barthow.

After leaving Lord Valentia on his first encounter, Barthow took his ship to Jedda looking for cargo. He was held up by the fearful winds and was forced south. When he arrived at Jedda, the promised freight was denied, for the Vizier gave the freight to native vessels. Barthow docked his ship at the Charles River and waited.[15]

As noted above, Barthow arrived in Suez on December 27, 1805. Lord Valentia arrived there in January 1806. On landing, Valentia was informed that Barthow, which he now spelled Bartou, was ashore and requested a meeting. So the two men met. This is when Barthow assured Valentia he had sent on his letters and updated him on events in Cairo, where Mohammad Ali was still securing his reign in the city and surrounding countryside. While at Suez, Valentia again depended on Barthow's expertise and knowledge of the language and the traditions of the region. Any person entering the Suez port had to have his baggage inspected by the customs officials. Valentia was no exception. Barthow acted as interpreter:

> The Dola sent off, early in the morning, the chief officer of the Ascari to invite me on shore, and to say that, if I pleased, a house should be prepared for my residence. Soon after breakfast I quitted the ship, and proceeded to visit the Dola.... I then entered on business, by stating, through Captain Bartou, that it was my wish to depart for Cairo as soon as possible, and that therefore I begged his permission to hire camels for the journey, and make an arrangement with the Arabs for my protection.... I next stated to him, that I was no merchant, and.... I hoped he would permit my trunks and boxes of shells, to pass unopened. He appealed to Captain Bartou if they had even opened his trunks; how much less, then, would they do so by me; and as for the coffee, if I had ten bales, they should not think of charging any duty on

them. I expressed myself very much pleased and obliged and it was determined that I should hire a warehouse, and send my boxes on shore, as I packed them....

February 2 Early in the morning Captain Bartou came off to the ship, with answers to my letters.... He informed me that Mohammed Ali Pacha had issued his orders for my being treated with every mark of respect at Suez, and that my baggage should be Passed free; I was therefore under no obligation to the Dola for his civility....[16]

As Lord Valentia prepared to join the caravan for Cairo, Barthow assisted him. While he was doing so, a man offered Barthow freight to Jedda, which he had to refuse for lack of men and supplies. Valentia took a few provisions from Barthow's few stores and departed for Cairo. He never mentions the captain again. Of course, further evidence would be helpful, but there is enough evidence within the words of Valentia to believe that his captain was indeed Francis Barthow.

Barthow as Dragoman

A dragoman was an interpreter, guide, and purveyor — a problem solver who was quick to action and willing to take risks. This was an easy transformation for a sea captain, as illustrated by Barthow's assistance to Lord Valentia. Usually a dragoman was a native of the Middle East, whose expertise served almost every establishment in Egypt, including businesses, government offices, wealthy families, and foreign consular offices. Westerners who became dragomans were rare, but they did exist.

America's great dragoman in Egypt was Francis Barthow. He did not become famous, as few travelers put his name in print. We do not know if he ever dressed in Arab robes, but one source notes that as late as 1815, "Both he and Francois Barthow had retained their European dress."[17] We know that he knew how to deal with dignitaries along the Nile, boatmen on the river, river pirates, villagers, and unusual situations encountered in Nile travel because his exploits appeared in a few books. Finally we know, as noted, that he helped Lord Valentia travel from Suez to Cairo in 1806 and, as described below, he led at least two important expeditions up the Nile in the second decade of the nineteenth century: Thomas Legh and Rev. Charles Smelt in 1813, and William John Bankes in 1815.

Thomas Legh and Charles Smelt Expedition of 1813

Thomas Legh, illegitimate son of Thomas Peter Legh of the Lyme Park estate in Cheshire, England, graduated from Oxford and visited the Near East twice: once in 1812–13 and again in 1816. The 1813 journey was Charles Smelt's only trip to Egypt. The pair hired Francis Barthow in Cairo on January 12, 1813. Legh confirms in his book *Narrative of a Journey in Egypt and the Country Beyond the Cataracts* that he "engaged Mr. Barthow, an American, who had resided many years in the country, to accompany us and act as our interpreter...."[18] At Bulaq, Grand Cairo's port on the Nile, they secured a *maish*, a Nile boat with two masts, one cabin, and an eleven-man crew. It cost them £20 a month.[19] True to what would become a typical Nile journey in years to come, they stored away non-perishables like rice, brandy, biscuits, oil, vinegar, pepper, spices, and mustard. They thought to bring exotic items for gifts to important people on their journey.

Before their journey the men had to acquire a *firman*, a passport, from Mohammad Ali. This document informed all the governors from Beni Suef, a city just below Cairo, to Aswan, the southernmost city in Egypt, that Mohammad Ali granted the party permission to travel as far as the First Cataract at Aswan. At each port of call the men were obliged to visit the governor and present their *firman* to him. He in turn was accountable to Mohammad Ali for their protection and granted them safe passage through his domain. In truth, the men had no intention of stopping their journey at Aswan. Accompanied by their guide, Francis Barthow, their ambitious agenda was to go where few Europeans had managed to penetrate previously: beyond the second cataract.

On the upward journey the *maish* flew before the wind, making only a few stops, another process that would define a Nile journey throughout the nineteenth century. It was a logical decision, one many future travelers did not understand. The Nile, in addition to bringing the inundation to replenish the soil each year, brought one other gift to Egypt: easy navigation. The Nile flowed north, so a boat at Aswan in the south could float easily its entire length to the Delta. Conversely, a strong wind blew from the north, allowing for sailboats to hoist their sails and travel against the current from Cairo to Aswan. It was a two-way highway, one of the few that existed in the world. The wind usually began at dawn and faded at sunset. Sometimes the wind was gentle; other times it blew a gale. So the caprice of the wind dictated traveling upstream as quickly as possible and slowly returning downstream with the current at a more controlled and leisurely pace.

On February 11, a little over a month after departing from Cairo, they arrived at Aswan. The journey was now turning into the expedition they hoped it would become, as few Europeans had penetrated into Nubia along the Nile in recent times. Near Philae they requested permission to pass through to Ibrim. After coffee and gifts, permission was granted, and the men returned to their boat with yet another *firman*, this one from the governor of Aswan. At Derr they had to obtain yet another *firman*, the final permission to Ibrim. They presented the Cacheff with the customary gift: a watch. He did not want a watch. A watch had no purpose in his world. He wanted one of their fine swords. Swords he understood. Swords had status. That is what he got. In return he gave Legh a young Negro boy, whom Legh took back to England at the end of the journey. Now the three men asked permission to go to Ibrim. With the sword in hand, it was quickly granted.

They set out on foot the next morning. It was a hot and difficult journey through the mountains. Within a few hours they left the mountains behind and moved along the eastern shore of the Nile. It took five more hours to reach Ibrim, an ancient fortress that stood on a dramatic rise commanding a strategic view the river. There was a village at Ibrim, but it had been completely destroyed by the Mamluks as they fled south to Dongola after Mohammad Ali massacred most of their brothers in arms at the Citadel in Cairo in 1811. The inhabitants had been taken away to form part of the Mamluk army:

> In about five hours we arrived at Ibrim, situated on the east side of the Nile, at the southern extremity of a ridge of mountains, which, for nearly two miles, rise perpendicularly from the Nile, scarcely leaving space for the road which lies between them and the river.
>
> The town lay on the eastern slope of the mountain, and the citadel, which was built on the summit, must have formerly been a strong position. Its height may be estimated at about 200 feet above the river, that washes the foot of the rock on which it stood, and which is, at this point, about a quarter of a mile broad. We were, however, so far deceived by the extreme perpendicularity of the precipice, that standing on its edge, we were induced to make several vain attempts to fling a stone across the Nile.
>
> The walls that inclosed the citadel and the ruins of the house of the Governor are still to be traced. We entered this fortress through a ruined gateway, and sat down to dine on the provisions we had brought with us from Dehr, consisting of goat's flesh,

the last remains of some biscuits from Cairo, coffee and tobacco. Not a vestige of life was to be seen about us; the destruction of Ibrim by the Mamelukes, when they passed two years ago into Dongola, had been so complete, that no solitary native was to be found wandering amongst its ruins; there was not even a date tree to be observed. The walls of the houses, which are in some places still standing, alone attest that it has once been inhabited. The population was partly carried off by the Mamelukes, and has partly removed to Dehr.[20]

The trio, after months of anticipation, stayed only a few hours at their destination. They ate lunch, and made an important decision: they decided not to continue further upriver. Money was an issue. Paper currency was not a recognized form of barter on this part of the river. That meant their scant supplies were not enough to take them further. There was another reason: Mamluks. Running into them was a distinct possibility. They turned their boat around to head north. Despite their forced retreat, the men were satisfied with their success. It had been a major adventure, and for Europeans eager for details about the upper Nile, it filled in important information. It was also short-lived. A few months later, John Lewis Burckhardt would penetrate beyond Ibrim to one of the most important river temples in all of Egypt, Abu Simbel, pushing exploration even further. He honorably credited "Captain Barthod, an American" and his employers as the first modern foreigners to explore the ancient sites above Philae (seen by Napoleon's men) to Qasr Ibrim, some thirty-five miles further up the Nile.[21]

Eager to penetrate deep into the Nile, the men had passed a number of historic sites on their journey south. Now, with more time and a sense of accomplishment in their craws, they slowly moved from one important ancient site to another. In almost every instance they left graffiti. The first stop on the return journey for Legh, Smelt, and Barthow was the rock-cut temple of Dehr (al-Derr), followed in the afternoon by the sandstone temple of Amada, which

The temple of Philae as it appeared in the early 1800s. In the twentieth century the High Dam was built over the Nile and the temple was dismantled and moved to a nearby island (in Frederick C. Penfield, *Present Day Egypt*).

they found to be inundated by sand. Barthow carved his name into the soft sandstone. Additional stops on their journey north included: Ramses II's temple of Sibhoi (Seboua), the Greco-Roman temple of Dakki (Dakka), the small Kiosk of Qertassi, the sandstone temple at Dendur (where they carved their names), and the temple of Kalabsha.[22]

They paused long enough at Aswan to make various visits in the area, including a second visit to the island temple of Philae, and continued to the town and temple of Kom Ombo, then el-Silsila, where the Nile is channeled between two mountains forming the narrowest point in the river (here they left graffiti). After Edfu and Esna, the temple and tombs at El-Kab (graffiti), they reached the largest and most important temple of Medinet Habu on the West Bank of Thebes (modern Luxor), where both Legh and Barthow left their mark. Smelt, as far as is known, put his name in only one place: the Tomb of Ramses VI in the Valley of the Kings at Thebes.[23] They reached Asyut on March 20. The excitement of exploration may have been coming to an end, but the greatest adventure of their journey was about to begin, for near the Nile village of Manfalut, known since ancient times for its pomegranates, they almost lost their lives.

The three men had heard that a mummy pit, an ancient site of multiple burials, existed near the village of Amabdi and thought it would be an interesting adventure. It was, but not as they had hoped! Foolishly, they mounted donkeys and stepped off into the desert without a guide. They were not alone. An Abyssinian merchant and three crewmen joined them. For four hours the odd party in their varied dress wandered around the desert. No luck! Then they met a few Arabs who said they knew where to find the mummy pit. Barthow understood one to say, "If one must die, — all must die," and reported it to his associates. They grew apprehensive. Yet they continued their journey, hiring those very men to guide them.

As they neared the pit, the guides told them to take off all their clothes. Of course that was out of the question, so they stripped to shirts and trousers, keeping their modesty and their caution intact. Only Legh, Smelt, and Barthow entered the pit, for the other four men decided it was not something they wanted to do. Once they climbed down into what appeared to be merely a hole in the ground, they found a tunnel headed underground. Lighting torches, they stepped into the darkness and slowly crept along the dark and dank tunnel, not knowing what to expect. Soon the leader emerged into a huge chamber. One by one their torches began to illuminate the chamber. There were no mummies. Instead there were hundreds of hanging bats dangling at various angles from the ceiling and dropping guano everywhere.

A number of dark holes indicated there was more than one way out of the chamber. It was a labyrinth of galleries. One at a time, Arab, traveler, Arab, they entered one of the galleries. Slowly they crept along as the gallery twisted and turned. After some time they reemerged into the chamber with the hanging bats. The Arabs denied it was the same chamber, but on being pressed agreed that they had taken the wrong turn and that they must begin again. Foolishly, the trio of travelers agreed. They entered another gallery. This time they had to jump a trench. The gallery began to decrease in size. Soon they had to crouch. Then they had to crawl. The gallery twisted and turned like a maze. Finally they entered a smaller chamber and were able to stand. No mummies.

Things got worse. It grew excessively hot. Breathing became difficult. Legh reported:

> We felt we had gone too far, and yet were almost deprived of the power of returning. At this moment the torch of the first Arab went out: I was close to him, and saw him fall on his side; he uttered a groan — his legs were strongly convulsed, and I heard a rattling noise in his throat — he was dead. The Arab behind me, seeing the torch of his companion extinguished, and conceiving he had stumbled, past me, advanced to his assistance, and stooped. I observed him appear faint, totter, and fall

in a moment—he also was dead. The third Arab came forward, and made an effort to approach the bodies, but stopped short. We looked at each other in silent horror. The danger increased every instant; our torches burnt faintly; our breathing became more difficult; our knees tottered under us, and we felt our strength nearly gone.

There was no time to be lost—the American, Barthow, cried to us to take courage, and we began to move back as fast as we could. We heard the remaining Arab shouting after us, calling us Caffres, imploring our assistance, and upbraiding us with deserting him. Be we were obliged to leave him to his fate, expecting every moment to share it with him. The windings of the passages through which we had come increased the difficulty of our escape; we might take a wrong turn, and never reach the great chamber we had first entered. Even supposing we took the shortest road, it was but too probable our strength would fail us before we arrived. We had each of us separately and unknown to one another observed attentively the different shapes of the stones which projected into the galleries we had passed, so that each had an imperfect clue to the labyrinth we had now to retrace. We compared notes, and only on one occasion had a dispute, the American differing from my friend and myself; in this dilemma we were determined by the majority, and fortunately were right. Exhausted with fatigue and terror, we reached the edge of the deep trench which remained to be crossed before we got into the great chamber. Mustering all my strength I leaped and was followed by the American. Smelt stood on the brink, ready to drop with fatigue. He called for us "for God's sake to help him over the fosse, or at least to stop, if only for five minutes, to allow him time to recover his strength." It was impossible—to stay was death, and we could not resist the desire to push on and gain the open air. We encouraged him to summon all his force, and he cleared the trench. When we reached the open air it was one o'clock, and the heat in the sun about 160°. Our sailors, who were waiting for us, had luckily a *bardak* (jars, made at Kenne [Qena]) full of water, which they sprinkled upon us, but though a little refreshed, it was not possible to climb the sides of the pit; they unfolded their turbans, and slinging them round our bodies, drew us to the top.[24]

Their ordeal was not over. When the villagers saw them returning without the guides, they were naturally concerned. Where were their men? Legh, Smelt, and Barthow lied. They told them the men were hauling mummies up out of the pit. Then they raced to the Nile on their donkeys, crossed the river on a ferry, boarded their boat, and tried to sail away. They did not escape. The remaining Arab had returned to his village, and told the families their sons and fathers were dead. He insisted the foreigners had killed his friends by magic. Under normal circumstances the three men would have been well on their way to safety. The Nile, however, was not cooperating with the foreigners. The wind, which blows one way, and the current, which runs another, were of equal force, stalling them in their tracks. Perhaps their crew had something to say about the matter as well. After all, they would remain behind and on the river long after the three foreigners were gone. Whatever the reason, they returned to face their fate.

The Cacheff, surrounded by menacing villagers, blasted them in Arabic. Barthow translated. Then the Cacheff left the room. The Arabs pushed closer. Barthow, Legh, and Smelt were afraid. The Cacheff called them into the inner rooms to face him once again. The Cacheff, now alone, was sympathetic, but told them the villagers outnumbered his small force and they might all be killed. He suggested that the trio escape as quickly as possible while he detained the villagers. So once again they headed toward the Nile. Nothing had changed. The wind and the current were still uncooperative. They began to tack, but made little headway. Horsemen began to gather. They were ordered ashore. Legh described the scene: "We rowed our boat as quickly as possible to the other bank, and consulted amongst ourselves what measures to take. Our danger was imminent, we were surrounded on all sides by enemies, our friend the Cacheff at Manfalout was unable to protect us, and the distance to Miniet was seventy miles."[25]

Once again they were forced to return to the shore, where they were immediately surrounded by mud-clad women and children. They were the families of the deceased and the mud was a symbol of their mourning. The men made their way to the Cacheff's house. He was surrounded by the villagers and the Sheikh from Amabdi. With them, the trio recognized the third Arab from their excursion, the one they had left behind:

> Our dragoman repeated our story again, and called upon the survivor to confirm the truth of it, but in vain; on the contrary he maintained we had taken him and his companions by force, and compelled them to conduct us to the place. In this falsehood he was supported by the Arab who had remained on the outside of the cavern, and whom we now saw for the first time among the crowd. In our defence we replied it was not possible we could have used any means of compulsion, as we were unarmed. This we boldly asserted, as the brace of pistols I had with me was never produced. Besides, we recalled to his memory that on our way thither one of the guides who had died, had replenished our bardak with water from a well near Amabdi.—This proved that we had gone amicably together.[26]

The Arab insisted they use magic. Finally, Barthow was sent in to negotiate once again. In they end they paid for the deaths and returned to the Nile for the third time. The wind subsided. The current cooperated. They headed for Cairo.

The William John Bankes Expedition of 1815

Two years later in 1815, Barthow was still leading expeditions on the Nile. This time it was the first journey of the Englishman William John Bankes. Bankes (not to be confused with Joseph Banks, the member of the African Association who had helped John Ledyard) was a rich young gentleman who traveled and collected antiquities. He was educated at Cambridge and later became a Member of Parliament. Like Barthow, Bankes never published. Unlike Barthow, his cache of drawings and journal notes has been preserved and his journeys in Egypt have been pieced together.[27] His influence on events in Egypt during this time is extraordinary. He joined in the early study and exploitation of Egyptian antiquities. On this visit to Egypt, Bankes coveted the fallen obelisk at Philae, which on a subsequent visit in 1818–19 he acquired and sent back to England to adorn his garden at Kingston Lacey in Dorset. Bankes would go on to edit a number of manuscripts from travelers like himself. Among them was one written by Giovanni Finati and another by George Bethune English, and perhaps it was he who decided the other manuscript found a few years ago in the Henry Salt Papers of the British Library was of no consequence (see next chapter).

The Finati manuscript is important to our discussion. Finati was an Italian from Ferrara who had served with the French army in Egypt and remained behind to serve in the Egyptian army. In both instances he deserted. At some point he met Barthow and they became friends. Perhaps Richard Burton, in his book *Personal Narrative of a Pilgrimage to Al-Madinah and Meccah,* was referring to Barthow when he reported that Finati "happened to meet his 'original friend the captain-merchant,' and in March, 1809, obtained from him a passage to Egypt."[28] In 1815 Finati met up with Barthow in Cairo just as the Bankes journey was about to commence, and Barthow urged him to join the expedition. In his book *Narrative of the Life and Adventures of Giovanni Finati* (translated and perhaps written by Bankes), Finati acknowledged his friendship to Barthow.

I resumed my habit of frequenting it [the foreign quarter of Cairo], having several friends there among the Italians and others, but none in the number whom I esteemed more than Francois Barthow, who was, I believe, a French subject born in St. Domingo ... he proposed to me that I should accompany him into Upper Egypt, adding that my passage and living would be free of all expense, and that I might expect some remuneration besides, for that he was to make the voyage upon the Nile with an English gentleman of fortune, in the capacity of his guide and interpreter.[29]

On September 16, 1815, the three-month journey began. Aboard the two-mast, two-cabin *maish,* in addition to Bankes, Barthow, and Finati, were Bankes's Portuguese servant Antonio da Costa; an additional interpreter, Haleel, whom Bankes had hired in Alexandria for his earlier trip to Sinai; and a number of men hired as laborers.[30] This was a much larger expedition than the Legh journey. They swiftly moved up the Nile and made Thebes in twelve days. There they had to pause for ten days as Bankes had contracted ophthalmia, a debilitating eye disease endemic in Egypt that plagued the peasantry through to the twentieth century. Barthow was free to roam the antiquities of Thebes during that time. He, too, would soon become a purveyor of Egyptian antiquities. Then they continued their journey south.

At Philae they traded in their spacious *maish* for a "diminutive" boat with planks without nails, a blue cotton sail, and a cabin that was only a mat of palm leaves over a pole.[31] From that point all but Bankes would sleep ashore. A two-man crew took them through the cataract and south past Ibrim and Abu Simbel to Wadi Halfa, making them the second credited Westerners to penetrate that far up the Nile. Both Bankes and Barthow wore European clothing and created great curiosity wherever they went.

They turned the boat around at Wadi Halfa, stopping often as they returned downstream with the current. Abousombul (Abu Simbel) was one of the first stops. Rediscovered by Burkhardt a few years earlier, the colossal rock-hewn temple was still buried up to the faces of the giant statues on its façade. The smaller temple of Hathor was not as fully covered and its entrance was visible. Bankes wanted to try to uncover the great temple but it was impossible. Instead he drew images of the colossal statues. He often drew what he saw and took many of the images back to England with him.

Next was Ibrim, the temple Legh, Smelt, and Barthow had reached in 1813, and further north they examined the temples at Amada, Sebua, Mharraka, Qertassi, Gerf Husein, Dakka, Dendur, Tafa, Kalabsha, and Dabod. Barthow's actions at these temples are mostly unrecorded, for no account which describes his movements has been discovered. Then the company returned to Philae for an extended stay. To the ancients, Philae was sacred, and the temple adorned with two granite obelisks was the chief center for the worship of Isis. Thousands of pilgrims from all over the Greco-Roman world traveled to Philae to pay homage to Isis. Now William John Bankes ensconced himself in one of the sacred sites for an extended stay while coveting its fallen obelisk. That obelisk bore the name Cleopatra and would become the key to unraveling the secrets of the ancient hieroglyphics.

It was Barthow who saved the day when Bankes encountered one of the few incidents with the inhabitants on the journey. Barthow had gone to Aswan to prepare another boat for their trip north, while Bankes and Finati remained on the island. Bankes was drawing.

> One morning a small crowd had collected round him whilst he was drawing in the portico of the principal temple, and one of the number became very importunate and troublesome in demanding a present, and at last even thrust his hand across the paper, in token that the work should not proceed without it; this rudeness had produced some irritation; and when, upon hearing the stir, I came in, I found that the Nubian had drawn his little crooked knife, which is worn buckled upon the left arm, and was holding it in the most menacing position.

> I was putting my hand to my pistols (for Mr. Bankes himself went unarmed), and
> the natives were beginning to take part with their countryman, when, luckily,
> Barthow appeared in sight upon the shore opposite, accompanied by the Cashief of
> Assouan, who came thus far to do honour to the stranger, and to the recommenda-
> tion with which he was furnished by the Pasha of Egypt.[32]

The arrival of the Cashief ended the fray, as the villagers scattered, jumped into the river, and swam away.

Continuing north, the party visited the caravan village of Derawi, and the temple villages of Kom Ombo, Edfu, Esna, and Thebes, where they enjoyed an extended stay. Just as Bankes had tried to carry off the obelisk at Philae but had to abandon the project because of the lack of men and equipment, he now tried to take a section of the two colossal statues on the Theban plain known as the Colossi of Memnon.[33] After Thebes the party visited Dendera, the weaving village of Echmim (Achmim), and Siout (Asyut), where they went looking for Coptic tombs. They returned to Cairo on December 16, 1815. Upon their return to Cairo, Bankes paid Barthow and Finati handsomely and asked Finati to join him on a journey to Jerusalem. Barthow did not go.

Barthow as Antiquarian

The practice of acquiring Egyptian antiquities for European interest and pleasure was well underway when Barthow began his excursions on the Nile. It would develop, in his life-time, into a lucrative, bizarre industry. Europe turned Egypt into a battleground of commerce similar to the confrontations taking place on the world's seas and oceans. Two leaders would emerge: the French Proconsul Bernardino Drovetti (see Chapter 3), who sold his collection mostly to France and Italy, and British Consul General Henry Salt, who sold to England and France. Drovetti was Napoleon's Proconsul. In that post, which he held until 1815 (he would be reinstated to the position in 1829), his influence over Mohammad Ali and the development of a modern Egypt was phenomenal. Once freed of the restrictions of office he turned to the quest for antiquities: first for his own collection, and later for museums and other clients in Europe. His personal collection of 5,000 objects was sold to the University of Turin between 1816 and 1819. Italy founded the Turin Museum to house it. It is, perhaps, the largest collection of all those amassed at this time.

Henry Salt was Drovetti's biggest competitor. He was appointed British consul general in 1815 and over the years acquired massive power. In addition to aiding British merchants and travelers in Egypt, he began to gather papyrus, statues, and other ancient artifacts. The two men created an industry, each employing agents along the Nile who looked for and labo-riously removed items, shipping them down the Nile to Alexandria and on to Europe: an amazing, monumental task. Sometimes the two men's agents were in direct conflict over specific items and ultimately they agreed to divide the Nile Valley, each working within his own area. Salt sold many items to the British Museum and the Louvre while amassing a col-lection of his own. Among his earliest acquisitions was an 1818 collection of colossal statues excavated by Giovanni Battista Belzoni (who eventually worked for himself). In addition to Belzoni, Giovanni d'Athanasi, nicknamed Yanni, worked at Thebes as Salt's main agent from 1817 to 1827.[34]

Barthow appears to have been an independent agent. Once again his sea captain training made him well equipped for hauling, storing, and shipping antiquities down the Nile and across the sea. By 1818 he was in communication with Bernardino Drovetti. In two separate letters, Drovetti corresponded with Barthow, who was in Europe at the time. On May 3, 1818,

Drovetti sent a letter to Barthow via Pierre Balthalon, a merchant from Marseilles whose father had established a trading house in Alexandria years earlier. The Balthalon family were related to Drovetti. Drovetti's note to Balthalon stated that he must give the letter directly to Barthow and if he did not find Barthow at Marseilles he was to return the letter to him.[35] On July 6, 1818, Pierre Balthalon received a further communication from Drovetti. This time it was a package for Barthow, who was now in Port Mahon, on his way to Marseilles.[36] The contents of the letter and the package are unknown. At the time, Drovetti was involved in the negotiations with Turin, mentioned earlier, for a collection that included over ninety statues and numerous papyri.

Likewise Drovetti received correspondence from friends and colleagues that refer to Barthow. In January of 1826 François Carignan, Prince of Savoy, wrote a letter mentioning that he had dealt with Barthow to acquire antiquities.[37] Even more convincing that Barthow was working independently in antiquities is a passage in yet another letter to Drovetti: "Preghiera di far recapitare lettera a Bartheau, con cui è in trattative per l'acquisto di una piccolo collezione de antichità egiziane; anzi a lui scrive perché complete opportunamente la medesima a fine d'trovarla de proprio gradimento al prossimo...." (Pray to deliver a letter to Bartheau, who is in talks to buy a small collection of antiquities from Egypt, even to complete properly....)[38]

Barthow's visits to Port Mahon put him in continuous contact with the men, ships, and events of Americans in the Mediterranean. Port Mahon is an ancient deep-water port on the southeast coast of Minorca, a 33-mile-long island to the east of Spain between Mallorca and Sardinia. It has a long and intriguing history. Located close to the Barbary Coast, it served as a harbor for almost every Mediterranean power at one time or the other, and the ships and sailors of many nations met and mixed within the port. By 1815 the naval yard, on a small hexagon-shaped island in the center of the harbor, was leased to the United States and used by the American navy as its winter base. It remained as such until 1848, when Spain took Mahon and the American navy moved its facilities to Malta and Spezia in Sardinia.[39] It appears that Barthow frequented Mahon regularly, for a year after Drovetti's letters to him, on June 23, 1819, Barthow returned to Mahon to acquire an American passport from the governor at the "request of the American Vice Consul of that city." After Barthow secured his American passport he returned to Egypt and registered as an American through the Austrian Embassy in Alexandria, as there was no American consul in the country at the time.[40]

In addition to communicating with Drovetti, Barthow was involved with Giovanni Anastasi, for what appears to be a lengthy association. Giovanni Anastasi (1780–1860), not to be confused with Salt's agent Giovanni d'Athanasi or Yanni, was the son of a Greek merchant by the name of Anastasiou, who supplied the French army while it was in Egypt from 1798 to 1803. When Napoleon abandoned Egypt, the French also abandoned its debt to Anastasiou, who went bankrupt. Giovanni began anew and rebuilt his father's business. He was among the Greeks who were friends of Mohammad Ali and was rewarded for his efforts on Egypt's behalf by being named Swedish-Norwegian consul in Egypt, a position in which he served from 1828 to 1857. Anastasi had a fleet of merchant ships that plied the Mediterranean. Anastasi also sold antiquities, mainly from Sakkara, and especially to northern European countries like the Netherlands and Sweden. He and Barthow became a team in buying and selling antiquities. One of their early customers was Jean-Baptiste de Lescluze (1780–1858), a merchant and ship owner from the Netherlands. Lescluze was probably the first trader from the Netherlands buying and selling antiquities in the Mediterranean.[41]

Barthow, the possible naval officer, the sea captain, the dragoman, and the antiquarian, continued trading in antiquities for some time. In 1827 he was involved with Anastasi in yet another sale of antiquities. In a letter written in French and signed by Barthow and Costantino Tossizza, a Greek operating as a merchant in Livorno and Alexandria under the name Fratelli Tossizza (Tossizza Brothers), Barthow confirmed a memo and catalogue sent to Guiseppe Terreni in Livorno (Leghorn) Italy.[42] By this time the antiquities business had matured enough for Anastasi and Barthow to have prepared a 110-page catalogue of 5,600 objects predominantly from Saqqara and Memphis, and a supplement with the artifacts they wished to sell "pictured." They were in competition with several other collections including one from Salt, who died that year, and another one containing 335 pieces from Maria Cimba, the widow of a doctor in Cairo who had served as Henry Salt's personal physician.[43] The negotiations took over a year. A representative from Leiden "inspect[ed] the collection, which was spread over various storehouses in the city [Livorno]. He saw beautiful objects: monumental statues, sarcophagi, mummies, bronzes, jewellery, glass, vases and many papyrus scrolls."[44] They started negotiations in August of 1827. Giuseppe Terreni represented Leiden, while Costantino Tossizza, "the American Francois Barthou and, at a later stage, the Italian Francesco de Castiglione, [represented d'Anastasi]. The latter two traded in Egyptian antiquities and some of their pieces came to the collection in Leiden separately from the Anastasi collection. The price asked for the whole collection was 400,000 French francs, about 200,000 Dutch guilders."[45] By September 21, 1827, Reuvens was evaluating the collection to determine if the price was good. He compared the collection to the Drovetti and Salt collections.

By this time many parties were involved in the Dutch purchase, including the king. The king would not give his consent, feeling much more information was needed before committing to the collection. The Anastasi team sent Francis Barthow to the Netherlands to reopen negotiations.

> In November 1827 Francois Barthou arrived in Holland, where he had talks with Van Ewijck and with Reuvens at Arentsburg, an excavation site between Leiden and The Hague. Barthou showed himself a perfect diplomat. During his conversation with Reuvens he admitted some weak points in the d'Anastasy collection and even mentioned some faults which Reuvens had not noticed. His approach had the desired effect. Reuvens wrote to the department that the collection had risen in value because of more confidence in the negotiators and valuable information about alabaster urns, small pyramids, bronze statues, mummies and papyri. Barthou had clarified catalogue statements about the collection which Reuvens had earlier disqualified as "downright charlatanry." He admitted that d'Anastasy's collection was less important than that of Drovetti, but said it had to be placed above Salt's because of the unique collection of mummies, the number of papyri (126 against 98) and the total number of pieces (5,600 against 3,000). Reuvens began to think of placing d'Anastasy on a level with Salt.[46]

A few months later a bid of 230,000 francs was made and accepted by Anastasi.[47] The negotiations were over, but the logistics of moving the objects from Italy to the Netherlands was not. The objects were heavy. They were fragile.

There was one more issue: a few items Tossizza was hoping to keep for himself. Anastasi, in order to sweeten the negotiations, had offered a bonus to the buyer in the form of "a Byzantine bronze helmet, a Greek manuscript and a bilingual papyrus in Greek and Demotic."[48] Tossizza never mentioned these items to the Dutch. "Barthou, in every respect a gentleman, informed Humbert about this misconduct of Tossizza before leaving for Alexandria."[49] Tossizza had to turn over the booty.

Having outlasted Drovetti and the late Mr. Salt to win the sale, Barthow and Anastasi had outmaneuvered the masters. They had set the standard for international negotiations of Egyptian antiquities. And there was more to come. In 1832 they did it again. They sold a small collection of antiquities to the first American commercial collector to arrive in Egypt: Colonel Mendes Cohen. Cohen was a Baltimore philanthropist whose Egyptian artifacts became one of the first important American collections.[50] Upon arrival in Alexandria at the end of his journey, Cohen purchased the last of his Egyptian collection. He wrote on the last page of his journal: "*Anastasies*— M Barthoe collection $1500."[51] That was all Cohen wrote of his fellow American, but it is enough to confirm that the Anastasi-Barthow partnership was still in the antiquities business in 1832. In 1839 Anastasi sold another large collection of Egyptian antiquities to the British Museum.

The full relationship between Barthow and Anastasi has not been completely explored. Anastasi had ships. Barthow was a sea captain. Anastasi shipped goods around the Mediterranean. It is well documented that Anastasi, friend to Mohammad Ali, supplied ships and armament for Egypt's various adventures on the high seas. Mohammad Ali was asked for assistance against the Greek insurrection by his Ottoman leader. He sent his son Ibrahim at the head of the Egyptian fleet. It met its fate at the Battle of Navarino on October 20, 1827. Greece, like Egypt, was attempting to gain its independence from the Ottoman Porte. Russia, France, and Great Britain, unlike Egypt, put their navies behind the Greek cause. America vacillated. Among the Egyptian ships at Navarino were those Anastasi had been asked to supply.[52] Like the rest of the vessels, they now lie at the bottom of the sea. It is said that on a calm day one can still see the sunken ships in their watery grave. What was Francis Barthow's role in this event?

Barthow the Baker and Family Man

After selling antiquities to Cohen in 1832, Barthow fell from traveler's tales. In 1820, after his journey to Port Mahon to acquire a new American passport, and communications with Bernardino Drovetti, Francis Barthow bought a bakery in Alexandria from an Austrian. It was the first "European" bakery in the city, and under Barthow it included extensive mills, granaries and machinery.[53] He married and had two sons, Joseph and Victor.[54]

In 1844, Francis Barthow's son, Victor, appeared at the American consulate requesting an American passport. He identified himself as the son of Francis Barthow and told John Gliddon, the United States consul, that both his father, Francis, and his brother, Joseph, were dead. Francis died around 1840. Attached to his petition were two passports, one for Francis. The second passport belonged to Joseph and was prepared by the vice naval agent of the United States residing in Marseilles. John Gliddon, the first American consul to be appointed to Egypt, was not well at the time and died shortly thereafter, so the matter was not resolved. Alexander Tod, John Gliddon's successor and son-in-law, sent several dispatches to Washington in the following years in the hopes of receiving an answer. In the meantime he offered Victor Barthow American protection.

In 1846 Victor Barthow reappeared at the consulate on another matter: a portion of the bakery was to be destroyed by the Egyptian government in order to widen the street. The episode and its aftermath were to last for almost ten years and become a diplomatic incident of gigantic proportions. The bakery was established as a *waqf,* a permanent endowment, duly recorded and protected by the Egyptian government. In August of 1847, with the affair now in its second year, Victor Barthow asked the consulate to petition the American ambassador in Constantinople to deal with the matter. He informed the consulate that a French Bakery in similar circumstances was compensated by the Egyptian government. He was unsuccessful. Nor was the family compensated for the loss of their livelihood.

In 1849, Victor Barthow wrote yet another letter, this time to Consul Tod's successor

Daniel McCauley, summarizing events up to that time and requesting intervention by the United States. McCauley was a different caliber of consul and considered the Barthow bakery incident a challenge to American power. McCauley warned that the incident was an affront to the American government and suggested the secretary of state should "show the colors" in the Mediterranean.[55] In February of 1852, seven years later, McCauley wrote to Secretary of State Daniel Webster that he had "informed the Minister of Foreign Affairs that should the case not meet a satisfactory conclusion within three weeks I should suspend the display of the American flag at Alexandria and await your instructions."[56] Since nothing happened to rectify the matter, the flag was struck. Then on February 15, 1852, McCauley wrote "that the display of the American flag at Alexandria is suspended as a matter of indignity at the manner in which an American claim, founded on the strictest principles of equity and justice has been received, discussed and disposed of, by the Government of His Excellency the Viceroy."[57] In a letter dated February 7, 1852 (the month March written above it with a question mark), McCauley stated that the Egyptian government offered $6,000 to Victor Barthow for his bakery. McCauley did not feel it was enough. On March 10 all the demands of the American consul had been met. The American flag was hoisted on March 11 "under a salute of 21 guns from the Batteries of Alexandria and a united display of all the flags of the respective European powers represented in Egypt."[58] American newspapers reported: "The American flag, which has been struck for some time, pending the satisfaction of a claim made upon the Egyptian Government for damages to property of a United States subject, was re-hoisted on the 11th ult., under a salute from the batteries of 21 guns."[59]

After the incident of the bakery, Victor Barthow became associated with the American Consulate in various positions until his death in 1872. He became an assistant to consuls Thayer and Hale. He developed into one of the leading foreign expatriates in the country, enjoying a great social position. On July 14, 1870, Victor Barthow, still employed at the Consulate in Alexandria, applied for the position of consul of the United States in Cairo.[60] At that time the Cairo Consulate was still subordinate to Alexandria, where the notorious George H. Butler, eventually dismissed for an incident which occurred between him and several of the American officers in the Khedive's army, then reigned as consul. Butler approved Victor Barthow's petition and acknowledged his lineage and his position in a letter to Hamilton Fish, Secretary of State: "Mr. Barthow is the son of an American Naval officer who visited this country many years ago, and has passed nearly all his life here, although an American citizen. He is consequently thoroughly acquainted with the laws, manners, customs, and language of the country and holds also a social position which will much facilitate his intercourse with the local officials."[61] Victor Barthow was appointed consul in Cairo in 1871. He died in that post on August 26, 1872.[62]

There is so much we still do not know about Francis Barthow. He was a man of many talents and great courage. He remained an American in Egypt for at least 35 years and probably more. He founded an American dynasty in Egypt and many of his family probably still survive there.

5

George Bethune English and the Egyptian Army Expedition of 1820–21 (Explorer)

Since the days of the pharaohs the Egyptians had coveted Nubia, the lands mostly south of Aswan. Although Nubian riches were sometimes under the control of ancient Egypt, and a Nubian dynasty once ruled Egypt, the conquests or unifications were never permanent and Nubian treasures remained elusive. Mohammad Ali's Egyptian Expeditionary Force of 1820–21 was one more attempt to bring the region under Egyptian control. The plan was to expand Egyptian territory and kill the hundreds of Mamluks who had escaped Mohammad Ali's wrath in 1811. More important, Egypt would once again gain control over the caravan routes and acquire the lucrative gold, ivory, and slave trade. Most important, conquest of the Sudan was the first step to control all of the Nile Valley and build a modern Egyptian empire. Egypt intended to do to the Sudan what the Ottoman had done, and what Europe was about to do, to Egypt: subjugate it.

This invasion, like its predecessors, was an ambitious venture, which, despite only a few battles, took several years to complete. It would bring about the end of the Funj Sultanate, which had been in power in the Sudan since the sixteenth century. In turn the conquest would establish a period called the *Turkiyya*, which would last until 1885 when the British began the conquest of the Sudan in the name of Egypt: one imperialist replacing another.

In charge of the expedition was Mohammad Ali's 25-year-old-son Ismail. Ismail's 4,000 soldiers were an accumulation of loosely disciplined men from around the Mediterranean world. In addition to Albanians from his father's homeland, Maghribeen from the edge of North Africa, and traditional Egyptian conscripts from the villages along the Nile, the army included Turkish Janissaries dressed in pantaloons, Kurds wearing medieval breastplates and conical hats, and desert Bedouins in flowing robes. They were armed with everything from spears to pistols to cannons, and rode everything from horses to camels to donkeys.

Preparations began in Cairo, where a flotilla of boats, reported to be as many as 3,000 by French merchant Felix Mengin, was assembled at Bulaq.[1] Camels were gathered at the southern Egyptian town of Esna, long known for its camel markets.[2] The army began its journey during high flood of the Nile to make navigation easier. Responsible for the artillery, English estimated the army at 4,000 men and the artillery as: "Ten pieces of field artillery, one mortar 8 inch caliber, and two small howitzers, [and] one hundred and twenty cannoneers...."[3] English maintained 120 boats of all shapes and sizes floated supplies and munitions

1st Cataract ⟍ ● ASWAN

EGYPT   RED SEA

ABU SIMBEL ●

2nd Cataract ⟍ WADI
                    HALFA

                            Koroso Road

3rd Cataract   SUDAN

                                    ● ABU HAMED

DONGOLA ●   Mahela Road
        Dongola Reach   4th Cataract
                    KAREMIA   5th Cataract

                                        ● BERBER
        Wadi Howar DEBBA ● KORTI   ATBARA
                        Bayuda Road

0   300 km   Atbara River
                            Shendi Reach ● SHENDI
6th Cataract ⟍

                        KHARTOUM

                        Blue Nile

                    White Nile

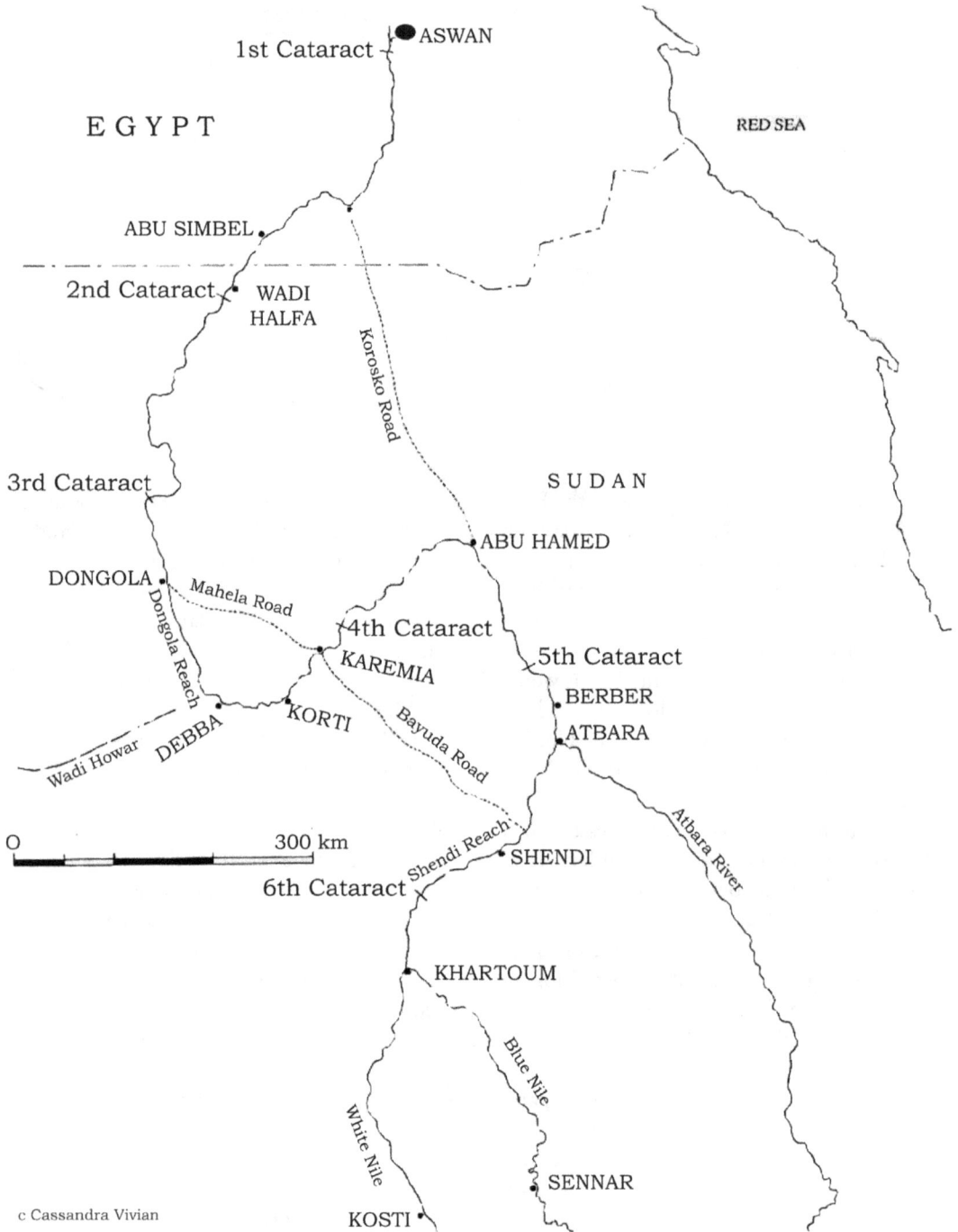

c Cassandra Vivian   ● SENNAR
                    KOSTI ●

**Map of the Nile at Sudan showing all the Cataracts and the great S-Curve between Cataracts 3
and 5 (map by the author).**

up the Nile, while Ismail and his cavalry marched along the shore for over two thousand miles from Cairo to Sennar. The sound of their drums was so formidable that as the army approached, village after village surrendered without a shot being fired.

The River and Its Deserts

The true enemies of this expedition were neither the kingdoms nor their inhabitants. The river and the desert were the real adversaries. More soldiers died from exposure or drowned in the cataracts of the Nile than on the field of battle. The army could not travel via desert routes because no one lived in the desert, so there was no one to conquer. Instead of taking the traditional land route from Korosko to Abu Hamid, as James Bruce and John Lewis Burckhardt had done, (and the future railroad would do) saving 600 miles, the army traveled next to and on the river so it could subjugate the inhabitants of Nile villages.

The Nile in the Sudan is diabolical. It is where the river earns the epithet "Father of Rivers." Where Khartoum would soon be founded, the docile White Nile, slowly working its way north from its source beyond Lake Victoria, meets the forceful Blue Nile, with its source in the Ethiopian highlands. In the 18th century nothing stopped its northern flow, especially during the high flood. The flood turned land masses into islands: some barely large enough to hold a few bits of shrubs; others miles long and dangerous obstacles to navigation. Precambrian granite basement rock could not stop the river. Instead the river cascaded and fell over the barriers, called cataracts, as it continued its downhill race to the sea. Six cataracts, called *shellals*, each with many rapids or falls, barred the river, all nearly impossible for navigation. English reported that Mohammad Ali had cut a channel through the northernmost or First Cataract, and a canal was under construction designed to bypass difficult portions of the second (vii). The remainder were untouched. The army had to deal with all of them. Boats were constantly hauled out of the water for repairs, or a hundred men would labor on shore to pull a single boat through a single rapid, of which there were hundreds along the river. For example, at the Second Cataract it took expedition boats over 30 days to travel 100 miles, a distance that a typical Nile sailboat could do from Cairo to a little beyond Beni Suef in a few days.

If that were not enough, the river held a huge bend that doubled the army's effort without doubling the distance. Called the Great S-Bend of the Nile, it finally forced the army overland through inhospitable desert while the river craft were left to navigate through two of the river's most horrific cataracts: the Fourth and the Fifth. The heat was oppressive. Marching through loose or blowing sand was exhausting. The wind was contrary: blowing a gale one day and at dead calm the next. To the east of the Nile was the Nubian Desert which ran from the river to the Red Sea. To the west was the southern section of the Libyan Desert. It was a most incredible journey, one that was recorded by a handful of Eastern[4] and Western explorers who suffered the consequences of their curiosity by traveling with the soldiers and sailors. Among these men were three known Americans: George Bethune English, Khalil Aga, and Achmed Aga.

George Bethune English

The pale and delicate 33-year-old American, George Bethune English (1787–1828), was a *Topgi Bashi*, a chief of artillery, for the expedition (x). The events that brought him to this point in his life were not only dramatic, but shocking. English was born in Cambridge, Massachusetts, on March 7, 1787, to Thomas English and Penelope Bethune English. He graduated from both Harvard Law School and Harvard Divinity School. While at Harvard, he worked at the library, where his inquisitive mind led him to old documents stored in the library basement. Among them were a number of seventeenth-century religious manuscripts. English became enthralled with the handwritten epistles and their main theories, which philosophically and theologically discredited the establishment of Christianity as a true religion. This was a shocking theory in the eyes of ultra-conservative nineteenth-century religious thought. English, a man more liberal than conservative, discussed the theories whenever he had a chance. Against the advice of his Christian friends, he published a pamphlet in 1813, *The Grounds of Christianity Examined by Comparing the New Testament with the Old*, which questioned the basic religious theories related to the establishment of Christianity.[5]

The publication was a bold move at the beginning of the nineteenth century, especially in Protestant New England, where independent religious ideas were not tolerated. In presenting a different view, English lost his job at Harvard, was attacked from pulpits in New England, and was maligned in published pamphlets throughout the United States. English was vilified. Finally, a committee was called at the First Church of Christ of Cambridge in New England and they excommunicated English.[6] English appealed to fellow Massachusian John Quincy Adams, then Secretary of State and fledgling America's primary visionary on foreign policy. Through Adams, English was appointed second lieutenant in the Marines on February 27, 1815.[7] He left his shattered reputation behind him and started a new life.

Stationed at Washington, D.C., English was attached to the U.S. sloop *Peacock* and the diplomatic party that took Ambassador Albert Gallatin to France in 1816.[8] Naval records confirm English was posted to the Mediterranean in 1816–1817, that he was promoted to first lieutenant on April 18, 1817, and resigned his commission three years before the Egyptian expedition of 1820.[9] After his resignation, the naval register continued to carry English's name. He was out of the Navy and in Constantinople by late 1817. Yet as late as 1819 his name was still on the naval register, albeit "crossed through with the notation 'out' and 'in Turkey.'"[10] No evidence has been discovered to date to indicate that English was on a mission for Adams, a well-documented service he performed after 1823. There is a high probability that he became that "secret agent" as early as 1816 when he journeyed to France with Albert Gallatin, whose views on trade and American involvement in European matters opposed Adams's views. Placing a spy in the "enemy" camp was an astute political move. English's mission could well have been continued during the prelude to the Greek War of Independence from the Ottoman Empire in 1821. That war, which involved Egyptian forces, was a volatile political issue in the United States, with Adams against American involvement and Albert Gallatin supporting alignment with the Greeks. These events could have ultimately brought English to Egypt before the Greek war began.[11] The United States had no official standing with the Ottoman Porte and thus Egypt. If English was sent to Egypt to gather information on trade and observe the political environment for Adams, as he would do in Constantinople after his time in Egypt, the record is yet to be unearthed.

By the time English arrived in Egypt, he had spent over five years in and around the Ottoman world. Not only was he prolific in Arabic, he wore Middle Eastern clothes, and took the Muslim name Mohamed Effendi. A bit of insight into a more relaxed English is given by James Ellsworth De Kay, an American zoologist studying the cholera in Turkey, in *Sketches of Turkey in 1831 and 1832*: "I had some years ago the pleasure of an acquaintance with this gentleman, and still recollect with pleasure the fund of anecdote and information which his various wanderings in different parts of the world had furnished him with. He had adopted completely the Turkish immobility of feature, and would frequently set the table in a roar by some amusing anecdote, while not a single muscle of his own face would be discomposed."[12]

In Cairo English sought and was given aid by the British, through the offices of the British Consul General Henry Salt. It was through Salt that English was offered and accepted a command in the Egyptian Expeditionary Force just as it was about to invade the Sudan in 1821 (10). The relationship with Salt would have far-reaching consequences for English, his companions, and Salt. No fewer than two of the American manuscripts of the Sudan journey would end up in Salt's hands. One, thanks to Salt, would be published. The other would languish unidentified in his papers for nearly two centuries.

While preparing for his journey to the Sudan, George Bethune English took the time to respond to his critics. He sent his manuscript off to America to be published and turned his mind and his face south, to the Sudan.[13]

Khalil Aga and Achmed Aga

There were two other Americans on the Egyptian Expeditionary Force: Khalil Aga and Achmed Aga. What is known of the two men is limited and comes from journals written by travelers who joined the expedition. These journals maintain that Khalil Aga was a native of New York, and Achmed Aga was a Swiss who had become a naturalized American. English only referred to them by their newly adopted Arabic names, a decision which has complicated the understanding of the events of the journey and its place in American history. Additional information appeared in a book by two British ministers who were on the Nile and met English and company near Merowe (ancient Napata, not Meroë). Their views of Khalil and Achmed were not kind.[14]

English wrote, "Khalil Aga, a native of New York, took the turban a few weeks before the departure of Ismail Pasha from Cairo. Learning that I was to accompany his Excellence, he requested me to obtain of the Pasha that he might be attached to me during the expedition" (205). The naval records that would confirm these observations and yield the Western names of the two men are difficult to trace. The ships of the Mediterranean Squadron from 1818 to 1821 included the USS *Franklin, Erie, United States, Constitution, Peacock,* and *Columbus.*[15] The two men were probably aboard one of these ships. The log books and muster rolls, numbering in the hundreds, are in the National Archives in Washington, D.C. Only one of these ships can be ruled out. According to the USS *Constitution* Museum, the *Constitution* did not depart for the Mediterranean until May 13, 1821, too late for this expedition.

Khalil survived the journey. In fact, in 1831 De Kay recalled, "He is still in Egypt, where, I hear, that he is distinguished for his courage and good conduct."[16] Achmed did not survive the journey.

More Westerners with the Expedition

The Egyptian expedition was a magnet for European travelers and adventurers who sought its safety in order to survey the mysterious Nubian lands. One man who took up the challenge was eighteen-year-old Linant de Bellefonds (1799–1883). He was a midshipman and draftsman born in Lorient, France, who came to Egypt in 1817, with the Conte de Forbin Expedition, remained to work as an engineer on a number of projects for Mohammad Ali, and became an important figure in Egyptian history. On this expedition he became the first Westerner to find the Temple of Musawaret and the Temple of Naqaa, both important desert temple complexes south of Meroë.

Linant was accompanied for part of the journey by Dr. Alessandro Ricci, a Siennese physician and artist. Like Linant, he was given a number of commissions to do drawings for a variety of clients.[17] After the journey he became Ibrahim Pasha's doctor. His collection of antiquities was acquired by the Egyptian Museum in Florence, Italy, in 1832. Ricci's journal was published by the Société Royale Geographical in Cairo in two volumes in 1930.[18]

Linant's second companion was the Italian explorer Giovanni Finati. Finati kept a journal too. It was translated and augmented by William John Bankes, who also oversaw the publication of English's text. Bankes translated, perhaps edited, and definitely footnoted Finati's manuscript, and published it in England in 1830. Finati seems to have marched his way south. Finally, near the beginning of the Fourth Cataract, Finati was assigned to a boat and given the job of procuring men from the different villages along the Nile and pressing them into service hauling the boats.[19] However, when the army left the Nile and crossed the desert, Finati and Linant went with it.

In the footnotes to Finati's book, Bankes took the liberty to attack English's manuscript, despite the fact that he was instrumental in its publication. In addition, and despite his negative views, he used English's account to supplement or substantiate Finati's narrative.[20] This alone should counter Bankes's careless assessment of English. Although he never acknowledged English by name, Bankes identified English by saying "The American," or "An American." He found English's use of Islamic dates an "absurd affectation." This was a fair criticism. He assessed English's contributions: "The ophthalmia and ill health also seem to have prevented the author from profiting much by his journey, and it is a work, therefore, of very little attraction."[21] This is a poor assessment of the book. Unfortunately Bankes's attitude is still held by some scholars today, damaging their evaluation of English and his contributions.

Frédéric Cailliaud (1787–1869) and his companion, the painter, astronomer, and draftsman Pierre Constant Letorzec, whom English called Mr. Constant, were often in the same flotilla as English, and the men became friends. Cailliaud and Letorzec are credited with the rediscovery of Meroë, which they saw for the first time on April 25, 1821. They were not the first Europeans in modern times to see it. That distinction belongs to James Bruce, who saw and identified Meroë in 1772, nearly fifty years before the Egyptian invasion got underway. What Cailliaud did was author and publish a most extraordinary book with dynamic illustrations and plans. *Voyage à Meroë, au Fleuve Blanc, au-delà de Fâzgol dans le midi du Royaume de Sennâr, à Syouah et dans cinq autres oases* was published in Paris in 1826. The two men returned to France accompanied by about 500 antiquities.

Other Europeans on the Egyptian expedition included an Italian named Rossignoli who traveled in the same boat as the Americans (actually the Americans were guests on the medical boat). He was part of the intriguing and dangerous medical staff headed by the Protomedico, or first physician to Ismail. The latter was a Smyrniot Greek and a conniving, intriguing man. At some point, after Dr. Gentile, the most competent doctor on Ismail's staff, was poisoned, Rossignoli feared for his own life. Around Christmas-time he asked permission to return to Cairo with George Waddington and Bernard Hanbury. The request was denied.[22]

Domenico Ermenegildo Frediani (1783–1823), an Italian soldier and traveler, also joined the expedition. He had a long association with Egypt — arriving around 1817. Mohammad Ali, at the recommendation of French Consul Bernardino Drovetti (with whom Frediani would travel to Siwa Oasis in early 1820), appointed Frediani as a Cavaliere and tutor to Ismail on the journey.[23] There was conflict between Frediani and the Protomedico too, and that intrigue created a great deal of friction. According to English, Frediani met an awful death at Sennar, where he contracted fever and had to be placed in chains because he had gone mad (xiv). *Who was Who in Egyptology* maintains that Frediani returned to Cairo and died there, but English is quite clear about Frediani's death.

From time to time, the expedition encountered additional independent travelers who joined it for a while. Among these were the two Englishmen mentioned earlier, Waddington and Hanbury. They left Cairo a day or so after English, accompanied by their Irish dragoman James Curtin. The Waddington party suffered much the same fate as the other Europeans: hunger, sickness, fatigue, and anxiety. They left the expedition at Ismail's request before the Fourth Cataract.

The Lost Journal[24]

There was another person who kept an English-language journal on the voyage up the Nile and offered a little more insight into the adventures of the expedition. The 56-page manuscript, long buried in the Henry Salt Papers of the British Library in London, forms the only complete record of the expedition from Wadi Halfa to Sennar.[25] The narrative of the journal concentrated mainly on the day-to-day ordeal of the boatmen as they tried to navigate the unknown and often savage river, and the hardship of the army as the men battled the elements and the lack of supplies. It was written in Naval log style with sailing times, wind directions, and visual landmarks listed for every day of the journey. Nautical terms like "got under weigh" and "warping," as well as the ability to perform naval tasks, endorse the idea that the author had a nautical background. He wrote, "I took to pieces one of the spyglass belonging to the Selectar to wipe and clean it the man in charge of the things not knowing how" (April 6).

Not only did the author of the manuscript have a naval background, he also had a personal knowledge of America. Within the pages of the manuscript are such American terms and descriptions as "shaking Aspen" (Nov. 29), "Indian corn" (Dec. 9), "American black bird" (Nov. 29), "barter as the Indians in America," (Dec. 3), and "savages of America" (July 4). Comparing the text with the entries of Waddington and English further cements an American background. Although he is not identified by name, what we glean from these comparisons is that the person who wrote the newly discovered manuscript was an American and he accompanied English on this visit. The journal belonged to either Khalil or Achmed, or both.

Achmed died on the journey and the manuscript does not end until the completion of the journey at Aswan. There is no reference to Achmed's death in the 1922 English edition of English's book, but in the American edition of 1923, English wrote:

> I had with me two soldiers, one Khalil Aga, an American of New York and the other Achmed Aga a Swiss by birth but an American by naturalization, both excellent swimmers. They prepared for me a small raft of logs on which I embarked [to check the damages to his ship].... When I was placed on my raft with Khalil and Achmed swimming by its sides and pushing it along. In the hilarity of the moment we cheered our passage by singing "Hail Columbia," which was probably the first time that the wilds of Africa ever re-echoed to a song of Liberty. Achmed Aga died on the third Cataract as Khalil his comrade believed, but upon uncertain grounds, of poison given him by a Greek in consequence of a quarrel.[26]

If Achmed were poisoned by a Greek, it would be in keeping with the intrigues among Ismail's staff. As noted, a Smyrniot Greek had been appointed Protomedico, or first physician, to Ismail. Every Western journal condemned him as a rogue. As mentioned above, he had one of his staff, an Italian named Dr. Gentile, poisoned in lieu of repaying him for a loan. Waddington retold the incident.[27] As reported by English, the Americans believed Achmed met the same kind of death. This was augmented by Frederic Cailliaud, who commented on all the strange deaths among the Europeans: "Ibrahym lost his first doctor, who died of an inflammatory fever; he was Genoese and called Scot. This gentleman's pharmacist died later in the same way. An American had previously succombed. Death seemed to want to claim all the gentlemen around me. Already six Europeans were no more...."[28]

With Achmed dead, precise identification of the writer of the lost journal emerges in the entries regarding the return to Wadi Halfa from Sennar. The journal was still being written. The person who wrote it finished the journey with English. When English began his homeward-bound journey he did not mention who was with him. But as the journey out of Nubia progressed he wrote of a "verdant island called Kandessee, in a small island adjoining which Khalil Aga, my traveling companion, says," etc. (203); and, "At about four hours after the noon of the 8th we quitted the banks of the Nile, and turned into the desert, carrying as much water as we could, myself taking four water-skins for myself, Khalil Aga, and a black slave of mine" (211). So there is enough evidence to say that the unknown writer of the mysterious and long-lost journal was in fact the American Khalil Aga. In the last few lines the journal refers to Khalil Aga in the third person. So who wrote this passage? All other passages could have been written by Khalil. Did he write this passage? Did Achmed write this passage? For now, there is no answer. The majority, especially the journey from the Fourth Cataract to the end, was written by Khalil.

Who was Khalil Aga? Some scholars have suggested Luther Bradish, on a mission to Turkey for John Quincy Adams, was Khalil. He was not. Bradish was not with the army at all. In a letter written by him to Thomas Appleton in 1824, Bradish stated he arrived in Egypt in February 1821. So he was too late to accompany George Bethune English up the Nile, for by that time English was well past the Fourth Cataract, deep in Sudan on his way to Meroë.[29] So Khalil was not Luther Bradish.

Khalil's journal is not just "one more account" of events. It provides a number of important functions. First and foremost, it clarifies English's dates. Not all of them, for the journals of all the Westerners contradict each other from time to time. What makes English's dates more complicated than the other journal writers is that he used the Islamic calendar to date his book. Where the western calendar has 12 months and 365 (+ -) days, the Islamic calendar is a lunar calendar of 12, 30-day months, for a total of 354 (+ -) days. It moves forward on the Western calendar by approximately ten days every year. The western calendar begins with the birth of Christ, while the Islamic calendar begins with the emigration (Hijrah) of the Prophet Mohammad from Mecca to Medina. Meshing the two is a bit complicated. On the first page of his text, English provided a date for the beginning of his journey from Wadi Halfa: "Zilghadge 16, 1235."

In a footnote to the American edition he explained the date as the "end of September, or the former part of October, A.C. 1820."[30] The English edition gave the date as September 24, 1820 (1). Then he, or Bankes, who had the responsibility of publishing the manuscript, abandoned the reader to Islamic dates. Khalil's journal is the key to interconnecting English's dates with other texts most of the time. Not always, for even the very first date is a contradiction. Three different journals give three different dates for English's arrival at Wadi Halfa. Waddington stated English arrived on November 10, 1820, "express in nineteen days from Cairo."[31] Khalil's journal recorded the arrival at Halfa as September 29. So none of the starting dates agree. However, Khalil's journal and English's journal agree more often than they disagree.

The second thing that the newly discovered journal does is to provide an explanation of the Henry Salt graffiti found along the Fourth and Fifth cataracts of the Nile. Salt did not sign his name. Khalil did. More important, Khalil's entries present English as more honorable and more competent than the reputation his name has carried for two centuries. Waddington, as discussed, assassinated English's character. Bankes, in a footnote in Finati's book, dismisses

Pulling boats through rapids (from Frederic Cailliaud's *Voyage à* Meroë, *au Fleuve Blanc, au-delà de Fazgol dans le midi du Royaume de Sennar, à Syouah et dans cinq autres oases*).

English as too sick to be of any value. In fact, orders from Ismail and intrigues among the Europeans tell another story. At times, such as at Wadi Halfa, English was ordered not to proceed with the main army. At other times, such as preparing to cross the Bayuda desert, it appears he too was a victim of the Protomedico, who kept supplies from reaching him, which delayed English and forced Khalil to travel with the boats through the great S-Bend. The latter is, perhaps, the most important contribution of the lost journal: not only does it show the intrigues against English and English's value to the expedition, it is the only day-by-day narrative of the *entire* river journey. No other European traveled the entire S-Bend of the Nile. Not only does Khalil provide details about the landscape and the river throughout the bend, he provides information about distance and difficulty, and also gives the names for the hundreds of rapids. As late as 1903, Khalil's journal appears to have been the only information available on this section of the Nile. It would be decades until the true character of that area was known to the West.

English and Khalil's Narrative of the Journey

The tale of the journey is what is important here: the daily struggle of a group of human beings moving through horrific and mostly unknown territory on an amazing journey. Equally important are the men who tell the tale: they are Americans. It is assumed that they are the first Americans to cast their eyes on the ancient monuments, the terrain, the S-Curve of the Nile, the confluence of the two Niles, and the legendary city of Sennar. We do not read much of Ismail and his main army in these pages. Our reporters are far down the chain of command, despite English's designation as General of Artillery. Ismail and his army were already at Wadi Halfa preparing to ascend the Nile when English and the other two Americans arrived.

English received his assignment from Ismail, but before the army began to ascend the Second Cataract, he had a severe attack of ophthalmia, a debilitating eye disease similar to trachoma: "My eyes were closed up and incapable of supporting the light, and occasioned me such acute anguish that I could get no sleep but by the effect of laudanum" (3). Intermittent attacks of ophthalmia would remain with him for fifteen months. When Ismail and the "4000 fighting men, Turks, Arabs, and Abadi, and ten pieces of cannon," left Wadi Halfa by land on October 3, 1820, English was left behind with the supply boats (2–3).

The adventure begins with the Second Cataract, which English described as not a single obstruction, but a succession of nine falls and rapids stretched over a hundred miles. It was then, and remains today, difficult to navigate. Before they arrived at Ambigol, two boats were crashed into the rocks of the rapids, two men were lost, and, in an oft-repeated labor, natives along the shore were conscripted to man the ropes hauling the boats through dangerous areas (5). In years to come, pushing boats over the rapids would become lucrative employment as tourist boats ascended the Nile.

The party arrived at Dal, ninety-eight miles from Wadi Halfa,[32] on November 10, 1820. English was not happy. The cataract proved to be much longer than expected. He wanted and needed to catch up with Ismail, in order to take up his position. Being the responsible man that he was, he tried to hire camels and go by land. He did not succeed. He was running out of food and the men in his command were reduced to eating bread, rice, and lentils. Finding food became an additional crisis because the natives would not accept Egyptian paper money (11–12). Finally, the hungry team managed to purchase a sheep from a farmer. Finati was far more clever than the Americans. He found a way to solve his supply problem by pretending he was one of Ismail's soldiers and drawing down on the army's supplies.[33]

English described in detail one of their encounters with the Second Cataract:

> The passage was dangerous, and the boat thrice in imminent peril. We struck once on rocks under water, where the current was running probably at the rate of six knots an hour. The current, after about ten minutes, swept the boat off without having received a hole in her bottom, otherwise we must probably have perished. Shortly after we were jammed between a great shallow whirlpool and a large boat on our starboard beam. This boat was dashed by the current against ours, and menaced to shove her into the whirlpool. The long lateen yards of the two boats got entangled, and I was prepared to leap into the other boat, in anticipation of the destruction of ours, when the wind freshened, and the large boat was enabled to get clear of ours. Not long after, the same boat fell aboard of us the second time, in a place where, if our boat had drifted twice her length to leeward or astern, she must have run upon rocks [15–16].

Then the Nile calmed and the men enjoyed good sailing through miles of fertile land.

On November 19 (English called it the 12 of *Safi*), the supply fleet was in the midst of a series of islands, and English's boat paused at the large island of Syéé (Sai), 130 miles from Wadi Halfa.[34] Here they viewed a forest of palms, seven villages, and an ancient temple (21–22). The ruins on Sai, we now know, date from four ancient civilizations and include the Temple of Amara, a number of Napatan temples, and a Pharaonic New Kingdom fortress with inscriptions by Thutmoses III and Amenhotep II. English and Khalil did not know that. The region was dominated by ancient ruins, including a number of temples on the west bank of the Nile at Saddenga (Sedinga) (142 miles from Halfa) and Soleb (143 miles). English described one of them as "two hundred feet long ... ten of the columns only are standing ... composed of separate blocks of a brown stone ... front faces the East; west bank of the river about two miles beyond the territory of Succoot" (27). Khalil set the date of their visit as November 22. A few days later, on the 25th, Khalil noted more ruins:

> About 8 miles from this narrow passage Saw the ruins of an antient temple. Four pillars were still standing, but the wind being very fresh was unable to go on Shore to examine it. Five miles higher up I went on Shore and passed through very fertile land cultivated in appearance in the European manner. Passed two islands one about five miles in length the other 3½ miles both fertile, came to a village named Coke [Koke] where they make wine and rum. Saw a lake about 2½ miles in length, inland. The wind failing at Sunset we stopped at the rapids of Kisebar [Kaibar, 203 miles from Wadi Halfa], having made the day about 25 miles.

Nearby was the city of Kerma, the ancient capital of the Kerma Culture (2500–1500 B.C.). In former times it was a major trading center for African goods, which were transported to the Mediterranean along the desert trade routes. The area surrounding it was fertile and plenteous. A few boatmen from the expedition went ashore to seek provisions and found the fields were fed by water wheels, which lifted the water from the river and sent it along canals to other wheels that irrigated the land (35). This system, used all along the Nile in Nubia and Egypt, was still in use in the 1970s. On November 26 they arrived at one of the major ancient sites along this section of the Nile: the 25-mile-long, 5-mile-wide island of Argo, 252 miles from Halfa.[35] It was a friendly place to the army; its ruler, Mek Tumbol, was assisting Ismail in his triumphal march south to Sennar. Amid the fields and palm trees were five temples, one identified as the New Kingdom Temple of Tabo, erected on the island during the reign of the Nubian Kushite kings (42). The next day English tried to accompany Khalil to see the ruins but was too sick with "a bloody flux" (dysentery).

Beyond Kerma the scene changed as the Nile narrowed, the islands disappeared, and high cliffs channeled the river. The wind was rising as they arrived at the Third Cataract of the Nile north of Dongola:

> We had been informed, two days ago, that there was a dangerous rapid between us and Dongola, and we congratulated ourselves that the wind was fair and strong to push us through it; we passed it happily, though not without peril.... The passage lay where the river rolled furiously over rocks under water, and between shores there was no approaching, on account of the shoals and rocks above and under water which lined them. The strong wind forced our boat alongside of another that was struggling and reeling in the passage, to the imminent danger of both. To clear this boat, our rais ventured to pass ours over a place where the foam and fury of the water indicated latent rocks. We hardly dared to breathe, but we did not strike here, but half a minute after we were fast upon a sand bank. We stayed in this condition for about a quarter of an hour, having in view close by us the wreck of a boat lost here. With considerable difficulty our boat was disengaged, when we put her before the wind and again faced this truly infernal pass. By the force of the current, the boat neared a large and furious whirlpool, formed by an eddy on the side of the passage. The steersman endeavored, in vain, to counteract this drift of the boat by the aid of the rudder. The side of the boat approached to within a yard of the white foam which covered this dreadful spot. Our rais tore his turban from his head, and lifted his clasped hands to Heaven, exclaiming, "We are lost!" The rest of the boatmen were screaming to God and the prophet for aid, when, I know not how, but by the good Providence that watched over us, the boat cleared this peril, and others that beset us in passing yet two more rapids almost as dangerous [28–40].

This scene would be reenacted dozens if not hundreds of times as this army of boats, men, equipment, and supplies tried to wend its way along the Nile. It was enough to turn back the most formidable of men. But Ismail and his men moved on.

About this time the independent travelers Waddington and Hanbury, who had been exploring the region by camel, asked for and received permission to join the boats and travel along the river with the expedition. Both Khalil and Waddington recorded the date as November 26 at New Dongola, while English called it the 6th of Rebi. English, Khalil, and Achmed were still to the north of Dongola and did not see the two Englishmen at this time.

The Americans had a problem. They knew the town of Dongola was near, but could not identify the legendary community from the villages scattered along the shore of the Nile. At one village English was told there were two Dongolas: New Dongola, which would be found on the west bank, and Old Dongola, which was further up the Nile. The latter had been recently destroyed by the Mamluks fleeing from Egypt. As for Ismail, the villagers told English he was still three days' march beyond. The Pasha and his troops had easily subdued the area and were forging ahead, leaving only 24 soldiers behind. English did not know the details of these events until much later.

At the end of November (Khalil dated it to November 29[36]), news came from Ismail, who was in Dongola, to hurry the supply boats along the river. So the fleet pushed forward with greater zeal. Khalil was much impressed with the entire province, as he wrote on December 3:

> 3rd Walked out to See the country which only wants inhabitants and cultivation to become the finest in the world. — Cut down a date tree to get the heart of it, found it very good eating. Something like the West Indian cocoa-nut both in taste and color. These people are very different from those of the lower country and it is only by force they can be enduced to part with any of their produce for money, but they will barter as the Indians in America for flour or rice or any kind of cloathes, linen, and cotton cloth which they wear round them, having no other kind of dress. We could not Sail this day the wind chopping round to the Eastward and blowing very fresh the river running to the ESE and unfortunately our boats like all those of the country not adapted to Sailing on a wind....

Waiting for calm, they found more evidence that a major battle had occurred. Yet they had no details and no idea of the scope of the encounter. When the boats reached New Dongola the winds forced them to put in to shore again. It gave them time to look about. They found a village of 300 houses. Fifteen inhabitants informed English that this was their home until the "brigands of Shageia [Shaqiya] infested and ravaged the country." (The Shaqiya were a formidable enemy with origins in Arabia.) Upon hearing that the Pasha Ismail had conquered the region and asked the natives to return home, they had come back (48). The area was still unstable, for that night, December 3, 1820, there were musket shots across the river and English feared it might be the Shaqiya, who were known for their fierce fighting ability. The boatmen fearfully gathered their arms, but nothing materialized.

When the party finally reached Old Dongola (351 miles from Wadi Halfa),[37] the capital of ancient Christian Nubia, they found the ruins of a large fortified city. It was Khalil who provided the most detailed description of the town on December 5:

> 5th Sailed at ½ past 5 with the wind at NW blowing very fresh. The country all deserted by the inhabitants for the Space of 30 miles being infested by a band of robbers amounting in number to five thousand.
> Fifteen miles from the place where we sailed passed a town on the East bank of the river about a mile and a quarter in length, built on a hill part of it inhabited and part of it in ruins. Observed two very large houses, partly built after the Spanish fashion. When we came too in the evening discovered this town to be Dongola [Old Dongola]. About 4 miles from the town saw another about ¾ mile in circumference all in ruins. The appearance of bastions Still remaining.

The wind encreasing to gale endeavored to fetch the Shore, but had the misfortune to ground on a bank of Sand, where we remained ¾ of an hour before we Succeeding getting off after much exertion however we gained the shore where we remained until about 3 when the wind lulling we got again under weigh. About 12 miles from the town on the East side of the river, passed another on the Western Side, not quite So large but all in ruins made this day 17 miles.

They did not stop to examine the ruined town, for the Pasha was only two days ahead, and the wind was continuing to impede their travel. They were now approaching the most terrifying part of their journey.

The S-Curve of the Nile

Ever capricious, the river presented the Americans with a great surprise: below Dongola at Debbe (371 miles) and Abu Dom it turns to make a huge U-turn, now called the Korti Elbow. It actually reversed direction. It flowed south while continuing to head north. Then, hundreds of miles later, before Abu Hamed, the Nile reversed itself again, returning to its normal pattern of flowing and heading north to the Mediterranean. This is the gigantic S-Curve (parts are now flooded in a new dam project). The entire expedition, which by this time was spread out along the Nile for hundreds of miles, had to pass this dangerous area not knowing what lay ahead. They would face two major cataracts, one more ghastly than the other. The river was and is so violent in this area that the decision was made to abandon it and cross through the desert between the two bends. It was a 250-kilometer (155-mile) detour through a volcanic wasteland.

Each evening as the various boats along the river pulled in to shore, it was easy to share information or, when available, a humble meal. As the task force approached the region of Napata a rumor circulated that the two Englishmen had joined the flotilla. It was here, at the edge of terror, that George Waddington and Barnard Hanbury met George English and the other two Americans again. Waddington and Hanbury had been riding camels and donkeys on their journey south. Their journey to that point was more leisurely than English's and their descriptions of the various ancient sites were much better than his. So was their description of the battle at Korti, which English was yet to comprehend and Khalil did not mention at all.

English was anxious to meet them, so on December 12, 1820, he walked the shoreline for three hours trying to find their boat.[38] During that walk he "observed some hundreds of bodies of men and animals that had perished in the late engagement and during the pursuit, and the stench which filled the air was almost intolerable" (61). Undeniably, a battle had taken place.

When the Americans found the Englishmen's boat, Waddington and his party were not on board. They settled in to await their return. English observed: "They were suffering privations, as were all in the boats, and I regretted that my being in similar circumstances put it out of my power to ameliorate their situation" (59). Waddington, as reported earlier, saw the men upon his return from a hunting expedition. Whether Waddington perceived English as a threat to his own exploration of the Nile, or was caught up in a bit of snobbery, or truly disliked him, he was not kind to English (nor to Cailliaud). Waddington questioned why he should be hospitable to a person who had deserted his religion.

English, to say the least, was not happy when he read Waddington's account of their encounter along the Nile. When he arrived in England after this journey he confronted Mr. Waddington about his comments and asked for a retraction. Waddington agreed to do so in the next edition. There was never a retraction, for no new edition appeared. Upon English's return to the United States the *Religious Intelligencer* quoted the *Philadelphia Union* newspaper, which repeated Waddington's admonitions almost verbatim when announcing the publication of English's own book of his adventure:

> Mr. George Bethune English, whose eccentric conduct has attracted so much attention, changing his religion from Calvinism to Arminianism, from Arminianism to Unitarianism, from that, to Judaism, and that again to Mohammedanism, has returned to Boston, his native place, in good health, after an absence of nearly ten years. A volume of his travels on the Nile, has recently been published in London, and from the uncommon incidents with which his adventures have been replete, it cannot but prove very interesting.[39]

There is no doubt that the remarks caused English a great deal of harm. His religious preferences were once again brought into question.

Back on the Nile, it took the main army over a month to begin to pass the treacherous rapids. While awaiting their turn to begin the navigation of the cataract in late December 1820 and early January 1821, the foreigners went sightseeing. The province holds five major ancient sites: Gebel Bakal, Kareima, Napata (also called Merowe, 447 miles from Wadi Halfa),[40] and Nuri. Most have evidence of the great Napatan (900–270 B.C.) and Meroitic (270 B.C.–350 A.D.) cultures that dominated the region and created many of Sudan's remarkable monuments.[41] English asked the natives the name of the area, which he believed held important archaeological remains. They replied, "Meroë!" One can only imagine the excitement of the foreigners at hearing the name of the lost site that surely they had discussed on the long journey south from Wadi Halfa. They were wrong. In a footnote to his 1822 London edition, English acknowledged the site was *not* Meroë, but Merowe, the ancient Napata. The two sites are often confused, for the names are pronounced exactly the same. By that time Cailliaud had truly rediscovered Meroë, which was further along the Nile near Shendi. English was the first in print with the information. He reported that Meroë has "the ruins of a city, temples, and fifty-four pyramids. This, I am inclined to believe, was the site of the famous Meroë, the capital of the island of that name" (133–34ff).[42]

On the 12th of Rebi (English's calculation), English arrived at Ismail's camp. Two days later he met the leader and offered many apologies for his delay and his failure to participate in the great battle. Khalil, who helped English prepare for the visit by giving him a shave, fixed this date at December 26. Once within the camp of the Pasha, English got a full description of what had transpired during the previous weeks. He wrote:

> His Excellence, as said before, set out from Wady Halfa on the 26th of Zilhadge last. In ten days of forced march he arrived at New Dongola. A little beyond this village, the Selictar, at the head of a detachment of about four hundred men, surprised and dispersed about fifteen hundred of the enemy, taking many of their horses and camels. Four days' march beyond new Dongola, the Pasha, at the head of the advance guard of the army, came up with the main body of the Shageias and their allies, strongly posted on the side of a mountain near a village called Courty [Korti], on the westerly bank of the river. The Pasha at this juncture had with him but six hundred cavalry and some of the Abbadies mounted on dromedaries, of whom we had about five hundred with the army, but none of his cannon. The enemy advanced to the combat with loud screams and cries, and with great fury. The Abbadies could not withstand their charge, and were driven rearward. At this critical instant, his Excellence gave the order, and the cavalry of the Pasha charged and poured in the fire of their carbines and pistols. After a conflict of no long duration, the cavalry of the enemy fled in dismay, while those who fought on foot fell on their faces, throwing

their shields over their heads to secure them from the tramp of the cavalry, and implored mercy.

In consequence of the result of this affair, all the country between the place of combat and Shageia, i.e. the country occupied by the castles and immediate subjects of the Makels of Shageia, submitted and were pardoned. The pasha pursued his march a mile in width, which at the time was covered with plantations of durra. The enemy were posted on the side of this mountain and among the durra in the open ground between the mountain and the river; so that their rear was secured by the mountain, and their right covered by a strong castle at the foot of its extremity lying off from the river. Malek Shouus, Malek Zibarra, and the other chiefs of Shageia, and their immediate followers, composed the cavalry of the enemy. They had assembled, either by force or persuasion, all the peasantry subject to their dominion, the whole forming a mass which blackened the whole side of the mountain. Their arms consisted of lances, shields, and long broad swords double-edged. These wretched peasants, who were all on foot, their masters posted in front in order to receive and exhaust the fire of the Pasha's troops; while Shouus and the cavalry occupied the rear in order to keep the peasants to their posts, and to have the start of the Pasha's cavalry in case they should find it necessary to take to flight. The Pasha posted his troops parallel to the enemy, placing the greater part of the cavalry opposite the open ground between the mountains and the river, and pushing the artillery in a little in advance. The enemy with loud cries and uplifted lances rushed forward. Some of the peasants in advance of the others, with no other arms than lances and shields, threw themselves upon the cannon and were blown to pieces. The castle on the right of the enemy was stormed. After feeling the effects of a few rounds from the artillery, which dashed horse and man to pieces, the cavalry of the enemy fled in dismay, leaving their infantry to be rode over and shot down by our cavalry, who destroyed many hundreds of them in the battle and during the pursuit. Malek Shouus and his cavalry did not discontinue their flight till they reached the territory of Shendi, leaving their numerous and strong castles, their dependant villages, and a rich and beautiful country, in the hands of the conqueror [80–84].

English was sympathetic to the natives who threw themselves against the cannons. He called it "the desperate courage of these wretched peasants," and lamented that the firepower of Ismail did not give them a chance (84).

Ismail was more concerned about what was yet to come. English asked for and was told he would receive camels and horses to aid him in continuing the journey, but at the present time there were more pressing matters. Over the next nine days Ismail secured the region. He showed a wisdom beyond his years and English was impressed with the way the young leader received and dealt with the defeated rulers and their subjects. In addition to respectful treatment for the dignitaries, the Egyptian army was kept from pillaging the region. Then on the 21st of Rebi, the army began to move forward as 300 cavalry headed to Berber, and Ismail reestablished his camp 8 hours further up the Nile (88–89). Khalil reported this took place on December 27.

By Khalil's description, the party visited the Pyramids of Nuri on the day the prince began to move the army. English also recorded the event:

They stand about half a mile from the right hand bank of the river. I counted twenty-seven, none of them perfect, and most of them in ruins; the greater part of them are built of stone, and are evidently much more ancient than those of Meroë. The largest is probably more than a hundred feet square, and something more in height. It presents a singularity in its construction worthy of notice. It is a pyramid within a pyramid; i.e. the inner pyramid has been cased over by a larger one; one of its sides being in ruins makes this peculiarity visible. By climbing up the ruined side, it is easy to reach its summit. No remains of a city or any traces of temples are visible in the immediate vicinity of this place, which is called by the natives "Turboot" [90–91].

Then he too began to move. One can hardly imagine the hardship of moving an army through the desert and along the Nile in the 1820s. Sickness, lack of medications, poor transportation, and inadequate provisions, were just the beginning of the hardships. English described the horrific physical punishment the men of the expedition had to endure. English himself suffered intermittently with dysentery and ophthalmia: pus filled his eyes, and the pain was excruciating. He needed laudanum to sleep, and feared he would die. It took thirty-nine days for English to navigate fifty miles along the river (91). He complained that the river was "spotted by an infinity of islands and rocks." In some places the current was like a mill-sluice and in others they had to draw the boat up by pure force, with its hull dragging along the rocks at the bottom of the river. The scenery had changed dramatically too. The green farms gave way to sterile desert once they reached the great S-Curve. Here the rocks and sometimes the river bed were white: thus the name *merui* or Merowe. Occasionally they saw an ostrich, or the ruins of old monasteries, but mostly it was desolate. Khalil painted the horrific details of moving boats and men along the wild and uncharted river. Page after page of his journal describes the difficulties the men encountered at this point on the river: boats collided, natives refused to help, and the rapids were unending, one upon another, which provided no time to rest. In the meantime English was summoned to the Pasha's camp and ordered to abandon the river and accompany him across the desert between the great bends and continue on to Shendi. The desert route that eliminated this loop in the river ran through the Bayuda Desert, a volcanic, stony trace with few wells and a different kind of suffering: no water, intense heat, and a blinding sun created unendurable pain. It could be crossed by different tracks leading to three different destinations: Berber, Meroë (not Merowe), or Shendi. The army and English would take the tract to Berber, then move along the river to Shendi.

English began to make preparations. However, on the day the Pasha departed, English's camels and baggage had not arrived. Whether this was another intrigue of the Chief Surgeon, the Protomedico, English does not say. Khalil's journal makes it look like it was:

> 18th Feby This morning the camels were prepared for conveying our effects to the camp but having nothing to mount for myself was forced to perform the journey on foot a long distance to in these hot climates.—On our arrival in the camp we were informed by the Chief Surgeon of the army from this Excelly that there were no horses to spare for us.—As there were no spare horses both my self and my partner remonstrated on being treated in this manner having volunteered our Services for the campaign on the faith of the promises that had been made us by His Exy that we should be provided with all that was necessary.

English mounted a horse and went looking for his provisions. He found one of the camels had fallen and the men were waiting for a replacement. So once again English was unable to travel with the Pasha.

However, he was not left alone: 300 soldiers were awaiting camels and 700 Mogrebin infantry were waiting their provisions, so all would travel together through the desert once the provisions arrived (96–98). Khalil recorded:

> Feb 21st this morning the half of the camp moved to join the boats the other half could not move for want of camels. About ½ way to the boats the army obliged to halt many of the camels dying from being overloaded and of hunger. I and my partner [Ahmed] were obliged to remain behind there being no pack saddles for the two camels that were given us to carry our baggage.

23rd This morning the Surgeon of the army came to visit the Chevalier with a view of pacifying him for the intrigues he had lately carried on with the chief Doctor in order to injure him — a pack of rascals together–

I was informed that all the large boats had received orders to abandon the attempt to pass the remainder of the third cataract of the Nile. They had already, with great difficulty, got through about fifty difficult passages, and it was reported that there were nearly one hundred more ahead.

Remember, this was still the Third Cataract. It is clear from this passage that only the smaller boats were to attempt to navigate the Fourth. This point is important because in one of his footnotes to Giovanni Finati's book on the journey, William John Bankes criticized English for saying the Pasha had "only nine boats to pass this river." Bankes was wrong. As we see in this passage, more than nine boats accompanied the expedition, but only nine, the smallest of the fleet, tried to navigate the S-Bend.[43] English was wrong too. He felt that once the boats were through, they had fairly easy passage to Berber. They did not.

All of these accusations–the failure of English to keep up with the Pasha (Finati and Bankes); the mistake as to the number of boats in the army (Finati and Bankes); remonstrations as to his religious preferences (Waddington)–have led to a 200-year misrepresentation of the character and integrity of George Bethune English on this journey to Sennar. In addition, they are being perpetuated today by modern scholars who do not delve into the materials of the day and see through early prejudices.

Khalil's Solo Journey

We may never know what caused the two Americans to be left behind to endure the Fourth and Fifth cataracts of the river. Was it more intrigue on the part of Ismail's physician, or was there a real crisis that often exists in expeditions? If it was a conspiracy it was one more factor in Achmed's death, for he died at the beginning of this leg of the odyssey. On the other hand, it should have brought glory to Khalil. According to English, Khalil was the "first person [Westerner] to travel the entire length of the Nile from Rosetta to Sennar" (205). Most travelers, like the army, avoided the huge S-bend between Dongola and Berber by crossing one of several desert tracks, thereby saving hundreds of miles (see map). Khalil did not do this simply because he did not have the transportation to cross the desert, and was therefore forced to stay with the boats, enduring the horrific cataracts. It should have made him famous. But his manuscript was never made public. As late as 1905 the ruins and the rapids in this region were still unknown.[44]

For fifty-seven days, from February 21 to April 29, Khalil Aga faced the rapids of the 100-mile Fourth and 14-mile Fifth Cataracts of the Nile. He describes the rapids and the particulars in detail. It is the only daily account of that section of the river as it was at that time. The journey was gruesome and the villagers were pressed into labor to tow the boats up and over rapids and waterfalls. During the passage of the Fourth Cataract the men would have to fight the river as it descended 160 feet. The river was running downhill. They were pushing against the stream: uphill all the way.[45]

In the meantime English had crossed the desert in the company of the Selictar, who had been on reconnaissance to collect *durra* for the army (100). The shorter distance through the Bayuda Desert was from Merowe to Berber, and that was the route the army took. English did not offer much information about that journey except that he suffered "much from the heat of the sun, which had burned the skin off my face;— from fatigue and want of sleep;— from hunger, as we had barely time to prepare a little rice and bread once in twenty-four hours;— and from exasperation of my ophthalmia, which had never entirely quitted me since I was attacked by it at Wady Halfa" (103). They took eleven days to reach the camp of the Pasha near Berber. Again English had to explain why he was delayed.

Ismail promised to supply English with good camels from his own herd, so that he would not have transportation problems again. Then he turned to the business at hand. Previous to the desert crossing, envoys from Shendi had come to Ismail and asked for peace. Ismail agreed and asked them to surrender their horses and arms. They, of course, refused. So now they had to face his army. But the wise chief of Shendi sent Ismail a number of valuable presents as a token of peace. They were accepted. So were the overtures of peace made by a number of Mamluks who were too long away from home and eager to return to Egypt. Ismail not only did not kill them, but sent the Mamluks back to Cairo unchained with the promise of a good life and a thousand piasters in each pocket. Later English acknowledged that Moham-mad Ali honored his son's decree (108–112). With this conciliatory gesture the long battle between Mohammad Ali and the Mamluks, which had begun in 1805, came to an end; so did any dreams of a Mamluk renaissance.

Eventually the King of Shendi arrived in camp and brought with him more presents, including two horses. English had never seen such magnificent animals. He wrote, "They were stallions, eighteen hands high, beautifully formed, of high courage and superb gait. When mounted, they tossed their flowing manes aloft higher than the heads of their tur-baned riders, and a man might place his two fists in their expanded nostrils" (117). English's admiration was justified. The horses of the region were legendary. As far back as the Kushite Kingdom, the horses were lauded. James Bruce reported about them on his journey of 1768 to 1773:

> What figure the Nubian breed of horses would make in point of fleetness is very doubtful, their make being entirely different from that of the Arabian; but if beauti-ful and symmetrical parts, great size and strength, the most agile, nervous, and elastic movements, great endurance of fatigue, docility of temper, and an attachment to man that seems beyond that of any other domestic animal, can promise anything for a stallion, the Nubian is, above all comparison, the most eligible in the world.[46]

At this point the cannon were being pulled by camels so that the horses could rest. English thought this a method that every army in the East should practice (190–192).

As it broke camp and headed south, the army passed the region of Meroë. The army did not go there. As stated earlier, Cailliaud did. The cataracts had been crossed. The army had regrouped. The final objective was within reach. Ismail and his army began the last leg of their journey.

On to Sennar

The army remained at Shendi for a few days, and on May 15 they began the journey to Sennar. On the 16th, while the army was resting and awaiting fodder for the horses, the Malek Shouus, King of the Shageias, finally came into camp and gave up his sword and horse. He came with such dignity and had fought with such ferocity that Ismail made him a Bimbashi and brought him into the army. He was a large, stout, 40-year-old black man who was con-sidered to be the greatest warrior on the Upper Nile:

> Malek Shouus, on learning that the Malek of Shendi had made his peace with the Pasha, threatened to attack him. On this it is said the Malek of Shendi called out twenty thousand men to line the easterly bank of the Nile, to prevent the approach of Shouus. Shouus, however, had the whole country of Shendi on the western side

entirely under his control before our arrival, he and his cavalry devouring their provisions and drinking their bouza at a most unmerciful rate. On our approach, he went up opposite Halfya, where the country, on the western shore, is desert. He demanded of the chief of Halfya, to supply him with provisions: on his refusal, Shouus, in the night, swam the river with his cavalry, fell upon the town of Halfya by surprise, and ransacked it from end to end, and then repassed the river before the chief of Halfya could collect a force to take his revenge. The cavalry of Shouus, in the course of the campaign, have swam over the Nile five times: both horse and man are trained to do this thing, inimitable, I believe, by any other cavalry in the world. Shouus, since his joining us, has rendered very important services to the Pasha, as he is thoroughly acquainted with the strength, resources, and riches of all the tribes of the Nile, from the second Cataract to Sennar and Darfour: his horses' feet are familiar with the sod and sand of all these countries, which he and his freebooters have repeatedly traversed. On our march from Berber to Shendi, I ran some risk of falling into his hands, as Shouus was continually prowling about in our neighbourhood, from the time of our quitting Berber. Two nights before we reached Shendi, I stopped on the route, at a village, to take some refreshment, letting the army go by me. About an hour and a half after, I mounted my horse to follow the troops, but, owing to the state of my eyes, I missed my way; after wandering backwards and forwards to find the track of the troops, about two hours after midnight, I descried the rockets always thrown aloft during our night marches, to direct all stragglers to the place where the Pasha had encamped. I put my horse to his speed, and arrived there a little before dawn [141–42].

Then the army moved on until on the 22nd, when they arrived at the large village of Halfya. They remained there for four days to purchase durra. Within a few days the Egyptian Expedition reached the fork where the White and Blue Nile converged and where Khartoum would soon be established. English attributed the "overflow of the Nile ... to the rise of the Bahar el Abiud [White Nile], which this year at least, commenced its annual augmentation nearly a month sooner than the Nile" (146). He believed he was the first Frank to drink from this river. He also believed it to be a different river from the one Bruce had discovered decades earlier and that it might, in fact, join with the Niger. We now know his last two observations were inaccurate.

To get to the fork, the expedition, including the additional warriors they had acquired along the way, had to cross the White Nile. This was easily done by the Shageia and Abbadies, natives to the country, who swam their horses across, but was not so easy for the Egyptians, who considered it their duty to outshine their enemies. After resting a few days the expedition commenced the march to the ultimate destination: Sennar, the city believed to be filled with gold. It was a very difficult journey. Because of the heat, the army began each day at midnight and marched until 9 A.M., when they stopped for a few hours' rest. Then they marched again. The troops had only durra to eat. English lost his supplies, due, he said, to the "carelessness of a domestic," and had no food at all.

Like most of the towns and villages along the route, Sennar proved no problem to the conquering army. In fact, the Sultan of Sennar had sent an envoy to Ismail six days before the army was due to arrive in his town. Two days later he set out himself to greet the enemy that had marched all the way from Egypt. Two days after that, he arrived at Ismail's camp. There would be no siege and no battle for the conquest of Sennar. It was theirs. English, one of the first to describe the town in modern times, found Sennar to be nothing but heaps of ruins, a far cry from the streets of gold of the legend. His description is outstanding and was the first to be in print:

> After the camp was pitched, and I had refreshed myself with a little food, I took a walk around the town. At almost every step I trod upon fragments of burnt bricks,

among which are frequently to be found fragments of porcelain, and sometimes marble. The most conspicuous buildings in Sennaar are a mosque, and a large brick palace adjoining it. The mosque, which is of brick, is in good preservation; its windows are covered with well wrought bronze gratings, and the doors are handsomely and curiously carved. The interior was desecrated by uncouth figures of animals, pourtrayed upon the walls with charcoal. This profanation had been perpetrated by the Pagan mountaineers who inhabit the mountains thirteen days march south of Sennaar, and who, at some period, not very long past, had taken the town, and had left upon the walls of the mosque these tokens of possession.

The palace is large, but in ruins, except the centre building, which is six stories high, having five rows of windows. By mounting upon its roof you have the best possible view of the city, the river, and the environs, that the place can afford. I judged that Sennaar was about three miles in circumference. The greater part of this space is now covered with the ruins of houses, built of bricks either burnt or dried in the sun. I do not believe that there are more than four hundred houses standing in Sennaar, and of these one-third or more are round cottages, like those of the villages. Of those built of bricks, the largest is the house of the Sultan [162–65].

English wrote of the shape of the city, the environs, its occupants and the various goods and vivid activities of the three marketplaces. He wrote nearly twenty pages describing the pageantry that was enacted during these days, including the final military expeditions to bring the outlying districts under Egypt's control, and the origins of the various rivers that fed the Nile. It remains the best description of the village by a Westerner:

Sennaar has three market-places. On our arrival we found them deserted, but on assurances from the Pasha that all sellers should receive a fair price for their commodities, the principal one in a few days began to be filled. The articles I saw there during my stay in Sennaar, were as follows: Meat of camels, kine, sheep and goats; a few cat-fish from the river, plenty of a vegetable called meholakea; some limes, a few melons, cucumbers, dried barmea, a vegetable common in Egypt; beans, durra, duchan, tobacco of the country, plenty of gum Arabic, with which, by the way, Sennaar abounds, (the natives use it in their cookery;) drugs and spices brought from Gidda, among which I observed ginger, pepper, and cloves; and great quantities of dried odoriferous herbs found in Sennaar, with which the natives season their dishes; to which must be added, a plenty of the long cotton cloths used for dress in Sennaar. Such were the articles offered for sale by the people of the country. In addition to which, the settlers of our army offered for sale, tobacco, coffee, rice, sugar, shirts, drawers, shoes, gun flints, &c. &c. all at a price three or four times greater than they could be bought for at Cairo. In some parts of the market-place the Turks established coffee-houses, and the Greeks who accompanied the army, cook-shops. These places became the resort of every body who wanted to buy something to eat, or to hear the news of the day. There might be seen soldiers in their shirts and drawers, hawking about their breeches for sale in order to be able to buy a joint of meat to relish their rations of durra withal, and cursing bitterly their luck in that they had not received any pay for eight months; while the solemn Turk of rank perambulated the area, involved like pious Eneas at Carthage, in a veil of clouds exhaling from a long amber headed pipe. All around you might hear much hard swearing in favor of the most palpable lies; the seller in favor of his goods, and the buyer in favor of his Egyptian piasters. In one place a crowd collects around somebody or other lying on the ground without his head on, on account of some misdemeanor; a little farther on, thirty or forty soldiers are engaged in driving, with repeated strokes of heavy mallets, sharp pointed pieces of timber, six or eight inches square, up the posteriors of some luckless insurgents who had had the audacity to endeavor to defend their country and their liberty; the women of the country meantime standing at a distance, and exclaiming, "that it was scandalous to make men die in so indecent a manner, and protesting that such a death was only fit for a Christian," (a character they hold in great abhorrence, probably from never having seen one). Such was the singular scene presented to the view by the market place of Sennaar [166–68ff].

As for the people, he found them "exceedingly avaricious, extortionate, faithless, filthy, and cruel" (187). According to English, they ate mice, rats, cats, and although Muslims, pork. He found the women the ugliest he had ever seen, but observed them enough to know that the young eligible girls wore little but a leather apron of thongs around their waists. For commerce the people made earthenware bowls, wore cotton clothes, used knives, and had a waterwheel, hoes and ploughs.

Return to Cairo

After exploring Sennar for seven days, English asked Ismail for permission to return to Cairo. It was granted. So he and Khalil began making preparations for the long journey back. When a courier arrived from Cairo the Pasha agreed to let English and Khalil accompany him back. The journey back to Berber was not easy. It took five miserable days.

Henry Salt

Finally the expatriate Americans arrived in Alexandria. When English went to see Mohammad Ali sometime in December of 1822, the Pasha refused to pay him the $20,000 contracted for his work. He had just received news of his son Ismail's murder. He had been burned alive in his tent at Shendi. The ruler felt the American had to bear some of the responsibility.[47] In the end, however, Mohammad Ali did pay English some funds. In a letter to French Consul Bernardino Drovetti, whom English befriended in Alexandria at this time, he wrote: "When I had last the pleasure of seeing you at Alexandria I think I mentioned that the Kilhya Bey had withheld from me twenty-two hundred piasters of my appointments, notwithstanding an express order from the Pasha that the whole soud be paid me."[48] So English was broke, and therefore stranded in Egypt. He turned to Henry Salt, the British consul in Cairo. For the fare of his passage home, English gave Salt the manuscript of his travels and the artifacts he had collected on his journey. Salt, in turn, sent the manuscript to William John Bankes in England, explaining to Bankes that he had helped English get back to the United States, and in turn English had given him his writings of the journey to Sennar. He asked Bankes to sell the manuscript to a publisher.[49] That is what happened. *A Narrative of the Expedition to Dongola and Senaar, under the command of His Excellence Ismail Pasha, undertaken by order of His Highness Mehemmed Ali Pasha, Viceroy of Egypt* was published in England in 1822 and in the United States in 1823. In gratitude to Salt, English dedicated his book to him. If there were more letters, journals, and other items, there is no evidence.

It is likely that Khalil knew Salt prior to the journey as well. If not, how does one explain the discovery of Khalil's journal in Salt's papers and the acknowledgment by Khalil that he carved Salt's name in a number of places along the journey? Through the journal of the Reverend Wolff, a convert from Judaism to Christianity who became a missionary in Egypt, we find that when Khalil returned from Sennar he was a guest of Henry Salt. Wolff reported that he "bought an English Bible for eight piastres, and gave it to Khalil Agha, an American renegade, who is in a very distressed state."[50] Wolff again referred to Khalil while relating his conversations with English: "At present, an American gentleman, who turned Musselman through despair, is in his [Salt's] house, and thus he was enabled to hear the world of God by me; and I sometimes pray with this poor American."[51] What happened to Khalil Aga after that we do not know, except, as related previously, that he remained in Egypt for some time. His identity is still a mystery.

English in America

When he arrived in America, English discovered that the manuscript *Five Pebbles in a Brook*, which he had sent home from Egypt before his journey to Sennar, had not been published. Against the advice of his friends, he published it. In the preface he wrote: "This book is not the work of an Infidel. I am not an infidel; what I have learned and seen in Europe, Asia and Africa, while it has confirmed my reasons for rejecting the New Testament, has rooted in my mind the conviction that the ancient bible does contain a revelation from the God of Nature, as firmly as my belief in the first proposition of Euclid." Then he contacted his old patron John Quincy Adams, who sent him off on another secret mission to Constantinople (see Chapter 6).

As if his life were not already mysterious enough, what happened to George Bethune English in the final months of his life is also intriguing. On July 21, 1828, John Quincy Adams once again "agreed on the arrangements for dispatching G.B. English as bearer of dispatches to Commodore W.M. Crane, in the Mediterranean." English was brought up to date on events surrounding the Ottoman Porte, especially at Smyrna (Izmir, Turkey). On the 22nd a letter was sent to Commander Parker, master commander of the *Fairfield*, "instructing him to receive G.B. English as a passenger, to carry dispatches to Commodore Crane, in the Mediterranean." Adams himself informed English of the appointment, noting, "He received notice of his appointment with expressions of warm gratitude." Two days later everything had changed. Adams recorded on the 24th:

> Mr. Brent was here, and afterwards Mr. Southard. No letter of appointment had been delivered to G.B. English, and no advance of money made to him. I determined to revoke his appointment, and, after consulting with Mr. Southard, to send Edward Wyer in English's place. I sent for Wyer and informed him of this new appointment, enjoining upon him the closest secrecy, and that he must be ready to leave this city on Monday morning; both of which he promised. Life is full of disappointments, and among the most mortifying of them to me had been the misconduct of persons whom I have peculiarly befriended. The case of English is one of the most mortifying that have occurred. I have repeatedly procured employment for him in the public service, and, notwithstanding his eccentricities, approaching to insanity, have continued to favor him till now. I can now no longer sustain him. In consequence of the change of the messenger, it becomes necessary to alter almost every one of the papers that I had prepared.[52]

What could have happened in a single day to cause such dire consequences? It is obvious to think of English's religious stance. But much of the religious controversy which followed English was well known to Adams and probably accounts the reference to "his eccentricities, approaching to insanity." This was different. It seems to be personal. George Bethune English seems to have performed some act that condemned him. What was it? Was it so *tabu* as to be unmentionable? It cannot be found in any public document related to English. Even private papers do not mention what had transpired. Two months after Adams rejected English, English was dead. His obituary in a Washington, D.C., paper shed no light on the event that angered Adams enough to end his career. Nor does it say how he died! Somehow it does not seem plausible that he died of natural causes. Did he commit suicide? Where are the records? It seems Mr. English left life as he lived it, in controversy.

6

The Gliddons and the Beginning
of American-Egyptian Relations
(Consular Service, 1832–1840)

When the Albanian Mohammad Ali wrested power from the Mamluk rulers in 1805, Egypt was not in charge of its own destiny. It was still a vassal of the Ottoman Empire. It could not form diplomatic ties or trade with foreign nations without Ottoman blessing. Mohammad Ali stabilized the country, but in order to prosper, Egypt needed everything: machinery, factories, transportation, and communication services. What it did have was agricultural products: sugar cane, cotton, grain, fruit trees, and a variety of produce such as onions and beans. It needed to modernize its agricultural base, find an industrial one, and then seek trading relationships. Over a forty-year period Mohammad Ali did just that. He sought foreign experts and welcomed them to Egypt. With their help he modernized, sent explorers into the far reaches of his domain to look for raw materials for the new factories, and expanded his territories by subjugating the Sudan to the south and invading Syria to the east.

The United States was equally unsophisticated in the world of trade. It was still trying to trade within itself, from state to territory, from territory to state, and cast no official eye toward the Atlantic and beyond. Having said that, and despite George Washington's warning to the American government not to become embroiled with foreign powers (a policy known as non-intervention), commercial relations with the Ottomans were discussed by the Continental Congress as early as 1774. By the beginning of the nineteenth century some individual politicians slowly began to test the waters of international trade by sending special agents on secret missions to see if commerce was viable. The problem then and in the years to come was that in the Ottoman Empire the United States was under the banner of the Levant Company and therefore owed allegiance and a tariff to the British.[1]

For the Americans, subjugation to the Levant Company extended the colonial yoke recently tossed aside by the Revolutionary War and added salt to an already festering wound. As they had refused to pay in Barbary when William Eaton and the American marines marched on Tripoli in 1804, the United States refused to pay in the Levant for the privilege of trading with the Ottoman Empire. It was one more battle the Americans would have to fight to confirm their independence, to gain respect among nations, and to acquire an important position among the trading countries of the world.

America's Secret Agents

New York attorney Luther Bradish (1783–1863) was appointed by Federalist Secretary of State John Quincy Adams to be a "secret agent" to determine the possibility, the problems, and the process of procuring trade with Constantinople and the Ottoman Empire, free of British interference. In 1820, just as the Greek battle for independence against the Ottomans was beginning to stir, John Quincy Adams appointed him as a special trade emissary to the Sublime Porte.

Bradish arrived in Smyrna on October 12, 1820, and met David Offley, an American merchant who had been a pioneer American trader with the Porte since 1802. Offley had established a commercial house in Smyrna called Woodmas and Offley, which brought him into conflict with the Levant Company. In retribution his company was charged additional tariffs by the Ottomans, instigated by British traders. Offley had been fighting for change in the trade rules for several decades. Once the long process of establishing trade with the Ottoman Empire was concluded, Offley would become American consul and commercial agent at Smyrna.[2]

Bradish went on to Constantinople, where he confirmed his secret mission was not much of a secret. That fact undermined everything he was trying to do. In a letter to Adams, Bradish confirmed that if the European powers saw the opportunity, they would create obstacles.[3] He further pointed out that gifts were essential in beginning negotiations. The United States was not prepared to present gifts as they had done in Barbary, so Bradish was not able to complete his mission. Adams was not pleased.[4]

The second person John Quincy Adams sent to Constantinople was George Bethune English (see previous chapter). English's Middle Eastern experiences and linguistic abilities made him useful, and John Quincy Adams appointed him a secret agent, perhaps for the second time. In 1823, Adams requested English "to proceed on the voyage suggested in your letters of the 26th and 28th ultimo and for the purposes expressed in them."[5] English took up his Muslim name once again, donned Eastern clothing, polished up his Arabic, and went to live in Constantinople. He thought he could keep his mission a secret, especially since the Greek war for independence was being waged against the Ottoman Empire and Adams spearheaded the position to keep America neutral. English wrote to Adams that he was "considered by the Europeans here merely as one who has heretofore travelled in the East and who visits Constantinople in an oriental dress to have the greater facility to observe what is worthy of notice."[6]

English accomplished more than Bradish. He acquired a copy of the treaty between France and the Porte, had it translated from Turkish, and sent back to Adams.[7] By December of 1823 English had made an assessment of trade with the Ottoman Porte:

> The only articles, it appears to me, which the vessels of the United States could profitably bring to it, are in my apprehension, coffee, sugar, indigo, cochineal and dollars; wheat, and, of course, flour, rice and tobacco, the empire produces in abundance. In return, it can furnish the United States drugs, gums, dried fruits, fine copper, and some articles of luxury. The Europeans carry home, besides the articles above mentioned, immense quantities of hemp, cotton, wool, and raw silk, for their manufactories, which are not, I believe, in demand in the United States. But by far the greater part of the profits derivable from a free intercourse with Turkey would consist in freight. The superiority of the American ships and sailors would give them a great advantage over most of their competitors; and it is the apprehension of this which makes most of the European powers so jealous of our obtaining a participation, in the carrying trade of the Ottoman empire, of which the British, French, and Imperialists, have at present almost the entire monopoly.[8]

In a letter to Adams on February 8, 1824, English explained why he thought the Bradish mission failed. "Mr. Bradish's failure was the influence of a certain European ambassador, (whom he [the Captain Pasha] did not name)."[9] It was the rivalry between nations once again. The Captain Pasha felt that a meeting at Constantinople would never produce results, so he suggested meeting elsewhere. English's report to Adams encouraged the United States to send an agent to the Porte. English wanted to be that agent, but Adams eventually gave the assignment to Commodore John Rodgers.

America had relied on her naval officers to carry sensitive messages and be tactful themselves from the advent of the American navy in 1775. Many a ship had sailed into Alexandria to leave important papers with Egyptian rulers. So Rodgers was an old hand at political maneuvers in the Mediterranean. He had taken command of the naval squadron there in 1804–5 when the Americans landed William Eaton and his marines on foreign soil in an attempt to bring an end to problems with the Barbary nations. Now he was being considered to hold the position again. It was a long and important process and Adams and his men took their time.

David Offley, who was also involved in the negotiations, was made consul to the Porte in 1824 while the Greek war of independence was raging. Once he was in place, negotiations for a new treaty were underway. This final team of negotiators included Offley, Naval Commander James Biddle, and Philadelphia merchant Charles Rhind. The trade treaty was ultimately signed by Rhind on May 7, 1830, and ratified by the Senate of the United States on February 1, 1831, while Egypt was at war with Syria.[10] This treaty granted the United States most-favored-nation status. Uncle Sam could now trade with all of the Ottoman Empire, including Egypt. The first appointment under the new treaty was on April 15, 1831, when Commodore David Porter became the charge d'affaires of the United States to the Sublime Porte.[11] His job was to establish the tariff on American goods trading with the Ottoman Empire. Once this was accomplished Porter could select the consular agents for the various trading countries. Porter chose Alexandria as the site of the first American mission to Egypt, as did all foreign powers at the time. After all, Alexandria was the main seaport of Egypt and sea trade was growing. Cairo, some 200 kilometers inland, was not as significant to trade in the nineteenth century as it had been from the thirteenth to the fifteenth centuries when trade came via the Red Sea.

The Gliddons

Earning a living as a trader in Alexandria since 1818 was Englishman John Gliddon. John Gliddon had been assisting Americans in Egypt for some time prior to his appointment. American traveler George Rapelje mentioned his name and his services as early as 1822. At that time he was in effect carrying out consular agent tasks.[12] On January 12, 1832, Porter appointed Gliddon to be "the non-salaried consular agent in the Dominions of the Bey of Egypt" for the United States.[13] The British tried to block the appointment. Failing that, they tried to regain their Levant status over American trade. Since Gliddon was a British subject, he was asked to pledge allegiance to England and thereby subjugate the United States to it in Egypt, as had been done earlier in Constantinople through the Levant Company. None of these maneuvers worked. America was now a permanent trading partner with the countries of the Ottoman Empire. The long story of American diplomacy in Egypt had begun. It would be a fascinating tale, especially in the nineteenth century as the United States continued its belief in non-intervention. Non-intervention was a complex path for America in Egypt, especially when European powers consistently interfered in Egyptian affairs. America was sympathetic to Egypt's predicament. It had thrown off the English bondage for far less.

Tall, blue-eyed, red-faced John Gliddon had attended the Free School in his hometown of Exeter in England. He went on to be a London banker and husband to his cousin Eleanor Gliddon. Shortly after their first son, George Robbins Gliddon, was born in St. Thomas in Devonshire in 1809, John took the family to Malta, where his daughters Ellen, Joanna, and Emma were born.[14] He remained there trading for eight years. In August of 1818 business took him to Egypt, where he spent the rest of his life. He died in Malta on July 8, 1844, twelve years after his appointment as consular agent.

George Gliddon grew up in Egypt, became proficient in Arabic, and when old enough returned to England to continue his education. After attending Burton Crescent and Monmouth schools, he joined a counting house in Glasgow for a short time before returning to Egypt.[15] In Egypt he went to work for his father, who, in addition to his elevation from consular agent to consul, had become the Director of the Alexandrian Insurance Company. By 1829 George was in Greece settling insurance accounts related to the war of independence, and in 1832 he was based in Cairo as agent for the Insurance Company of the Nile. Up to that point there was only one American consular office in Egypt and that was in Alexandria. On September 11, 1833, George Gliddon was officially appointed as the American vice consul at Cairo, subject to the consular office in Alexandria.[16] He served in that position for only a short time, but his far-reaching influence and outstanding contributions, as outlined below, earned him an important place in the legacy of Americans in Egypt in the nineteenth century.

More Secret Agents

In August 1834, William Brown Hodgson arrived in Egypt to explore commercial opportunities for the U.S. government: yet another "spy" appointed by John Quincy Adams. Hodgson, a native of Savannah, Georgia, had been trained in Arabic, Turkish, and French. He was appointed to Algiers until 1829, then became affiliated with the American consul in Constantinople. His mandate in Egypt was to discover if the ruler had the power to make commercial treaties with foreign nations. Hodgson, in the reports he submitted to the government in March of 1835, did not believe the Pasha could make the treaties the United States hoped he could make. He pointed out, much to John Gliddon's delight, that foreign powers had consul generals in Egypt, not consular agents, the position the United States had given him. He also felt that trade with Egypt would be rewarding. Of course, Hodgson requested the position for himself. Shortly thereafter John Gliddon was raised from a consular agent to a consul, and the United States began to look directly to Egypt for commercial projects. As for Hodgson, he went to London in 1836, Washington in 1837, and Tunis — as consul general — in 1841.

The entire ritual of one country sending representatives to others is a complicated procedure dating to the beginning of time. Ancient Egypt both received and sent envoys to other nations in such a manner. From those ancient beginnings grew the world of diplomacy. By the time of Mohammad Ali the system had become so convoluted that there were degrees by which various government agents were to be recognized. From the least important they were consular agents, consuls, diplomatic agents, consuls general (capital letters), envoys extraordinary, and ministers plenipotentiary. The lowest position was the consular agent, often established where no consulate existed. He was an eye in a foreign country letting his employer know what was happening. This was John Gliddon's first appointment. Once a consul was established, consular agents were established in cities within the foreign country. For example, the United States eventually established consular agents in Cairo, Luxor, Asyut, and Rosetta, all reporting to the main agency in Alexandria.

A consul had added responsibilities. He was charged to deal with the commercial interests of his country and, when necessary, to aid citizens living in or visiting foreign lands. He supervised consular agents. Once a country established more than one office in more than one location in a foreign country, the person in charge of all the offices was a consul general. (Diplomatic agents could not be appointed to Egypt because it was not an independent country.) Regardless of a person's title, his mission was to place the United States in the most advantageous position possible when it came to commerce and its related problems, such as tariffs, trade agreements, and restrictions. It was not easy.

Help from American Travelers

The Gliddons pampered Americans in Egypt, solved their problems, arranged audiences with the Pasha, and housed them, often in George's own medieval Cairene mansion. The Gliddons booked excursions to the pyramids, the tombs of the caliphs, and Roda Island, and then put the travelers on George's private *dahabeyyiah* for a journey to Upper Egypt. The father and son were indispensable and their efforts would reward them well, for George was making lasting and influential friends.

When George Gliddon petitioned the American government to elevate the status of the Cairo consular offices, he called upon the American travelers to both confirm and defend his petition. The first was Mendes Cohen, an American collector from Baltimore, who spent five months in Egypt in 1832. He reported that on the return to Cairo after a lengthy journey in Upper Egypt, "I found an American Consular agent in Mr. Geo R. Gliddon who had been appointed by his Father to that post, he rendered me very useful services in that city."[17]

Next Gliddon turned to the family of John Lowell. Lowell and his traveling companion, Swiss artist Charles Gleyre, arrived in Alexandria on December 27, 1834.[18] John Lowell died on this journey. Despite his death, George Gliddon asked for and received a testimonial from Lowell's brother F.C. Lowell, who reported that Gliddon went into the streets during a raging plague to procure provisions for Lowell's trip up the Nile.[19]

The next person to assist Gliddon was redheaded John Lloyd Stephens of New York, who arrived in Egypt in 1836. He published *Incidents of Travel in Egypt, Arabia Petraea, and the Holy Land* in two volumes in 1837, under the pseudonym "An American." Both Stephens and John W. Hammersley, a businessman from New York who was in Egypt in 1833, would join Gliddon and a few other men in business ventures between Egypt and the United States. John Lloyd Stephens testified, "In Egypt no man is superior to Mr. Glidden," and no man "uses his knowledge and influence more fairly and effectively for the benefit of the travelers."[20] Hammersley provided the Gliddons with a worthy reason to be elevated to a higher status with a more distinguished title, because he was able to avoid quarantine for Hammersley while "two English Gentlemen who made application to their consul for similar favors which were refused."[21]

New York merchant Richard Haight and his wife Sarah credited Gliddon with the success of their journey and in return provided many a financial favor to him in future years. Richard was son and grandson of a famous and successful New York merchant family trading in Lower Manhattan since 1784. Sarah wrote the tale of their adventure (see next chapter).[22] The Gliddons appear throughout Sarah's book. It was Richard who responded to George Gliddon's appeal. He wrote: "Mr. Gliddon having had a first rate repel built for him expressly for the accommodation of such of our countrymen as might make the voyage of the upper Nile.—..."[23]

Traveling with the Haights, at least in Egypt, was Richard Randolph of Philadelphia, who probably introduced George Gliddon to Samuel Morton, the anthropologist. Gliddon was to send Morton hundreds of skulls from Egypt for his extensive studies, which would be published in *Crania Egyptica*, at the dawn of the discipline of anthropology. Randolph acknowledged Gliddon's excellent assistance in quarantine, on his journey up the Nile and added, "It is exceedingly important that our Consuls should possess a knowledge of the languages of the country where they reside, as well as the customs of the people and the institutions of the Government: Mr. Gliddon does possess all these advantages."[24]

The power of these visitors to Egypt who lent their prominent voices to George Gliddon's plea for the proper American consular status in Cairo did not fall on deaf ears in Washington, and George was duly elevated to that position.

The Gliddons were also effective because they were well connected in Egypt. In addition to cultivating men in the Egyptian government, George knew and wrote to all the Egyptophiles from all the countries associated with Egypt. He studied with Frenchman Jean François Champollion, who deciphered the hieroglyphics; Samuel Birch, who became the head of the British Museum; and Karl Lepsius, the Prussian linguist and pioneer Egyptologist. He went into business with the British artist Joseph Bonomi, the French physician Clott Bey, the English businessman Thomas Waghorn, and the French explorer, artist, and Egyptian government official Linant Bellefonds. He traveled with the Alexandria merchant Anthony C. Harris, who discovered the now-famous Harris papyrus. He confided in British artists Frederick Catherwood and Robert Hay, the architect J.W. Wild, the writer Edward Lane, and adventurer James Burton. On July 9, 1836, he became a charter member of the Egyptian Society, an organization established by foreigners living in Egypt.[25] These prominent men offered the Gliddons important contacts in the foreign community in Egypt. Within the Egyptian government the Gliddons were equally connected.

Encouraging Trade

The biggest and most difficult task of the American consuls was to find a way to develop trade between Egypt and the United States. To that end the Gliddons encouraged a number of projects. The first was introducing rice and cotton machinery into Egypt, and the second was exporting giraffes to America. In what had to be considered a brilliant achievement, the Gliddons convinced Mohammad Ali to buy American equipment for Egypt's rice industry. That was George Gliddon's mission on his first trip to the United States in 1836. In a letter to John Forsythe, secretary of State under President Andrew Jackson, he outlined his mission:

> 1st. To execute orders for a Rice Hulling Mill to clean the Rice of Rosetta and Damiata; as well as for a Cotton seed Oil Mill, which last will, if successful, draw a new revenue to the Pasha of a million dollars per annum, from an article hitherto of no possible value.
>
> 2ndly. To send out 6 American Mechanics and Engineers to superintend the erection of the above.
>
> 3.dly To collect accounts estimates, drawings, plans, models, and suggestions on all such subjects as may prove of advantage hereafter to Egypt; and to further the introduction of American machinery etc where any benefit might acure to the Pasha.
>
> 4thly To furnish to the American Merchant all such information relative to Egypt, and its trade, as may induce the creation of direct intercourse for which object the writer has all the necessary elucidations, as well as samples, with him; or he possesses the means of furnishing them.

In the course of 4 or 5 months it is presumed the machinery and men will be
ready for embarkation, and be sent out from New York to Alexandria.[26]

Accompanied by his brother William, George Gliddon left Egypt for America on September 24, 1836, and landed at Newport, Rhode Island, four months later after a "tempestuous voyage." He went directly to the West Point Foundry at Cold Springs along the Hudson River in upstate New York. The foundry, which employed 150 people, would become known in later years for manufacturing munitions and building locomotives. The owner, William Kemble, agreed to build and ship the required machines. Kemble sent Alexander Marshall, John P. Bee, Charles Palmer and a fourth engineer and the machines to Egypt. They set sail March 19, 1838, aboard the ship *Carroll* and reached Alexandria on May 21, 1838.

The Eastern Question and Mohammad Ali's Bid for Freedom

What was happening in the Mediterranean during these years would not only affect Americans in Egypt but would have far-reaching ramifications on the history of the region and Americans in Egypt in the future. On June 9, 1815, Great Britain, Russia, Prussia, and the Austro-Hungarian Empire signed the Congress of Vienna with which they hoped to determine who owned what and did what in the Mediterranean. France, which had helped Egypt considerably since Napoleon's invasion in 1798, was not included.

Greece, with encouragement from France and Russia, began its quest for independence from the Ottoman Empire with a rebellion at Morea (the Peloponnese peninsula) in 1821. By 1824 the Ottoman ruler Sultan Mahmud II called on Mohammad Ali for assistance. Egypt, with the aid of France, had built a powerful army and navy, and agreed to join the Porte to quell the Greek rebellion. By 1825 they were on the verge of victory when Britain, France, and Russia formed yet another agreement: the Protocol of London. It demanded a cease-fire and liberation for the Greeks. The Porte, flush with its victories, refused. This maneuver culminated in the Battle of Navarino, where the powerful fleets of Great Britain, Russia, and France defeated the Egyptian (French-trained) and Ottoman navies on November 20, 1827, leaving the Ottoman fleet at the bottom of the sea. Russia went further: it declared war on the Ottoman Empire in April of 1828 and declared victory in September of 1829 (Edirne Peace Treaty). With France occupying the Peloponnese, Great Britain forming an agreement with Egypt to withdraw her troops, and Russia closing in from the east, the Ottoman Empire accepted the Protocol of London and the Greeks had their independence. America, urged to enter the fray on the side of Greece, refused to become embroiled in Mediterranean affairs. America stayed true to George Washington's concept of non-intervention, and despite many leaders who opposed the position, did not support causes, sign protocols, or become involved in the fate of other nations either in Europe or the Americas (the Monroe Doctrine aside). This held true more or less throughout the nineteenth century.

Since the Greeks had won their freedom, Egypt hoped that Europe would help it gain its own independence. When the Ottoman Sultan called for aid against the Russians, Mohammad Ali refused. Further, because the Sublime Porte failed to give Syria to Egypt for their efforts in the Greek affair, Egypt invaded Syria. Ibrahim Pasha and 24,000 troops conquered Acre and stood within striking distance of Istanbul. It was 1832. The Sultan now viewed Egypt as a threat and plotted to remove Mohammed Ali from power. Mohammad Ali not only felt that independence was at hand, but that the entire Ottoman Empire could be his.

The Sultan turned to his former enemies, the Europeans, for help. The British, French, Russians, and Prussians did a turnabout and did not assist Egypt, but sided with the Ottomans. It was not in their interest for Egypt to build an empire. Each of the European powers had something to gain by keeping the status quo. Mohammad Ali backed down. On May 5, 1833, he signed the Treaty of Kutahya; and for his signature he was given Syria and his son Ibrahim received Jeddah.

But the problems continued. Russia and Constantinople signed the Hunkar Iskelesi Treaty on July 8, 1833. It had a secret agreement: more turmoil among the plotting nations. Mohammad Ali took advantage of the turmoil to rebuild his military, and continued to move toward independence. The Porte concluded the trade agreement with the United States in the hopes of American aid in shipbuilding and military equipment, but the United States would not officially assist the Porte. England was not pleased. By 1838 England forged a new trade agreement with the Porte, too. France at first revolted, but shortly signed the new trade practices. Mohammad Ali knew his chance was now or never. He demanded more concessions. They were denied. He declared independence from the Porte. The Porte invaded Egypt held Syria. The armies met at Nezib on June 24, 1839. The Egyptians made easy work of the Ottoman forces at the battle on June 29. A few days later the Sultan died and his son, Abdulmecid, only 18 years old, assumed power. Egypt took the Ottoman fleet, much of it built by the Americans Henry Eckford and Foster Rhoades, and brought it to Alexandria.[27] Enter England, France, and Russia, as well as Austria and Prussia. All but France signed the Convention of London on July 15, 1840. It demanded that Egypt's independence be denied. Mohammad Ali would get the right of succession he so desperately wanted if he would return the fleet, and he had ten days to agree. He said, "No."

An Anglo-Turkish force invaded Egyptian-held Beirut in 1840 and encouraged rebellion against Egyptian forces. Then they placed a British fleet off the coast of Egypt at Alexandria (which they had done before and would do again). Egypt could not fight all of these forces. It brought its military home and signed the Charter of Concessions on February 14, 1841. Independence was lost. Egypt was forced to return Syria and other recently conquered territories, except the Sudan. The agreement also gave and took away certain powers for the ruler. Mohammad Ali had to give up all his monopolies in Egypt, allowing free trade to operate in the country. This was good for Egypt. He had to redesign the tariffs on imported goods so that they favored the importers. This was bad for Egypt. It would kill many of the fledgling industries, such as the new rice mills, and eventually forced the newly imported cotton factories out of business. He also had to return the American-built Turkish fleet.

One cannot help but wonder what the world would be like today if Mohammad Ali had won the day and the Egyptians had built a new empire.

Of course the machinations of the Mediterranean nations were much more complicated than what is summarized here. The devastation it caused modern Egypt was unforgiving and sat at the heart of the events for the next 100 years. Releasing Egypt from the grasp of the Ottoman Empire was a goal of Egyptian rulers from Ali al Kabir in the 1770s to the last of Mohammad Ali's dynasty in 1952. That was two hundred years. When it finally happened after World War I, the Egyptians simply fell from one foreign ruler to another, as the British continued to dominate Egypt for at least half of the twentieth century.

Gliddon, Animals, the American Circus, and Samuel Morton

In the 1830s Africa and its animals were curiosities to the rest of the world. No zoo in America held such exotic animals as giraffes, elephants, or hippopotami. Since the fall of the Roman Empire, when thousands of exotic African animals were slaughtered in the arenas for the enjoyment of the audience, few if any African animals had been seen in Europe. The first giraffe to arrive in France was sent by Bernardino Drovetti, the French consul, in 1824. America now wanted its share of these exotic creatures. The first to bring such wonders to the American shore would reap huge profits. Gliddon began a business association with former visitors John Lloyd Stephens and John Hammersley, and Francis Griffin, a New York attorney and relative of James Augustus Dorr (in Egypt by 1834). This venture was to last for the remainder of Gliddon's tenure as consul in Egypt. His task was to find and ship giraffes to America, which he did. George and his father took full shares in the first adventure. Unfortunately, the giraffes died and a competitor arrived, so the expedition only covered expenses.[28]

Less than two years later the idea of importing giraffes into the United States reemerged. In 1838 Benjamin Brown and Steb June were sent to Egypt by June, Titus, Angevine and Co., a group which would become leaders in developing the circus in America. The mission was to procure not more than six giraffes, and Gliddon was hired to assist them.[29] Brown started up the Nile to get giraffes almost immediately. June, nephew of one of the partners, lingered in Alexandria and Cairo, taking side trips to various places. While Brown was in Dongola and places south searching for animals, George Gliddon went on an excursion to Upper Egypt and the Eastern and Western deserts with the English merchant Anthony C. Harris, trading in Alexandria as Harris and Company.

A true crisis arose when Benjamin Brown went missing. No one had heard from him for some time when Gliddon began his long journey with Harris. Gliddon sent letters up and down the Nile looking for him. June was very anxious in Cairo and Alexandria and finally came down with an illness for five weeks, for which his anxious nature could be partially to blame. Then news came down from Dongola that Brown was dead. Gliddon, learning the rumor was untrue, wrote to Brown from Wadi Halfa on Dec 28, 1839:

> ... neither June or I had received a single letter from you since you left us last April.... This anxiety was greatly measured a few day ago with the report of a Berber named Dries, who told me at Asswan that you had died before the Ramadan at Dongola....
>
> Derr—I stopped on purpose to ascertain this fact at Derr on the 25th instant, and I saw Haroun, who said, that Dries was a liar, as he, Haroun, left you all well at Dongola about the Ramadan....
>
> PS Griffin wrote me that he and Stephens have taken a deeper interest in your speculation, as besides Giraffes they with your partners undertake all the risks in Monkeys [illegible] beasts and broad Curiosities antiques etc. etc. So make a good collection while you are about it.[30]

Brown kept a journal of his Nile adventure, yet another elusive treasure. Years later, in an interview with an American newspaper, Brown retold the story:

> Well, we went up the Nile about 1,000 miles to Wady Halfaya, and then we left the Nile and took camels. We had ten camels.... Soon after leaving the Nile I was taken ill, and I lay on the ground for forty-four days with the fever, in one of those little Arab villages. [While] I was sick, Jeffrey, another servant, tried to rob me, but I had buried my money in the sand and lay on it.... But after a while I got well, and we went on. I went to the Pasha of the Upper Nile, and showed him my firman, and he sent for the sheiks to come in with their men. I offered $25 each for giraffes and paid for the grease.... Those fellows want grease to grease themselves with to keep off the sun, and I paid for that. It cost about $15 for each company.... Three companies went out and brought in five giraffes. They were calves about a month old. My firman only called for four giraffes, and so the Pasha would not let me have but the four.... We had to lead them three hundred miles across the desert, and we made about twenty miles a day, or rather a night for we couldn't travel by day it was so

hot. It was 130° in the sun. We fed the calves on buffalo milk, and I had sometimes to send ten miles for milk for them. We had lots of narrow escapes.... I got back to Cairo one year and two days from the time I started, I having been very nearly a year without seeing the face of a white man. I looked like an Arab when I got there. I did not burn with the sun, but tanned until I was nearly black, and my beard was immense reaching nearly to my waist. My head was shaved and I wore the costume of the country. When I went to Glyddon's house he was entertaining some newly arrived missionaries, he told them that he'd introduce a countryman of theirs. "He may be a countryman," said one, "but he is certainly a black man."[31]

The letters flew back and forth. In addition to Clott Bey, Dr. Abbott, a British physician living in Cairo and collecting antiquities, became involved in purchasing animals. He begged June not to let Gliddon know of his intentions or of his planned trip to America.[32]

It was during this period that George Gliddon received a letter from a Philadelphia scientist named Samuel Morton, who asked him for ancient Egyptian skulls. Gliddon was willing to cooperate. Mr. Morton was attempting to analyze the various races to determine their origins and wanted to study bone structure as a method of determining race. In this new age, when the sciences of anthropology, ethnology, and archaeology were in their infancy, many strange conclusions were drawn. For those who viewed the Negro as inferior to the white, the Egyptian civilization (not to mention the Chinese, or the Japanese, or the Inca, or the Mayan, etc.) posed problems. How could western civilization have sprung from the Negro race if the Negro race was inferior to the white? The conclusion had to be that the Ancient Egyptians were not black; they were white. Skulls, thought Morton, could provide evidence. Morton's book, flawed as it was, would be the birth of anthropology in America.

Gliddon wrote to Samuel Morton:

> You have been chiefly benefited by a vagabond spirit that has kept me traveling since last summer wandering in the Eastern and Western Deserts, visiting all localities interesting to the Antiquarys, or exciting to the Hunter, and making a close examination of all the Monuments of Egypt and Nubia to the Second Cataract. Besides acquiring a tolerable correct idea on most subjects connected with Egypt, from the flood downwards, (not to speak of occurrences in the antiluviar material) I have been able to drag from the innermost recesses of tombs and Sanctuaries myself, the best portion of the Collection now sent. Some of these Skulls are above 4500 years old, affording vast field to conjecture, and measurements of the positive demonstrations your studies will present, I may be able to add elevations on many points that may turn up in conversation, in a manner that may enhance their value. Egypt is exhausted, so far as I am able to aid you — perhaps in other climes I may yet further your pursuits, to which I have a congenial fancy.[33]

Gliddon put the skulls and a number of other interesting items aboard the *Helme*, the ship chartered by what he called the Zoological Institute of New York to carry the giraffes back to the United States.[34] He planned to travel back to the United States himself aboard the same ship and asked the government for a leave of absence.[35]

On September 7, a leave of absence from his position as U.S. consul in Cairo was granted. George Gliddon made preparations to sail to America. His first plan was to sail with Brown and June aboard the *Helme*. June had teased, "Tell George if he will accompany us to America we will give him something besides *Fried onions* and *Fried cheese* for dinner — alias our trip in the desert."[36] Gliddon packed the *Helme* with box after box of items he wanted to send to various persons and institutions in America, including 143 skulls for Morton.[37] Those skulls are currently at the Philadelphia Academy of Natural Science.

The *Helme* sailed to America on May 30, 1840, without George Gliddon, but with seven tons of items that Gliddon consigned to Samuel Morton to use or to hold for his arrival in the United States. They included, in addition to Morton's skulls, a mummy and "oriental wooden ceilings"[38] for the Naval Lyceum in New York, 24 skulls from Thebes for the collection of Barlow and Fowler, phrenologists,[39] and a crate of Creto Maristream wine to be sold in New York.[40]

A single giraffe became a part of the June, Titus, Angevine and Company circus. "This giraffe appeared in Newark, New Jersey in early May (arrived in town ... drawn by a coach and six, with a long retinue of attendants.... He carries his head high in the world, and obtains the attention of thousands." Brown seems to have taken the others from America to England in December of 1840. The American giraffe did not survive very long, for by June of 1841, June, Titus, Angevine and Company were exhibiting a stuffed giraffe in New Jersey.[41]

On July 16, 1840, George Gliddon was terminated as consul in Cairo, effective September 1. The Cairo consulate closed. On April 18, 1841, Dr. Abbott wrote to Steb June, who was now in London, "George Gliddon left here to sail in the English steamer next week.... Recheck not to tell him I am writing you about animals." [42]

George Gliddon in America: The Awakening of Egyptology

George Gliddon closed all his obligations to the United States and many private business ventures and sailed for his native England in an attempt to start a new life. The first thing Gliddon did in England was write two important pamphlets: *An Appeal to the Antiquaries of Europe and the Destruction of the Monuments of Egypt* and *A Memoir of the Cotton of Egypt.* Called "perhaps the first expression of archaeological conscience in print" by *Who was Who in Egyptology,*[43] the *Appeal* criticized the wholesale exodus of antiquities out of Egypt. Gliddon must have had an about-face for he certainly helped Mendes Cohen, John Lowell, Francis Barthow and other Americans export thousands of antiquities out of the country, not to mention the shipload he sent to America himself. In addition to foreign nations, Gliddon blamed Mohammad Ali for allowing the exploitation of the ancient monuments in his country.[44]

By 1842 Gliddon sailed to America for the second time. He arrived in New York on January 7 and stayed at the Globe Hotel in Manhattan.[45] At last George Gliddon was about to accomplish what he had always wanted: he did more for the advancement of ancient Egyptian scholarship in the United States than any other single person to this time. He was at the vanguard of scholarship in the new fields of archaeology, anthropology, and ethnology. He was an accomplished, intelligent, interesting, experienced man and was about to prove it. He very cleverly contacted all the travelers he had assisted in Egypt, including members of his Egyptian Society, and asked them to assist him in the United States. Over the next ten years, they did.

Gliddon did not enter this adventure with his usual bluster and self-assurance. He was concerned lest he fail at giving public lectures on such a complicated subject and felt that America did not have important books like Ippoito Rosellini's *Monumenti.* To speak on such complex matters unprepared, he wrote to Morton, "will be to expose oneself to errors, to endless controversy, and to satire, without the means of defence derived from the evidence of *Monuments,* while any one else, who has read the whole, will be ahead of us." [46] In the end it was Richard Haight, the New York merchant and visitor to Egypt in the 1832, who bought the necessary books and loaned them to Gliddon (eventually they were given to the New York Historical Society). The books included Ippolito Rosellini's *Monumenti* and Karl Lepsius's *Denkmäler aus Aegypten und Aethiopien.* It is believed they were the first copies of the titles to arrive in the United States.[47]

A series of lectures was arranged for Boston. Gliddon made considerable preparations,

EGYPT'S REVELATIONS.

FOUR ARCHÆOLOGICAL LECTURES!

Entirely Distinct from the PANORAMA OF THE NILE,

Will be commenced by

MR. GEORGE R. GLIDDON,

FORMERLY U. S. CONSUL AT CAIRO,

AT ODD-FELLOWS' HALL, WASHINGTON,

ON TUESDAY EVENING, APRIL 8.

Continued on the ensuing FRIDAY and TUESDAY, and closed on FRIDAY Evening, APRIL 18.

ILLUSTRATION OF CHEV'R LEPSIUS'S DISCOVERY, IN 1843, OF

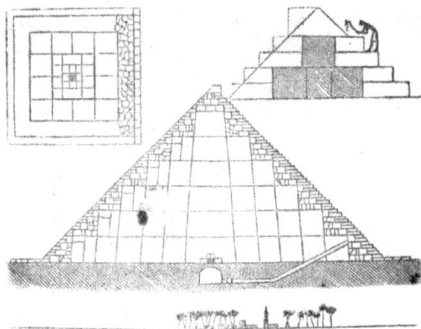

THE LAW OF PYRAMIDAL CONSTRUCTION.

Twenty-five months spent in personal visits to the Museums of London, Paris, and Berlin, and the kindness of his Egyptian colleagues in Europe, have enabled Mr. GLIDDON, since he lectured in Washington seven years ago, to collect vast archæological materials, elucidatory of Biblical, Egyptian, Assyrian, and other Oriental *discoveries*, far in advance of publication, comprising information on some scientific *results* arrived at in the last six years, which are yet inaccessible in popular literature.*

In oral descriptions of a "Moving Panorama" it is, of course, impossible to digress upon themes, however interesting, not immediately connected with the scenes passing before the audience; at the same time that past experience of the attention bestowed in this city upon questions of science, and the expressed wishes of many friends, lead Mr. GLIDDON to infer, that a Course of *Archæological Lectures* would, in Washington, receive support and patronage.

To accomplish these objects in a manner satisfactory to his friends and the public, best calculated to insure comfort and facilities to his auditors, and at the same time compensatory to himself, Mr. GLIDDON submits the following sketch of a *Programme*.

* See Appendix, 1846, to Gliddon's "Chapters on Early Egyptian History," 15th edition, *T. B. Peterson*, Philadelphia, 1850 ; and "Address to my friends in America," in the "Hand-Book to the Panorama of the Nile," London, 1849—for sale at the door.

ORDER OF THE LECTURES.

(TWO A WEEK.)

Lecture I.   *Tuesday Evening, April 8, 1851.*

INTRODUCTORY.—EGYPT's *Place in the World's History,* at the middle of our XIXth century, since the return of the *Prussian Scientific Mission* under Chev. LEPSIUS. Sketch of their explorations. The Royal Museum of Berlin. What is doing in Egyptology in England, France, Italy, Germany, and the United States.

Lecture II.   *Friday Evening, April 11.*

THE PYRAMIDS, and the tombs around them—the most ancient vestiges of primeval humanity now extant on earth. Discovery by LEPSIUS of the true *Labyrinth,* and of *Lake Mœris.* Ante-Abrahamic epoch of these Monuments.

Lecture III.   *Tuesday Evening, April 15.*

THESE PRIMORDIAL SCULPTURES, copiously *illustrated.* Their scientific teachings in respect to *Language, Alphabets, Writing Materials, Numerals, Divisions of Time, Painting, Sculptures, &c.* Arts known at that remote age in Memphis, about B. C. 3500.

Lecture IV.   *Friday Evening, April 18.*

ETHNOLOGY.—EGYPT's testimony. How and why the *Monuments* of the NILE, in the debated question of the aboriginal "Unity" or "Diversity" of human Races, corroborate the Xth *Chapter* of GENESIS. Families of man known to the Egyptians 1500 years B. C.—Antiquity of *Negro* Races.—Rectification of some misunderstood points of Hebraical geography.

including enlargements of images from his borrowed books. He had to transport those enlargements, a number of antiquities he needed to illustrate his lectures, and himself and his personal effects from New York to Boston and back to New York again. It was an expensive project. The morning after his first lecture the Boston newspapers gave Gliddon mixed reviews.[48] Gliddon remained in Boston and presented thirteen lectures, while enjoying the social life with aplomb. When he returned to New York he found that he had spent too much money preparing his lectures and his income did not cover his expenses. In order to recoup his losses, Gliddon tried to publish his lectures.[49] He turned to Richard Haight and Haight, as usual, agreed.

> It is arranged *definitively* and *confidentially* between Benjamin, Mr Haight, and myself that my *first 8 Lectures*, augmented by hierological wood cuts, are to appear in an *Extra News Work*, fine type, well got up and *stereotyped*. All hands to work at it secretly, as fast as possible; and when it is ready and I deliver my *Introductory*, and the *next day* it is to be spread from Maine to Lousiana to Georgia and thence to bright Iowa and Back with the Manner the New World's influence, I shall be *advertised* enough giving away a Copy of my Lectures with my Tickets for the course. I supervise every step till this is done. The reasons are all urgent and will be to *you*: more than *satisfactory*. By the 15th March it will be *done*.[50]

The booklet, called *Ancient Egypt*, became a sensation. It sold over 24,000 copies and made George Gliddon the "first writer on Ancient Egypt in the USA."[51] Gliddon continued his lectures in New York and Philadelphia. In 1843 he had a private demonstration in New York. By 1845 he was in Baltimore at the University of Maryland unwrapping a mummy belonging to Mendes Cohen.[52] In the end, the American lecture series proved to be a success.

Samuel Morton published the book *Crania Egyptica, or Observations on Egyptian Ethnography, derived from the History of the Monuments*, in four volumes in 1844. It concluded that 6,000 years ago the races were as defined as they were in Morton's day. So, according to Morton, human beings did not all derive from the same source, but from a variety of sources. In studying the skulls Gliddon had sent to him from Egypt, Morton concluded that the elite of ancient Egypt were Caucasians and the servants and slaves were Negroes, just as in 1840s America. George Gliddon accepted this theory.[53]

Panorama of the Nile

In July 1844, while still in Philadelphia, George Gliddon wrote to Joseph Bonomi in England about Bonomi's planned Panorama of the Nile.[54] George suggested a liaison with his own illustrations and Bonomi's Panorama. It would take years for the project to reach fruition for Bonomi had not yet gone back to Egypt to propose the idea to the Pasha and receive his blessing. In the meantime, John Gliddon died and the consular post fell to his son-in-law Alexander Tod. George returned to England and Europe, at the expense, once again, of Richard Haight, who had agreed to support Gliddon as he studied with Egyptian scholars in Paris and Switzerland.

In April of 1846 George Gliddon married his 39-year-old cousin Anne Gliddon, the artist and illustrator. They would have one child, Charles Americus Quaharite Gliddon, who inherited his mother's artistic ability, but was born with birth defects and died as a young man. Four months after his marriage, Gliddon left London and headed back to America for his third visit and second, briefer, lecture series. He arrived in the United States on October

Opposite: **Poster announcing George Gliddon's lecture series (from Broadside Collection, ncdeaa B0022, Library of Congress, American Memory).**

6 and began his second lecture tour with a series of six lectures at the Brooklyn Institute beginning November 29.[55] In January of 1847 he lectured at the New York Historical Society at the request of Richard Haight.

He was in Pittsburgh in March and Cincinnati in April.[56] In May he gave a four-part lecture in Chillicothe, Ohio, at the behest of Ephraim George Squier, the American archaeologist who would become a fast friend and brother in the birth of anthropology and ethnography in America.[57] In September, Gliddon was in Philadelphia; in November, Charleston, South Carolina.[58] He left New York for England in August of 1848 after spending a month as the guest of Richard and Sarah Haight in their new "palazzo" on Fifth Avenue and Fifteenth Street in New York City.

In England, George Gliddon busied himself at the British Museum and published again: *Otia Egyptiaca*, a book related to his most recent lectures, and a *Handbook to the Nile*, a booklet to accompany his new lectures and adventures. While in England he took a trip to Berlin to visit Dr. Karl Lepsius and discuss his most recent work.

Then he set sail for America for the fourth time. Accompanying him were the *Handbook*, a number of mummies, more Egyptian antiquities, and the transparent, moving Panorama of the Nile. It was the same Bonomi Panorama that had been exhibited at the Egyptian Hall in Piccadilly Circus in London. It was mounted on two huge cylinders, was unwound from top to bottom in a vertical manner, and was backlit like a lantern slide. The narrator, standing beside it, gave the presentation. In that manner only one tableau, or scene, was viewed at a time. In the title of the *Handbook*, which Gliddon wrote to accompany his presentation, he acknowledged that he purchased the Panorama from its painters and proprietors, Messrs. H. Warren, J. Bonomi, and J. Fahey. It contained 28 tableaus going up the Nile to the Second Cataract, and 22 going down the Nile to Cairo. That was 50 images, an enormous undertaking for the artists and an incredible bulk to be shipped across the Atlantic and from city to city in the United States.[59] Gliddon would lecture standing beside the Panorama. Surrounding him would be a display of artifacts, including mummies. To accompany him, Gliddon had arranged for Egyptian, Greek, Turkish and other oriental music to be played.[60] He was quite the showman.

The Panorama opened at the Chinese Theater in New York just before the Christmas season of 1849 and ran until the week of February 8, 1850.[61] In June of 1850 it was in Boston, which nearly proved to be the last stop, for Gliddon made a major error. In addition to the Panorama, Gliddon sold 300 subscriptions at $5 apiece to a three-lecture series on unwrapping a mummy. Each subscription entitled the owner to four tickets, and 1500 souls were present at the Tremont Temple on Monday, June 24. Among them were the elite of Boston, including the poet Henry Wadsworth Longfellow, the president of Harvard University Jared Sparks (author of *The Life of John Ledyard*), and the statesman Oliver Wendell Holmes.

The show began at noon. Gliddon told the audience the inside lid hieroglyphics indicated that the mummy was the daughter of a high priest of Thebes at the time of Moses and that A.C. Harris had obtained it at Thebes three years earlier in 1846.[62] Then the unwrapping began. The mummy's coffin was placed upright in front of the audience. Gliddon's aide sawed open the coffin. Gliddon lectured on the *Book of the Dead*, yet to be fully translated. He talked about mummification and the embalming process. He explained how the process differed between Thebes and Memphis and told his audience how they could recognize the type of animal that was encased in mummy wrappings. By that time the coffin was open. The mummy was taken out and placed on a revolving pedestal for all to see. That is where the session ended. George Gliddon had become the consummate showman.

The unwrapping proper took place two days later on Wednesday. When the unwrapping reached its climax and the final wrappings were removed, the audience was in shock: the mummy had a penis. Newspapers throughout the United States carried the story of the blunder. This event is one of the defining moments of Gliddon's reputation in America. It shouldn't be. Gliddon was a true scholar and entertainer. Caroline Ransom Williams of the New York Historical Society reported: "There is no more remarkable passage in the history of American interests in ancient Egypt than that of the activities of George Gliddon, writer and lecturer, during the years 1842–50.... But in addition to abilities as a lecturer which held the crowd, Gliddon presented matters of such importance in so acceptable a way as to elicit commendation from men of the standing of John Pickering, Charles Lowell, and Charles Sumner."[63] Once again the Gliddon project fell short of the projected income. Gliddon wrote to Joseph Bonomi in England in January of 1850 that the weather was bad, there were too many balls and parties, and that on one Sunday they only took in $7.[64]

Next the Panorama of the Nile went to Washington, D.C., where a tabloid announced it and the four lecturers to be presented independently of the Panorama. The *Graham's American Monthly Magazine of Literature, Art and Fashion* announced the Panorama was in Philadelphia in May 1850.[65] In December of 1850 the *Saturday Evening Post* announced, "Gliddon's *Panorama of the Nile* is still at the Chinese Museum."[66] In late January 1851, Gliddon was unwrapping yet another mummy at the Philadelphia Museum. The audience was over 1000 people.[67] In April of 1851, he was in Washington where the Panorama and his lectures went well until Passion week, when attendance fell. He moved on to Baltimore on April 28.[68] In November of 1851 he was in Pittsburgh.[69] The tour continued until March of 1852. New Orleans was the last stop, and that is were Gliddon closed his Panorama forever.

Gliddon's Artifacts

The whereabouts of the Panorama remains a mystery. As for the mummies, several have had longstanding homes. While in New Orleans at the University of Lousiana, now Tulane University, George Gliddon unwrapped a mummy named Nefer Atethu. This time, since he was at the end of his tour, he left it behind, along with three coffins and a number of other antiquities. "Gliddon donated them to the Medical School's Anatomical Museum."[70] Their journey into the 21st century is quite a story. They were subsequently transferred to Gibson Hall, then put in storage under the bleachers of the football stadium. There they witnessed several Super Bowl games before they were salvaged in 1997 and given a number of scientific tests.

In fact, George Gliddon left his Egyptian artifacts all over America. Several collections were on exhibit in the National Gallery in Washington, D.C., in 1857.[71] In 1867 the Smithsonian acquired their "earliest pieces of African ethnology," which the catalog stated were donated by Gliddon himself: an earthenware water jug "received with two Ethnological specimens from Egypt and Persia," and a second, "a Nubian basketry 'tree-server,'" from G.R. Gliddon.[72]

Gliddon settled into Mobile, Alabama, with his friend Dr. J.C. Nott to research and write the book *Types of Mankind*. There he gave several lectures. The bulk of his energies were spent producing an elaborate ethnological work complete with massive drawings done by his wife Anne. The book was completed in the summer of 1853 and published by subscription by Lippincott and Grambo of Philadelphia in 1854. His publisher then paid for his trip back to England and Europe. By the 1870s *Types of Mankind* had gone through ten editions. It is still in print.

It was not a pleasant journey to England, for his only son was ill and may have died at this time. George went on to study on the Continent and remained in Paris until June 1855. In May 1856 he was back in New York. He did not remain long, for he traveled to Philadelphia, where he began work on the book *Indigenous Races of the Earth*. It was published in March 1857.

Squiers, Honduras, and Panama Fever

George Gliddon was about to enter into the last phase of his life, and it was completely different from anything he had done before. In 1857, through the good graces of his longtime friend E. George Squiers, he accepted a post as deputy agent of the Honduras Inter-Oceanic Railroad Company.[73] This agency was peopled by railroad men from Philadelphia — men who had built the Pennsylvania Railway. Their plan was to cut the isthmus that separated the two American continents and cut the time of ocean travel from the East Coast to the West Coast of the United States.

George Gliddon arrived in Honduras on April 16, 1857, and brought along his younger brother Henry Gliddon, who served as secretary of the agency.[74] But George Gliddon did not last long in the post. He contracted Panama fever, also known as Yellow fever, and by October 10, 1857, tried to resign his commission and go home. The company gave him a three-month leave, hoping he would recuperate and return.[75] But he did not make it. George Robbins Gliddon died in Panama on November 16, 1857, at the age of 48.[76] Henry Shelton Stanford, his superior in Panama, wrote to E.G. Squier: "Gliddon is dead! He expired yesterday of pulmonary paralyses at ¼ to 5 o'clock. His widow must not know the cause of his death: his own stubbornness and self willed obstenance, which led him to doctor himself— to take overdoses of laudanum and opium unknown to his physician...."[77] He was buried at the American Cemetery in Panama. Nearly ten years later his true friend Squiers returned to Central America on business. He wrote:

> This delay at least gave me time to perform a melancholy duty in caring for the remains of my old friend, George R. Gliddon, known to the world in general as former Consul of the United States in Egypt, and as agent of the Viceroy of Egypt in the United States; known also to the scientific world by having supplied Dr. Samuel G. Morton with most of the material for his "Crania Egyptica," and as the associate of Dr. J.C. Nott in the production of the "Types of Mankind," and "Indigenous Races." He was also the friend of Humboldt, Jomard, and Lepsius; was a fascinating lyceum lecturer, and contributed largely towards popularizing Egyptian research in America. Having several years before had important business relations in Honduras, Mr. Gliddon acted as my agent in that country. On his return to the United States, he was attacked by sudden illness, and died at Panama.
>
> During the flush period of emigration to California, and before the Panama Railroad was built, and while there were no adequate means of speedy communication with California, hundreds and thousands of American emigrants were stricken down with fever at Panama, and died there. The then prefect of the city assigned a piece of ground in the suburbs as a burying-ground for them. In this Gliddon was buried; and, acting in behalf of my associates, I sent to the American consul the materials for erecting an inclosure around his grave, and a marble slab to mark the spot. It was a sad duty for me now to visit the grave of my old friend. I early directed my steps to the "American Cemetery." I found it literally a golgotha — "a place of skulls." The shrubbery which had covered it had been cut away, and from numerous little hillocks projected skulls and human bones; many others had been piled up in heaps and burned. A somewhat pretentious building was in course of erection in one corner of the area, and into the walls were built the bricks and head-stones of the few graves

which had ever been so marked. The ground had been made over to one of his friends by the very prefect who had originally conceded it for an American cemetery. I sought in vain for the tomb of my friend; all that I could find were two or three half-calcined fragments of the marble slab which I had sent out. I found out a German carpenter, who had acted as undertaker, and with him returned to the cemetery, and with great difficulty we were able to identify the grave, and that only by my recognizing the bricks which I had sent for the foundation of the monument. I caused the remains to be gathered together and sent to Philadelphia, to Mr. Lippincott, his friend and publisher, by whom they were deposited in the Laurel Hill Cemetery, the spot being marked by an appropriate monument.[78]

George Gliddon was blessed to have found such a friend.

If you look George Gliddon up on the Internet, you will find very little about all the contributions he made to Egyptology. Instead he is placed at the center of the controversy related to the origin of the races. Not only did Gliddon become an Egyptologist, he was also an anthropologist and ethnologist. Just as Egyptology was in its infancy, so were the other two disciplines. In the early decades of the 19th century no one believed the world consisted of a single race. There was the red race of Native Americans from the Americas, the yellow race from the Asian continent, the black race from Africa, and the white race from Europe. Early anthropologists set out to prove that the origins of the different races were not the same. They further decided that the white race was the superior race. We now know that all races sprang from a single source. George Gliddon was much involved in the early process. It is not within the scope of this book to deal with this issue, except to say that George Gliddon's legacy takes him far beyond the early mistakes in anthropology.

7

Sarah Rogers Haight Steamin' to Egypt: The American Traveler Is Born (Traveler, 1836)

It was the steamship which turned the tide of travel from America. It had taken three months to reach Europe by sail, so a further passage to the Orient was prohibitive and few Americans undertook the journey. Steam cut the Atlantic passage to fifteen days, a sixth of the time. The P.S. *Savannah*, an American part-steam, part-sail ship, began the very first steam-propelled transatlantic crossing in 1819, making steam the propulsion system of choice for the world.[1] By 1833, just as America was finalizing its relationship with the Ottoman Porte, regular steam packets from Liverpool opened up the Mediterranean ports of Alexandria, Smyrna (Izmir), and Beirut. These events combined to lure rich Americans to Egypt and cause David Finnie in *Pioneers East: The Early American Experience in the Middle East* to write, "By the winter of 1838–39 it was said there were more American travelers in Egypt than any other nationality but the English."[2]

Of the growing number of visitors who published their adventures, it was a woman, Sarah Rogers Haight, who left us one of the most outstanding early accounts of Egypt by an American traveler. Richard K. and Sarah Rogers Haight were in Egypt in 1836. Richard was son and grandson of a famous and successful New York merchant family who was involved in trade in Lower Manhattan from around 1784. Walter Barrett in *The Old Merchants of New York City* called the "very handsome" Richard "English Clever."[3] The Haights had four children and were known for giving lavish parties in their mansion at the southeast corner of Fifth Avenue and Fifteenth Street. Beginning while still a very young man (in 1821), Richard made several visits to Europe for his company and was the toast of the town. When Richard married Sarah, she accompanied him on his journeys. Sarah came from a prominent Long Island family and was known for her beauty. In the waning years of her life she lived in Paris, and the elegant mansion on Fifth Avenue became the home of a New York club.

A tour of Egypt was quite an adventure for a New York lady in 1836. Few American women had ventured to Egypt before her: families of sea captains sometimes accompanied them on voyages, and we know that Elizabeth Cabot Kirkland was in Egypt in 1832.[4] Sarah may not have been the first American woman in Egypt, but she is probably the first published American woman travel writer with Egypt as her subject.[5] When she returned to the United States, Sarah published the events of her journey in the two-volume *Letters from the Old World by a Lady of New York*.[6]

The letter format was the typical style of women's travel writing at the time, for it "protected" so-called sheltered women from presuming to "go public" with their experiences. Sarah repeated that she did not want to publish her letters, but on hearing that someone else was going to, she took on the job. This, too, is the typical feminine justification for presenting a public voice. It vindicated Sarah for being so bold. Publication difficulty is not the only way the plight of women travelers is dealt with in Sarah's book. As we shall see, she was denied many of the adventures the men enjoyed simply because she was a woman and considered too delicate. In addition to being a travel writer, Sarah Haight was also an early feminist.

The 1840 publication by Harper and Brothers covered the Haight's entire journey from Constantinople through Palestine. Of the twenty-

Portrait of Sarah Rogers Haight (Sarah Josepha Hale. *Woman's Record: Sketches of All Distinguished Women.* New York: Harper and Brothers, 1853).

three letters in volume one of the two-volume set, seventeen letters deal with the journey in Egypt. They cover every aspect of the journey from supplies to sites to emotions.

Quarantine

When Richard and Sarah Haight peered over the boat railing and saw the minarets and domes of Alexandria for the first time, they were heading straight into quarantine. From the days of the ancient Egyptians, epidemics and pandemics had swept the known world. The ancient Egyptians fled to Sinai. The medieval Cairenes shut themselves up in their homes. The thirteenth-century Venetians, often carriers of communicable diseases in their merchant ships, finally began to isolate incoming ships in the harbor for forty days (*quaranta giorni*— thus the name quarantine) before allowing them to dock and unload their sailors and cargo. None of it worked. Tens of thousands of people died each time cholera, smallpox, or the plague found its way into populated areas.

For centuries Europe believed that Egypt was the origin of the plague. This was detrimental to the plans of Mohammad Ali. He wanted to modernize. He did not want illness to stop the progress he was making in the country. So he instituted a quarantine for ships from the Turkish Empire as early as the 1820s and established a Quarantine Board by 1831, cleverly "entrusting that board to European consular representatives."[7] Although it did not last long, it was "the first international body charged with disease control."[8] It would take the international community until 1893 to reach consensus on quarantine control.

The Haights should have been concerned about being caught in an epidemic. There had been a devastating cholera epidemic around the Mediterranean in 1831 (during which time the Quarantine Board in Egypt was established). Egypt, with a population of around 3 million (compared to 81 million today) was devastated. It killed 150,000 people, 30,000 of them in Cairo.[9] In 1835, mere months before the Haights' arrival in the Mediterranean, the plague hit and hit hard. In fact, in Egypt that epidemic was not officially over until October 30, 1837 (It would hit again in 1848 and 1865).[10] The Haights had been skirting disaster on their entire journey. Obviously it not only took money and time to travel in the nineteenth century, it also took courage. Sarah explained their quandary: they could continue their travels south and wait out the plague in Nubia or Abyssinia, or leave Egypt and head to Syria via Sinai. They decided on the former and returned north as far as Thebes, where George Gliddon would have a message waiting for them. If it was bad news they would cross to the Red Sea (153). None of these carefully laid plans had to be implemented, as the Haights managed to escape any semblance of disease on their journey.

Arranging the Journey

Once in Egypt, they had tasks to perform. The Haights, admired and respected in New York and Europe, just as travelers before and travelers after, had to establish their good character and financial status when they traveled abroad. Very few travelers of the day set out on such a journey without letters of recommendation and letters of credit, both designed to ease the journey. These documents were the passports and the traveler's checks of the day. Next the Haights had to find a place to stay. Hotel owners would send emissaries to the docks when ships arrived in the hopes of luring travelers to their establishments. There was little accommodation for Western travelers in Egypt. In Alexandria the Haights stayed in a mansion formerly owned by an English merchant.

Once accommodation and finance were in order, the Haights had to establish their itinerary. It was a formidable task, something Thomas Cook and American Express would do years later once travel turned to tourism and the masses were on the move. For now, the American agent took on the difficult task. He procured a dragoman, an interpreter and guide, to escort them as they rode their donkeys through the streets; he found a hotel where westerners could be comfortable; he fixed an itinerary to include all the major sites; he made advance bookings for boats to sail to Cairo, and then did the same for Cairo and the rest of the Nile journey. That included purchasing all the equipment and stores for a four-month journey on the Nile and dipping the boat into the water to rid it of rats, fleas, and other vermin. In fact, among his other duties, the representative of a country in a foreign land often served as a travel agent. For the Haights this task fell to George Gliddon, who as we have seen was well rewarded for his efforts.

Having "done" Alexandria and being quite satisfied at seeing Pompey's Pillar, the remains of the Pharos, and the Catacombs, the Haights headed for Cairo. But arrangements went astray and what was to be a short journey, like John Antes's baptism into Egypt, turned into a nightmare. Sarah in Letter IX advised the traveler to spend a little more money and get a good boat and enough boatmen to travel this stage of the journey. It was faster and safer. When they arrived at Bulaq, Cairo's Nile port, hundreds of boats were lined up along the shore. Bulaq was the heart of commerce for Grand Cairo from its founding in 969 through the grand eras of the Mamluk and Ottoman empires. Along its shores were the remnants of the warehouses through which had once transited the goods of the world (and probably an equal number of *hammams*, bath houses, where the travelers and sailors would wash the journey away). They shared space with customs houses where duty was assessed on goods coming by camel caravan as well as boat. Under Mohammed Ali the great port of Cairo began to thrive as it had done in medieval times. He added to Bulaq's landscape by erecting many of his spinning, weaving, and cotton factories there. Amid the warehouses he made room for the government printing presses (to this day Bulaq remains the center of the printing industry in Egypt) and continued and improved the boat building center.

When the Haights arrived, the Bulaq docks were busy with loading and unloading goods to be transported up the Nile into the interior of Africa or down the Nile to Alexandria and the Mediterranean Sea. They had to prepare themselves to go through customs once again. Once that was accomplished, all their goods were before them upon the dock, but there was no one there to lead the Haights on to their hotel. They did not speak Arabic and Sarah feared for their fate. She wondered how to say, "Mrs. Hill's boarding-house in the Frank Quarter," when along came "the first Frank we had seen near Cairo, in the shape of a very genteel, remarkably well-dressed Frenchman or Italian, as we thought." But he wasn't French. He was British. And he knew of their arrival. He saw to it that the animals were loaded and the party was headed in the right direction. Later Sarah discovered their hero was Dr. Alfred Walne, whom Sarah describes as "residing here, to study the monuments and inscriptions of the country." He was the British vice consul (106–108).

Cairo had changed considerably since the days of John Antes and George Bethune English. New areas had grown up outside the walls of the Fatimid City of 969. There was a Coptic Quarter, a Greek Quarter, a Frank Quarter, the Muski, and the Ezbekiyyah. Each was unique. Each had a history. Sarah described the journey from Bulaq to the Frank Quarter in great detail.

> We first rode through a great square, next squeezed through a narrow and crowded street, then plunged under an archway into an alley so narrow as to admit only one horse at a time. Again crossing another apology for a street, we rode directly into a house, where we groped about for ten minutes, threading dark passages, without being able to see each other, under the vaulted basements of a square of houses, and guided by the voice of the donkey boys, who piloted us through these nether regions. We emerged again into open day, and passing a huge wooden gate, we found ourselves in the Frank Quarter, and were set down opposite a low-arched doorway, into which we were desired to walk. As we had to spend some time at Cairo, my heart failed me when I saw we were to be ushered into a stable for our abode.
>
> Frequently, "ce n'est que le premier pas qui coute;" so in this instance, after clearing the barrier of low-arched passages and double gates, we came to a spacious court, surrounded by a fine four-story house, with beautiful and singular arabesque carvings in stone and wood. Here we found the best apartments — those that had been used for the *hareem* of the former possessor — allotted to our use [107].

Sarah's description is one of the earliest records of the famous hotel used by travelers during these early years of modern travel: Hill's Family Hotel, sometimes simply called the British Hotel. Sir John Gardner Wilkinson, in the guidebook *Modern Egypt and Thebes* (the 1842 edition), said that Hill's was also called the Eastern Hotel.[11] Richard Vyse in 1837 explained that Hill had been a superintendent of copper mills "worked by steam in the Citadel" before he opened his hotel.[12] Hill's was the forerunner of the famed Shepheard's Hotel. A young Samuel Shepheard came to work for Hill, and around four years later, Hill left and Shepheard took over the business. Later Shepheard moved the hotel from the Frank Quarter into the former Alfi palace in *Ezbekiyyah*. Renamed Shepheard's Hotel, there it would remain until it was burned in the riots of the revolution of 1952, when Egypt finally obtained the freedom which Ali Bey al Kabir, Mohammad Ali, and the Khedive Ismail had so valiantly fought to achieve for nearly a hundred years.[13]

In Letter X, after a good night's rest, Sarah was surprised by the dramatic view of the pyramids seen from her rooms on the upper floor.

The next morning, after a most delightful night of sweet repose on a good and clean English hair mattress (a luxury unknown to me this side of Moscow), I was awakened by such an extraordinary glare of light, that I at first fancied myself in the open air, on some terrace or portico. Taking a rapid survey of the premises, I found that there was scarcely any *wall* around the apartment. Casting an inquiring look upward, I saw that there was indeed a roof of some sort over my head, but so far off that I could not discover of what it was composed. That and the floor gave me the assurance that I was really within doors. All the rest was *window, window....* Being in the highest story of the house (always considered the best and pleasantest in Oriental houses), my apartment overlooked all the houses around; but then the wainscot was so high that I could not see over it. Impatient to get a sight of something in the vicinity of my abode that might give me an idea of its *locale,* I hastily threw on a *robe-de-chambre* and slippers, and ascended the little staircase leading to the terrace. The sun had just risen. Turning suddenly round, I was astonished and surprised to see the three great Pyramids, appearing so near to me that I thought one might walk to their base, ascend to the top, and return to breakfast.... It was to me a glorious sight, and as gratifying as it was unexpected. I had not seen them on our approach towards Cairo, owing to the hazy state of the weather; but now a change of wind had brought us a fine sky and a clear prospect.

At the early hour at which I first saw the Pyramids, the western horizon had yet its deep blue tinge of departing night; and the light, cream-coloured stone of those gigantic masses being lighted up by the rising sun, they stood in extraordinarily bold relief against the western sky [108–109].

Through George Gliddon, with whom they also dined, donkeys were rented by the week, an itinerary was put together, and the Haights dutifully set forth to "see" Cairo. One more travel necessity enjoyed by the Haights and travelers before and after them was a dragoman's services. The Gliddons provided them with one in Alexandria and another in Cairo. One evening they were invited to Gliddon's home. Now Sarah wrote:

We were invited to spend an evening at the bachelor's hall of our very polite and agreeable young consul. We accordingly sallied out after dinner with our paper lanterns, and, groping our way through dark alleys, came at last to almost as forbidding a little stone arched doorway as that of our own stable-faced hotel. A nearer inspection, however, showed the stone imposts and architrave to have once been very elaborately sculptured in beautiful arabesques of the best days of the califate, indicating that the mansion we were about to enter had probably belonged to some Arab of note, or, at least, to some rich merchant of Venice or Genoa....

A second door brought us into a court similar to that of our hotel, except that one side opened on a garden. On the side towards the street (alley) is the dwelling, opposite to the garden. One wing is for the bureau and magazine (for our consul is not an idle man, but carries on an extensive commercial agency); in the opposite wing are stables for his Arabians.

A winding staircase brought us to the state apartments of this singular mansion; our names being passed up from one well-dressed brown Arab to another, until we were ushered into the great receiving room, where our host was reclining *a la Turc.*

You, of course, have often read of the "highest seat" in Oriental houses, yet perhaps you quite as little understand the true meaning of the term as I did before visiting the East. In all the state apartments of the better sort of houses, that part of the room near the door (generally about twenty feet square) is paved with marble, in mosaic work, with a marble fountain in the centre, always active. This part of the room is for the servants in waiting. One or two steps take you to a platform, of the same size as the first compartment. On the two sides of this are the usual low and wide Oriental divans. This part of the room is the permanent place for guests of inferior grades. Beyond, three or four more steps lead to the place of honour for visitors of distinction. On two sides of this place are also divans of the usual dimensions, but more richly covered than those below. At the farther side of this place of honour is a small platform, raised generally two or more steps above the last floor, and on this is another divan. This is the "highest seat in the synagogue," the supreme place of honour, where the master of the mansion reposes in state, and all those whom he deigns to honour he places on his right and left. This is the *general* arrangement of the best houses, but they frequently differ in unessential details....

The consul placed us on the highest seat, and shortly after several other visitors came in. Pipes, coffee, and sherbet were introduced, of course. Coffee is served here... [117–118].

Letter XIII is about medieval Cairo. It did not please Sarah. She saw it as a shadow of its former glory and wasted little effort describing it. But the visit followed the typical tour of Cairo which all travelers were destined to follow through the next decades: into the exotic eastern bazaars, on to the slave market where black Africans were for sale, and up the hill to the Citadel, that bastion of Cairo military power. All were done with the assistance of the trusty dragoman and donkeys.

Sarah, the Pyramids and Women's Rights

George Gliddon accompanied the Haights to the pyramids. Sarah was game for the pyramids. Emulating Elizabeth Cabot Kirkland, she was willing to attempt the climb and endure the manhandling needed to get to the top. She reported:

When about to ascend the great Pyramid of Cheops, we were very glad to avail ourselves of the services of another tribe of Bedouins, who reside in a village near at hand. I had four of them assigned to me as conductors, with a promise of a good backshee in case they took me safely to the top, and returned me again where they found me. The gentlemen had each two to attend them.... before I had time to reflect on the danger of ascending, the gentleman hurried me onward, and I soon found myself lifted from shelf to shelf, without time to look behind me. After about half an hour's climbing, we came to a part of the edifice where it appears attempts have been made to penetrate the interior. [Sarah was about two-thirds up the side.] But, when we looked down and saw the precipice below us, some of our hearts, or rather nerves, failed. My husband insisted that I should proceed no farther and such was his anxiety on my account that he prevailed on me to return. Early the next morning, however, he ascended to the top in a very few minutes. Not having the anxiety and responsibility of my precious self he felt no nervousness, and enjoyed the fine prospect exceedingly. The gentlemen cut their names on the summit; but I was obliged to content myself with doing it by proxy... [127–128].

Does Sarah's use of the words "obliged," "content myself," and "some of our hearts ... failed," mean she was not pleased? She didn't say it was *her* heart which had failed at climbing the pyramid. She may have enjoyed the adventure and have desired to cut her name herself into the stone at the top of the pyramid, as opposed to "doing it by proxy."

Elizabeth Kirkland, striking a blow for women everywhere, was up to the challenge, and her husband did not stop her. She told her sister in a letter of April 18, 1832:

We lodged in one of the catacombs and rose at sunrise to ascend the outside. Dr. Kirkland accompanied us with the intention of mounting, but altered his mind as it looked rather formidable, especially as they tell you of a young man, who fell and was dashed to pieces a few months since. But this is a very unaccountable fact to me unless he was by himself and was giddy or had an ill turn. The fatigue was great, the charges small. We had three Bedouin Arabs, one on each side and one behind. They were very active and strong and assisted you greatly in getting up. Many of the stones you ascend are four feet high and it would be impossible for you to climb them without these assistants. The only objection to them, for they are very obliging and good tempered, is that they are so filthy both to the nose and the touch. Dr. K. got a number of creeping things but I was lucky enough to escape. You have nothing to reward you for mounting but an idea of the vastness which you cannot otherwise acquire. We were forty minutes in going up, and twenty two in descending. Mr. Coster a gentleman residing with Mr. Galloway who went with us, cut our names in the imperishable stone, probably the most enduring memento of us (one which will survive all others) for although Mr. K was only at their feet I had his name engraved on the top. We were unfortunate in our weather, the wind from the desert excessively hot, with a scorching sun.[14]

As Sarah attempted to visit other sites on the Giza plateau, she fell victim to sexism yet again. We have already seen Sarah's prejudices against the Bedouin and low-class Arabs around her. Now, we see how prejudice affects her. Just as she was sent down from the pyramids, at the Ibis cemetery we find her once again denied access to an adventure she seemed willing to take. She had to wait above ground while her husband and friends descended into the catacombs, and she had to rely on their descriptions of the scene, which she relayed to us: "I remained above ground while the gentlemen descended a perpendicular shaft, about three feet diameter, by holes cut in each side wherein to put their feet. They represented the place as divided into various chambers, all filled with these jars, piled up in regular order" (143). The same thing would happen a few days later when Mr. Gliddon arranged a visit to the Pasha. Sarah could not go. Sarah, with her astute mind, her way with words, her keen observations, and her sense of adventure, was vexed and she spoke out, making her an early advocate for women's rights.

Sarah and the Gothic Tale

Of all of Sarah's letters home, the fourteen-page Letter XII, which gives a description of their lodgings in a local tomb for the night, is the most famous passage in her book. It is often quoted, for it moves her into the world of Gothic literature. That world, heralded in America by Nathanial Hawthorne, Washington Irving, and Edgar Allan Poe, is filled with terror, tyrants, villains, ghosts, vampires, demons, and mummies.

> Our place of rest for the night was a large tomb, excavated in the solid rock, in the side of the hill, with one end opening upon a sort of terrace. Being well swept out, and spread with carpets and mattresses around the sides, it formed a tolerably comfortable parlour, with divans, &c. In the centre a table was arranged, by placing several canteen boxes side by side, which, with a clean white tablecloth and sundry articles of dinner furniture, wore quite a promising aspect.
>   My impatience for dinner led me to make a domiciliary visit to the quarters of Monsieur Francois, who I found had appropriated to himself another of these chambers of the dead, which he had transformed into a pretty good restaurant for the living, and in which, with the aid of a little charcoal from Cairo, and sundry portions of mummy from a neighbouring pit, he made out to produce for us several courses of viadans in his best style. This was the first time in my life that I ever bivouacked for a night, or made a meal seated *a la* Turc upon the ground [133].

After they were well fed, they bedded down for the night. All the men fell asleep. Soon the darkness and the night crept in on Sarah Haight. She rose from her divan and made her way to the entrance.

The night was one of true Egyptian darkness. Such a background, together with what I then saw, formed the very beau ideal of a subject for the pencil of *De la Notte*. In the distance, a few dying embers served to throw an uncertain light on sundry forms lying about, so like the human as easily to be mistaken for man or mummy. In the foreground were several camp-fires, around which were seated the half-naked Bedouins, silently and voraciously devouring some fragments of food.

While gazing at these hideous creatures, my imagination transformed the hooded females who flitted by the blaze into Hecates and witches, the swarthy myrmidons into devils incarnate, and the half-consumed mummy-fuel into some victim they were tormenting.... To give the last finishing touch to the picture, and to exalt my excited feelings to the highest pitch, in every direction lay fragments of mummies. Their resinous cerements were scattered in all directions; each puff of wind drove them across the embers, where, instantly igniting, they caused a transient blaze to flash a lurid glare upon hundreds of "death's heads and cross-bones." At each step of these busy demons we heard the sharp crackling of dried human skeletons; a sound which together with my already surcharged vision, so overcame all my remaining courage, that I tottered back to my sepulchral couch, and there endeavoured to overcome my excitement, and, if possible, partake of the repose around me.... To me, who had never before passed a night out of a house, it was not a very amusing matter to be thus lying in a cavern of the Libyan rocks, in the very centre of the greatest necropolis the world ever knew, where were entombed countless millions of human bodies, scarcely changed in feature, the accumulated relics of ages, and the unbroken ranks of nations and people existent more than three thousand years ago. Not only the Egyptian, but the most distinguished individuals from many nations lie here entombed; for such was the celebrity of this sacred spot, such the known skill of its adepts in the art of embalming; such the gorgeousness of the funeral habiliments; such the luxury and splendor of the obsequies, that no higher honor could be conferred, nor a more consoling promise made, than that contained in the significant words of Scripture, "MEMPHIS SHALL BURY THEE" [135–136].

She did not sleep through the night and was happy when the dawn came and they departed. The Haights went on to Sakkara and Memphis before they returned to Cairo to prepare for their Nile journey.

Up the Nile

The Nile begins its journey north deep in Africa. It runs downhill through present-day Uganda, Sudan, and Egypt on its way north, dispensing its waters through the most arid regions on earth. It is the mythical river travelers from Herodotus to Baedeker said it was. Its significance to Egypt is that it begins its flood in summer, when most rivers run dry, thus allowing a third growing season every year. That is because the Blue Nile, commencing in the highlands of Ethiopia, picks up the melting snow of the mountains and swells as it races downhill. Eventually the roaring river crashes into the placid White Nile at Khartoum. The two rivers do not merge for many miles but run side by side, each distinctly visible to the other with the naked eye. Merging, they flow north overflowing their banks to flood fields and turn villages into islands. Cresting sometime in September, the receding waters leave the rich Ethiopian soil, or silt, behind, renewing the land year after year. The ancient Egyptians made it a god; the modern Egyptians not only dammed it but are pushing its waters deep into the Western Desert.

There were no dams on the river in 1836 when the Haights left Cairo and made their way south, up river to Thebes. They sailed in George Gliddon *dahabeyyiah* under the safety of the national flag. Sarah explains to us that the flag is necessary "in order to command respect from the natives, and to protect the boat from being seized by petty government officers, who are in the habit of pressing into their own service every boat, vehicle, or animal they can get hold of" (160). At the end of the second full day of travel, Sarah reported that they moored near the quarries of the pyramids. That means they were at Tora, between modern-day Maadi and Helwan. Today one can drive in heavy traffic from the Haights' point of departure at Bulaq to Helwan in an hour (at 3 A.M. with no traffic, in 15 minutes). In fact, their boat would travel in a day what a car can now do in an hour. It took the *dahabeyyiah* fourteen days to travel 650 miles into Africa. Then the great boat turned around just before the cataracts at Aswan and down the Nile they floated, stopping at will to visit the sites of this incredible land.

Letter XVI is devoted to Aswan and environs, including the island of Philae with its temple complex, the granite quarries where many of the obelisks of Egypt were cut, and Aswan itself. Letter XVII is the west bank of Thebes, where the ancient Egyptians buried their dead. Letter XVIII is the east bank, where the city of Luxor and Karnak Temple are located, and Letter XIX is an evening in the Valley of the Kings, yet another Gothic tale. It becomes obvious that Thebes captured Sarah's heart:

> The first day we passed principally on horseback, galloping from one monument to another, and scouring the plain of western Thebes from north to south and from east to west, in order to get a correct idea of the locale. We were too much excited by the idea that we were actually riding over the very ground once covered by the greatest and one of the most ancient cities of the world, to stop and observe even superficially any one of the multitude of interesting objects which presented themselves on every hand to our astonished view.
>
> We returned at evening to our boat, fatigued both in body and mind. We could neither read nor write, and our communications were rather a string of ejaculations and exclamations than a regular and satisfactory conversation [193].

Sarah was impressed. And in her own way, she attempted to help us see what made her so happy in Thebes.

In probably one of the most interesting passages in travel literature, Sarah sits a reader on the back of a swift steed for a grand tour of the monuments and graves of the elite of ancient Egypt. Sarah enchants the reader with her spirit and her words. "I will direct Ali to 'saddle white Surry for the field tomorrow,'" she begins; and then she moves "upon yon hill," for an overview of what we are about to do. Then our magic journey around glorious Thebes atop a spirited horse at the side of Sarah Haight commences. She quotes Denon, Belzoni, Ovid, and Juvenal to prove her enthusiasm is not misplaced. We begin at what we call the Temple of Seti I, but she refers to it as the temple of Gornon. We do not tarry and speed on to the Memnonium (Ramaseeum) where we are warned to be careful as an earthquake has left the ruin shaky and dangerous. She yells, "Turn round the angle of that fragment of wall, and behold the prostrate Memnon! Before it was dashed to pieces, this was, perhaps, the greatest monolith ever transported by man to any distance from its native quarry." Of course she is referring to the red granite statue of Ramses II, portions of which still lie within the courtyard today, and is correct, for it is the only known colossus still in existence. It weighed 1,000 tons and was transported by the ancient Egyptians overland 170 miles from Aswan to this spot on the Theban plain. It would be an amazing feat even today, but even more spectacular they raised it upright! Sarah tries to tell us its size and exclaims that the chest alone is 54 feet around (198–199). After an extensive tour, we mount our steeds once again and travel to the temple at Medinet Habu, where Sarah complains of how the temple has been usurped by Arab huts, garbage, and a church. After a tour of the west bank, Sarah takes her reader across the river to the east bank.

Colossal statue of Rameses the Great at the Memnonium, the mortuary temple of Ramses II around 1854. Located on the West Bank of Thebes, the temple is now called the Ramesseum (in *Photographic Views of Egypt, Past and Present* **by Joseph P. Thompson).**

Sarah Haight brings Thebes alive: even the most jaded of us, who have tramped over Thebes for many seasons, are refreshed with her images. Nowhere is this clearer than at Luxor Temple:

> I have purposely kept your attention fixed upon the water, in order to manage a surprise for you. Look up, and behold the towering walls of *Luxor* above your head, with its aspiring obelisk, ready in anger to dart at the sun for not having annihilated, at a stroke, the barbarous Gaul who so lately robbed it of its mate.* [* The French, by permission of the pacha, have taken one of three beautiful obelisks to Paris, where I saw it lying on the quay.]
>
> We are now arrived at the water-steps of the temple, by which devotees used to ascend to worship at the shrine within. The river front is not as imposing as the opposite one which faces the north. Before we land I will call your attention to the sudden turn in the river at this point, by which it runs nearly parallel with the south facade of the temple. We will ascend the steps and make a *detour,* in order to get a front view of the great north entrance of Luxor, where it is to be seen to the best advantage.
>
> If we had time at this moment, I would make a morning call, and introduce you to an English lady, who, with her husband, arrived here yesterday overland from India, and is at present living in yonder tent, delightfully pitched under the shade of some palm-trees. But they will be our guests at dinner this evening, when you shall see them. So *allons,* to our work.
>
> Step, now, from behind that mud hut, and behold the sublime entrance to a sublimer temple. That propylon is two hundred feet wide at its apparent base. (The real base is thirty feet below the present level of the soil.) On one side is the widowed obelisk, mourning for its lost companion. May the Briton have more good taste than

the Gaul, and leave it here, under its own bright skies, where the sun, of which it is a type, never for a day withdraws from it the light of his countenance. Fancy it now standing among the dripping and moss-covered trees of St. James's Park, and, after two years' smoking, coated with an inch of coal soot! It would then be under the ban of Typhon with a vengeance! That row of enormous heads and shoulders, which you see twenty feet above the soil, belongs to as many huge statues of red granite, buried thirty feet in the earth. We will pass through the propylon only, in order to see a succession of courts very similar to those of the Memnonium, a temple in very little better preservation than the latter, and much less perfect than that of Medinat Abu.

She continues through the first court and the "forest of columns" beyond. We climb the propylon with her to see the magnificent view of the Nile and the town, and Karnak beyond. Then we climb the gateway and Sarah comments on what lies below the surface, including the "double row of colossal sphinxes" leading to Karnak (207–211).

And then Sarah moves on to Karnak, where she outdoes herself and transfixes us with her words and deeds:

> The grand propylon before us is the southern entrance to the great court of Carnac. You have now to enjoy the greatest treat the world can afford in the way of ruins. If you enter that gate as I did, such will be your surprise that you will be riveted to the spot without the power of advancing any farther for an hour. As I am your *cicerone,* you must not only be guided by my advice, but you must obey my commands. It is my intention to transport you suddenly into the centre of the great area of ruin, in order that you may at once attain the only point of view where the whole may be seen to advantage. There, without stirring from the spot, you may, by simply turning round to every side, behold all the wonders of this most extraordinary locality. Therefore I will draw your shawl over your eyes while I conduct you thither; but be prepared for a surprise when you shall be unhooded, and string your nerves to their utmost degree of tension. You need not fear that any of those tottering walls would reach you should they fall; for, such is the immense diameter of the court, that, should another earthquake occur while you are there, no harm could happen to you, even though every one of the immense fabrics were overthrown at once.
>
> There! be seated on the capital of this overthrown column. I will now remove the veil from your eyes, and leave you for half an hour to your own reflections. None can tolerate the least intrusion at such a moment of intense excitement, when the rapt soul is absorbed in contemplating the most sublime conceptions and wonderful executions of that creature whom God made after his own image.
>
> I leave you with this caution. Divest your mind of all association with the vulgar name of *Carnac,* and of the heathen uses to which these temples were profaned. Elevate the mind to the point where an enlightened, though partially corrupt, priesthood caused these vast piles to rise in honour of the great Creator of the universe, so far as he was then known to them, under the type of *Jupiter Amman.* These are greater and more glorious temples than were ever dedicated *directly* to the true and only God since the creation of this world. I now leave thee for an hour [210–211].

We, too, will leave Sarah at Karnak.

Collecting Antiquities

At this point in the narrative Sarah's husband and their traveling companion, Richard Randolph of Philadelphia, were about to practice a bit of cultural imperialism of their own. Randolph traveled with the Haights on this journey in Egypt. Sarah wrote little about him, but upon his return to Philadelphia both he and Richard assisted George Gliddon in America. Richard Haight was not alone in his desire to bring a piece of Egypt home. Almost every visitor told of an encounter with antiquities dealers. In Letter XIX Sarah told their tale. Of course, she was not allowed to attend the event.

The pacha had some time since forbidden, under very heavy penalties, any excavation or search for antiquities and treasures to be made in any part of his dominions, giving as a reason that the *fellahs* neglected the cultivation of the soil, and, consequently, curtailed his revenues. Another reason is alleged for this arbitrary order; it is, that several collections of Egyptian antiquities have been sold in England lately at enormous prices by private speculators. This has excited the old Shylock's cupidity, and he has forbidden the exportation from the country of the least article of *virtu*. The Greek's house was watched day and night by some of his arguses. We thought, however, that by a little backshee soporific, the guards might be put *hors du combat*. The old Greek was too much in fear of the bastinado to break the law, and the negotiation resulted much to our disappointment. Our principal object was to obtain one of the beautifully ornamented mummy-cases, with its Pharaoh or pontiff within it untouched. He showed my husband a great number which he had obtained some time previous, but dared not part with one. All that could be obtained were the spoils of one beautiful female mummy, supposed to have been a person of great distinction. It was enclosed in three distinct coffins, one within the other; the innermost splendidly decorated with painting and gilding. We obtained the face which was carved on the inner case, and supposed to be an exact resemblance to the person enclosed when alive. The face is heavily gilded, and the gold perfectly fresh. From this same body we obtained the bead ornaments, idols, and a small basket of biscuit, in as perfect a state as when it came out of the oven three thousand years ago. Also a small wooden tablet covered with white linen, on which are painted certain hieroglyphics, said to be a funeral prayer by those learned in this mystic lore. Last of all was a large shawl or funeral pall, three yards long by one and a half wide, with a fringe on each end. It is made of linen, and as perfect as when it came from the loom of Egypt or India.

The Greek said that he had hidden in a tomb in the edge of the desert a great number of this superior order of mummies, from which we might select a couple for a small price, if we could prevail upon some Arab to smuggle them on board in the night; but our time was then too short to enter upon this contraband speculation. From the point where the Greek's house was situated, my husband determined to scale the mountain wall, and meet us at the tombs of the kings, which he did, while the thermometer stood at one hundred and thirty. He found the altitude of this rocky barrier to be seven hundred and fifty feet at this its lowest point.... [225–227].

And then they really got down to business. Sarah began another Gothic tale:

Every night we lay alongside the shore at Thebes, we had messages sent to us through our interpreter Giovanni, from some fellahs on shore, that, if the gentlemen would land at midnight, and meet them at a given point, they would sell them any quantity of "anticas." But they must come alone with their money, and with no witness to betray them.... So one dark night, precisely at twelve, they put themselves under the charge of their swarthy guide, first arming themselves well with a double brace of pistols each and a dirk. After wading a mile through wheat fields up to their chin, they came to the edge of the desert, and another half mile brought them and their conductor to the outskirts of an Arab village. They entered a mud-walled court, which was built in front of a ledge of rock.... This excavation in the rock proved to be a tomb of ancient times, but now perfectly black with smoke. They descended several other flights of steps to other chambers, and wound through an intricate passage until they came to a small, low apartment, about ten feet square, at least two hundred feet from the first entrance.... In this chamber the great negotiation for anticas were to be made. The guide made a sign to them to be seated on the side of an

old sarcophagus. Soon after which came in another, and another dingy imp, each
with something wrapped up in the skirt of his garment. The torch was stuck in the
ground in the centre of the room, around which half a dozen squalid creatures seated
themselves. One brought out a large stone image similar in form to the musical
Memnon, very roughly cut, and evidently a counterfeit. Next a half bushel of
scarabei, as large as terrapins, also counterfeits, and made from the soft chalk rock,
and then boiled in asphaltum, to give them the genuine mummy odour.

... They then produced a large bronze vessel, covered with hieroglyphics, a genuine
antique; at the sight of which the antiquity hunters from the New World could not
restrain their emotion. Taking advantage of this, they demanded ten times its value,
nor would they abate a piaster. Twenty dollars, or even fifty, were not too much for
an old kettle in which Pharaoh's chief butler was wont to boil his rice. Their price
was a hundred [225–229].

In the end the travelers made a few purchases and set off down the Nile for Cairo. They
were on their northward journey from March 17, when they left Aswan, until April 10, when
they arrived back at Bulaq. There are more encounters on their journey, but we must stop here.

As the journey neared its end, Sarah began her adieus. For us it is one more glimpse into
the workings of a Nile journey. Fellow travelers were a lifeline for delivering messages, letters
from home, newspapers to keep up with events in the world, and supplies to refill the boat
larders. So it was important to salute a boat on the Nile, for they might know of dangers, like
the plague's advance along the river. Sarah Haight made it very clear that the journey was a
hardship. The adventure was difficult, and done with courage. To modern readers, a nineteenth-
century Nile journey is a romantic interlude. To those who lived it, everything was complex:
living at close quarters with a crew of strangers for four or five months; lacking any form of pri-
vacy; at the whim of the wind and the river; forced to walk long distances over difficult terrain;
fearing disease, fearing pirates, fearing cobras, crocodiles, and scorpions. She wrote:

> Few travellers that ever ascended the Nile have had so pleasant and comfortable a
> time as we have had, and for the reason that we had the most comfortable boat on
> the river, and an abundant supply not only of necessaries, but of luxuries seldom
> thought of by the generality of travellers. For the boat we were indebted to our con-
> sul, Mr. Gliddon; for our larder and stores, to our worthy landlord, Mr. Hill; and as
> for the European luxuries with which our table was daily supplied, I was much
> indebted to the forethought of Mr. R. and my husband, who spared no pains to ren-
> der my situation in the uncivilized regions we have just visited as agreeable as it was
> possible to make it. Mr. R., who has been before in tropical climates, and much
> accustomed to travelling, was perfectly *au fait* with everything required to guard
> against discomfort, besides having had much experience in medical matters, which is
> an invaluable thing to us all in these uncivilized regions. Notwithstanding the pecu-
> liarly auspicious circumstances under which I have visited the upper country of
> Egypt, yet, had I been previously apprized of all the unavoidable disagreeables which
> must be gone through with, I never should have had the courage to undertake the
> voyage; for no one who has not visited the wonders of Thebes can estimate the
> amount of sacrifice they must be willing to make to accomplish so desirable an object
> [246].

To many in America, Sarah Haight's descriptions of the wonders of Egypt were their first taste
of life on the Nile. Her enthusiasm maximized their interest and went a long way to promote
Egypt to an American public eager to visit foreign sites. Further, the Haights' journey on the
Nile and their obvious infatuation with what they saw encouraged them to aid George Gliddon
on his various journeys to the United States, donate their artifacts to American museums, and
assist in bringing Egyptology to America.

8

Bayard Taylor's Twice-Told Tale
(Traveler, 1851–1852 and 1874)

The American travel writer Bayard Taylor was in Egypt twice, once in 1851–52 and again in 1874. Each journey produced a book. Some consider Taylor America's best travel writer. Surely he was the first who traveled exclusively to write about the experience. And he was good. He was a poet, an author, a journalist, and a diplomat, and in each vocation he was among the cream. In the introduction to *A Journey to Central Africa*, Bayard Taylor made it clear why he wanted to travel to Egypt:

> The journey was undertaken solely for the purpose of restoring a frame exhausted by severe mental labor. A previous experience of a tropical climate convinced me that I should best accomplish my object by a visit to Egypt, and as I had a whole winter before me, I determined to penetrate as far into the interior of Africa as the time would allow, attracted less by the historical and geographical interest of those regions than by the desire to participate in their free, vigorous, semi-barbaric life. If it had been my intention, as some of my friends supposed, to search for the undiscovered sources of the White Nile, I should not have turned back, until the aim was accomplished or all means had failed.... I have aimed at giving representations of the living races which inhabit those countries rather than the old ones which have passed. I have taken it for granted that the reader will be more interested — as I was — in a live Arab, rather than a dead Pharoah.[1]

That is exactly what he did.

Bayard Taylor, as with many of our travelers, was from Pennsylvania. He came from the small Quaker village of Kennett Square, southwest of Philadelphia in Chester County. Today, the charming community that is known as the mushroom capital of the world considers him its most famous son. As a youth Taylor became an apprentice in a print shop. He had to buy his freedom in order to make his first voyage to Europe in 1844. He could not travel in the grand style. He was one of the first American writers to have a patron who would support his journey. Both the *Saturday Evening Post* and the *United States Gazette* paid him to send back articles about his adventure. On that first voyage he left on July 1, 1844, and after traveling through England and Europe returned to America in 1846. Upon his return to the United States he published his first book and with the royalties bought a newspaper in Phoenixville, Pennsylvania, which he renamed *The Pioneer*. Within the year he sold the newspaper and headed for New York. He ended up on Horace Greeley's *New York Tribune*. The *Trib* became his home for life.

When his wife died just a few months after his marriage in 1850, Taylor was devastated. Even his writing suffered. As was the custom in the Victorian world, Taylor traveled to cure his ills. He headed for the Holy Land. The trip up the Nile as far as Khartoum, well off the beaten path of the traditional American traveler of the day, was just the beginning of his journey. After Egypt he would move on to Constantinople, Japan, and China; there he joined Commodore Matthew Perry, whose "gunboat diplomacy" persuaded Japan to open its doors to the West. This journey made both men famous. Taylor quickly capitalized on this fame by writing three quick books, all based on the letters he had sent home to the newspaper: *A Journey to Central Africa, or Life and Landscapes from Egypt to the Negro Kingdoms of the White Nile* in 1854; *The Lands of the Saracen: or Pictures of Palestine, Asia Minor, Sicily, and Spain* in 1855; and *A Visit to India, China, and Japan in the Year 1853* in 1855. After a lifetime of travel and travel writing he returned to Egypt in 1874, and afterward wrote *Egypt and Iceland in the Year 1874.*

Beginning the Journey

Bayard Taylor gave America what it wanted: a view into other worlds. Not only did he describe famous things such as pyramids and temples but, as he told us, Taylor saw and enjoyed describing the simple things which helped his readers not only to see but also to taste and to smell as well. He met and traveled with a Smyrniote merchant of 30 and a 45-year-old portly German whom he called A.B. of Saxe-Coburg-Gotha. This man was August Bufleb, to whom Taylor dedicated his book (Taylor would marry Bufleb's niece c. 1857). There are hints by Taylor's biographers that the two men were romantically involved. It is doubtful. "Mr Bufleb in his letters to his wife at this time, spoke in the strongest terms of his new-found friend. 'A glorious young man,' he wrote. 'If it were not for you I would go with him. His company is a gain to me in every respect. He, with his clear head and pure heart has preferred to travel with me, while many of his countrymen are following or sailing ahead of us.... He has won my love by his amiability, his excellent heart, his pure spirit, in a degree of which I did not believe myself capable.'"[2]

Portrait of Bayard Taylor in native dress (from *A Journey to Central Africa*.)

The trio would forgo the fairly new steamer to Cairo and rent a *kangia*, settling for the time-honored method of reaching Cairo. The Mahmoudieh Canal, a 50-mile-long manmade canal which linked Alexandria with the Nile, was now complete, and there was no need to go on to Rosetta in the Delta. Steamers now made a quick few hours' trip to Cairo. As they approached Cairo, the *kangia* had to wait in line to pass through the docks or barrage. Travel in Egypt was changing. Inns and hotels dotted the Frankish quarter of Cairo, where most travelers stayed. Taylor signed the register of the *Hotel de Europe* and immediately went out to sip coffee in a café. It was not long before he was mounted on a donkey and dodging his way through the narrow streets. Navigation was not easy: "You dodge your head under a camel-load of planks; your leg brushes the wheel of a dust-cart; you strike a fat Turk plump in the back; you miraculously escape upsetting a fruit-stand; you scatter a company of spectral, white-masked women, and at last reach some more quiet street, with the sensation of a man who has stormed a battery...." (38–39).

Taylor did not tarry in Cairo. He was anxious to begin his journey south to the confluence of the White and Blue Nile at Khartoum, the city established after George Bethune English had traveled in the region in 1821 (see Chapter 4). He named his boat the *Cleopatra*. Thanks to the American Vice Consul at Cairo Mr. Constantine Kahil, Taylor got permissions from the Pasha, settled on Achmet el Saïdi (Achmed the Upper Egyptian) as his dragoman, changed his money into Egyptian silver and, more importantly, Spanish pillar-dollars (the common currency of the world of travel and trade at the time), and sent his cook Salame to the market for fowls, eggs, butter, and vegetables. He was on his way. Taylor did not take a three-day excursion from Cairo to the pyramids, but sailed south to Giza (Gizeh) and began his pyramid journey from the banks of the Nile.

The ten-mile journey with the pyramids growing larger and larger as they neared must have been one filled with joy. Once he was there, Taylor's entire journey up the side of the pyramid was marred by the demands for *backsheesh* from the men who were helping him up, a lament that would plague visitors to the pyramids well into the 1980s. He insulted them at the top by handing them a meager tip and saying he would take it back if they were not quiet. They gave it back, but one by one took it back again when the others were not looking.

His party was rewarded for their poor experience at the pyramids by meeting Auguste Mariette at Memphis. Mariette was a French Egyptologist who excavated at many sites in Egypt. He would become a dominant voice in salvaging and preserving Egyptian antiquities. He founded the Egyptian Antiquities Service and the Bulaq Museum (and wrote the libretto to Verdi's *Aida*). When Taylor met him he had to remain content to dig up Memphis and rebury it again. Anyone who has visited the site may ask why. Well, Taylor may have the answer. Once Mariette discovered Taylor was an American and not an Englishman he was willing to show him the site and talk about it. Taylor wrote:

> ... The French influence at Cairo was then entirely overshadowed by that of England, and although M. Mariette was supported in his labors by the French Academy, and a subscription headed by Louis Napoleon's name, he was forced to be content with the simple permission to dig out these remarkable ruins and describe them. He could neither protect them nor remove the portable sculptures and inscriptions, and therefore preferred giving them again into the safe keeping of the sand. Here they will be secure from injury, until some more fortunate period, when, possibly, the lost Memphis may be entirely given to the world, as fresh as Pompeii, and far more grand and imposing [66–67].

Marietta was not protecting the antiquities from the English. He was protecting them from all of the hunters who were trekking the Nile looking for prey. For by this time everyone was digging and taking Egyptian artifacts away from their homeland. The demand turned Egyptian farmers into hunters. In the 1870s, when New York wanted an obelisk, Marietta was one of the major voices against it.

Taylor was not sure about his Nile journey. He did not know if he would return down the Nile or continue his adventure via the Red Sea, so he made many stops on the upward journey for fear he would not return. He wrote: "Opportunity is rare, and a wise man will never let it go by him. I knew not what dangers I might have to encounter, but I know that it would be a satisfaction to me, even if speared by the Bedouins of the Libyan Desert, to think: 'You rascals, you have killed me, but I have seen Thebes!'" (71–72). Regardless of which route he decided, one thing is sure: Bayard Taylor discovered the wonders of a *dahabeyyiah* on the Nile. He described it in detail and then joyously exclaimed:

> The Nile is the Paradise of Travel. I thought I had already fathomed all the depths of enjoyment which the traveler's restless life could reach — enjoyment more varied and exciting, but far less serene and enduring than that of a quiet home — but here I have reached a fountain too pure and powerful to be exhausted. I never before experienced such a thorough deliverance from all the petty annoyances of travel in other lands, such perfect contentment of spirit, such entire abandonment to the best influences of nature. Every day opens with a *jubilate*, and closes with a thanksgiving. If such a balm and blessing as this life has been to me, thus far, can be felt twice in one's existence, there must be another Nile somewhere in the world [86].

Bayard Taylor found the mystery of the Nile. It is everything he said it was. It must have been so for the ancient Egyptians, who made it a god. It was surely so for the Fatimid dynasty, who crossed the Western Desert to build their city on its eastern shore. It was definitely true for Napoleon, who sent his explorers deep into Africa seeking its wonders. And it was true in the mid–twentieth century when Cairo was the cosmopolitan jewel of the East and the river held the magic of centuries along its shores. Taylor revels in the freedom the river provided. Taylor was not finished with his praise. He spent several pages writing about his traveling companions, showing that he, too, was enamored not only with the East but the men with whom he enjoyed it. Then, he described the joy of writing in such an environment:

> I could say much more, but it requires no little effort to write three hours in a cabin, when the palms are rustling their tops outside, the larks singing in the meadows, and the odor of mimosa flowers breathing through the windows. To travel and write, is like inhaling and exhaling one's breath at the same moment. You take in impressions at every pore of the mind, and the process is so pleasant, that you sweat them out again most reluctantly. Lest I should overtake the remedy with the disease, and make to-day Labor, which should be Rest, I shall throw down the pen, and mount yonder donkey, which stands patiently on the bank, waiting to carry me to Siout once more, before starting for Thebes [97].

Dendera to Aswan

By the time he reached Thebes, Bayard Taylor had seen a boat with a New York physician,[3] tried to observe the dervishes "who finished howling" before he could find them, walked through a village market place where the men "were taller and more muscular than in Lower Egypt," commented on pilgrims returning from Mecca "carrying the red flag, with star and crescent," and saw "fields of sugar-cane about Farshoot" which he found to be "the richest I saw in Egypt." Then the *Cleopatra* stopped to see the Temple of Hathor at Dendera before making its way to Thebes. At Thebes, Bayard Taylor added his voice to the growing number of protesters who observed the removal of artifacts from the shores of the Nile. Where he mostly protected the names of fellow travelers he met, he named names at Thebes. When in the tomb of Ramses I, he lamented:

> This tomb has already fallen a prey to worse plunderers than the Medes and Persians. Belzoni carried off the sarcophagus, Champollion cut away the splendid jambs and architrave of the entrance to the lower chambers, and Lepsius has finished by splitting the pillars and appropriating their beautiful paintings for the Museum at Berlin. At one spot, where the latter has totally ruined a fine doorway, some indignant Frenchman has written in red chalk: "*Meurtre commis par Lepsius.*" In all the tombs of Thebes, wherever you see the most flagrant and shameless spoliations, the guide says, "Lepsius." Who can blame the Arabs for wantonly defacing these precious monuments, when such an example is set them by the vanity of European antiquarians? [118–19].

Of course he has much more to say about Thebes, much of it offbeat and unusual, such as: "Memnon now sounds at all hours of the day, and at the command of all travelers who pay an Arab five piasters to climb into his lap" (123); or, "The temple of Luxor is imbedded in the modern village, and only the front of the pylon, facing towards Karnak, and part of the grand central colonnade, is free from its vile excrescences" (137). He adds, "The English Vice-Consul, Mustapha Agha, occupies a house between two of these pillars" (138). More criticism against pilfering: "I cannot conceive the passion which some travelers have, of carrying away withered hands and fleshless legs, and disfiguring the abodes of the dead with their insignificant names. I should as soon think of carving my initials on the back of a live Arab, as on these venerable monuments" (126). And finally, "Ah, there is Karnak! Had I been blind up to this time, or had the earth suddenly heaved out of her breast the remains of the glorious temple?" (140).

The Dancing Girls of Esna Flee to Luxor

Mohammad Ali had banished the dancing girls from Cairo. They were *ghawazee* (gypsies) and the public would call upon the dancers to entertain at special events. Some were prostitutes. That is why they were banished to Upper Egypt and became famous as foreigner after foreigner enjoyed their services and wrote about them. Edward Lane introduced them to the traveling public in *Manners and Customs of the Modern Egyptians* in 1836.[4] Among the American visitors who mentioned them were, George William Curtis in 1849, who published *Nile Notes of a Howadji* in 1851;[5] William Cowper Prime in *Boat Life in Egypt and Nubia* in 1857;[6] and Charles Dudley Warner in *My Winter on the Nile* in 1876. He was in Egypt in 1874.[7] Then in 1979 one more book appeared. Francis Steegmuller published the forgotten letters of the French writer Gustave Flaubert under the title *Flaubert in Egypt A Sensibility on Tour: A Narrative Drawn from Gustave Flaubert's Travel Notes & Letters.*[8] It became a sensation and Flaubert's description was hailed as a masterpiece. The famous French author of such books as *Madam Bovary* went to Egypt with the French artist Maxime de Camp, and the two men seem to have enjoyed the raunchier side of Egypt.

Bayard Taylor called the dancing girls *Almehs.* Just as Gustave Flaubert and Maxime du Camp had done the year before (1849–50), he paused in his Nile cruise to enjoy an evening of dance, pipes, and debauchery in Luxor. Taylor believed the ladies had been banished from Esneh, and were now in Luxor. By Warner's day they were in most of the major Upper Egypt tourist towns: Asyut, Luxor, Esna, and Fashut. Taylor devoted more time describing this experience than he did at any one monument along the Nile. Some think he has outdone Flaubert!

We were politely received and conducted to the divan, formed impromptu of a large *cafass*, or hen-coop, covered with a carpet and cushions. We seated ourselves upon it, with legs crossed Moslem-wise, while our attendants ranged themselves on the floor on the left, and Ali stood on the right, ready to replenish the pipes. Opposite to us sat the two Almehs, with four attendant dancers, and three female singers, and beside them the music consisting of two drums, a tambourine, and a squeaking Arab violin. Our crew, shining in white turbans, were ranged near the door, with a number of invited guests, so that the whole company amounted to upwards of forty persons. On our entrance the Almehs rose, came forward and greeted us, touching our hands to the lips and forehead. They then sat down, drank each a small glass of *arakee*, and while the drum thumped and the violin drawled a monotonous prelude to the dance, we had leisure to scrutinize their dress and features.

The two famed danseuses bore Arabic names, which were translated to us as the Orange-Blossom and the Apple-Blossom. The first was of medium size, with an olive complexion, and regular, though not handsome features. She wore a white dress, fitting like a vest from the shoulders to the hips, with short, flowing sleeves, under which a fine blue gauze, confined at the wrist with bracelets, hung like a mist above her arms. Her head-dress was a small red cap, with a coronet of gold coins, under which her black hair escaped in two shining braids. The Apple-Blossom, who could not have been more than fifteen years old, was small and slightly formed, dark-skinned, and might have been called beautiful, but for a defect in one of her eyes. Her dress was of dark crimson silk, with trowsers and armlets of white gauze, and a red cap, so covered with coins that it nearly resembled a helmet of golden scales, with a fringe falling on each side of her face. Three of the other assistants were dressed in white, with shawls of brilliant patterns bound around the waist. The fourth was a Nubian slave, named Zakhfara, whose shining black face looked wonderfully picturesque under the scarlet mantle which enveloped it like a turban, and fell in long folds almost to her feet. Among the singers was one named Bemba, who was almost the only really beautiful Egyptian woman I ever saw. Her features were large, but perfectly regular; and her long, thick, silky hair hung loose nearly to her shoulders before its gleaming mass was gathered into braids. Her teeth were even, and white as pearls, and the lids of her large black eyes were stained with *kohl*, which gave them a languishing, melancholy expression. She was a most consummate actress; for she no sooner saw that we noticed her face than she assumed the most indifferent air in the world and did not look at us again. But during the whole evening every movement was studied. The shawl was disposed in more graceful folds about her head; the hair was tossed back from her shoulders; the hand, tinged with henna, held the jasmine tube of her pipe in a hundred different attitudes, and only on leaving did she lift her eyes as if first aware of our presence and wish us '*buona sera*'—the only Italian words she knew — with the most musical accent of which an Arab voice is capable.

Meanwhile, the voices of the women mingled with the shrill, barbaric tones of the violin, and the prelude passed into a measured song of long, unvarying cadences, which the drums and tambourine accompanied with rapid beats. The Orange Blossom and one of her companions took the floor, after drinking another glass of *arakee* and tightening the shawls around their hips. The dance commenced with a slow movement, both hands being lifted above the head, while the jingling bits of metal on their shawls and two miniature cymbals of brass, fastened to the thumbs and middle finger, kept time to the music. As the dancers became animated, their motions were more rapid and violent, and the measure was marked, not in pirouettes and flying bounds, as on the boards of Frank theatres, but by a most wonderful command over the muscles of the chest and limbs. Their frames vibrated with the music like the strings of the violin, and as the song grew wild and stormy towards its close, the movements, had they not accorded with it, would have resembled those of a person seized with some violent nervous spasm. After this had continued for an incredible length of time, and I expected to see the *Almehs* fall exhausted to the earth, the music ceased, and they stood before us calm and cold, with their breathing not perceptibly hurried. The dance had a second part, of very different character. Still with their lifted hands striking the little cymbals, they marked a circle of springing bounds, in which their figures occasionally reminded me of the dancing nymphs of Greek sculpture. The instant before touching the floor, as they hung in the air with the head bent forward, one foot thrown behind, and both arms extended above the head, they were drawn on the background of the dark hall, like forms taken from the frieze of a temple to Bacchus or Pan ... [132–35].

Taylor continues for a few more pages, but space limits our view.

On December 8, 1851, Bayard Taylor and friends left the dancers behind in Luxor along with the temples and the tombs and wended their way south to Esna, Aswan, and Philae. At Philae they ran into M. Linant, whom Taylor identified as the explorer of Petra. He was, of course, the same Linant de Bellefonds who, as a youth, accompanied the Egyptian expeditionary force up the Nile in the company of George Bethune English (see Chapter 4).

Aswan and the Cataract

Aswan is the gateway to Africa. It has always stood as Egypt's frontier to the exotic. Nubia begins earlier, at Kom Ombo, but Aswan personifies Nubia in Egypt. Its inhabitants are dark-skinned Africans who have their own legends, their own history, their own music, and their own architecture.

Taylor left the boat and his newly found but beloved friends north of the First Cataract, jumped on a donkey, and picked up another boat on the southern side. He was headed to Khartoum and there were many, many cataracts, more rapids, and the great S-Curve of the Nile ahead of him. He was about to follow in the footsteps of George Bethune English and Khalil Aga, who had conquered the river thirty years earlier. He was anxious to give up his traveler's mantle for an explorer's cloak. For now, the first thing he noticed was that the river changed:

> Those who do not go beyond Thebes are only half acquainted with the Nile. Above Esneh, it is no longer a broad, lazy current, watering endless fields of wheat and groves of palm, bounded in the distance by level lines of yellow mountain-walls. It is narrower, clearer and more rapid, and its valley, after the first scanty field of wheat or dourra, strikes the foot of broken and rocky ranges, through the gaps in which the winds of the Desert have spilled its sands. There is not the same pale, beautiful monotony of color, but the landscapes are full of striking contrasts, and strongly accented lights and shadows. Here, in Nubia, these characteristics are increased, and the Nile becomes a river of the North under a Southern sun. The mountains rise on either hand from the water's edge; piles of dark sandstone or porphyry rock, sometimes a thousand feet in height, where a blade of grass never grew, every notch and jag on their crests, every fissure on their sides, revealed in an atmosphere so pure and crystalline, that nothing but one of our cloudless mid-winter days can equal it. Their hue near at hand is a glowing brown; in the distance an intense violet. On the western bank they are lower; and the sand of that vast Desert, which stretches unbroken to the Atlantic, has heaped itself over their shoulders and poured long drifts and rills even to the water. In color it is a tawny gold, almost approaching a salmon tint, and its glow at sunrise equals that of the snow-fields of the Alps [163–64].

Like the Scotsman James Bruce from 1768 to 1773 and the Swiss explorer John Lewis Burchkardt around 1813, Taylor left the Nile at Korosko before Abu Simbel and joined a desert caravan to go through the desert. The caravan had just arrived from Sennar. It was here that

Taylor, now traveling alone except for his trusted Achmet, met the son of M. Linant by an Abyssinian woman. He was a merchant funded by his father and traveling south to trade. With Linant was the son of the former Mek (king) of Shendy, "the same fierce old savage who burned to death Ismail Pasha and his soldiers..." [168–69].

Then, he set off through the desert with six camels and four Arabs. While encamped on the second day he met a stranger: Captain Peel of the British Navy. William Peel was a Royal Navy officer and recipient of the Victoria Cross. He would publish his journal of his travels, *A Ride through the Nubian Desert,* the following year. Taylor met a few other travelers on this journey, but finally they reached Abu Hamid, the small village at the top of the S-Curve where the Fourth Cataract ended and the railway from Wadi Halfa would one day reach. They had been many days in the desert and dehydration was settling upon them. "Achmet and I began to feel thirst, so we hurried on in advance, to the mud hamlet of Abou-Hammed. We dismounted on the bank of the river, where we were received by a dark Ababdeh.... Achmet gave him a large wooden bowl and told him to fill it from the Nile, and we would talk to him afterwards. I shall never forget the luxury of that long, deep draught. My body absorbed the water as rapidly as the hot sand of the Desert, and I drank at least a quart without feeling satisfied" (193). He continues:

> I left Abou-Hammed at noon the next day, having been detained by some government tax on camels, which my Bisharees were called upon to pay.... The people were glorious barbarians — large, tall, full-limbed, with open, warm, intelligent faces and lustrous black eyes. They dress with more neatness than the Egyptian Fellahs, and their long hair, though profusely smeared with suet, is arranged with some taste and clothes their heads better than the dirty cotton skull-cap. Among those I saw at Abou-Hammed were two youths of about seventeen, who were wonderfully beautiful. One of them played a sort of coarse reed flute, and the other a rude stringed instrument, which he called a *tambour.* He was a superb fellow, with the purest straight Egyptian features, and large, brilliant, melting black eyes. Every posture of his body expressed a grace the most striking because it was wholly unstudied. I have never seen human forms superior to these two. The first, whom I named the Apollo Ababdese, joined my caravan, for the journey to Berber. He carried with him all his wealth — a flute, a sword, and a heavy shield of hippopotamus hide. His features were as perfectly regular as the Greek, but softer and rounder in outline. His limbs were without a fault, and the light poise of his head on the slender neck, the fine play of his shoulder blades and the muscles of his back, as he walked before me, wearing only a narrow cloth around his loins, would have charmed a sculptor's eye. He walked among my camel-drivers as Apollo might have walked among the other shepherds of King Admetus. Like the god, his implement was the flute; he was a wandering minstrel, and earned his livelihood by playing at the festivals of the Ababdehs. His name was Eesa, the Arabic for Jesus. I should have been willing to take several shades of his complexion if I could have had with them his perfect ripeness, roundness and symmetry of body and limb. He told me that he smoked no tobacco and drank no arakee, but only water and milk — a true offshoot of the golden age! [195–97].

It was an amiable time walking along the shore of the Nile, taking shortcuts through the desert while enjoying teasing about weddings and joining the tribe. Among his many talents, Taylor was a linguist and picked up languages easily. By this time his Arabic was good enough to enjoy conversations with his new traveling companions, including the beautiful Eesa. Whether this conversation took place in Arabic we do not know, but it is a wonderful view into the pleasure Taylor enjoyed on his journey:

> We had a strong north-wind all day. The sky was cloudless, but a fine white film filled the air, and the distant mountains had the pale, blue-gray tint of an English

landscape. The Bisharees wrapped themselves closely in their mantles as they walked, but Eesa only tightened the cloth around his loins, and allowed free play to his glorious limbs. He informed me that he was on his way to Berber to make preparations for his marriage, which was to take place in another moon. He and Hossayn explained to me how the Ababdehs would then come together, feast on camel's flesh, and dance their sword-dances. "I shall go to your wedding, too," I said to Eesa. "Will you indeed, O Effendi!" he cried, with delight: "Then I shall kill my she-camel, and give you the best piece." I asked whether I should be kindly received among the Ababdehs, and Eyoub declared that the men would be glad to see me, but that the women were afraid of Franks. "But," said Achmet, "the Effendi is no Frank." "How is this?" said Eyoub, turning home. "Achmet is right," I answered; "I am a white Arab, from India." "But do you not speak the Frank language, when you talk with each other?" "No," said Achmet, "we talk Hindustance." "O, praised be Allah!" cried Hossayn, clapping his hands with joy: "praised be Allah, that you are an Arab, like ourselves!" And there was such pleasure in the faces of all, that I immediately repented of having deceived them. They assured me, however, that the Ababdehs would not only admit me into their tribe, but that I might have the handsomest *Ababdiych* that could be found, for a wife. Hossayn had already asked Achmet to marry the eldest of his two daughters, who was then eleven years old [199].

On New Year's Day 1852 Taylor broke his thermometer. He lists all the temperatures he had recorded through the desert: in winter the days were between 90 and 100 degrees and the nights were near 60 degrees Fahrenheit. Finally they entered the Berber region and stopped at the village of El Mekheyref. Taylor was greeted with great respect. He met the Albanian governor, to whom he gave cigars, and was invited to a wedding, given a boat for the remainder of his journey, and enjoyed visits from the Civil Governor Mustapha Kashif, who called him Yeiikee-Doonea:

> A remark of the Governor gratified me exceedingly, as it showed that all the attention I received was paid me, not on account of my supposed rank, but from the fact of my being the first American who had ever visited the place. "I have been in this country twenty-four years," said he, "and in all that time only some French and two or three German and English travellers have passed through. You are the first I have seen from *Yeiikee-Doonea*. (This sounds very much like Yankee-Doodledom, but is in reality the Turkish for "New World.") You must not go home with an unfavorable account of us." He had once, when in Alexandria, visited an American man-of-war, which, it appeared, had left a strong impression upon his mind. After mentioning the circumstance, he asked me how many vessels there were in our Navy. I had mastered the Arabic language sufficiently to know the necessity of exaggeration, and answered, without hesitation, that there were one hundred. "Oh no!" said Mustapha, turning to Mahmoud, the Secretary: "His Excellency is entirely too modest. I know very well that there are *six hundred* vessels in the American Navy!" I had fallen far below the proper mark; but Achmet tried to straighten the matter by saying that I meant one hundred ships-of-the-line, and did not include the frigates, sloops-of-war, brigs and corvettes [211].

The next morning Taylor settled into the boat prepared for him by the governor and set off for Shendi. He was now on the last part of his Nile journey. He named his boat *America.* He would pass the Atbara River, view his first hippopotamus, and enjoy the ride. By the third day on the river he noticed "that warm vermilion tinge of clouds, which is frequently exhibited near the Equator, but is nowhere so striking as in Central Africa. Lying heavily along the horizon in the warm hours of the day, they appeared to glow with a dead smouldering fire, like brands which are soft white ashes on the outside, but living coals within" (223–24).

Then he reached the ancient Kushite ruins of Meroë. Lost for centuries, the mysterious

Ruins of Meroë as seen by Bayard Taylor in 1852 (from *A Journey to Central Africa*).

pyramid structures had been rediscovered by the Frenchman Frederic Cailliaud in 1821 on the Egyptian Expeditionary Force to the Sudan, but now the site was easy to find, for Taylor had it marked clearly on his map. Yes, a map! Whose map? Taylor told us he "provide[d] myself with Berghaus's great map of Arabia and the Valley of the Nile, which, with a stray volume of Russegger, were my only guides. In Khartoum, afterwards, I stumbled upon a copy of Hoskins's Ethiopia" (49). Showing it to the rais and reading the names of the villages was a surprise: "I ... told him that I knew from it, the name of every mountain, every village, and every river, from Cairo to Abyssinia. The men crowded around and inspected it with the utmost astonishment, and when I pointed out to them the location of Mecca, and read them the names of all the villages as far as Khartoum, they regarded it with an expression of reverential awe. "Wallah!" exclaimed the rais: "this is truly a wonderful Frank!" (225).

The nights, which Taylor wrote "possessed a charm which separates them from all other nights I have known," led to talks of Arabian Nights. The days took on more adventure, for they were at the very end of the S-Curve and were about to encounter the rapids and violence of the Nile. At Shendi, Taylor reminded his readers: "... in 1822, Ismail Pasha and his soldiers were burned to death by Mek Nemr (King Leopard) ... [and] bloody revenge taken by Mohammed Bey Defterdar (son-in-law of Mohammed Ali), for that act, sealed the fate of the kingdom. The seat of the Egyptian government in Soudan was fixed at Khartoum... (260). The next day a gale was blowing and they almost had a shipwreck, but in a few more days they reached Khartoum:

> The city presented a picturesque — and to my eyes, accustomed to the mud huts of the Ethiopian villages — a really stately appearance, as we drew near. The line of buildings extended for more than a mile along the river, and many of the houses were embowered in gardens of palm, acacia, orange and tamarind trees. The Palace of the Pasha had a certain appearance of dignity, though its walls were only unburnt brick, and his *hareem*, a white, two-story building, looked cool and elegant amid the palms that shaded it. Egyptian soldiers, in their awkward, half-Frank costume, were

lounging on the bank before the Palace, and slaves of inky blackness, resplendent in white and red livery, were departing on donkeys on their various errands. The slope of the bank was broken at short intervals by water-mills, and files of men with skins, and women with huge earthen jars on their heads, passed up and down between the water's edge and the openings of the narrow lanes leading between the gardens into the city. The boat of the Governor of Berber, rowed by twelve black slaves, put off from shore, and moved slowly down stream, against the north wind, as we drew up and moored the *America* below the garden of the Catholic Mission. It was the twelfth of January. I had made the journey from Assouan to Khartoum in twenty-six days, and from Cairo in fifty-seven.

At the time of my arrival in Khartoum, there were not more than a dozen vessels in port, and the only one which would pass for respectable in Egypt was the Pasha's dahabiyeh. I had but an open merchant-boat, yet my green tent and flag gave it quite a showy air, and I saw that it created some little sensation among the spectators. The people looked at the flag with astonishment, for the stars and stripes had never before been seen in Khartoum. At the earnest prayer of the rais, who was afraid the boat would be forcibly impressed into the service of the Government, and was anxious to get back to his sick family in El Metemma, I left the flag flying until he was ready to leave. Old Bakhita, in her dumb, ignorant way, expressed great surprise and grief when she learned that Achmet and I were going to desert the vessel. She had an indefinite idea that we had become part and parcel of it, and would remain on board for the rest of our lives [269–270].

Bayard Taylor's belief that he was the first American to fly the flag at Khartoum might not be correct. The American collector and philanthropist John Lowell preceded Bayard Taylor to Khartoum, arriving there with Swiss artist Charles Gleyre on November 14, 1835.[9] One can assume that he flew the American flag. Where Lowell went on to Suakin along the Red Sea in December, Taylor would continue south, and there it is highly likely that he was the first American to fly the flag that far south along the Nile.

Where Taylor had slept in his tent in all other places, he now went looking for a house with the assistance of the Austrian consul. At the time of Taylor's visit a gathering was taking place in Khartoum of the rulers in the region. There was discontent. He had a wonderful time visiting the Catholic mission and Dr. Knoblecher, who had written of his adventures on the White Nile in a number of German journals. Of course, Taylor had read them. He also visited Lattif Pasha, the Egyptian ruler. They talked of America, then of steam navigation on the Nile: "An engraving of the Turkish frigate *Sultan Mahmoud*, which was built by the American Eckford, hung on the wall opposite me" (286–87). The Pasha's palace was sumptuous and the dinner he hosted for the American was grand. Most of the Frank population attended. It was not a large group, consisting mostly of "Dr. Reitz and the priests of the Catholic Mission, of Dr. Peney, a French physician, Dr. Vierthaler, a German, and an Italian apothecary, the two former of whom were in the Egyptian service" (293).

Taylor lingered in Khartoum, taking advantage of this hiatus in his travels to go on excursions around the city. But he was eager to push even further into the interior of Central Africa. He was wise enough to know that it was not safe for a boat to travel on its own and sought the company of additional traveling companions. He thought it came in the form of a Maltese trader who was outfitting two boats to travel south. But he was going to tarry longer than Taylor could. There was only one other small boat in port and Taylor rented it. It was clear from the beginning that the captain would only go as far as the island of Aba, 250 miles south of Khartoum. Taylor agreed and christened his boat the *John Ledyard*, after the American explorer who died in Cairo in 1789 while on a mission to walk across the Sahara in search of the Niger River (see Chapter 2).

On January 22, 1852, they pointed the bow south and began their journey into history. The crew was not so sure, as Achmet told Taylor: "If it were not that we left Cairo on a lucky day, O my master! I should never expect to see Khartoum again." He feared what lay beyond (319):

> The men pushed away from shore with some difficulty, as a violent north-wind drove the boat back, but the sail once unfurled, we shot like an arrow between the gardens of Khartoum and the green shores of the island of Tuti. Before reaching the confluence of the rivers, a jut of land obliged the sailors again to take to their poles and oars, but a short time sufficed to bring us to the turning-point. Here the colors of the different streams are strongly marked. They are actually blue and white, and meet in an even line, which can be seen extending far down the common tide.... A flock of the sacred ibis alighted on the sandy shore of the island, where the tall king-heron, with his crest of stately feathers, watched us as he walked up and down...
>
> All the afternoon I sped before a strong wind up the magnificent river. Its breadth varied from two to three miles, but its current was shallow and sluggish. The shores were sandy, and covered with groves of the gum-producing mimosa, which appeared for the first time in profusion.... The sand-banks were covered with wild geese and ducks in myriads, and here and there we saw an enormous crocodile lounging on the edge of the water. The sun went down; the short twilight faded, and I was canopied by a superb starlit heaven. Taurus, Orion, Sirius and the Southern Cross sparkled in one long, unbroken galaxy of splendor. The breeze was mild and light, and the waves rippled with a pleasant sound against the prow. My sailors sat on the forward deck, singing doleful songs, to which the baying of dogs and the yells of hyenas made a fit accompaniment. The distant shores of the river were lighted with the fires of the [natives].
>
> ... About sunrise the rais ordered the sails to be furled, and the vessel put about. The men were rowing some time before I discovered the cause. Whilst attempting to hoist my flag, one of them let it fall into the water, and instead of jumping in after it, as I should have done had I seen it, suffered the vessel to go some distance before he even announced the loss. We were then so far from the spot, that any attempt to recover it would have been useless, and so the glorious stars and stripes which had floated thus far triumphantly into Africa, met the fate of most travellers in those regions. They lay imbedded in the mud of the White Nile, and I sailed away from the spot with a pang, as if a friend had been drowned there. The flag of one's country is never dearer to him than when it is his companion and protector in foreign lands [320–23].

Taylor continued south to Aba. He believed that he had traveled further along the Nile than any other European or American traveler. He was probably right, at least as far as the Americans were concerned. Taylor's spirit of adventure was not satiated. He wanted more:

> As we weighed anchor, I found that the men had taken down both sails and shipped the oars for our return to Khartoum. We had reached the southern point of the island, in about lat. 12°30' north, and the north-wind was still blowing strongly. The rounded tops of the mimosa forests bent southward as they tossed; the flowery arms of the ambak-trees waved to the south, trailing against the current, and my heart sank within me at the thought of retracing my steps. We had sailed two hundred and fifty miles in forty-eight hours; the gateway to the unknown South was open, and it seemed a treason against Fortune to turn my face towards the Mediterranean. "Achmet!" said I, "tell the men to set the *trinkeet* again. We will sail to the Bahr el-Ghazal." The Theban's face became ghastly at the bare idea. "O Master!" he exclaimed, "are you not satisfied with your good fortune? We are now nearly at the end of the earth, and if we go further, it will be impossible to return." Rais Abou-Hammed declared that he had kept his word, and that he should now return, as it

had been agreed, before we left Khartoum. I knew there was certain danger in going further, and that I had no right to violate my agreement and peril others as well as myself; but there lay the great river, holding in his lap, to tempt me on, isles of brighter bloom and spreading out shores of yet richer foliage. I was in the centre of the Continent. Beyond me all was strange and unknown, and the Gulf of Guinea was less distant than the Mediterranean, which I left not three months before. Why not push on and attempt to grasp the Central African secret? The fact that stronger, braver and bolder men had failed, was one lure the more. Happily for me, perhaps, my object on commencing the voyage had been rest and recreation, not exploration. Had I been provided with the necessary means and scientific appliances for making such an attempt useful, it would have been impossible to turn back at that point.

I climbed to the mast-head and looked to the south, where the forest archipelago, divided by glittering reaches of water, wove its labyrinth in the distance. I thought I saw — but it may have been fancy — beyond the leafy crown of the farthest isles, the faint blue horizon of that sea of water and grass, where the palm again appears and the lotus fringes the shores. A few hours of the strong north-wind, now blowing in our faces, would have taken me there, but I gave myself up to Fate and a pipe, which latter immediately suggested to me that though I was leaving the gorgeous heart of Africa, I was going back to Civilization and Home [343–44].

Back to Cairo

Taylor returned to Khartoum and prepared for his journey north. He made the rounds of newly acquired friends to bid them adieu probably for the last time. While he was preparing to leave, M. Drovetti, the French consul's son, arrived and immediately fell ill. The hot season, always filled with sickness, was arriving. For his journey north Taylor plotted a different route: he would "cross the Beyooda Desert to Napata, the ancient capital of Ethiopia, thence to Dongola, and through the Nubian kingdoms to the Second Cataract of the Nile at Wadi Halfa" (379). He would do in reverse the route of George Bethune English on his return journey from Sennar to Cairo. The only part of the Nile he did not traverse was the formidable Fourth Cataract, which Khalil Aga had been forced to do.

After the camels were purchased and the provisions packed, he bid goodbye to one more group: the menagerie that lived in his garden.

I felt a shadow of regret when I reflected that it was my last night in Khartoum. After we walked home I roused the old lioness in her corner, gave her a farewell hug and sat down on her passive back until she stretched out her paws and went to sleep again. I then visited the leopard in the garden, made him jump upon my shoulders and play his antics over once more. The hyenas danced and laughed fiendishly, as usual when they saw me, but the tall Kordofan antelope came up softly and rubbed his nose against my leg, asking for the dourra which I was accustomed to give him. I gave him, and the gazelles, and the leopard, each an affectionate kiss, but poked the surly hyenas until they howled, on my way to bed [383].

He left Khartoum on February 5, 1852, made his way back to Shendi, and began to cross the Bayouda Desert, to which he devoted an entire chapter. Another chapter was devoted to the temples and pyramids of Napata, a third to Dongola, a fourth en route to Wadi Halfa past the temples of Argo, Soleb, and Sai, and a fifth past the granite quarries and the Second Cataract to reach Wadi Halfa. The journey was all by camel. At Halfa he rented a ferryboat and headed north to Abu Simbel:

There is nothing in Egypt which can be likened to the great temple of Abou-Simbel. Karnak is grander, but its grandeur is human. This belongs rather to the superhuman fancies of the East — the halls of the Afrites — or to the realm of the dethroned Titans, of early Greek mythology ... [492].

On March 16, 1852, he reached the Egyptian frontier. It had been forty days since he left Aswan. He quickly found a *dahabeyyiah* and went looking for news from home. The governor of Aswan told him, "Ninety-six vessels and eleven steamboats had reached the harbor of Assouan, and of these the greater number were Americans" (507). Taylor went looking for his fellow citizens. Instead he met two Europeans with no news from America. Then, in company of the boat carrying the young M. Drovetti, he began his journey north: at Edfu his eye trouble began and he could not read or write; at Esna, they encountered a storm: "...a fresh gale arose, and kept us tossing about in the same spot all night. These blasts on the Nile cause a rise of waves which so shake the vessel that one sometimes feels a premonition of sea-sickness. They whistle drearily through the ropes, like a gale on the open sea. The air at these times is filled with a gray haze, and the mountain chains on either hand have a dim, watery loom, like that of mountains along the sea-coast" (510). They paused at Luxor for one more day of contemplating its wonders:

> The ruins had now not only a memory for me, but a language. They no longer crushed me with their cold, stern, incomprehensible grandeur. I was calm as the Sphinx, whose lips no longer closed on a mystery. I had gotten over the awe of a neophyte, and, though so little had been revealed to me, walked among the temples with the feelings of a master. Let no one condemn this expression as presumptuous, for nothing is so simple as Art, when once we have the clue to her infinite meanings.
>
> While among the many white days of my travel, that day at Thebes is registered; and I left with pain, and the vast regret we feel on turning away from such spots, at least I took with me the joy that Thebes, the mighty and the eternal, was greater to me in its living reality than it had ever been in all the shadow-pictures my anticipation had drawn. Nor did the faultless pillars of the Memnonium, nor the obelisks of Karnak, take away my delight in the humbler objects which kept a recognition for me. The horses, whose desert blood sent its contagion into mine; the lame water-boy, always at my elbow with his earthen bottle; the grave guides, who considered my smattering of Arabic as something miraculous, and thence dubbed me "Taylor Effendi"; the half-naked Fellahs in the harvest-fields, who remembered some idle joke of mine, — all these combined to touch the great landscape with a home-like influence, and to make it seem, in some wise, like an old resting-place of my heart. Mustapha Achmet Aga, the English agent at Luxor, had a great deal to tell me of the squabbles of travellers during the winter: how the beach was lined with foreign boats and the temples crowded day after day with scores of visitors; how these quarrelled with their dragomen and those with their boatmen, and the latter with each other till I thanked heaven for having kept me away from Thebes at such a riotous period [511–12].

They reached Cairo on April 1, 1852. Bayard Taylor remained in Cairo eight days. He then took a steamer to Alexandria and left for new adventures on new continents.

Epilogue

Over twenty years later, Taylor returned to Egypt. This time the adventure was not so grand. He visited Alexandria, Cairo, and the Fayoum, where he met and toured with some of the American missionaries. While in Cairo he went looking for his old dragoman Achmet es Saidi who had accompanied him throughout his journey into central Africa nearly a quarter of a century before. He found him and was happy to see he had prospered and "no longer needs to accompany the Frank traveler on his eccentric pilgrimages...."[10] He asked Achmet what he thought of the changes taking place in the city: the wide straight roads, the gas lamps, the opera house. The answer seems unclear, but then, near the newly erected bronze statue of Ibrahim Pasha, he inquired again, "'Oh, Egyptian!' I said to a native; 'what do the people think of this?' 'O, stranger!' he answered, 'they ought to think it a great sin'" (32).

9

Charles Hale: An Enigma
(Consular Service, 1864–1868)

The American consular mission in Egypt had been in operation for over thirty years when Charles Hale was appointed agent and consul general. The responsibilities of the office had grown since the days of George Gliddon. The rituals of office were more frequent and more sophisticated. Commercially, trade between the United States and Egypt remained problematic. The two nations offered similar products such as grain, sugar, and, above all, cotton. American cotton became unavailable to the European market during the American Civil War (1861–65), so Egyptian cotton enjoyed an enormous boost. In fact, it was a bonanza, and the Khedive Ismail poured the profits into his grand plans for Egypt.

The changes were far-reaching. Ismail enhanced transportation. Steamships were ordered from England. Railroad engines and armaments were imported from Europe and America. The Alexandria-Cairo-Suez Railway had been completed in the 1850s under Sa'id. It linked the Mediterranean with the Red Sea and thus to the Overland Route to India. John Antes took eighteen days to travel between Alexandria and Cairo; Charles Hale could travel between the two cities in four hours at thirty miles per hour. Other communications were also improved. The Transatlantic Cable linking Europe to America by wire was completed in the 1860s, giving speedy access to information. Mohammed Ali had begun a primitive telegraph service in Egypt years earlier; now Egypt was linked not only to Europe but to the Red Sea and India too. Hale could send or receive dispatches from Washington, D.C., in twenty-four hours.[1] It was a new world.

Charles Hale

Charles Hale was born into a prestigious political and literary family in Boston, Massachusetts. His father, Nathan Hale, founded the *Boston Daily Advertiser* newspaper and was one of the co-founders of the *North American Review*, America's first literary magazine (1815). Charley, as he was known by his family, wrote for both of them. As his father's name implied, Charles Hale was related to the American patriot Nathan Hale, who served in the Continental Army during the American Revolution, was captured by the British, and was hanged as a spy. Nathan Hale is remembered for saying, "I regret that I have but one life to give for my country." Charles went to Harvard, was elected to the Massachusetts House of Representatives in 1855, went on to the Massachusetts Senate, and made his way in the political world.

Thin as a rail and in poor health, Charles resigned his state office in 1861 and, in the same manner as many travelers in the nineteenth century, began an extended tour of Europe to improve his health. On December 19, 1861, he arrived in Egypt to visit his former Harvard classmate and very good friend William Thayer, agent and consul general to Cairo for the United States.[2] Planning on staying only a few days, he remained for over four months, touring the country and assisting Thayer in his consular work. In his journal Thayer called Hale "my special friend," and throughout his 1861–62 journal it was easy to see that the two men were lifelong friends. In a letter to a friend dated January 12, 1862, Thayer wrote: "Charley Hale has been here since Dec. 20th.... He is now writing next to me making up my quarterly accounts...."[3] Hale remained until April 1862.[4] Thayer died in office in 1864 and Hale was asked to replace him.[5] He did. Following his six-year term as agent and consul general in Egypt, Hale became Assistant Secretary of State under Hamilton Fish from 1872 to 1873, and then returned to Boston, where he practiced law. He died in 1882. He was only 51 years old.

Throughout his Egyptian service there was a mystery about Charles Hale. Allusions and innuendos from friends and enemies alike put his character in question; yet, nothing concrete emerges. Lucy Duff Gordon, the Englishwoman who came to Egypt for her health and penned the famous *Letters from Egypt*, was a special friend of William Thayer. She wrote: "Mr. Thayer's underling has been doing Levantine rogueries, selling the American protégé's claims to the Egyptian government...."[6] She is referring to Mr. Wilkinson, Thayer's vice consul, but the event took place while Hale was in Egypt and others suggest that he was also involved. The *New York Times* in January 1872 also suggested that Charles Hale may have been indiscreet while in Egypt: "It is reported today that the Foreign Relations Committee of the Senate have requested the President to withdraw the name of Charles Hale, nominated to be Assistant Secretary of State. However this may be, it is not true that the Committee have decided to report against him, nor is the other statement true, that Mr. Hale was removed from his former position as consul-general to Egypt on charges affecting his personal character. He resigned with no charge on record against him."[7] The article continued with an outline of the Dainese affair. Francis Dainese, in his book *The History of Mr. Seward's Pet in Egypt*, made a very clear accusation regarding Wilkinson and Charles Hale: "It has even revived the old clamor against him [Hale] for an intrigue attributed to him in former times, while he acted as a clerk or assistant to Mr. Thayer, in 1862, and Mr. Vice Consul Wilkinson, whereby it is affirmed that they obtained from the late Viceroy, Sa'id Pacha, a present of fifty thousand dollars, or ten thousand pounds sterling, on a promise not to prosecute Sorian's and Kindineco's claims."[8] (These complicated issues are discussed below.) Despite the accusations, Charles Hale was appointed as assistant secretary, but he only served for about a year, during which newspapers of the day suggest further, or continuing, issues.

Even Charles Hale's death is controversial. His obituary in the *New York Times* stated: "Mr. Hale gave up his Consulship in 1871, a malarial disorder having attacked him." The same article goes on to say, "In 1876 he had the first of a series of paralytic strokes, and subsequently lived in retirement."[9] *Appleton's Cyclopedia of American Biography* was not very clear either: "During the latter part of his life he lived in retirement, occupied in literary work, and was much of the time an invalid."[10] Perhaps the most trusted source, *The Hale Family Papers, 1787–1988*, at the Sophie Smith Collection at Smith College, stated: "Charles returned to Boston after two years and was again elected to the state House of Representatives in 1876 and 1877. Declining mental and physical health, probably the result of syphilis, led to his eventual institutionalization. He died in 1882."[11]

Charles Hale on the Khedive Ismail
and Cairo in the 1860s

If one reads the British reports of his reign, most say Ismail was a despot, an excessive spender who brought his country to financial ruin. If one reads the American sources, especially the dispatches and the books of the American consuls general who lived and worked in Egypt during Ismail's reign, one finds the exact opposite. Charles Hale gave the American public a view of the Egyptian royal family in an article, "The Khedive and his Court," in the *Atlantic Monthly* in May of 1876.[12] He remembered Ismail as a 45-year-old short and stout man, "with a face whose expression indisputably betrays the fact that he is a statesman of ability."[13] Hale found a "hard-working and hardworked man; this is no doubt the necessary lot of every ruler who really attends to the affairs of government, and it is especially the case in an arbitrary government like that of Egypt."[14]

Other Americans agreed. Elbert E. Farman, who was the American agent and consul general from 1876 to 1881, was especially assertive. In his book *Egypt and its Betrayal*, Farman defended Ismail and put the blame for the ills of Egypt directly on the Europeans, especially the French and the British: "European Powers claim infallibility for all their acts in the Oriental non–Christian countries and, however great their mistakes, or those of their agents, they always insist that they were in the right."[15] Farman elaborated this, providing an impressive list of Ismail's accomplishments and an equally impressive indictment against the foreigners in Egypt:

> Most of the writers of the history of the period are English. Many of these have written with a semblance of fairness. They are, however, constantly searching for an excuse for being in Egypt, and find no other than that of the claim of the bad administration of Ismail Pasha. It is not my purpose to undertake a defense of his Government. It would be difficult, with our ideas of what constitutes good government, to justify the acts of any Oriental prince.
>
> ... The people were governed arbitrarily, and what we should term harshly, as in all Oriental countries. There are few prisons and, in the larger number of cases, the *koorbash* and the *bastinado* took the place of confinement.
>
> But there were no riots, no periodic slaughtering of Christians, as throughout the whole of the rest of the Ottoman Empire....
>
> During all the reign of Ismail Pasha, the Christian was as secure in his rights of property, liberty and life as the Mussulman. The stranger, of any nationality or religion, could travel throughout all his dominions, from the sea to Central Africa, as safely as in any country in the world. Had he remained Khedive, with his authority as a ruler untrammeled, the same conditions would have continued. There would have been no revolts in 1881–82, no rule of Arabi Pasha, no bombardment, pillage and burning of Alexandria, with all their attendant horrors, and no $20,000,000 indemnity to be paid by the Egyptian Government and added to the national debt.
>
> There would have been no Tell el-Kebir with its slaughter of unarmed natives, no successful Mahdi, no defeat and massacre in Kordofan of Hicks Pasha and his ten thousand Egyptian soldiers, no terrible defeats and slaughters at Suakin, no disastrous expedition up the Nile in a vain effort to rescue Gordon Pasha, no loss to Egypt of the Sudan and the other provinces of Central Africa, and no expedition of Egyptian and English soldiers, at great expense to the Egyptian treasury, to recover the lost territories.
>
> All of these events, with their attendant losses of tens of thousands of lives and scores of millions of dollars, were the direct result of the removal of a strong and competent ruler and the placing of the Government in the hands of irresponsible agents of the Paris and London bankers. And this removal was a sequence of Lord

Portraits of the Mohammad Ali Dynasty, clockwise from top left: Mehemet Ali Pasha, Ibrahim Pasha, Saïd Pasha, Tewfik Pasha, Ismail Pasha, Abbas Pasha (in Frederick C. Penfield, *Present Day Egypt*).

> Beaconsfield's consent to join with France in an attempt to extort excessive interest
> on loans of which only fifty to sixty per cent had actually been received by the
> Egyptian Government....
>
> Ismail Pasha was in many respects a most remarkable man. In energy, administra-
> tive ability and intelligence, he far surpassed all other Oriental rulers. Under his
> guiding hand, Egypt advanced more in all that pertains to modern civilization during
> the sixteen years of his reign than it had in the previous five hundred years. In the
> promotion of education, in the preservation of the monuments of antiquity, in vast
> explorations — scientific and geographic — in the construction of railways and tele-
> graphic lines, in the matter of steam navigation and in reclaiming land from the
> desert, it accomplished more than had been accomplished by the whole Ottoman
> Empire since the days of Osman, its founder.[16]

Farman continues with page after page of the specific accomplishments of Ismail and how
foreigners interfered and doomed him to failure.

Hale, on the other hand, focused on a few observations. In fact, he found that once
again, as in the case of piracy along the Barbary Coast (William Eaton) and the cleanliness
of the streets of Cairo (John Antes), the East was judged by a different standard than the West.
In a speech he made before his fellows in Alpha Delta Phi, his college fraternity, on the cel-
ebration of their reunion, Charles Hale continued to praise Ismail:

> This able Prince has given indisputable proofs of statesmanship, and many impor-
> tant changes have been made during his administration. Some of these, it is true,
> may appear at first view to relate rather to his personal convenience or aggrandize-
> ment, but upon closer inspection, it will probably be found that they enure at least
> indirectly to the advantage of Egypt and of its inhabitants. He has been largely
> instrumental in placing the relations between Egypt and the Porte upon a well-
> defined footing....
>
> ... he has changed the order of succession ... [and agreed] that the annual tribute
> paid by Egypt to the Porte under the arrangement insisted upon by the Great Powers
> of Europe shall be increased from 80,000 purses to 150,000. These are purses of
> Turkish piastres, and the amount of the present annual payment is very nearly
> $3,300,000 in gold. In the prosecution of the various public improvements under-
> taken by the Khedive and his immediate predecessors, a considerable debt has been
> created. At present, there are three classes of debt; under the first, there remain to be
> made thirty semi-annual payments of about $650,000 each; under the second, four
> semi-annual payments of about $1,500,000 each, and under the third, forty-two
> semi-annual payments of about $2,380,000 each. The annual revenue of the Govern-
> ment is equivalent to about fifty millions of dollars in gold.[17]

The two observations are samples of additional comments made by other American representatives in Egypt, including Edwin de Leon, Fredrick Penfield, General Charles Stone, and
Colonel Charles Chaillé-Long, men close to the Khedive, men who were relied upon to make
astute remarks.

Consular Duties

To understand the life of the consular agents in Egypt one can read the article Charles
Hale wrote for the *Atlantic Monthly* in 1877. Hale was an agent and consul general (in charge
of a number of consuls) as opposed to John Gliddon's post of consul. The very first American
of this higher rank was Daniel S. McCauley in 1849. A consul general had much more responsibilities than John and George Gliddon but was still below the rank of an ambassador (see
Chapter 6 for more). At this time the American ambassador was established at the Sublime

Porte in Constantinople. Egypt, after all the years of trying to gain its independence from
Ottoman rule, was still a vassal state. In the Gliddons' days as consul, the United States had
two men in Egypt, one at Alexandria, a second in Cairo. Thirty years later Hale had vice-
consuls at Alexandria, Damietta, and Suez, with consular agents "at several of the inland towns
in Lower Egypt and upon the river."[18] Hale explained:

> At the time of my service in Egypt, sixteen nations had consuls-general there.
> These nations, besides the United States, were the following: Austria, Belgium,
> Brazil, Denmark, France, Great Britain, Greece, Italy, the Netherlands, Persia, Portu-
> gal, Prussia, Russia, Spain, and Sweden and Norway, the last two kingdoms counting
> together as a single power. The grade of all these officers in their consular service was
> "consul-general," but some of them bore the full title of "agent and consul-general,"
> which is understood to imply at least a *quasi*-diplomatic rank.[19]

Hale continued to present details of the service, especially explaining the difference between
diplomatic status in Egypt and elsewhere. This is important for events that would take place
during Hale's tenure in Egypt:

> This conjunction of the title of agent with that of consul-general for the officer in
> Egypt was expressly sanctioned by Congress in 1864, and serves to mark one of the
> important differences between our service in that country and elsewhere. The post in
> Egypt is the only one so distinguished, and the functions which the incumbent is
> called upon to discharge are so various that it would be difficult to describe them in
> detail.... But besides the ordinary consular duties of the position, a peculiar impor-
> tance attached to the office of consul-general in Egypt, arising from the character
> which the place possesses in common with other posts in Mohammedan or non–
> Christian countries, the treaties with which we recognize the principle of "exterritori-
> ality," as it is called, as pertaining to the citizens or subjects of the Christian or
> Western powers residing therein. It was due to the recognition of this principle that
> no technical difficulties stood in the way of the surrender of John H. Surratt to the
> government of the United States, when he was found in Egypt. Congress has
> imposed judicial functions on the consuls of the United States in such countries by
> express enactments, the validity of which was always generally recognized, and has
> been recently upheld by a decision of the supreme court, so far as they fall within the
> terms of the treaties. Our treaties with the sublime porte have been interpreted as
> giving to the citizens of the United States residing within the Ottoman dominions, of
> which Egypt forms a part, the privileges enjoyed by the subjects of Christian nations
> under the ancient treaties of the sultans and caliphs with the principal European
> powers. By virtue of these "capitulations," as they are called, the Frank residents in
> Egypt are suffered by the authorities of the country to enjoy an entire immunity from
> local laws and local tribunals, and are regarded as subject to the jurisdiction of their
> several consulates. It follows that it is of the utmost importance for every Frank who
> wishes the benefit of this privilege to register himself at his consulate, to acknowledge
> and accept its jurisdiction. He desires that the consulate should take notice of almost
> every act in his life: he goes there to be married and to record the births of his chil-
> dren; and, "after life's fitful fever," it is through the consulate that a permit is
> obtained for the burial of his body, and there his worldly estate must be settled. All
> formal communications between subjects of different nationalities are made by their
> respective consulates, and their intervention is invoked in many matters of ordinary
> business. The consuls have the powers of notaries public, and are constantly called
> upon to exercise them. The laws of most of the Continental nations of Europe pre-
> scribe a great number of formalities, attaching to the various relations of the life and
> work of every individual; these laws follow their people when they take up their resi-
> dence in the East, and are administered through their consulates.[20]

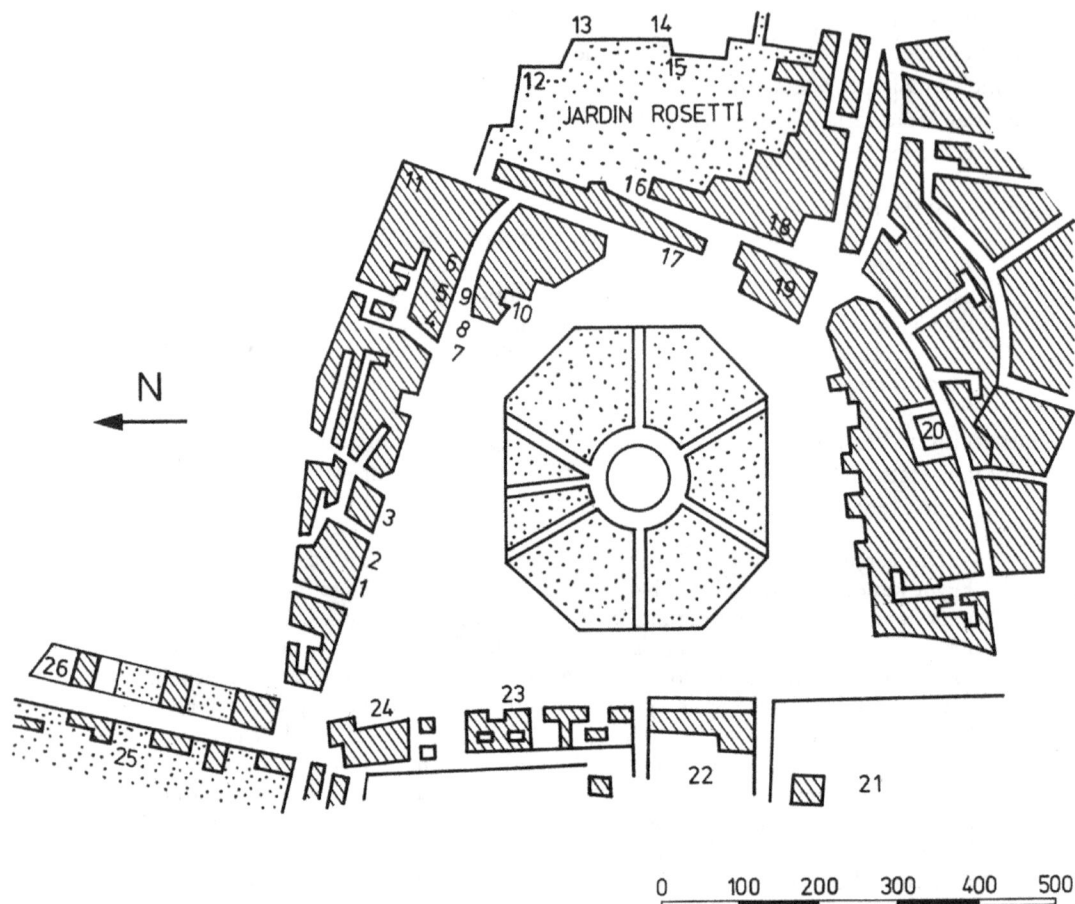

1) Russian Consulate
2) Portuguese Consulate
3) Austrian Consulate
4) Cercle Oriental
5) French Consulate
6) Café Eldorado
7) Cercle du Globe
8) Hôtel Royal et des Messageries
9) Hôtel des Ambassadeurs
10) Hôtel d'Orient
11) Hôtel du Commerce
12) Prussian Consulate
13) Observatory
14) Swedish Consulate
15) Italian Consulate
16) Hôtel de France
17) Dutch Consulate
18) Greek Consulate
19) Police & Court
20) Palace of Ḥalim Pasha
21) Palace
22) Hôtel de la Cie Peninsulaire Orientale
23) Hôtel Shepheard
24) British Consulate
25) Residence of the French Consul
26) Hôtel d'Europe

Ezbeyyikia and the location of the various consular offices in 1868 (courtesy of Doris Behrens-Abu Seif from her book *Azbnakiyya and Its Environs from Azbak to Ismail 1476–1879*).

Simply told, and therefore easily understood, Hale has defined one of the most complex relationships between nations. These distinctions are very important to our understanding of Americans in Egypt. As Hale reported, they are unique to nations formerly of the Ottoman Empire. Included within the capitulations and the court system they spawned is the protégé system.

The American Colony and the Protégé System

By the time Charles Hale arrived in Egypt there was an American colony living there. It was not large, but it was big enough to have a presence and to assemble for American holidays and other celebrations; however, there were more foreigners under American protection in Egypt than there were actual Americans. The non–Americans were called protégés. As Hale explained, there was a series of laws surrounding the rights of foreigners in Egypt. First came the capitulations. They were in place as early at the 1500s and were a series of agreements between Christian Europe and Muslim Turkey, defining the rights and privileges of Europeans within the Ottoman Empire. When these items grew to include the right to be judged by one's own nation for crimes committed within an Ottoman country, a problem arose: some of the European residents had no consular representation. It was determined that they were entitled to obtain asylum from another country's existing consulate. If accepted, they were considered a protégé of that country and were to be protected by that country if Egypt brought charges against them, or were tried and punished by that country if they committed a crime against Egypt.

Over the centuries a system of courts was created to deal with these matters. These included Consular Courts and Mixed Courts. The Consular Courts were presided over by consular agents. The Mixed Courts were presided over by judges from the various countries. This system allowed foreigners living in Egypt the right to be judged by their own country and its laws through their consulates. The capitulations were abolished in the Turkish Empire by the Treaty of Lausanne in 1923. They continued in Egypt, under British rule, until 1949.

Among the first American protégés were members of the Hamet Karamanli family of Tripoli. When William Eaton and the American marines crossed the Western Desert of Egypt in 1805 to attack the fort at Derna and free the American prisoners from the USS *Philadelphia*, part of their army consisted of Hamet Karamanli and his family (see Chapter 3 for details). Eaton had promised to place Hamet on the throne. The Americans won the day, but they struck a deal with Yusef, Hamet's brother, and Hamet was left out in the cold. Eaton was furious but could not do anything about it. Hamet had also been promised financial security. That never happened either. In 1862, nearly sixty years later, William Thayer notified the Secretary of State when the oldest Eaton protégé, Mohammed Habbat, had died in Cairo. He was Hamet's nephew. "In recognition of the services of Hamet Pacha, he and his family and suite, numbering about 50 persons, received at the time papers of American protection, but, notwithstanding his urgent petition, Congress was never induced to reward him in any other way; and 50 years later this Mohammed Habat, then an old man in great poverty, came from Cairo to Washington to supplicate in vain for what he considered our debt to the remnant of his uncle's descendants.... A wife and one child, a son of about forty, survive him."[21]

The protégé system created many problems, as outlined by Charles Hale's brother Edward Everett Hale:

> Charles wrote me while he resided in Egypt that he had the day before sat as judge in a trial of an "American," who had been stealing in the Egyptian post-office. "The man spoke Arabic; the witnesses testified in Arabic, Turkish, and Coptic; the lawyers

on both sides conducted their pleas in Italian, and I decided the case in French." The only language of which not one word was spoken by any accident was the language of the country to which the judge and the case belonged.

My brother redeemed all this system of trials from this absurdity. He drew up the plan by which a special court authorized by the Egyptian Government now tries all such prisoners.[22]

Hale, indeed, created a set of rules to govern such circumstances. Called the *Rules for the Consular Courts in Egypt of the United States of America,* the forty-five-page document outlined the process by which a person could lodge a complaint and the steps that would be taken in order to receive justice. It included thirty-two points.[23] The courts were filled with petitions both simplistic and complicated. Two of the many instances affected by consular law during Charles Hale's tenure were the Surrat Affair and the Dainese or Kindineco Affair.

The Death of Abraham Lincoln and the Capture of John Surratt

Charles Hale was appointed to his office by President Abraham Lincoln. During Hale's tenure the Civil War was coming to an end. Lincoln was assassinated by John Wilkes Booth at Ford's Theater on Good Friday, April 14, 1865. He died the next day. It took a while for the news of Lincoln's death to arrive in Alexandria. Some diplomatic dispatches were sent in confidence and were not trusted to the telegraph or the post. Because of the capitulations and the consular court system, Charles Hale was one of the few persons in the consular system around the world who could actually detain, arrest, and even put on trial an American in a foreign country. Among the conspirators to assassinate President Lincoln was a woman named Mary Surratt. Surratt was a controversial figure who may or may not have been a participant, but definitely was a Southern sympathizer and carried out many missions for the Confederacy. She was tried by a military court, found guilty, and hanged on July 7, 1865. She was the first woman ever executed by the United States government.

Her son, the tall, slim, sandy-haired, blue-grey-eyed John H. Surratt, was also a Confederate sympathizer. He participated in sending messages about troop movements and other information of interest to the Confederacy. He also participated in a plot to kidnap President Lincoln. That attempt, on March 17, 1865, failed. No one will ever know if he was really involved in the assassination attempt. When his mother was arrested, the 20-year-old fled to Canada, beginning a twenty-month manhunt that spanned three continents. His entire journey was recorded by a number of American consuls who were attempting to capture the fugitive. In addition to a detailed account of Surratt's adventure, the messages provide an interesting view of international law. Surratt's arrival in Egypt put a stop to his flight and sealed his fate.

In Canada, Surratt was assisted by a priest from Quebec and remained hidden for five months. When his mother was hanged, he took passage to Ireland, but soon made his way to Liverpool, then London, and on to Italy. Perhaps without funds, John Surratt joined the Papal army and put on the Zouaves' uniform.[24] That did not last long either. A person who had known Surratt reported his presence in Rome to General Rufus King, the American minister in Rome. King immediately requested extradition. His arrest was ordered by the Papal State. Once again, Surratt escaped.[25]

On November 21, 1866, Frank Swan, American consul to Naples (Italy was not a united country at this time and the Papal State to this day is still a separate state), reported to fellow consuls:

On Sunday morning, November 19, I received a despatch from Hon. Rufus King, minister at Rome, of which the following is a copy: "Surratt, conspirator against Lincoln, under the name of Watson, went to Naples the 8th. Arrest him if possible." I immediately went to the quistore here, and at three o'clock learned from him, through the police, that Surratt had sailed the evening before by the English steamer [*Tripoli*] for Alexandria, touching at Malta. I immediately telegraphed to our consul at the latter port, informing him of the fact....

... He [had] remained here till Saturday, giving them some trouble at the English consulate, and exciting sympathy by his position of a young man of good appearance, without means, they not knowing of the money which the police had found. He expressed at the consulate the greatest desire to return to Canada, and through the influence of the consul he obtained passage on the steamer to Alexandria, some English gentlemen paying for his board during the voyage, and giving him a few francs. He still wore his uniform when he sailed.

The steamer left here Saturday evening at nine o'clock, clearing for Alexandria, but not having time to coal here, the captain intended to stop at Malta to do so, which would detain him all day Monday.[26]

Swan sent a dispatch to Malta to have Surratt arrested.

Winthrop, America's man in Malta, sent an urgent message to the British Acting Chief Secretary in Malta, Mr. Legh, asking him to arrest Surratt.[27] He did not. He felt he did not have authority to arrest or detain an American. It was a matter of international law. He explained to Winthrop in a message sent on the same day that he needed evidence of wrongdoing to arrest him. Conspiracy was not an arrestable offense:

In your letter you do not say that the conspiracy in which Surratt had taken part was the same which obtained its object by the murder of the late President, Mr. Lincoln. Nor does your letter point to any evidence that the man going by the name of Walter or Watson is the conspirator Surratt.

Without some evidence giving satisfactory reasons to believe that the man Walter or Watson is indeed Surratt, and connecting him with the murder of Mr. Lincoln as an accomplice, that man, if apprehended, would within a very short time be discharged, and might then bring an action of damages for unlawful arrest, for which you would be responsible.

I am, therefore, directed to request that you will be good enough to furnish my government with any evidence which you may possess regarding the identity of the individual.

I have the honor to be, sir, your most obedient servant.[28]

It was not that Mr. Legh did not send someone to board the *Tripoli*. He sent the superintendent of police, who "reported that there is no person of the name of Watson, or of any name like it, on board the vessel, and that the only person who is dressed as a zouave is a passenger who calls himself John Agostini, a native of Candia."[29]

The clever John Surratt, now sailing as John Agostini, had managed to evade capture once again. Now he was on his way to Alexandria where Charles Hale was American consul general, and thanks to the rules concerning foreigners in Egypt, Hale had the authority not only to detain, but to arrest, and to put Surratt on trial if necessary. On November 19, Winthrop sent a message to Hale, telling him, "If Surratt came in the vessel *Tripoli*, he is on board now. I do not see his name Walters, or Watson, among the list of passengers; but as there are seventy-nine laborers, it is difficult to tell if he is among them. I have no doubt you will do the needful, that such a murderer may not escape."[30] To be sure Hale received the message he sent a second message to the *Tripoli*, the boat Surratt was reputed to be on. He was more than concerned that Surratt might slip the trap and "may hurry off to India."[31]

When the *Tripoli* arrived in Alexandra it was subject to quarantine. To complicate matters, the telegraph cable between Alexandria and the outside world was not working. Finally, on November 27, Hale sent Secretary of State Seward the following message:

> Sir: I have the honor to report that, in consequence of a telegram received, via Constantinople, from Mr. King, United States minister at Rome, and of several letters received from Mr. Winthrop, United States consul at Malta, (the Mediterranean wire being, unfortunately, broken between Malta and this place,) I have this day arrested a man calling himself Walters, dressed in the uniform of a zouave, who arrived at Alexandria on the 23d instant in the steamship *Tripoli*, from Naples, and who is believed to be John Harrison Surratt, one of the conspirators for the assassination of President Lincoln.
>
> The telegram and some of the letters having been delayed in transmission, I was fortunate in finding the man still in quarantine among the third-class passengers, of whom there is no list whatever. It was easy to distinguish him among seventy-eight of these by his zouave uniform, and scarcely less easy by his almost unmistakable American type of countenance. I said at once to him, "You are the man I want; you are an American." He said, "Yes, sir, I am." I said, "You doubtless know why I want you. What is your name?" He replied promptly, "Walters." I said, "I believe your true name is Surratt," and in arresting him mentioned my official position as United States consul general. The director of quarantine speedily arranged a sufficient escort of soldiers, by whom the prisoner was conducted to a safe place within the quarantine walls. Although the walk occupied several minutes, the prisoner, close at my side, made no remark whatever, displaying neither surprise nor irritation. Arrived at the place prepared, I gave him the usual magisterial caution that he was not obliged to say anything, and that anything he said would be at once taken down in writing. He said, "I have nothing to say. I want nothing but what is right." He declared he had neither passport, nor baggage, nor money except six francs.
>
> His companions confirm his statements in this respect. They say he came to Naples a deserter from the Papal army at Rome. I find that he has no papers, and no clothes but those he is wearing.
>
> The appearance of the prisoner answers very well the description given of Surratt by the witness Weichmann, at page 116 of Pittman's Report, officially sent to me by the government, and is accurately portrayed in the likeness of Surratt in the frontispiece of the same volume. Mr. King and Mr. Winthrop speak in confident terms of the identity of the zouave Walters with Surratt, and, after seeing the man, I have not a shadow of doubt of it.
>
> According to the well established public law of this place, as the prisoner avowed himself an American, and submitted, without objection, to arrest by me on my statement that I acted for the United States, and especially as he has no paper to suggest even a prima facie claim for belonging to any other jurisdiction, there is no other authority which can rightfully interfere here with his present custody; and I have good reason for saying that no attempt at interference will be set on foot by any authority, whatever pretensions he may make. The prisoner's quarantine will expire on the 29th; he will then be received into the prison of the local government, which cordially gives me every assistance. It will readily occur to you that the only convenient way of transferring the prisoner to the United States will be by an American man-of-war, and I earnestly hope that one may soon come here to receive him. Although the arrest was finally made with ease, I ought to say that the necessary precautions to avoid possible failure caused some anxiety to the consulate general, and that I received valuable and faithful assistance from my clerks, Messrs. Edwards, Elias, and Charles Chevrier.[32]

Charles Hale arrested John Surratt on the 27th.[33] The warship *Swatara* was sent to Alexandria to collect him. Hale transferred the prisoner to the corvette on December 21 and it set sail for America. He was put on trial, but unlike his mother, he was tried by a civilian court. In the intervening time between his mother's trial and his, a new law was passed that a military court could not try civilians. The trial began June 10, 1867, and ended August 10. The jury was deadlocked at four guilty and eight not guilty. John Surratt was a free man. He became a teacher in Maryland and lived until 1916.

The Dainese or Kindineco Affair

An earlier incident related to citizenship and protégés concerned the Dainese or Kindineco Affair. At first the string of events of this incident seems like a simple matter that arose when a temporary leader, Francis Dainese, made one decision and his permanent replacement, Charles Hale, overruled him and made another decision. But it was a matter that went on for over a decade and tarnished not only the reputation of Charles Hale, but the American government as well. As noted, the official agent and consul general in Egypt from 1861 to 1864 was William Thayer. When he became too sick to serve he appointed Francis Dainese as acting consul general. Dainese dates this event to September 5, 1863.[34]

In the papers of William S. Thayer, Thayer addressed what seems to be the beginning of the Dainese Affair. "4th May [1863]. Thomas Kusdinsko [Kindineco] came at my summons to substantiate certain charges against Mr. Silkinson [Wilkinson]. I told Mr. W. that they must either be disproved or he must resign. W. was greatly excited. W. said if one of the four witnesses named by K. sustains him in his assertions, 'I resign.' The witnesses came and testified directly against K., so that W. was fully justified. Alexander C. Evangelides was present.[35] Two of the witnesses were Latif Effendi, and Sarafino Pittako."[36] Despite the denials, the accusations would not go away and were the heart of the Dainese-Hale conflict. Wilkinson was eventually dismissed for "having been detected in practices degrading to the character of an officer of our government."[37]

Dainese was an American citizen who formerly lived in Washington, D.C. He became involved with the ongoing Kindineco incident when the Egyptian government arrested Kindineco while he was under the consul's protection. Since Kindineco was an American citizen who had been doing business in Egypt from 1861, Dainese was concerned. Dainese reported to Mr. Seward that "an American domicile was brutally violated by some forty armed policemen ... its owner was beaten and imprisoned...." The Egyptian government reported that he had erected a steam engine and there was no steam engine.... This latter step can only be regarded as a direct and intentional insult to the consulate....[38]

The *New York Times* explained events this way:

> A quarrel has ensued between His Highness's Government and the Consulate of the United States. It appears that an American subject, a Mr. KINDINECO, in erecting a steam engine (which, according to a Government regulation, he has no right to do without the permission of the authorities,) has partly destroyed an aqueduct by which a portion of the town is supplied with water. The Consul of the United States [presumably Dainese], on being applied to by the authorities, stopped the works, but subsequently allowed them to be proceeded with. The consequence of this was, that the Government sent a party of Cawasses to the spot, who forcibly ejected the workmen. The United States Consul hereupon demanded satisfaction for the insult thus offered to the banner of the Stars and Stripes. He refused to accede to a proposal on the part of the Egyptian Government, that each party should send an engineer to inspect the alleged damage, agreeing to abide by their joint decision, and threatened to strike his colors unless satisfaction were given by the Egyptian Government within twenty-four hours. Accordingly, after that time had elapsed, the colors

of the United States were hauled down, and a dispatch, which arrived almost immediately afterward, from Cherif Pasha, was returned unopened. The United States
Consul is said to have telegraphed to Constantinople, and there the matter now
rests.[39]

Striking the flag was a very serious matter. In fact, it broke diplomatic relations between the
two countries involved and should not have been done in haste. When Charles Hale arrived
(August 17, 1864), he reversed Dainese's actions and refused protégé status to Kindineco and
Santi, another American involved.[40] Hale abandoned Kindineco and he was deported.

When the Egyptian police arrested Kindineco they also arrested Mr. Santi, an American
who supported Kindineco's claims. Santi was the editor of the newspaper *Il Popolo*, published
at Alexandria, and had gone to Egypt from New York in 1864. *Il Popolo* was a political weekly
that had created a niche by looking for and writing about corruption in Egypt at all levels.[41]
Dainese wrote that Santi, "the editor of the only American journal in Egypt, [had] displeased
Mr. Hale by his free expositions of liberal ideas, and by denouncing his conduct with reference
to the flag."[42] Dainese is referring to the fact that Santi depicted Hale as raising the American
flag cantilevered by a pot of gold, which presumably he pocketed. This was not only in reference
to Hale's (and Wilkinson's) having received a bribe in 1861 for not protecting Kindineco, but
to the likelihood that he had done it again. Dainese translated Santi's offensive article in *Il
Popolo*:

> The independent banner of the U.S. of America, which spreads abroad its stars as
> symbols of splendor and beauty, now waves draped with crape and bound with a
> chain of iron, a standing proof of the ignominy inflicted on America by its new rep-
> resentative! C. Hale, who passed the seas as the supposed champion of liberty, but
> who is, nevertheless, the upholder of despotism, has sold himself as an agent to carry
> out the despotic will of others. At the very moment when the honor of the American
> flag should have been preserved, and when Mr. Dainese was vindicating the honor of
> America, offended by the local government, the narrow mind of C. Hale intermed-
> dles and indecently disturbs the question, encroaches on the rights of third parties,
> and casts a slur on the free and noble nation of which he is the accredited representa-
> tive, reducing his country in public opinions, to the position of a weak and degraded
> power, *the least amongst the least...!* We hope, then, soon to see a speedy termination
> of all such abominations, and that Mr. Hale, dismissed from his public charge, may
> be sent to seek, within the walls of some temple, an inspiration to better actions from
> the sacred principles of the Bible.
>
> He would, at least, be more in place there than here.[43]

Dainese could do nothing to aid Kindineco or Santi. They left Egypt.

If that were all, the matter might have ended there. But the two men had various interests
in Egypt and associates in America whose losses needed to be addressed. Hale's judgment
related to these matters is questionable. Relations between Hale and Dainese rapidly deteri-
orated. Dainese continued his attack on Hale:

> Mr. Hale reached Alexandria the 17th of August, 1864. On his arrival your memo-
> rialist [Dainese] received him in his house as a guest, informed him of the state of
> affairs and of his course, *which he promised to sustain,* notified his colleagues of the
> new consul's arrival, made over to him the consular property, and withdrew from
> further connection with the office. A few days thereafter, and after a dozen of secret
> interviews between said Hale and a Jew banker a confidential agent of the Viceroy in
> pecuniary affairs, he changed tactics and again hoisted the consular flag *unavenged,*
> without any satisfaction for the violation of domicil and insult to the consular
> authority or the settlement of the pending American claims, through well founded
> public opinion accused him of having received in exchange from His Highness the

Viceroy a present of twenty thousand pounds sterling, for which he was denounced in every public place in Egypt and through the newspapers and was caricatured as *pulling up with one hand* the American flag by the weight of a bag of coin in his other hand![44]

Twice now, people believed that Charles Hale took bribes from the Egyptian government. Dainese felt that Hale's actions both in 1861–2 and 1864 were so well known and condemned in the American community that the American government was losing respect: "The outcry against him is general, and many of our 'protégés' have already abandoned American protection as worthless. His confidential man and go-between (a Greek, whom Mr. Thayer would not even admit into his presence) went round to collect signatures in his master's favor, but unluckily for the success of the scheme, not one of the reputable men in Alexandria would allow his name to be used for such a purpose; such facts are anything but credible to our great country...."[45] Further, Hale refused to help the American protégés to regain their various properties. He also took and sealed Dainese's property.

> Mr. Hale unceremoniously possessed himself of your memorialist's [Dainese] house with its contents, intercepted and opened his letters, broke open and plundered two locked rooms, and seized the money, books, effects, and private papers therein, among which was part of your memorialist's correspondence wherein his conduct was exposed ... and he did this while your memorialist was ill, crippled by rheumatism, and totally incapacitated of the use of arm and limb.
>
> Your memorialist thereupon quitted Egypt for the mineral baths to seek a relief from his disease, and thence proceeded home. In quitting Egypt he left in charge of his friends a large amount of American machinery, agricultural implements &c., &c., which he was introducing there and also many notes and claims for collection.... Mr. Hale, encouraged by the impunity which his misdeeds had met in the hands of Mr. Seward, by another stretch of consular power and the usurpation of jurisdiction, attacked and seized, and thereby prevented the sale of your memorialist's property, worth over $60,000, which he locked up so as to cause its destruction by dampness and rust, and prevented, also, the collection of over $40,000 due him and in other words, totally ruined his business in Egypt.... To give coloring to these high-handed acts, Mr. Hale alleged as excuse that he made that seizure with a view to protect a small claim of about £1,000, made up for the occasion by his New York friends, Messrs. R.H. Allen & C., for whom he was acting as agent and attorney.[46]

Thomas Kindineco verified much of what Dainese claimed. In a letter to Abraham Lincoln he wrote: "This was secretly arranged with Mr. Charles Hale, our Consul General for a large bribe, and was carried out without previous notice to me. I am at the same time, informed that simultaneously to the issue of that circular, the Egyptian Government took possession of my property, demolished one hundred and seventy shops belonging to me, and it otherwise persecuted my family and my interests in Egypt.... "[47] Sadly, Lincoln was assassinated. So Mr. Kindineco wrote another letter, this time to President Andrew Johnson. To further cement Kindineco's claim, a letter signed by seven New York manufacturers was sent to a senator and a representative of New York recounting their losses in the Kindineco Affair. The signatories were: Wm. D. Andrews and Brothers, pump and engine manufacturers; Bayley and Hill, rotary pump and fire engine manufacturers; Franklin H. Lummus and Co., cotton gins; Charles A. Buckley, cotton gins; E.H. Reeves and Co., agricultural implements; Horace L. Emery and Son, agricultural works; and Wheeler Melick and Co., agricultural implements.[48] All had lost property sent by them to Egypt because of the Dainese-Hale feud.

Dainese pursued his own claim vigorously and it went to the Supreme Court of the United States twice. In 1872, Charles Hale was asked to pay Francis Dainese. The *Chicago*

Tribune on May 6 of that year put the following paragraph in their personal section: "The Hon. Charles Hale, Assistant Secretary of State, at Washington was last Wednesday served with papers calling for $125,000, at the suit of one Francis Dainese, who alleged trespass by Mr. Hale when Consul General in Egypt. Mr. Hale did not happen to have the money at hand."[49] Nor did he accept the court's decision. The matter was appealed to the Supreme Court. The final decision was rendered in the October Term of 1875, eleven years after the incidents took place.

"The judgment of the Supreme Court of the District of Columbia must be reversed, and the cause remanded with directions to allow the defendant to amend his plea on payment of costs."[50]

To Conclude

It is hard to assess Charles Hale. His entire consularship in Egypt was overshadowed by the Dainese Affair. Yet, the rest of his work seems to have been not only efficient, but on a par with the best of American representatives. There appears to have been a great deal of family power expended in eliminating records that could call his honor into question.

10

Charles Chaillé-Long: The Man Who Fought an Empire (Soldier, 1869–1882)

Charles Chaillé-Long was an extraordinary American. He was a soldier, an explorer, a diplomat, and a writer. As a soldier he served his country in the Union Army during the American Civil War and the Egyptian army during the heyday of the Khedival era. As an explorer he expanded the Egyptian empire along the Nile and found the final link in the search to discover the river's source. His diplomatic career began in Egypt when he was asked to serve as interim consul general during the Bombardment of Alexandria in 1882 and continued when he was appointed consul general in Korea in 1887. As a scholar Chaillé-Long wrote a number of books, contributed dozens of articles in magazines, and sent hundreds of letters to newspapers, historical associations, and other organizations in America, France, and England.

On a more personal level, Chaillé-Long was a Southern dandy, a man who enjoyed fine and ostentatious clothes and wore them with flair. He took great pleasure in wearing the elaborate Egyptian uniforms with their gold embroidery and ornate medals. "[He] once won praise from the khedive [Ismail] for his traveling costume: a silk top hat, a black cape with crimson lining and patent leather shoes."[1] When General Gordon was hosting his first banquet in Khartoum to thank the local dignitaries for their reception, he intended to use daily military dinnerware: tin cups, tin plates and no tablecloths. Chaillé-Long went looking in the storerooms and found fine china left behind by Sir Samuel Baker: "Sèvres porcelain, fine knives and forks, damask table-linen, Bohemian glassware, and wines of the best *crues* of Médoc, Burgundy and Champagne."[2] Even the wilderness of Africa did not halt Chaillé-Long's sense of protocol and love of finery. In Uganda, after marching for over fifty days through jungle and savannah in the African rainy season, he greeted King M'tesa (Mutesa) in a uniform "similar to that worn by the officers of *Les Chasseurs d'Afrique*, in France."[3] The young American colonel understood the importance of standards and of maintaining or exceeding them at every opportunity.

His manners were only eclipsed by his arrogance. One of his biographers reported he was "ambitious and jealous of fame,"[4] which manifested itself against many famous men, including General Charles Gordon in Khartoum and Anglo-American Henry M. Stanley.

Born on July 2, 1842, on a small plantation in Princess Anne, Maryland, to a family which could trace its Huguenot roots in America back to 1645, perhaps Chaillé-Long had good reason for his arrogance. The Chaillé men helped forge the nation: great-grandfather Pierre Chaillé was a member of the Maryland Convention of 1775, served in the Continental Army during the Revolutionary War, and signed the United States Constitution in Philadelphia in 1788. Grandfathers Moses Chaillé and Solomon Long (hence the hyphenated name Chaillé-Long) were also officers in the Continental Army. Charles received his education in classical studies at Washington Academy, where he graduated in 1860. Then he continued the family tradition of service in the military. In 1861 he became a member of Company A of the Maryland State National Guard. In 1862 he joined the First Regiment of the Eastern Shore Maryland Infantry. That took him to the Civil War, where he served as captain of Company G of the 11th Maryland infantry. Along with the remainder of his regiment he was mustered out on June 15, 1865.[5]

In his lifetime he was honored by France, Egypt, and America. The French presented him with the Croix de Chevalier de la Légion d'Honneur, given in honor of excellence in civil or military conduct. The Egyptians honored him twice, with the Commander Order of the Cross Medjidieh for his work in Central Africa and with the Grand Cross Order of the Osmanieh for his assistance during the Bombardment of 1882. The United States State Department honored him twice too. He received a letter of appreciation in 1882 for his service in Egypt during the Bombardment of Alexandria, and another for his service as consul general to Korea in 1888. The American Geographical Society of New York presented him with the Charles P. Daly Gold Medal for his contributions to the field of geography. Finally, in 1904, his home state conferred an award upon him for his lifetime achievements.

Charles Chaillé-Long died March 24, 1917, at the age of 75 and is buried in Arlington National Cemetery with his Civil War unit.

Despite all this glory and the enormous efforts Chaillé-Long himself made to preserve his memory and his place in history, today he is a forgotten man. While America pays homage to many men — heroes and explorers such as Lewis and Clark, who sailed the Mississippi Watershed looking for the Northwest Passage; and a few women, including Clara Barton, who nursed soldiers during the Civil War — it often ignores American men and women whose achievements were on foreign soil. There is no glory for George Bethune English of the Sudan, or William Eaton of Tripoli. As Edwin Swift Balch of the American Geographical Society of New York wrote in his 1918 essay "American Explorers of Africa":

Charles Chaillé-Long in 1875.

Americans are different from Englishmen in regard to their great travelers. The British always make the most of their great travelers. They give them full credit for what they have accomplished, they keep on their charts all English names and all names given by English discoverers, and in so doing sometimes they eliminate the names given by earlier explorers of other nationalities. We Americans, on the contrary, do not stand up enough for our great travelers.... Chaillé-Long deserves a high place among world explorers. As yet he has not received the credit due him, and this is partly because he was an American. His labors cleared up a large part of the Nile mystery and entitle him to rank as one of the four discoverers of the sources of that river. His explorations were made while he was in the service of the Egyptian Government, and it was on this account that, when he discovered a third and a totally unsuspected great Nile lake, the Khedive Ismail named it Lake Ibrahim, after his soldier father, Ibrahim Pasha. But when the British declared a protectorate over Egypt, they were not especially desirous that the Egyptian control of Uganda and other provinces of the White Nile region should be remembered, and possibly for that reason, although they were careful to retain the names Victoria, Albert, and Albert Edward for the other three great Nilotic lakes, they changed the name of Lake Ibrahim to Lake Kioga.[6]

America's position among the European nations is another reason true American heroes are forgotten. A fledgling country with a non-intervention foreign policy (see Chapter 6 for details) lacked power in the world and tried to keep Americans focused on domestic issues. The British dominance of the nineteenth century made their view of history not only worldwide but also the popular and accepted view. Today, with revision very much in place, another look at past events may change history as we know it. In America's case, old heroes are receiving a new look and Chaillé-Long may re-emerge as one of the most important.

Welcome to Egypt

Charles Chaillé-Long arrived in Alexandria in 1869, amid the great building explosion that was taking place in Egypt. He was one of approximately fifty Americans employed by the Egyptians (see Chapter 11 for details). The Khedive Ismail was keen to continue to build an African and Middle Eastern empire. He originally expected to use the Americans for that goal, but the French and British strongly objected to the Americans and made Ismail's dreams of empire very difficult. Until Ismail could find a secret way, the Americans were given little to do. Chaillé-Long was appointed a lieutenant-colonel and was expected to teach French at the military school. Within a year he became chief of staff of the Egyptian Army in Alexandria, and by 1873 he was chief of staff to General of the Army Charles Pomeroy Stone with offices at the Citadel in Cairo. While in Cairo, Chaillé-Long embraced the social scene. He went to the newly erected Théâtre National de Comédie in Cairo, which featured French entertainers direct from Paris. He also attended the newly built Cairo Opera House and probably was there when the first performance of *Aida* was held (surely wearing his red-lined cape and top hat).[7] He may have been accompanied by Auguste Mariette, the Egyptologist and head of the Egyptian Museum at Bulaq, who had become a good friend. In fact, Mariette appointed Chaillé-Long as his first assistant.[8] Surely he visited the Samuel Remington mansion, also newly built along the route to the pyramids. Not only was it a showroom for E. Remington and Company's rifles, which were outfitting the Egyptian Army, but it was a major part of the social network of Cairo.

Chaillé-Long lived in the Ezybekkiah district of Cairo, where so many changes were taking place. The Opera House was there. The famous Shepheard's Hotel and its fantastic front veranda, where foreigners sat to be seen and to see, commanded the new square, while around the corner stood the *Hotel des Ambassadeurs* that many of the American visitors preferred. In the evenings, the well-dressed Chaillé-Long could prance his horse or sit back in a carriage along what had become "a Champ-de-Mars for the Europeans." The gardens of the Ezybekkiah had been created by French landscape gardener Gustave Delchevalerie, and contained fountains, a lake, and several grottoes set amid European-style cafés, "an alfresco theatre, and capital military bands.... Visitors could sample the Greek and German brasseries and musical cafes, in which mixed Bohemian bands and native performers played on the *kanoon*, 'ud and *kemnejeh*."[9] It suited the Marylander and expressed the changes taking place throughout the city. The streets were paved for the first time, had sidewalks for pedestrians, and were illuminated with gaslights. Cairo truly was the "Paris of the East."

With Gordon in Khartoum

Chaillé-Long's first significant military assignment came in 1874, when he was appointed second in command to Charles George Gordon in Khartoum, Sudan. Gordon, known to the British first as "Chinese" Gordon and, after his martyrdom, as "Gordon of Khartoum," sent him a message on February 19, 1874, that simply stated: "My dear Chaillé-Long: Will you come with me to Central Africa? Come and see me at once. Very truly, C.G. Gordon." Within days Chaillé-Long was on his way to Sudan and an amazing series of exploratory expeditions. Gordon's mission was under the auspices of the Khedive, who saw to it that several of his Americans were on the staff. Gordon reported to and sent dispatches back to Cairo to Charles Pomeroy Stone, the American at the head of the Egyptian army.

While Gordon, as governor-general of Sudan, began to organize the provinces, he reported to Stone that he had been visited by an embassy of King Mutesa of Uganda.[10] The king was seeking friendship with Egypt. Gordon assigned Chaillé-Long to visit the King in Uganda. That was the beginning of Chaillé-Long's adventure. Chaillé-Long maintained that his journey to Mutesa's kingdom was a special assignment from the Khedive Ismail. What better opportunity could Ismail find to expand his kingdom than by putting an American inside the British camp in Central Africa? If Mutesa joined Egypt, Egypt's authority in Africa would spread along the entire length of the Nile, cementing the African portion of the great empire of Mohammad Ali's dream. This was not something England and France wanted. But that is exactly what Chaillé-Long accomplished, and more. In fact, in his book *My Life in Four Continents*, Colonel Long described his mission as given to him by the Khedive:

> You have been chosen as his [Gordon's] Chief-of-Staff for many reasons. Chief of these is to guard the interests of the Egyptian Government. An expedition is being organized in London, under the command of a pseudo–American, named Stanley, ostensibly to succor Dr. Livingstone, but in reality to plant the British flag in Uganda. Go to Gondokoro, but lose no time in making your way to Uganda, anticipate the London expedition, make a treaty with the King of Uganda, and Egypt will owe you a debt of everlasting gratitude. Go and success will attend you, *Inshallah!*[11]

Pierre Crabites, an American member of the Mixed Courts of Egypt (1911–36) who had access to the Egyptian archives at Abdin Palace and used them frequently as sources in his book *Americans in the Egyptian Army*, did not find a record of Ismail's message to Colonel Long.[12] In fact, this is a much-criticized statement by Chaillé-Long and undermines his credibility.

In an article in *The North American Review* in 1899, Chaillé-Long presented his point of view:

> In 1875, the British Foreign Office, in accord with an English and American journalistic enterprise, sent an expedition to the African lakes, ostensibly in the interest of

discovery, but in reality to hoist the British flag in Uganda. [This was Henry Stanley's Expedition.]

Ismail Khedive forestalled that purpose by appointing, in 1874, an American officer, then in his service, Chief of Staff to Gordon, with instructions to proceed to Uganda in haste, and after executing a treaty with King M'Tesa, occupy the Nile with Egyptian military posts. This mission was promptly accomplished, and when, in April, 1875, the British expedition arrived at the capital of Uganda, bearing both a British and an American flag, it was confronted by the fact of an Egyptian occupation. Gordon's Chief of Staff had arrived nine months before, and returning to Gondokoro, had taken with him the coveted treaty by which M'Tesa recognized Uganda and the Nile basin as Egyptian territory.

Great Britain neither forgot nor forgave this unexpected check to its ambition, which aimed even in 1875, to take possession of Uganda and the head-waters of the Nile.[13]

According to Chaillé-Long, clever Ismail foiled the British and the British would get their revenge. Within a few years Ismail was deposed and banished from Egypt and his Americans were expelled from the country. Within a decade England changed its protectorate over Egypt to an occupation, set the Egyptian border at Aswan, cut Egyptian authority over Central Africa, and established authority over the entire length of the Nile.[14]

Thus the journey Chaillé-Long took to the Ugandan King Mutesa is at the heart of his fame and his frustration. He fought to acknowledge his claims for the rest of his life: one man against an empire. It is discussed in many books by various authors, but Chaillé-Long tells it at least three times: in *Central Africa: Naked Truths of Naked People, An Account of Expeditions to the Lake Victoria Nyanza and Makraka Niam-Niam, West of the Bahr el Ab'ad*; much later in his autobiography *My Life in Four Continents*; and officially in a report submitted to generals Gordon and Stone: *Expedition from Gondokoro to Lake Victoria and discovery of Lake Ibrahim* in *Provinces of the Equator*.[15] The book *Central Africa*, at 330 pages, is an embellishment of the report, which runs 44 pages. The report was issued in 1874, while the book was published in 1876 after some of the criticism and doubt were voiced.[16] The journey began April 21, 1874, when Chaillé-Long left Gondokoro, and ended October 16, 1874, when he was greeted by Gordon upon his return to Gondokoro.

He began the journal on April 24. It would take fifty-eight days to reach Mutesa's village. It was not an easy journey. The expedition did not halt to rest until May 6, when they reached Fatiko station, once a slaver's haven. When the American arrived it was garrisoned by the Anglo-Egyptian forces. Chaillé-Long had a fever and the expedition rested at Fatiko until May 11. Conditions did not improve, nor did Chaillé-Long: "May 13 — We marched at seven o'clock A.M. The country here is wild, uncultivated and uninhabited, save by elephants, deer and buffaloes. The ground is marshy and difficult to traverse. My horse slipped and plunged in elephant holes at almost every step. There was a fearful rain falling throughout the night."[17] By May 17 they reach the Nile. It was filled with "jungle-grass and papyrus." His horse pitifully leaped from one spot to another and was terrified. When they reached the river, boats sent by Mutesa were waiting for them. The horse was finally put into a canoe, a most horrifying experience for both man and beast. Chaillé-Long described the river at this point as 100 yards wide, deep, flowing westerly, and filled with hippopotami and crocodiles.[18]

By the end of May the drinking water was so bad they were all sick. The natives were sullen. The rain was so brutal they could march only a few hours a day. Chaillé-Long's gums and lips were bleeding. All they had to eat was durra and bananas. Indian corn was looked on as a luxury but occasionally a little was found. Their water was taken from the hoof prints of elephants. Then, on June 9, "three goats, three sheep, three dogs, and three women," were brought into the camp. On June 11 an envoy from Mutesa arrived with cows, potatoes, bananas, banners, and music.[19] They remained at this camp until the 18th. On the 20th the expedition, which had grown to 4,000 people, formed a column and began to march toward Mutesa's village, which was located near modern-day Kampala. Both the Ugandan and the Egyptian flags flew at the head of the column while horns and drums marked its approach. It made quite a sight. M'Tse's bodyguards,

> ... armed with lances, formed in solid column of forty to fifty front, the roads here permitting this formation; whilst on each side skirmishers dressed in a fantastic uniform, with fez of flannel ornamented with black feathers, performed the most remarkable evolutions, whilst firing the uncertain firelocks with which they were armed, with reckless disregard of aim. These were the body-guards of M'Tse,' and had this curious privilege. On each side of the column marched a numerous body of men, wholly dressed in plantain leaves curiously arranged around the body, who with grimace and wild gesticulation kept time in dance and shouts to the accompanying music. A curious throng of young girls peered out with startled gaze from the great banana forests through which the cortége passed; or fled with gazelle fleetness at the sight of man and horse! It was a proud day for Said, Abd-el-Rahman, and Selim, as they marched in front of me, dressed in their gay uniform kept for the occasion. "Ugunda," too, seemed proud of the distinction of being the first horse that had ever visited Central Africa.... I stood facing an elevation not 500 yards away, the palace of M'Tse, King of Ugunda! I forgot for the moment the physical pain to which I was a victim, in the strange coup-d'oeil that presented itself to my view.... On every hillside thousands of people were gathered: whilst directly in front of me, at the outer gate of the palace, stood M'Tse himself, surrounded by a great throng of men and women....
>
> ... in the immediate vicinity of my person the natives had prostrated themselves; whilst still mounted I surveyed the novel scene. Soon with lightning speed several messengers (Marsalah) came running towards me, and throwing themselves at my feet, conveyed to me the welcome of their king. Selim thanked them in my name, and they hastened back. These men merit description here. Chosen for their ferocious appearance, there is the wild glare of brutality in their gleaming eyes, and a long black beard proclaimed them of other origin than the Ugundi, undoubtedly Malay. Their dress consists of a pantaloon of red and black flannel, bordered with black: a tunic of red flannel with black stripes, dolman-like across the breast, from which hangs a fringe of a peculiar monkey skin; a red cloth turban, around which is wound in tasteful coils a finely plaited rope-cord, badge and instrument of their deadly office: for they are the *bourreaux* at the court, executioners of M'Tse's undisputed will! M'Tse' sends his messengers to ask that I will approach, that he may see the animal on which I am mounted. Only for a moment I felt a sense of repulsion to all this show; but I was no longer free to risk what had cost me so much suffering, the sympathy and confidence of the king. Gathering the reins in my hand, I drove my spurs into the flanks of Ugunda, and sped down the hill with fearful speed, amid the yells of delight of the assembled throng. An instant the horse slipped and stumbled in a depression of the uneven road; quickly recovering however, I rode towards M'Tsé and his hareem, who broke in flight with cries and screams of fright...![20]

Colonel Long was then led to his hut. It had been fifty-eight days since he and his men had departed from Gondokoro. Despite the noise and the hum of the mosquitoes, he fell into his hammock and slept.

The next morning there was a great reception. Chaillé-Long announced the purpose of his mission: to wish the king friendship and health. It was greeted with great rejoicing. Then something happened which would fuel attacks from Chaillé-Long's critics: the king ordered the slaughter of thirty people in honor of the envoy from Egypt. Here is how Chaillé-Long reported the event to Stone: "Last scene of all that ends this strange eventful history and interview is blood. Thirty of his subjects were seized, quickly bound with cords and, a few paces distance, crowned with dissevered heads the honor of the white man's visit to M'tesa! I asked the question if these were criminals that awaited such an event to expiate their crimes; the reply was 'No.' Thus, M'tesa, though more intelligent and more open to conviction, has yet this strange and bloody instinct common to African kings."[21] It would happen again when Chaillé-Long received permission from the king to travel on Lake Victoria. Chaillé-Long explained his thoughts and concerns about the slaughters a few years later in *Central Africa*:

> M'Tse suddenly rose from his seat; a slight but significant contraction of the eye had caused the disappearance of the "marsalah," who quick to do their master's will, snatched from their turbans the plaited cord, and seizing their unresisting victims, to the number of thirty, amid howls and fearful yells, crowned in blood the signal honor of the white man's visit to M'Tse. It required no common effort for me to repress my feelings at this moment, or to assume the careless air that concealed what was going on within: for all eyes were watching me intently, and a sign of feeling would, if nothing more serious, have subjected me to ridicule and loss of prestige. Singular contradictory combination in the negro, that cowardly himself, he most admires coolness in others.
>
> To protest would have been as useless on my part as impolitic. This was a custom common to all African potentates; a prerogative that went with the claim to African greatness. A protest from me would perhaps have consigned me to a like fate: and though impracticable philanthropists would have advised my throwing myself into the "bloody chasm," I confess to a certain selfish congratulation, that neither myself nor my soldiers had been included in the sacrifice....
>
> I cite these facts in the interest of truth alone, yielding to none in the desire to ameliorate the condition of the African. But in heaven's name, let those whose province it is to be the pioneers in the work, speak of him as he is, without regard to those who attribute to him virtues and ideas, that, if possessed, would render him no longer a subject for our commiseration and sympathy.[22]

The most important point in this mission was suzerainty, from the King of Uganda to the Khedive of Egypt. As noted above, it had to be accomplished on this mission or Egypt would miss the chance. Chaillé-Long saw to that too:

> M'tesa, at my request, called Ide to him and addressed a letter to the Khedive in which he acknowledged himself a *Vassal of Egypt*, asking at the same time protection and the means and aid necessary for constructing the houses and palace, with sketches of which I had acted on his imagination.
>
> He wished that priests might be sent to him, and lastly, begged for horses and carriages.[23] Col. Gordon subsequently sent to him the *flki* (priests). The carriage was sent from Cairo by H.H. the Khedive on receipt of the letter from M'tesa which I forwarded from Khartoum in November 1874.[24]

According to Chaillé-Long, "The treaty, dated July 19, 1874, was officially announced by the Egyptian Ministry to all the Powers, England included. It proclaimed the annexation of Uganda to Egypt, and its execution was realized without delay by sending, as Egyptian Minister Resident at the court of M'tesa: M. Ernest Linant de Bellefonds, son of the celebrated French engineer. He had resided for several months at M'tesa's capital, Rubaga, when the English expedition under Stanley arrived there (April 15, 1875)."[25]

Ismail had trumped the British Empire. The man who was being portrayed as a poor ruler was seen by the Americans as a formidable foe.

The Source of the Nile

Having completed his mission, Chaillé-Long asked permission to return to Gondokoro via Lake Victoria and the Nile. Mutesa granted only half of the request: the lake. After several bouts of illness and one more sacrifice of human beings to celebrate the trip to Lake Victoria, the expedition was on its way. It was this portion of the journey that was to prove the most significant, for despite Mutesa's not granting permission, Chaillé-Long did return to Gondokoro via the Nile.

The quest for the source of the Nile is one of the most famous adventures in the Age of Discovery and has been told and retold in every medium imaginable. Every European country with designs on the "dark continent" sought this elusive treasure. From the days of the ancient Romans through the Greeks, the Arabs, and the dynasty of Mohammad Ali, the source of the Nile remained a mystery to outsiders. Claudius Ptolemy, who lived in Alexandria in the first century during the Roman occupation of Egypt, created a map that had the Nile exiting from two lakes beyond which were the "Mountains of the Moon" (Ruwenzori Mountains).[26] Ptolemy was not wrong. Two Roman centurions went in quest of the source during the age of Nero but could not penetrate the Sudd, a swamp in what is now southern Sudan. Mohammad Ali sent his first expedition in 1820 (see Chapter 5), and another expedition which reached Juba in 1839. With funding from the Royal Geographical Society, Englishman Richard Burton, accompanied by John Hanning Speke, approached the Nile from Zanzibar looking for the great lakes in 1856. They are considered to be the first Europeans to see Lake Tanganyika, which they did in 1858, except Speke was too blinded by ophthalmia (similar to trachoma) to see it. Later Burton lay ill and Speke, now able to see, continued on to find the lake and name it *Victoria* after the Queen of England. Speke and Colonel J.A. Grant mounted a third expedition in 1860. They traveled along the edges of Lake Victoria and in July of 1862 discovered and named Ripon Falls. In 1863 the pair met Samuel Baker and his wife Florence at Gondokoro. The Bakers continued to travel in the area for two more years and found and named Lake Albert in honor of Queen Victoria's husband. At this point most literature continues the quest for the source of the Nile with Henry Stanley, who in 1874–75 went to Lake Victoria and Lake Tanganyika, which he circumnavigated. Stanley, who would begin his journeys as an American and end them as an Englishman, never credited Chaillé-Long with his contribution to the discovery of the source of the Nile.[27]

Book after book, newspaper after newspaper, and even modern Internet sites, American or foreign, omit Chaillé-Long from this illustrious group of explorers. A modern Princeton University map exhibit website wrote: "Not until the 1860s explorations of Burton, Speke, Baker, and Grant—further confirmed by Stanley in the 1870s—was the puzzle of the lakes resolved.... Alan Moorehead mentions Chaillé-Long in his book *The White Nile*, not as an explorer but as part of the "exploitation" (his word) of the Sudan carried out by Gordon and the British.[28] On line, Wikipedia, Answer.com, newworldencyclopedia, and a host more do not list Chaillé-Long at all.[29] As will be seen below, he certainly did contribute to the souce of the Nile. To this day Chaillé-Long's battle continues.

On July 14, 1874, Charles Chaillé-Long left the small comforts of King Mutesa's court and began his journey to Lake Victoria. The boats consisted of "thick bark, sewed together with rope made of banana-tree ... thirty to forty feet in length ... propelled by thirty or even forty rowers, two by two ... to say nothing of the drummers and musicians, making 1200 men that had been detailed to escort me."[30]

At this point Chaillé-Long made an observation that would haunt him forever. He claimed to see the far shore of Lake Victoria:

We embarked and started, the boats racing, and during the entire day we were
pushed about upon the lake. The water of the lake is extremely light and sweet, and I
drank to repletion of the delicious beverage. It is clear and transparent. The depths I
found were from forty to fifty feet. There was no perceptible tide, and I saw no
shells....

I discerned what I presumed to be land — the opposite shore. An unnautical and
unpracticed eye may have deceived me, but I judge it to be fifteen miles wide. Can it
be double that distance? Certainly I saw something that I think is land. Should this
be so, then the lake has not the width ascribed to it by Speke, and I recollect that
Grant says: "Sadi could descry nothing of land in a westerly direction except the very
faint outline of the summit of a mountain, far, far away on the horizon" [*].[31]

The asterisk denotes, "Col. Long in his published notes of travel says: 'The subsequent exploration of Stanley, in April 1875, ten months later, has proved that the land that gave me the
impression of a coast-line, was in fact a chaine of islands of which the lake is full.'"[32] We now
know this chain as the Sese Archipelago.

After visiting Lake Victoria, Chaillé-Long and his men returned to Mutesa and made
plans for their final departure. The journey home would be along the banks of the Nile. On
August 6, 1874, they came to the headquarters of the admiral of the river fleet. On the 7th
the party took to the Nile in four boats, with Colonel Long's long-suffering horse moving
along the bank with the native escort. All was not satisfactory, as Chaillé-Long had acquired
a few enemies among the natives. One named M'tongoli, had placed two natives with smallpox
in his boat. He threw them out of the boat. No sooner were they disembarked than "a large
black dug-out canoe, was seen approaching, heavily laden with men," and they put ashore.
He was told they "had now reached neutral ground (the place from which Speke had been
driven)," and that the approaching boat belonged to Keba Rega who was watching the river.
Chaillé-Long agreed to wait for permission to continue. They started out again on August 9
and found the river "300 yards wide and thirty to forty feet deep."[33] On August 11 they entered
a lake. In the official report to Stone Pasha, Chaillé-Long wrote:

We pushed off at four A.M. At noon, having on my right a high mountain called
by the natives M'tinge, I found myself in a lake, apparently about from twenty to
twenty-five miles wide. There was no land near us. We tried to follow a track which
was evidently frequented by the canoes of the savages. We followed it bordered and
shaded by high reeds for miles, looking in vain, for a chance to land. Finally, we discovered some savages on a floating island formed of aquatic plants. On this floating
island there was a hut built of canes. These savages are fishermen, whose sole food is
small dried fishes. Here we took out our only sheep, and after many difficulties,
standing upon the yielding surface knee deep in water, and having from twenty to
thirty feet of water below us, we made a fire and cooked our mutton.... I hastend our
departure and gained the open water of the lake where, as I had no compass, we were
at the mercy of the wind which drove us first to one side and then to another, while
rain, accompanied by thunder and lightning, continued all night, and we were
obliged to take turns in bailing out our leaking boats.[34]

That night they camped on top of a papyrus jungle in the middle of the lake and slaughtered
and ate a sheep. The next day, August 12, they paddled from 5 A.M. to midnight until they
found a landing to rest.

They continued their journey on the 13th amid yet another storm. They were still on the
lake, and try as they might, they could not find the river. Chaillé-Long believed the wind had
blown them away from its mouth. Sighting no land at all, the men were disheartened as it
continued to rain. The fragile boats were beginning to fall apart and they had to bail constantly.

Then, "at three o'clock in the morning of the fourteenth, the clouds cleared a little, I caught sight of the polar star, scarcely perceptible, and guided by that, I roused Said and Abdul and we worked at the paddles until sunrise, when we found a clear space which I thought to be the course of the river from the fact that there seemed to be a little current."[35]

Chaillé-Long had done it. He had found not only the unexplored portion of the Nile, but a lake as well. The first lake the expedition entered was Lake Victoria. As did Speke, Chaillé-Long found the mouth of the Nile and entered it. Speke was forced to stop his journey, but Colonel Long's expedition continued and discovered yet another lake (which Ismail named Ibrahim). Then he found the mouth of the Nile again and exited that lake to continue along the Nile and into Lake Albert: what Speke had guessed to be true, Chaillé-Long confirmed.

The Issues

There seem to be two major issues concerning the truth of Chaillé-Long's journey. The first was the failure to allow an explorer the right to name his discovery. The second was the failure to recognize Colonel Long's contribution to the discovery of the source of the Nile: the river flowing out of Lake Victoria was the same river which flowed into Lake Albert.

The right of an explorer to name his discovery is almost sacrosanct. Unfortunately, in the case of Lake Ibrahim, this right seems to have been ignored and various maps of the day ascribe different names. The Great Map of Africa that was created in 1877 by General Stone's staff, of course, called it Lake Ibrahim. A German map of the day credited Colonel Long by calling it Longs See. But the British, who had allowed Speke and Baker to call their discoveries Lake Victoria and Lake Albert, dismissed the name Lake Ibrahim and named it Lake Kyoga, maintaining that native names should be kept.

The first to criticize Chaillé-Long's achievement was the controversial Laurence Oliphant, a friend of John Speke. In an article in the *North American Review* in 1877, he denounced Colonel Long's "discovery" as insignificant:

> This portion was descended by Colonel Long, the year before last, who in conse-quence of this very moderate achievement also, like Mr. Stanley, puts in his claim to be a discoverer of a Nile source. He found that the Nile widened at one spot to a reedy lake about twenty-five miles long by ten or fifteen broad, to which he gave the name of Lake Ibrahim Pasha; therefore, in a work which he has recently published he exclaims: "The question of the Nile source is now no longer one of *Caput Nili quarere;* the problem of remote ages had been finally solved...."
>
> Colonel Long distinguished himself so very much by his courage in an encounter with the natives on this lake, that it is a pity he did not rest rather on his laurels as a soldier than as a solver of "Nile mysteries" which had ceased to exist.[36]

Oliphant continued for some time claiming that after Speke's and Grant's explorations there were no further mysteries to be solved. He was not the last critic of Chaillé-Long's achieve-ments. Sir Harry Johnston in *The Nile Quest* and again in *The Uganda Protectorate*, among other criticisms, maintained, "Chaillé-Long's one practical contribution to Nile exploration was the definite discovery of Lake Kioga, which had only been hesitatingly reported by the unlearned Piaggia,"[37] and that Gordon "sent two or more of his cosmopolitan white assis-tants — Belgians and Americans — to spy out the land in Uganda."[38] Johnston's attack on Col-onel Long is riddled with his own errors, and in a letter to the Paris Geographical Society, repeated in the *Bulletin of the American Geographical Society*, Chaillé-Long made a strong defense.

As late as 1909 Colonel Chaillé-Long felt it necessary to once again attempt to lay claim to his discovery. In an extensive letter to the American Geographical Society he listed his accomplishments, to which the Geographical Society appended a note: "This letter received from colonel Chaillé-Long, is a concise recapitulation of facts that are a part of history. They are again printed in the BULLETIN because it is desired to reiterate the notable service of Colonel Chaillé-Long as the pioneer discoverer of a part of the Upper Nile and in the belief that his just title to be known for the work he did, should, in no way, be obscured."[39]

What was all the fuss about nearly fifty years after the event? The Royal Geographical Society in London was celebrating "Fifty Years of Nile Exploration" in honor of the Jubilee of Speke's discovery of the Victoria Nyanza. In the Journal of December 15, 1908, Sir William Garstin, although acknowledging Chaillé-Long, did not credit him enough. Chaillé-Long exclaimed, "There is no connection, in Sir William Garstin's brief note, of my discoveries with those of Speke and Baker." He is also irate because Garstin believed that Stanley came before him and wrote, "Stanley did not precede me in the Nile Basin, but succeeded me." Garstin did, indeed, diminish Chaillé-Long's discoveries. His text, which was organized in chronological order, began with Burton, moved on to Speke, continued with Grant, then Baker, and ended up with Stanley:

> I now come to what is, perhaps, the most striking personality of all — in the roll of the discoverers of the Nile — that of Henry M. Stanley.... On November 17, 1874, he set out from Bagamoyo for the interior, arriving at the south end of Lake Victoria, in February of the following year. He circumnavigated the lake in a boat that he had brought with him — and corrected the errors of Speke's map, as to its shape and area....
>
> On arriving at Mtesa's capital, Stanley, like Speke, was immensely impressed by the remarkable civilization, and the powerful military organization, existing in the Baganda kingdom....
>
> Stanley had thus cleared up the last great problem with respect to the Nile sources. He had proved that this river had two separate and distinct systems of supply. The one is Lake Victoria, fed entirely by the rainfall over its catchment basin; the other comprises the Edward and Albert Nyanzas — connected by the Semliki — deriving their supply, partly from rainfall, and partly from the melting glaciers of the Ruwenzori snowfields....
>
> It is impossible to exaggerate the importance of Stanley's work. The main facts regarding the sources of the Nile were finally revealed by him, and nothing was left for future explorers but to fill in the details.[40]

There is no mention of Chaillé-Long in the history of the exploration and discovery of the source of the Nile in this address. That does not mean that Sir William did not mention him at all. He did. Under the achievements of Gordon Pasha over twenty pages later he wrote:

> During the same period, Gordon Pasha — who had succeeded Baker as Governor-General of the Sudan — did much in the direction of mapping the upper Nile.... Gordon also despatched Gessi Pasha and Mason Bey [an American], at different periods, to navigate and survey the Albert Nayanza.... In 1874, Colonel Chaillé Long explored the Victoria Nile and proved, beyond all question, that the river which entered the Albert Nyanza, at Magungo, was identical with that which issued from Speke's lake at the Ripon Falls. Colonel Long was also the discoverer of the reedy lakes known as Choga and Kwania, called by him Lake Ibrihim.[41]

One more time, Colonel Charles Chaillé-Long laid down his achievements in the hopes that he would be recognized for his accomplishments.

> American officer, Lieut.-Colonel of the General staff of the Egypt army since 1869, I was appointed chief of staff to Colonel Gordon, Feb. 19, 1874, and charged by

Ismail Khedive with a secret mission — to make a treaty with Mtesa, King of Uganda. I left Gondokoro accompanied by two soldiers, two servants and native porters, April 20, 1874, and arrived at the capital of Uganda, June 19, 1874. I visited the Lake Victoria, July 14, and, returning to the capital, executed the treaty between the Khedive and the King, July 10. On July 28, I regained the Nile, reached Urondo-gani, August 5, descended the river in two bark canoes, and discovered, August 11, a lake to which I gave the name of Hussein (after Prince Hussein, Minister of War), but to which the Khedive subsequently gave the name of Ibrahim in honour of his father, the "hero of Nezib."

The navigation of Victoria Nile and the discovery of Lake Ibrahim completed Speke's discovery of the Victoria Nyanza and finally solved the Nile source problem. I claim, therefore, with Speke and Baker the part attributed to me by General Gordon.[42]

Today, nearly 150 years later, on Google maps, Lake Victoria is listed as Lake Victoria, Lake Albert is listed as Lake Albert, and Lake Ibrahim is listed as Lake Kyoga.[43]

Chaillé-Long did other exploration in Africa, but for us his journey has come to an end.

Cairo, a Medal, a New Society, and an Aborted Journey

On March 17, 1875, Chaillé-Long began his journey back to Cairo. When he arrived at Berber, he met another of the Khedive Ismail's American explorers: Major Prout. Prout was on his way to explore and map Darfur and Kordofan to continue Ismail's empire. Then, Chaillé-Long crossed the Korosko Desert, took a steamer down the Nile past Aswan, Luxor, and the ruins of ancient Egypt, and then by rail to Cairo (May 22). Next day he reported to the Khedive at Abdin Palace. While in Cairo he spoke before the Geographical Society.

The Geographical Society is very important to the discussion of Americans in Egypt. Tucked into the archives of the Société Khédiviale de Geographie, now the Geographical Society of Egypt, are the maps and reports of the Khedive Ismail's American soldiers: Lockett's map of Africa of 1877 (listing Lake Ibrihim) as well as his plans of Goura and Haala, Mitchell's geological profile of the Eastern Desert, Purdy's maps of Darfur and reconnaissance of the Eastern Desert, and Major Prout's maps of Darfur and Kordofan, as well as the town plan of El Obeid, not to mention Chaillé-Long's discovery of Lake Ibrahim and the source of the Nile. There are Prout's and Colston's individual 1875 reports on the provinces of Kordofan, Mitchell's topographical report of Zeilah and the Abyssinian plateau, and Mason's mapping of Siwa and Fayoum. It goes on and on. They not only extended the boundaries of the Khedive's empire, they enhanced the knowledge of the African continent. These men spoke at the society. They discussed their findings and shared their thoughts. They wrote articles for its *Bulletin de la société khédiviale de geographie*, which began publication in 1876. All their reports, maps, and three-dimensional replicas remain in the great halls of this beautiful building just off of Midan Tahrir on Kasr el Aini Street awaiting the scholar's keen eye. But through the years western scholars have mostly ignored the society's holdings.

In the End

In the end it was all for nothing. When the British Protectorate gave way to the British Occupation in the 1880s, Britain maintained the Sudan was a burden on Egypt. Chaillé-Long disagreed and stated: "Their [central African] cost to the [Egyptian] Government were only in the insignificant presents made to the King and Sheiks of those regions, whilst valuable cargoes of ivory were in return brought back, and placed to Government account."[44] England cut central Africa from the Khedive's domain. Then Britain proceeded to build railroads and roads in the Sudan and declare yet another protectorate. It did the same in Uganda.

What Happened to Chaillé-Long?

After all the dramatic exploration, Chaillé-Long went on a six-months' leave to Europe. On his return he discovered that his Egyptian interlude was coming to an end. Over the next few years, Ismail's position as Khedive of Egypt and ruler of an African empire was slowly eroded by European interests. High usury on European loans contributed to the decline of Egypt.

On June 30, 1878, the remaining Americans were mustered out of the Egyptian Army and returned to the United States. Only one remained behind: Charles P. Stone, bowing to Ismail's last wish, stayed on to guide his son Tewfik through the difficult and perilous road ahead. In all, six American soldiers had died in Egypt.

The Egyptian experience would not be easily forgotten by these men. In addition to their achievements were their flaws, Union and Confederate men did not mix well. Some were drunks. Some were incapable of doing their jobs. Others achieved exceptional feats.[45] In the end they wrote books, articles for *The Century Magazine, Harper's Weekly Magazine,* the *North American Review* and others. They went on the lecture circuit. But eventually they were forgotten, as was their mission in Egypt. In fact, few Americans are aware of these interesting men. And so generations have grown up in America brandishing swords like Lawrence of Arabia, not realizing they had a few Middle Eastern heroes of their own to be proud of.

As for Chaillé-Long, in September 1877 Colonel Charles Chaillé-Long resigned his Egyptian commission. He went back to Europe, then on to America. But he did not step out of public life as so many of his colleagues did. He attended Columbia Law School and graduated in 1880, having specialized in international law. By 1882 he was back in Egypt. He went hunting in Luxor. When the city of Alexandria was bombarded by the British, Chaillé-Long became consul general. His most important task was dealing with all of the refugees trying to flee the city and the British. American warships stood ready to receive them in the Bay of Alexandria. He got the Americans safely out of Egypt and then returned to the Consulate. He opened it and stayed there until August 17. He also sent an American force to the aid of the Khedive Tewfik to protect him from Arabi (see Chapter 12 for details). In 1883 he represented many western clients trying to get back their losses in Alexandria. By 1887 he was consul general in Korea and he continued to explore. In Korea it was the Cheju Island. At the age of 48 he married Marie Amelia Hammond on July 16, 1890. Between 1890 to 1892 he was back in Egypt representing Europeans in Alexandria who held claims against the Anglo-Egyptian government for damage to their property during the Bombardment of Alexandria.

He may have been arrogant. He may or may not have sensationalized his story. But he did put in place an important piece of Nile history, and credit is long overdue to Colonel Charles Chaillé-Long.

11

Ulysses S. Grant: The King of America's Progress through Egypt (Traveler, 1877)

If a progress is "a ceremonial journey made by a sovereign through his or her realm," then that is what General Ulysses S. Grant and his escorts were doing as they toured the world in the 1870s. Grant was America's hero. He was the last and the best general in charge of the Union forces during the American Civil War. He went on to be elected president of the United States. Having devoted his life to the army and public service, Grant had never been further than Mexico. When he retired from public service he took a two-year voyage around the world. The Department of State sent a statement to all of the diplomatic and consular posts en route on May 23, 1877, asking each post "to make his journey a pleasant one."[1]

Ulysses Grant, his family, his friends, and his reporters left Philadelphia on May 17, 1877. He would return to American soil in San Francisco in 1879. After eight months in Europe the party arrived at the port of Alexandria on January 5, 1878, aboard the *Vandalia*, a U.S. man-of-war placed at the general's disposal for his entire journey. Elbert E. Farman, the American agent and consul general in Egypt, who had been appointed by Grant during his presidency, met Grant aboard ship. Just as George Gliddon had done for travelers fifty years earlier, Farman made arrangements for travel up the Nile and, unlike Gliddon, accompanied Grant on his journey. Farman wrote about it in *Along the Nile: An Account of the Visit to Egypt of General Ulysses S. Grant and his Tour Through That Country*. Farman's book was one of a number of publications that reported on Grant's progress. John Russell Young, correspondent of the *New York Herald*, had been asked to accompany the former American president on the voyage and send regular dispatches back to America. Young wrote *Around the World with General Grant*, published in 1879, a most astounding book with uncanny perceptions that once opened is hard to put down. There were nearly a dozen more.[2]

It is not surprising that so many books were written about President Grant's journey. First and foremost he was an American hero. He was the man in charge of the army when the nation was torn asunder and through his leadership patched together again. Next to Abraham Lincoln, Ulysses S. Grant epitomized the years of the Civil War. Grant began his military career along the western waters of the great Mississippi River watershed and distinguished himself in early Civil War battles along the Mississippi River at Fort Donelson, Shiloh, and Vicksburg. As the war progressed he commanded the Union troops successfully, and at the end of the war accepted the Confederate surrender of Robert E. Lee at Appomattox. When

Grant and Ismail in carriage.

Lincoln was assassinated in 1865, Grant was "the" hero and his popularity led him to the presidency of the United States, where he served two terms.

Travel had changed since Richard and Sarah Haight were on the Nile in 1836. Steamboats had arrived on the Nile. Those aristocrats who traveled abroad as part of their education on the Grand Tour of Europe or the Holy Land Tour had to make room for this new type of traveler: the tourist. These tourists did not have a year to travel. They didn't have six months. There was no time for a slow ride in a *dahabeyyiah*. The organization that made this all happen was the British company Thomas Cook and Son.[3] Cook's first Egypt and the Holy Land tour of 1869 took thirty-two persons on a Nile cruise aboard the steamers *Benha* and *Beniswaif*. It was looked on as appalling by the British elite, who did not welcome Cook's tourists to Egypt. This is the origin of the negative attitude attributed to the word *tourist* as opposed to *traveler*, a distinction still common today.

The Grant party had made no diplomatic plans for Egypt and expected to tour the country as any other tourist from America. But that was not to happen. Ulysses S. Grant was famous. He was accorded every honor due the "King of America." He would tour Egypt not as a Cook's tourist, but as an aristocrat, for once Khedive Ismail heard Grant was arriving he asked Farman if it would be proper to ask General Grant to be his guest in Egypt. That would include every service: "a palace, special trains on the railroad, and a steamer in which to make the voyage of the Nile." Grant was cautious too. He consulted some of his guests and Farman and then said, "If you see no impropriety in so doing, I will accept the hospitalities of the Khedive."[4]

The Khedive's caution was not just Middle Eastern politeness. General Grant was president of the United States when the ceremony celebrating the opening of the Suez Canal was held in 1869. The Khedive Ismail extended an invitation to the United States to attend the ceremony. His ability to send this invitation was questionable because Egypt was still under the rule of the Ottoman Empire and Ismail did not have such authority. So the invitation was extended via France. It was not accepted. This new invitation had to be correctly done. It was.

Grant in Cairo, the City Victorious

Grant headed to Cairo in the Khedive's personal rail coach, which had been sent to Alexandria expressly for him. For four hours the party sat and watched the Delta unfold from their windows. When they arrived in Cairo they were greeted by a crowd of Americans:

> The General, looking at the group, recognizes old friends. "Why," he says, "there's Loring, whom I have not seen for thirty years;" and "There's Stone, who must have been dyeing his hair to make it so white." The cars stop, and General Stone enters, presenting the representative of the Khedive. This officer extends the welcome of his highness, which General Grant accepts with thanks. General Loring comes in, and receives a hearty greeting from his old friend in early days and his enemy during the war. General Stone and General Grant were at West Point, and are old friends, and their meeting is quite enthusiastic. The General asks General Loring to ride with him, while General Stone accompanies Mrs. Grant, and so we drive off to the Palace of Kasr-el-Noussa — the palace placed at General Grant's disposal by the Khedive.[5]

General Grant's wife Julia added more "color": "The General had all the carriages he could possibly use. I had a beautiful little Victoria drawn by a span of beautiful Russian horses with flowing mane and tails. I often used it with my two handsome *syce* running ahead about twenty yards. The General dismissed his runners, saying it was inhuman, and wished me to do so, but I would not, as I liked to see them in their flowing white sleeves, velvet jackets, and full Greek skirts, with silver helmets and silver wands held high in the air, flying as it were like Mercury before my phaeton."[6]

The following day General Grant had an audience with the Khedive at the Abdin Palace. "A battalion of soldiers was drawn up as a guard of honor, in front of the main entrance and a carpet was extended to the carriage, where the General was met by the Master of Ceremonies.... The Khedive met the General at the foot of the stairs and conducted him up the broad stairway to what would be called the first floor in Europe, but with us the second.... The Khedive spoke in French and General Grant in English.[7]

This was not the Cairo of Mohammad Ali, Ismail's grandfather. The changes were traumatic and overwhelming. Cairo was no longer an exclusively Islamic city. Of all of Mohammad Ali's offspring, Ismail took Egypt as far west as it could go before being consumed. There were two Cairos now: the original Eastern city, filled with tight, winding, poorly lit Oriental streets, buildings, and shops; and the new Western city stretching south to the river's edge, absorbing the port of Bulaq and swinging west toward the pyramids and east to the base of the Mokattam hills. That new city had long, wide boulevards, fabulous French-style buildings and statues built by the most prominent architects of Europe, dozens of new elaborate western-style palaces for the royal family, new bridges across the Nile for easy access to Giza and the Nile islands. The streets were lined with trees imported from all parts of the world and well lit at night by gas lights. Cairo was Paris on the Nile.

Stone and his wife also accompanied the Grant party on their excursion to the pyramids. Of course the men climbed the pyramids, and standing at the top, Farman gave a good American comparison for their size and wonder: "If you stand at the foot of Niagara upon the

Canada side, as near the falling waters as possible, and look upwards you will perhaps obtain the best impression of the height, the grandeur of the Great Father of the Cataracts. The Falls are about one hundred and fifty feet high. You have only to treble this distance, to pile three Niagaras one on the top of the other, and you will have the perpendicular height of the Great Pyramid."[8]

While in Cairo, Farman too gave a dinner for the Grant party. The event was at the New Hotel. The guests were a who's-who of Americans in Egypt at the time: Judge and Mrs. Barringer, Judge and Mrs. Batcheller, both of the Mixed Courts; M. Comanos and Madame Comanos of the American consul; General Charles P. Stone, Mrs. Stone and Miss Stone; General Loring, Colonel Dye, all the American officers now in the Egyptian Army; Mme. Colestone, Colonel Graves, Colonel Mitchell; Rev. Dr. Lansing and Mrs. Lansing of the American Mission in Egypt; M. and Mme. De Ortego Morejon; Judge and Mme. Hagers; Mr. Tower, Admiral Stedman, Mr. Van Dyck and Dr. George H. Cook of the *Vandalia*.[9]

Grant Visits the Americans at the Citadel

Grant could be a little more relaxed on his visit to the Citadel. There, General Stone was in command and he toured the facility with his old friend. It was General Headquarters for the Egyptian Army and the main facility for the army's Americans. The Citadel is located atop a spur of the Mokattam Hills that flank the city on the east, forming a strong natural barrier for defense. That was the reason the Egyptian ruler Sala-a-din chose it for the seat of his power and for nearly a decade (1170s–1180s), fortifying it with walls, gates, and dozens of buildings. Rulers from Sala-a-din to the Mohammad Ali dynasty lived in its safety. They only moved down into Cairo when Ismail built the 500-room Abdin Palace (1864) with plans by French architect De Curel Del Rosso.[10]

The arrival and mission of ex–Civil War officers from both the Union and the Confederate armies is an interesting tale that affected not only General Grant and his tour of Egypt, but several other Americans in Egypt. It all began when the American Thaddeus P. Mott met the Khedive Ismail in Constantinople in 1868. Thaddeus was the son of Valentine Mott, the famous New York surgeon who traveled to Egypt in 1838 and wrote the book *Travels in Europe and the East* in 1842.[11] Thaddeus was a colonel in the Union Army and after the war he traveled to Turkey, where he was often at the Turkish court. There he met Ismail, whom he filled with stories about American military expertise and tempted him with the thought that some of these fighting men might be persuaded to join Ismail's military visions. When General William Tecumseh Sherman visited Egypt in 1869, Ismail also asked him for American officers. By 1870, the first American soldiers arrived in Egypt: William Wing Loring and Henry Hopkins Sibley.

The British and the French were not happy to see Americans aiding the Egyptian army. They went so far as to try to organize all the diplomatic corps against the Americans and to have them expelled from Egypt (which they finally succeeded in doing). American John P. Dunn, in his excellent book the *Khedive Ismail's Army*, concluded the Americans were mercenaries and they were doomed to failure because of Ismail's weaknesses. He called them the new Mamluks, and he was right, for the Mamluks were mercenaries too.[12]

The Americans set about the various tasks assigned to them. The Khedive Ismail was more than interested in building an empire in Africa. His father Ibrihim's army, trained and led under the ex–Napoleon officer Joseph Sève, which fought so magnificently against the Greeks and the Porte in Mohammad Ali's bid for independence in the 1830s and '40s had fallen to ruin (see Chapter 6). Stone and his staff, including William McEntyre Dye, restructured the Egyptian army along more modern lines, including a general staff, an ordnance section, a transport section, and an intelligence corps. Plans were laid to build a military rail-road for Alexandria-Rosetta-Damietta-Port Said and create a submarine fleet and a naval tor-pedo mining service. In addition Stone created a military library at the Citadel, started regimental schools for his soldiers, and when he saw the need, began schools for the children of military men.

Along the Mediterranean and Red seas, the Americans fortified coastal defenses by erecting gun emplacements (William Wing Loring, Henry Hopkins Sibley, James M. Morgan, Beverly Kennon, Cornelius Hunt), and built lighthouses from Suez to Aden (Charles C. Graves). The American soldiers handled the mail steamers from Alexandria to Constantinople and along the Nile (Alexander McComb Mason, William P. Campbell). They set up a submarine school in Rosetta (William H. Ward, John L. Lay). They explored and mapped the Nile, Darfur, Korodofan, Siwa, Fayoum, the Eastern Desert between the Nile and Berenice on the Red Sea, and contributed to the final discovery of the source of the Nile (Raleigh E Colston, Colonel Erastus Sparrow Purdy, William P.A. Campbell, Alexander Mason, Henry G. Prout, Charles Chaillé-Long). They accompanied Gordon to Khartoum (Chaillé-Long, Mason, Prout) and fought in the Abyssinian campaign (William McEntyre Dye, Samuel H. Lockett, Surgeon Major Thomas D Johnson). When the Americans were finished exploring and making expe-ditions, the Khedive could count the entire Nile valley and most of Darfur, Kordofan, and Uganda as part of his empire. Stone explained all of this to Grant during the visit to the Citadel and aboard the boat on the Nile.

Eventually the Europeans won the day, dethroned Ismail, and forced his Americans to leave. And so, on June 30, 1878, while General Grant was still on his tour around the world, the remaining Americans in the Egyptian Army were mustered out and returned to the United States. A few remained behind as private citizens, while Charles P. Stone, bowing to Ismail's last wish, stayed on to guide his son Tewfik along the difficult and perilous road ahead.

Heading to Upper Egypt

Long before the Grants arrived in Egypt, steamboats had arrived on the Nile. It was an entirely different experience from taking a sailing boat as travelers had done since antiquity. Steamers were faster and they held more people. For the Grants it was a special steamer: the *Zinet el Bohrer* (*The Light of Two Rivers*). To the shouts of the American community that had gathered along the shore, the party boarded at Bulaq on January 16, 1878. John Russell Young wrote home to New Yorkers anxious for news about the General:

> On Wednesday, the 16th of January, embarked on the Nile. As the hour of noon passed the drawbridge opened, farewells were said to the many kind friends who had gathered on the banks, and we shot away from our moorings, and out into the dark waters of the mighty and mysterious stream. One cannot resist the temptation of writing about the Nile, yet what can a writer say in telling the old, old story of a journey through these lands of romance and fable! The Khedive has placed at the dis-posal of the General one of his steam vessels, and she swings out into the stream with the American flag at the fore. We have all been in a bustle and a hurry to get away.... We bought each a Turkish fez, and some of us ventured upon the luxury of an Indian hat. Others went into colored spectacles, and the Marquis, a far-seeing man, who had been on the Nile and who was not in the best of spirits at leaving a palace to float for weeks between Arab villages, appeared with an astonishing umbrella. We had many friends to see us off— General Stone, Judge Batcheller, and Judge Bar-ringer, with their wives, General Loring, and others.... The General sits in a corner with Stone and Loring, talking about old days in the army, and making comments

upon famed and illustrious names that the historian would welcome if I could only dare to gather up the crumbs of this interesting conversation. At noon the signal for our journey is given and farewells are spoken, and we head under full steam for the Equator.

Our party is thus composed: We have the General, his wife, and his youngest son, Jesse. The Khedive has assigned us an officer of his household, Sami Bey, a Circassian gentleman educated in England. Sami Bey is one of the heroes of our trip, and we soon came to like him, Moslem as he is, for his quaint, cordial, kindly ways. I suppose we should call Sami Bey the executive officer of the expedition, as to him all responsibility is given. We have also with us, thanks to the kindness of the Khedive, Emile Brugsch, one of the directors of the Egyptian Museum. Mr. Brugsch is a German, brother to the chief director, who has made the antiquities of Egypt a study. Mr. Brugsch knows every tomb and column in the land. He has lived for weeks in the temples and ruins.... The Consul-General, E.E. Farman, formerly editor of *The Western New-Yorker,* is also of our party, and I have already spoken of the pleasant impression he made upon General Grant in Cairo.... The Consul-General is accompanied by a kind of Arabian Sancho Panza named Hassan. I am afraid it is because the Consul-General is tall and thin, and Hassan is short and brown and stout, that we call the latter Sancho Panza. However, the comparison comes from illustrious lips, and was made one evening when our Consul-General and Hassan were coming over the plains of Dendereh, mounted on donkeys. Hassan has been eighteen years in the legation. He speaks a ready, expressive, but limited English; wears an Arabian costume, including a cimeter, and is proud of two things — first, that he wears a gold American eagle mounted on a pin, with which he was decorated by Consul-General Butler; and second, that he captured John H. Surratt [see Chapter 9]. Hassan is a Moslem, the husband of two wives, and believes in Dr. Lansing, the missionary, who educates his children....

Our boat ... is a long, narrow steamer, with two cabins, drawing only a few feet of water, with a flat-bottomed keel. The Nile is a river of sand and mud, and as the bottom is always changing, you must expect to run aground every little while and to run off again. This in fact we do, and the announcement that we are aground makes about as much impression upon us as if a passenger in a Broadway omnibus heard the wheel of his coach interlocking with another. The Nile boats seem arranged to meet any emergency in the way of land — for this river is sprawling, eccentric, comprehensive, without any special channel — running one way to-day, another next day....

When evening comes our captain picks out the best point that can be found after sunset, and runs up to the land. The crew are sent ashore with torches and hammers, posts are driven into the soft clay, and we are tied to the shore. There, as if out of the earth they come, we have a group of Bedouins in their turbans, who gather on the river bank and make a bonfire of dried sugar-cane or cornstalks, and keep watch over us during the night.[13]

What is so wonderful about reading Young's vivid, dramatic, spellbinding accounts of their journey is that they are filled with minute details that make us jealous that we are not with the General: "The General is an early or late riser, according as we have an engagement for the day" (311); or, "We lounge on the deck. We go among the Arabs and see them cooking. We lean over the prow and watch the sailors poke the Nile with long poles and call out the message from its bed. Sometimes a murderous feeling steams over some of the younger people, and they begin to shoot at a stray crane or pelican" (311); or, "There are long pauses of silence, in which the General maintains his long-conceded supremacy. Then come little ripples of real, useful conversation, when the General strikes some thesis connected with the war or his administration. Then one wishes that he might gather up and bind these sheaves of history...."

Or perhaps our friend Brugsch opens upon some theme connected with Egypt. And we sit in grateful silence while he tells us of the giants who reigned in the old dynasties, of the gods they honored, of the tombs and temples, of their glory and their fall. I think that we will all say that the red-letter hours of our Nile journey were when General Grant told us how he met Lee at Appomattox, or how Sherman fought at Shiloh, or when Brugsch, in a burst of fine enthusiasm, tells us the glories of the eighteenth dynasty, or what Karnak must have been in the days of its splendors and its pride.[14]

Farman, too, talked of the conversations that were held as the steamer made its way along the Nile: Grant's life at West Point, the Mexican War, the battles along the Mississippi, his relationship with various Union officers including Sheridan, Halleck, and Buell, but especially Sherman and his march to the sea from Atlanta. "His narrations were concise, clear, complete," wrote Farman. He continued:

> His criticism of generals was always in a kindly spirit.... The circumstances were such that a very large part of these accounts were only heard by Mrs. Grant and myself, while sitting under the awning, on the deck of the steamer where we passed a large portion of nearly every day.... I have often wished that they might be preserved for history, as there was probably no occasion on which he spoke so freely, and so fully, as on the Nile voyage. He afterwards in his memoirs treated the same subjects. It is probable that he wrote what he desired to leave on record.... It would therefore be unjust for me to leave a record of very much of what he said. While in Luxor the General received his mail and among the letters was an English journal criticizing his leadership at the Potomac campaign. That, too, was part of the discussion."[15]

The King of America

Wasef el-Hayat, a Syrian landowner, was the U.S. consular agent in Asyut. The American presence in Egypt had grown to such an extent that there was a respectable American colony there, especially missionaries. There were consular offices throughout the country in many communities. Wasef el-Hayat took over the care and comfort of the party when they arrived in his city. The city of Asyut, as with most major Egyptian cities, was far from the banks of the Nile to protect it from the yearly inundation. This year, 1877, the Nile flood was poor, the river not overflowing far enough to coat the fields with its life-giving silt. Thus the trip from the river to the city was through parched land. True to form, after an all-day excursion, el Hayat put on a dinner for the Grants and their party. "Mr. Hayat sent his carriage for General and Mrs. Grant....

> We were bidden to an entertainment at the home of Wasif el Hayat, and, seven being the hour, we set forth. We were all anxious about our first Arab entertainment, and after some deliberation our naval men concluded to wear their uniforms. The Doctor rode ahead, in the carriage with General and Mrs. Grant and the consul-general. As the Doctor wore his uniform and the others were in plain dress, he was welcomed by the awestricken Moslems as the King of America. Hadden and the rest of us rode behind on our trusty and well-beloved donkeys, Hadden in uniform, followed by wondering crowds. I suppose he was taken for a minor potentate, as, in the Oriental eyes, all that lace and gold could not be wasted on anything less than princely rank. But we all had more or less attention, although we could feel that the uniforms were the centre of glory, and that we shone with borrowed splendor. As we came to the house of Wasif el Hayat, we found a real transformation scene. Lanterns lined the street, servants stood on the road holding blazing torches, a transparency was over the gate with the words, "welcome General Grant." ... Our host met us at

the gates of his house, and welcomed us in the stately Oriental way, kissing the General's hand as he clasped it in his two hands, and then touching his own heart, lips and brow. Here we met the governor, and, more welcome still, the Rev. I.R. Alexander and his wife. Mr. Alexander is one of the professors in the missionary college, and is under the direction of the United Presbyterian Church. The dinner came, and it was regal in its profusion and splendor. I should say there were at least twenty courses, all well served. When it was concluded, the son of the host arose, and in remarkably clear and correct English proposed the General's health. The speech closed by a tribute to the General and the Khedive. General Grant said in response that nothing in his whole trip had so impressed him as this unexpected, this generous welcome in the heart of Egypt. He had anticipated great pleasure in his visit to Egypt, and the anticipation had been more than realized. He thanked his host, and especially the young man who had spoken of him with so high praise, for their reception. The dinner dissolved into coffee, conversation and cigars. Mrs. Grant had a long talk with Mrs. Alexander about home — Mrs. Alexander being a fair young bride who had come out from America to cast her lot with her husband in the unpromising vineyard of Siout. And when the evening grew on, we rode back to our boat, through the night and over the plain. Torch-bearers accompanied us through the town. Donkey-boys and townspeople followed us to the river bank. The moon was shining, and as we rode home — you see we already call the boat our home — we talked over the pleasant surprise we had found in Siout and of its many strange phases of Oriental life.[16]

What Young does not mention is what the crowd was saying. Julia Grant asked Hassan to translate: "Hassan said: 'You foreign devils. Why do you come here?' I did not think the crowd looked friendly and now I knew their temper — as straws show the direction of the wind."[17]

Between Asyut and Abydos the party encountered two other groups of travelers, and Julia Grant reported who they were: Mr. and Mrs. Joseph Drexel in a *dahabeyyiah*, and later, near Girgah, Admiral Charles Steedman and Mr. Davis of Boston.[18] As Asyut was carriages and lights, Abydos was donkeys. Nothing in the annals of travelers' tales of Egypt intrigued the writers like the donkeys of Egypt. Young's tale is among the best.

It was rather a long distance from our landing place to Abydos, and Sami Bey had given orders that we should be ready at eight for our journey. I am afraid it was quite an effort for some of the party, whose names shall be withheld, to heed this command. But the General was first on deck, and very soon came Mrs. Grant eager and smiling. And as the General waits for no one, those who were late had to hurry their breakfasts and some of them were skurrying up the side of the bank with a half-eaten biscuit. There were our Arabs and donkeys all waiting, and the moment our company began to muster there was a chorus of screams — "Good donkey," "Goodmorning," "Backsheesh," and other limited forms of speech. The donkeys charged upon us in a mass, each owner screaming out the merits of his animal. It was only by vigorous efforts on the part of Hassan that we could see and select our animals. Hassan had given me a private bit of information as to which donkey I should select, and I found myself the master of a little mite of a creature, scarcely high enough to keep my feet from the ground, but vigorous and strong, and disposed to stop and bray for the amusement of the company.... The General himself had a horse placed at his disposal by the Pacha who rules the district, but he rode the animal with a protest, as it had a shambling gait, and wished that courtesy to his host did not prevent his taking a donkey.... So in time we were off over the country for Abydos. The fields were cracked, and the ditches, which in good times would carry irrigating streams, were dry. Each of us had two Arabs for an escort, and the duty of these attendants seemed to be to encourage the beast by a sound something between a whisper and a hiss, or shouting or beating him. I rather think the beating did not amount to much, for these people love their animals and live with them, and make them companions and friends. But the lady of our expedition would not endure the stick, and we were halted, and Hassan was summoned and told to say to the attendants that they must not beat the donkeys or they would have no *backsheesh*, not a farthing. There could be no more fearful punishment than this, and there was no more beating. But the Arabs had their satisfaction in kneeling and running at your side and seeking a conversation. Their observations became monotonous. "Good donkey," "My name Mohammed," "My name Ali," "Good donkey," "Yankee Doodle," "Good-morning," "Good donkey." Others came with bits of scarabei and bits of ancient pottery, fragments of mummy lids and shreds of mummy cloth, to drive a trade. I was on the point of making a moral observation upon the character of a people who would rifle the tombs of their ancestors and make merchandise of their bones and grave-ornaments, when it occurred to me that these were Arabs, and descended, not from the Egyptians, but from the men who conquered the Egyptians and occupied their land. I hope it is not against the laws of war for a conquering race to sell the bones of those they have defeated, for our Arabs were so poor and wretched that no one could grudge them any means of earning a piaster.... I became quite friendly with my Mohammed Ali, who had two English phrases with which he constantly plied me — "I am serene," and "Yankee Doodle." The latter phrase was the name of his donkey, and I was about to thank him for this kind recognition of my country when Hassan, from whom I draw great stores of information, told me that they had a variety of names — English, French, German, Italian — which they used according to the nationality of their riders. I had no doubt that my present plodding Yankee Doodle had done duty as Bismarck, MacMahon, and the Prince of Wales....

My first impression was to hold my animal well in hand and guide him, keep from going over his head into a ditch, and show him the safest paths. But I soon learned the elementary lesson in donkey riding — namely, that your animal knows more about the subject than you can teach him, and that you had better discharge your mind from all care and allow him to go in his own way wherever Mohammed Ali will lead him. Then if you can make up your mind to disengage your feet from the stirrups and let them swing, just as when a boy you used to swing over a gate, you will find it easier in the long run. I noticed that those of our party who had the most experience of Egypt rode in this fashion, and so, while some of our ambitious members who had learned horsemanship in the best schools and loved to brace themselves in the saddle were anxious about stirrups, I allowed myself to dangle. There is another reason for this, as I learned from practical experience one day at Assouan. The donkey is apt to fall, for the land is full of holes and traps. To fall with your feet in the stirrups might be a serious matter. But when Yankee Doodle took it into his head to throw his head upon the ground and his heels into the air, it only remained for me to walk from him, as though I had risen from a chair, and wait until he came to a better frame of mind.

"Here," said Brugsch, as we dismounted from our donkeys and followed him into the ruins of the temple, "'here we should all take off our hats, for here is the cradle, the fountain-head of all the civilization of the world."[19]

After visiting Abydos and Dendera, the steamer pulled into Thebes, modern Luxor. As one approaches from the north, the first thing that comes into view on the west bank of the Nile are the Colossi of Memnon. The party spied them through field glasses, then turned to face the east, where the entire population of Luxor was out to greet them. Amid the flying flags of the consulates and the *dahabeyyiahs* were buildings festooned with palm boughs. The U.S. consular agent there was Aly Mourad. Aly, too, intended to feast the Grant party. But the General was tired after spending the entire day on the West Bank and sent his regrets. Aly said he would lose face if the General did not attend. The General attended the dinner. While the party was at Karnak, lunch was to be aboard ship, but Aly Mourad had other ideas. He had arranged "for us a *collation a l'Arabe*, in the great hall of the temple. His hospitalities could not properly be declined. Nor did the fact that the lunch consisted principally of the uncarved viands of the previous evening render it less appreciable. The photographer was also present."[20]

Like so many before and after him, Young was overwhelmed by the glory of Karnak. Not only is he eloquent, but he gives us an American perspective so the folks back home could get some idea of the mass and the splendor of the ancient ruins.

President Grant (front row with white hood) and his party at Karnak (in *Along the Nile* by Elbert Farman).

It was because that Thebes was the centre of a rich and fertile province, sheltered from an enemy by the river and the mountains, that she was allowed to grow from century to century in uninterrupted splendor. What that splendor must have been we cannot imagine. Here are the records and here are the ruins. If the records read like a tale of enchantment, these ruins look the work of gods. The world does not show, except where we have evidences of the convulsions of nature, a ruin as vast as that of Karnak. Imagine a city covering two banks of the Hudson, running as far as from the Battery to Yonkers, and back five, six, or seven miles, all densely built, and you have an idea of the extent of Thebes. But this will only give you an idea of size. The buildings were not Broadways and Fifth Avenues, but temples, and colossal monuments, and tombs, the greatness of which and the skill and patience necessary to build them exciting our wonder to-day — yes, to-day, rich as we are with the achievements and possibilities of the nineteenth century. Thebes in its day must have been a wonder of the world, even of the ancient world which knew Nineveh and Babylon. To-day all that remains are a few villages of mud huts, a few houses in stone flying consular flags, a plain here and there strewed with ruins, and under the sands ruins even more stupendous than those we now see, which have not yet become manifest.[21]

Thus the Grants continued south. They visited Esna, Edfu, and finally Aswan and the Island of Philae. At each stop the Grants and their entourage visited, commented, learned, and enjoyed. And at each stop Farman and Young followed, noted, observed and wrote amazing vignettes. Then they turned the steamer around and headed downstream once again. Stops were made at Kom Ombo, Valley of the Kings, Memphis, where General Stone joined them, and Sakkara. In the final days of their stay in Egypt the Khedive gave the General yet another dinner. The de Lesseps attended this time. Julia Grant had been to visit Khedive Ismail's wife and asked for her at the dinner. The Khedive replied, "Oh, Madam, it is not the custom of the country."[22] A few days later, as they were giving their goodbyes, Julia Grant was to visit the Princess for the second time:

When I told the Princess how disappointed I was not to see her at the banquet, she repeated through her interpreter just what the Khedive said: "Oh, it is not the custom of our country." I at once declared it to be a very hard and unjust custom, and added, "In America we would not consent to such an unjust custom. We always were present at the entertainments given by our husbands if any ladies were." I am afraid in saying this I left the apple of discord for the Khedive in the heaping basket of delicious fruit on the table in front of us.[23]

How very American! Then the Grants were on their way out of Egypt and perhaps on a diet.

Epilogue

While traveling in China, Young had several interviews with General Grant. He specifically asked him about the "Eastern Question." Grant's response:

"I did not know much," said the General, "about the Eastern Question until I came to Europe. The more I looked into it, the more I was drawn irresistibly to the belief that the Russian side was the true one. Perhaps I should say the side of Mr. Gladstone. On the Eastern Question there is more diversity in England than elsewhere. As I was traveling through the East, I tried hard to find something in the policy of the English government to approve. But I could not. I was fresh from England, and wanted to be in accord with men who had shown me as much kindness as Lord Beaconsfield and his colleagues. But it was impossible. England's policy in the East is hard, reactionary, and selfish. No one can visit those wonderful lands on the Mediterranean, without seeing what they might be under a good government. I do not care under which flag the government flourished, English or French, Italian or Russian, its influence would be felt at once in the increased happiness of the people, toleration to all religions, and great prosperity. Take the country, for instance, that extends from Joppa to Jerusalem!— the plain of Sharon and the hills and valleys beyond. What a warden the French would make of that! Think what a crop of wheat could be raised there, within easy sail of the best markets! As I understand the Eastern Question, the great obstacle to the good government of these countries is England. Unless she can control them herself she will allow no one else. That I call a selfish policy. I cannot see the humanity of keeping those noble countries under a barbarous rule, merely because there are apprehensions about the road to India. If England went in and took them herself I should be satisfied. But if she will not, why keep other nations out? It seems to me that the Eastern Question could be settled easily enough if the civilizing powers of Europe were to sink their differences and take hold. Russia seems to be the only power that really means to settle it, and it is a mistake of England that she has not been allowed to do so with the general sympathy of the world."[24]

12

Fanny Stone: Diary of an American Girl in Cairo (Soldiers, 1882)

It was 1882. Egypt was in chaos. The American soldiers imported by the Khedive Ismail had come and gone. Only Charles P. Stone remained in his position as head of the Egyptian military.[1] As the previous chapters explain, the Khedive Ismail had been deposed, mostly through foreign intervention. His son Tewfik now ruled. The French and English continued their fight for control of Egypt. The French were winning the cultural war, but the English would soon occupy Egypt. Out of the military came a man named Ahmed al-Arabi, a soldier trained by Stone Pasha. He was to lead a revolt. The war cry was "Egypt for the Egyptians," and their aim was to depose the Khedive Tewfik and throw the foreigners out of the country. Foreign nations brought their ships into the bay of Alexandria poised to protect their interests in Egypt. Foreigners began to leave in great numbers. The British bombarded Alexandria for nearly ten hours. Then they came ashore. It was the third time British troops had invaded Egypt in modern times.[2]

The American timeline to the bombardment is clear. On January 17, 1881, Arabi made a *pronunciamiento* at Abdin Palace in Cairo against discrimination among officers. In September it was repeated with a demand for a constitution and an increase in the size of the army. By February of 1882, Cherif Pasha had resigned as prime minister and was replaced by Mahmoud Sami. Sami appointed Arabi Minister of War. On February 22, United States Agent and Consul General Simon Wolf held a banquet at the New Hotel. He invited every American in Egypt, plus Sami and Arabi. The consuls general of European countries did not attend.[3] Tension grew throughout the country. On April 4, 1882, the steamer *Arabia* arrived from Naples, and it was rumored that the Khedive Ismail was returning to take charge of the country. He was not. By May 31 Arabi had circulated a petition and called for the Khedive Tewfik to leave office. Cairo went silent. Rumors of a Christian massacre circulated. Tewfik could not leave Abdin. On June 1, American Agent and Consul General Simon Wolf resigned, leaving the United States without a leader at this volatile time. On June 8, the Porte at Constantinople, to whom Egypt was still subject, sent a special envoy to try to calm things down. The USS *Galena*, under command of O.A. Batcheller, arrived in Alexandria on June 10. Fifty Americans and 250 Europeans, mostly residents of Alexandria and Cairo, boarded the ship.

As summer approached it was obvious the country was headed for a confrontation. On June 11, 1882, 120 Europeans were murdered as an Egyptian mob rampaged through a residential area near the Place des Consuls, a section of Alexandria mostly inhabited by foreigners.

Arabi did not call out the army to stop the carnage. On June 14, foreign consulates in Cairo abandoned the city and headed to Alexandria with many of their important papers in hand. On June 15, Charles Chaillé-Long was appointed consuls general of the United States to assist Americans in Egypt at the time and care for American interests. Europeans were leaving the country by the thousands. On June 19, the entire European squadron of the U.S. Navy was sent to Alexandria. On June 23, a six-power conference of foreign countries was held, excluding the United States. The Sultan did not attend. On June 26, the conference agreed not to take political advantage of the situation.

Almost all of the Americans in Egypt had something to say about the events of these days. They wrote their firsthand accounts in journals, books, letters, and family papers. Charles Chaillé-Long saw it this way:

> It has been charged that the bombardment of the 11th of July was a crime. This was not the feeling of the foreign population in Egypt. The crime was committed in the refusal to land troops on the 11th day of June, and the bombardment one month after was a tardy recognition of this fact. It was universally asserted at the time, and I submit that subsequent events have proved it to be so, that it was only necessary to show to the fellah the slightest disposition to employ force, and the army of Arabi would have melted away like the rays of the morning sun. Egypt then would not have been lost to France. England would not have escaped by this act an occupation which may cost her more than her prestige, and, above all, humanity would not have been called upon to weep over the calamities which since have befallen Egypt....
>
> This apparent compromise with the crime of the 11th of June had been inspired, it was said, by the humane policy of the consuls to do all to avert a general massacre, and gain time to get their compatriots out of the country. The panic and exodus, even to the dull comprehension of the *prophet* [Arabi], was a proof that if *Egypt* was to be *for the Egyptians,* the legacy would be barren, for the *money* and *industries* were possessed by this *fleeing* people, who since Mehemet-Ali had acquired a right in the soil, and who, in fact, were as truly Egyptian as the *fellah.* The fellah gave to the country his labor, the European his money. Their interests were thus identified, and consequently the flight of the European and the withdrawal of his capital from the country meant little else than the ruin of the fellah. The cry which had been raised of "Egypt for the Egyptians!" was understood, when too late, to have been a deception and a snare....
>
> It has been asserted that England, for political reasons, really desired the destruction of Alexandria. Its mixed population of French, Italian, and Greek represented anything but English interests. The city burned beyond hope of resurrection, they would be driven away from Egypt. England could thus build upon its ruins an English city where Englishmen only would be invited or encouraged to reside.[4]

General Stone described the events in an introduction to his daughter Fanny's article in *The Century Magazine* in 1884.

> On the 6th of July I took the evening train for Alexandria, expecting to return on the 8th.... I felt that it was probable that the British Admiral would eventually bombard Alexandria, but I could not conceive that he could bombard an open sea-port after having proclaimed that he entered its harbor "as a friend,"—certainly not without giving such clear and timely notice that the thousands of Europeans residing in the interior cities (to whom no notice was given) would have opportunity to leave; for he and all the British authorities must have known perfectly well that the bombardment of Alexandria by any European fleet would cause the enraged inhabitants to work vengeance on all Europeans who might be in the country, of whatever nationality.

To my astonishment the notice of only *twenty-four hours* was given, and that notice was given late in the afternoon of the 9th of July, *after the departure from Cairo of the last train on that day for Alexandria*. At the same time the foreign warships and ships of refuge were advised to quit the harbor *at noon on the 10th!*

This barbarous disregard on the part of the British of the lives of citizens of all other nationalities caused me, as well as thousands of others, fearful anxiety, and caused the horrible death of scores of Europeans — French, Germans, Austrians, and Italians....

Then came the British occupation of Alexandria, and the campaign against Arabi. During this campaign I did all of which I was capable to aid the allies of the Khedive; well knowing that while such was my duty, yet the performance of that duty, day by day, and act by act, must necessarily add to the dangers clustering around my family in their isolation. In my position every act was, of course, well known and conspicuous to the enemies of the Khedive....

During the so-called "massacre" of June 11th, 1882, in Alexandria, European *men* were struck down by the infuriated populace, but not a woman or child was injured. During the Christian bombardment of Alexandria scores of Egyptian women and children perished, and their husbands, brothers, and fathers wreaked vengeance, a little later, on the innocent and helpless Europeans at Tantah and Mehallet-el-Kebir.[5]

Fanny's Diary

The Stone family included Stone's second wife Annie Jeannie Stone, his three daughters Hattie (Hettie), Fanny, and Sister (probably Todas), and his son John. They lived on a tree-lined street in an opulent home complete with beautiful gardens and abundant servants in the island community of Zamalek. At that time Zamalek was mostly a garden and only the elite of Cairo were living there. The Stones had a life of privilege, becoming their father's position as the head of the Egyptian Army.

Fanny's voice provides what many of the other voices do not: a look into the affect the bombardment had on families and ordinary people — Egyptians, servants, wailing women, and junior officers who were not sure what was happening or to whom their loyalty belonged. In the *Century* article, Fanny Stone's diary begins on July 6, 1882, the day her father left Cairo for Alexandria and only a few days before the Bombardment of Alexandria:

> *Cairo, July 6th, 1882.* — This has been a day of excitement, and mamma looks pale and tired, in spite of her efforts to bear up bravely. This morning papa announced his intention of going by the evening train to Alexandria, and proposed taking Johnny with him. I saw a pained look in mamma's eyes, and knew she would suffer much from the separation from her dear boy, even for two days only, as proposed; but he looked so wistful and longing when she asked him if he would like to go that she gave her consent....
>
> I had a wretched foreboding all day that some unhappiness was in store for us. The constant coming and going of the staff-officers, the pale faces of mamma and sister, and the alarming telegrams, all conspired to make me nervous and unhappy... [87].

July 8: Stone was to return to Cairo. It was also the day before the British issued the notice that people had 24 hours to leave Alexandria.

> *July 8th.* — Letter from papa. He thinks that Admiral Seymour will finally bombard Alexandria; and that if he cannot find a pretext he will make one. Mamma had an interview with some of the staff-officers, and they say that Arabi will betray the Khedive; that he is determined to rule Egypt, and whatever the Khedive may say or do, Arabi will try to put him aside, even should it mean assassination.

July 10: General Stone places his son onboard the *Lancaster*. Arabi says, "I will sink the entire Inglisee fleet within an hour if they dare attack me."[6] Foreign ships are ordered to leave the harbor.

> *July 10th.*—After passing an anxious day we were startled by having the card of Ali Pacha Cherif (a cousin of the Khedive) brought to the drawing-room. We thought he was with His Highness in Alexandria, and felt instantly that he was the bearer of bad news. He came in his *costume de voyage*, covered with dust, and looking very much agitated. He said: "Madam, I bring you news from Stone Pacha. Admiral Seymour has given notice that he will bombard Alexandria tomorrow. The Khedive has left the palace of Ras-el-Tin, and gone to Ramleh (which is a few miles east of Alexandria, on the shores of the Mediterranean). We had only twenty four hours' notice in which to escape from the city. The Christians have fled to the ships. The Mussulmans are scattered over the country trying to find safety. Stone Pacha desired me to say that he is with the Khedive at the palace of Ramleh, and your son John Bey is at sea, about ten miles out on the flag-ship *Lancaster*. The English threaten to keep up the bombardment twelve hours. After it is over the Pacha will return to the Hotel d'Europe, and your son may return after a few days."
>
> There is great excitement in the city of Cairo. The Arab women are going through the streets to-night wailing and covering their heads with dust.[7]

The Bombardment of Alexandra by the British navy began at 7 A.M. and ended at 5:30 P.M.

> *July 11th.*—The staff-officers came to the house in great numbers to-day to tell us there is no danger for us. The bombardment is said to have ceased at sunset to-day.

After the Bombardment of Alexandria in 1882 (unknown origin).

Official telegrams state that several fine buildings were destroyed, all the forts silenced, and large numbers of Egyptian soldiers killed. Some of the English ships were struck, and report says many English were killed and wounded.

Mamma tried to send a telegram to papa, but failed, as all the European employees, both here and at Alexandria, have fled, and we must wait until they can be replaced by the Egyptian operators who were turned out when the English took charge of the telegraph department; so they say. Neither can we send letters, as the post-office department is also in confusion; however, that will soon be regulated.

Mamma came to the desperate determination of sending our faithful Oster Mohammed to Alexandria with a letter to papa, asking him to send Johnny home, and imploring him to give her definite instructions as to what we shall do.

The panic is simply frightful. The trains going to Port Said and Suez are crowded. I thought all the Christians had gone in the panic following the massacre; but I suppose these now going are the poor *ouvriers*, who hoped to stay on. The different foreign governments are paying their passage to some safe port. Mamma has ordered Mohammed to go to the Hotel d'Europe, and if papa is not there to seek him at the Ramleh palace; and we expect him back to-morrow evening, as the express trains are stopped, and he must take any accommodation he can get. We felt very sad when we parted with the faithful creature; he has been with us for nearly thirteen years, and loves us better than he does himself. When he bade mamma good-bye he said, "My lady, I will find the Pacha if I live; and if he orders me to go to Johnny Bey, I shall go if I have to fight every step of the way." We trust him implicitly. Oh! if papa would only tell us to go, we might reach some safe spot. But, alas! Johnny is separated from us, and every hour that we must remain increases the danger of trying to escape. The railway stations are crowded with infuriated natives who insult Christians, and I hardly believe we could get permission to have a staff-officer accompany us, as these officers are already suspected of wishing ill to the "Arabi party." Mamma has busied herself all day in putting our clothes, or some of them, into trunks, hoping papa will tell us what to do.

July 12: Alexandria is covered with black smoke. The Egyptian army surrounds Ras el Tin with orders to kill the Khedive and burn the palace.[8] Massacre erupts in Tantah, Egypt's third largest city. Trains return to Alexandria on 13th loaded with "fanatics and loot."

July 12th.—Officers have been running in and out all day, bringing the wildest reports that are flying about the city. They say it would be extremely perilous for us to attempt to escape; at any rate, we must abide by papa's decision. Some of the staff-officers

Portrait of Arabi (from *The Three Prophets* by Chaille-Long).

applied for a guard for our house, and two policemen were sent to stand at our gate; but to-day mamma demanded that papa's two orderlies from the War Department should be stationed in the garden, near the door.

They came, and we feel safer; for two finer, braver men never lived. They came to mamma to thank her for having applied for them. They said: "We never had a friend until Stone Pacha came to Egypt. He took us from poverty and wretchedness, and made us what we are, happy, well-fed, well-dressed men, with our families living in comfort. We swear by the heads of our dear children, by the bread that we have eaten, and better than all, by the Prophet, that no harm shall come to the Pacha's wife and children until we lie dead on your door-step...."

It is nearly midnight. Sister is pacing up and down her chamber, waiting. As I look from my window, I see the four armed men looking like statues in the moonlight, and two faithful servants sleeping on the graveled walk before the door.

July 13: Chaillé-Long entered Alexandria and got permission for the Americans to put 120 sailors and marines on shore while the British secured the harbor.

> *July 13th.*—Mohammed returned about two o'clock this morning, and brought a letter from papa, but, alas! not Johnny boy. He had a frightful journey down and back. The train was crowded with horses and munitions of war going down, and with wretched fugitives coming back. He was twelve hours *en route* to Alexandria, and found papa at midnight at the Hotel d'Europe.
>
> The next morning papa took Mohammed with him to see the forts. Many were utterly demolished, and he saw several dead soldiers still lying under the great cannon. They visited the hospital. It must have been a heart-rending sight; the wounded were lying on the bare stone floors, covered with blood and dust, gasping for water, and some dying for want of proper care, as there were only three doctors there. Oh, how could Arabi bring such misery on his country...!
>
> Alexandria is in flames; the soldiers and low class of Arabs are pillaging and plundering, and Arabi is encamped near Ramleh.
>
> This morning, after breakfast, mamma called us all to her, and said: "My children, we are in great trouble, but we must look it bravely in the face, and try to help each other to bear it. Papa has a good reason, of course, for leaving us here; he may rescue us yet; only we may have to undergo great suffering in the meantime. You know he left me money enough only for a few days' expenses. That is all gone, and I must use your little store; I shall be forced to exercise great economy, as it will last but a short time. Now, I want you to promise me to be patient, to be cheerful, and always brave. Go on with your studies, keep always busy, and trust to me to save you, if it is possible, when the worst comes. We have fire-arms enough in the house to defend ourselves until we can get help from the staff-officers; and if they fail us, you can be brave and face death like good soldiers...."
>
> We went out driving this afternoon, taking an orderly on the box with the coachman; but even he could not prevent our being insulted in words, and we shall in future be forced to remain in the house. That will be hard to bear in this hot weather; but we must be cheerful and patient, as we promised this morning.
>
> The streets are crowded with wretched Arabs from Alexandria....

July 14: Chaillé-Long boarded the *Lancaster*, then joined the American landing party. American military from the *Lancaster*, *Nipsic*, and *Quinnebaug* moved into the city center, reopening the U.S. consular agency, put out fires, tried to restore order and are credited with saving the Palace of Justice. Khedive Tewfik was at Ras-el-Tin.

> *July 14th.*—Terrible news from Alexandria. The Khedive, they say, had all his preparations made to come to Cairo, where he might be with his people, and try to stop the English from taking the country. The royal train was ready and waiting for

him, when the palace was surrounded by soldiers sent by Arabi to massacre him and all the court! The Khedive sent to know the meaning of the movement. When the officers of the regiment came into his presence they said: "We have been sent here to fire the palace, and shoot every person who may attempt to leave it; but we cannot do it. We want to remain with Your Highness, and guard you." They all swore fidelity to him, but advised him to fly to the palace of Ras el-Tin, in Alexandria, and call upon the English to protect him, as Arabi was determined to take his life. Then there was a scene of confusion — a general rush for the carriages. Those who could get none went on foot, the soldiers escorting them. They were fired upon by soldiers, or Bedouins, on the way. One carriage carrying four ladies of the court had a horse killed, and they were forced to make their way on foot through the sand and dust for two miles, in their delicate satin slippers and trained dresses. The sister of the vice queen, Madame Daoud Pacha, who was dangerously ill, was carried on a mattress, and was so alarmed by the firing and confusion that she is in a dying condition. Not succeeding in their infamous designs, Arabi's troops went to the railway station and destroyed the beautiful railway carriages, smashing everything they could lay their hands upon.

The Khedive called upon the English admiral for protection, and is safe from Arabi; but oh! — God protect us! — we are in greater danger than ever, since the news has reached Cairo that General Stone remains faithful to the Khedive, even while he is with the English. We have no claim upon them now for protection. Even the staff-officers may desert us. Papa telegraphed them that he intrusted us to their honor; but at that time the Khedive was with his own people, and we were all in sympathy. Our dining-room servant was insolent to mamma at dinner to-day, and we heard him tell mamma's maid that "the Bashaw had gone over to the English...."

Midnight. — Sister has just left me. She came softly into my chamber an hour ago, followed by Todas, both looking like ghosts with their pale, frightened faces, and told me that she had been roused by a tapping at her window. She sprang up and found Mohammed standing below. He had thrown a handful of gravel to waken her, being afraid to call lest he should attract the attention of the policemen, whom he distrusts. His story is a terrible one. There has been a massacre of Christians at Tantah, a station on the railroad between Cairo and Alexandria. We have been sitting here shivering with horror for an hour, and finally determined not to tell mamma until to-morrow morning, as she gets so little sleep at the best.

July 15: The British landed. People aboard ships were disembarked and went to their homes. Lord Charles Beresford was made prefect of police.

July 15th. — This morning we heard that seven staff-officers had been ordered to Kafr Dowar. They are all in a terrible strait. All their sympathies are with the Khedive, and they detest Arabi. But if they refuse to obey the orders of the Minister of War, they will doubtless be shot. Mamma advised them to go, and to take the first chance to escape to Alexandria.

Mamma sent Mohammed with them, telling him to try to get permission to go to Alexandria. She has written to papa imploring him to give her permission to leave, to send her money enough to get us to Palermo, and to send Johnny to join us there.

Several of the staff-officers have offered her as much money as she needs; but she invariably makes the same reply: "You know how much I thank you for your generous kindness, but I cannot leave Cairo until I have permission from the General."

We told her the news from Tantah, but she is firm, and will not leave until we can be sure of papa's approval. We have faithful friends in Moktar Bey, Omar Bey, Latif Bey, Sadie Bey, Abdul-Razak Effendi, and Ismail Effendi Nazeem. All of them are staff-officers. Latif Bey has refused to serve Arabi, although he was offered the command of a regiment. All these officers have offered us refuge in their houses. They said to-day, "General Stone is the father of the staff; we will protect you with our lives...."

July 16: Various consuls returned to Alexandria and opened for business in whatever facilities they found. Arabi sent his soldiers into Alexandria dressed as fellahin. It was rumored he planned to attack the city with 60,000 men.

July 17: Chaillé-Long went to look at the damage to the battery Colonel Beverly Kennon had constructed in 1870 for the coastal defenses of Egypt.

July 17th. — Mohammed returned this morning. Alas! he did not reach Alexandria. When he arrived at Kafr-Dowar he went to an officer, and asked him if Stone Pacha was there. The officer turned upon him with an oath, and told him that Stone Pacha had joined the English. "But, thank God," said he, "we paid him well for it; for we burned him to death in the Hotel d'Europe, before we left Alexandria." Then he ordered Mohammed to return to Cairo, and told him that if Arabi caught him there he would be shot. Poor fellow! He was in an agony of distress. He dreaded coming back to us with such heart-breaking news, and was walking slowly back to the railroad when a soldier spoke to him. Mohammed asked him if it were true that Stone Pacha was killed, and the soldier said, with a shrug of his shoulders: "Perhaps, but I doubt it. I think the Bey you have been talking to only said that to torment you. However, if you value your life, go back to Cairo at once. If you will come with me, I will disguise you as a fellah; and you had better lie down in a cattle-car, and pretend to be sleeping when you see any one approaching."

So Mohammed went with him to his tent, put on a disgustingly soiled old galibeer, and hid himself in a cattle-car....

This morning sister came to her [mamma] and said that Ali and mamma's maid were closeted in the pantry, and that she had overheard them speaking disrespectfully of us, calling us "dogs of Christians," and threatening us. After a few minutes mamma called them to her in the morning-room, and even now, as I think of the interview, I tremble. She told them that they had proved themselves to be faithless wretches; that she had fed them for years, and been like a mother to them; and now, in the first moment of trouble, they had turned traitors to her. Then she told them they were mistaken in thinking they could frighten her. "There never lived the Arab," said she, "who could frighten me. No, not Arabi and all his troops can do it. Go to your work, you miserable cowards, and the first time you *look* insolent I will have you thrashed. Never dare to threaten me again until you are beyond my reach!"

I never saw creatures so completely cowed and frightened as they were. They went sneaking from the room, but begged, before leaving, to be allowed to kiss her hand. They didn't do it, however, and got a reply which must have burned their ears. This evening, when the staff-officers heard of it, they shook their heads and said that mamma was imprudent; but she fired up, and told them that her position was a desperate one and required desperate measures.

They say that the report that papa was killed is false.

July 18: The Americans had withdrawn from Alexandria and only seven marines remained on shore.

July 18th. — Sister, Todas, and I took a short walk early this morning. We were accompanied by the two orderlies. We went to the little English chapel, hoping to be able to get in and get some books from the library. We found the boab sleeping at the door, and having roused him, he opened it for us. I was astonished at seeing the orderlies follow us in, and more astonished when they took cushions from the seats, and placed them on the floor to kneel upon. I asked them, "Is it possible that you are going to pray in a Christian church?" "Why not, my lady?" said they. "We Mussulmans can pray anywhere. Do we not all pray to the same good God? Jesus Christ belongs more to us than He does to you. You call Him the Son of God, which He was not. He was a great Prophet, and we love and respect Him. We love His blessed mother, too, the Sitta Miriam."

We left them to their prayers, and went into the little library to get our books. When we reentered the chapel we found the orderlies looking with great curiosity at the organ; and when I told them it was a "musica," they begged me to play for them. I sat down and played "Nearer, my God, to Thee," and when I told them how our dead President loved it, they begged me to play it again....

Ten more staff-officers have been called.

July 19th.—Our troubles are increasing. This morning Major Abdul Razak Effendi requested a private interview with mamma, which lasted nearly an hour. When he left she called us all to her, and told us that there had been a massacre of Europeans at Mehallet-el-Kebir; that two European officials of the cadastre had been killed, cut into small pieces, and carried about the town by a procession, while the dogs were fed with their flesh! The women made what they call "the cry of joy," and waved their handkerchiefs. The sheiks of the mosques saved several families by shutting them up in the mosques, and afterward concealing them in their houses and one sheik saved a gentleman by shaving his head, putting him in *sais* costume, and letting him run in front of his horse to a place of safety, about ten kilometres away. Many of the sheiks have behaved well thus far. One of them (Sheik Ibrahim) in Alexandria saved a large number of men on the 11th of June, by shutting them up in his mosque and guarding them until the riot was over.

Abdul Razak Effendi says we must leave our house without delay, and advised mamma to prepare to go to-night to Omar Bey's house. He said we ought to get away without allowing our servants (except our Mohammed) to know where we are going. Shortly after he left, Omar Bey and Ismail Effendi came also to urge us to leave, and Omar Bey said that we would be safe in his house. Mamma said she would consider the matter, and give them an answer at sunset.

Then we had a regular *paw-wow* among ourselves. Mamma told each one of us to give the best advice she could, which made us very proud, so that we chattered like three magpies, while she sat and listened. Finally she said: "Well, girls, I will tell you what I think about it. It is all nonsense to suppose we could leave this house without our destination being known; for I have seen three men watching the house the last three nights past, and they will follow us. I shall not run away from my servants like a coward, and leave my house to be pillaged. Omar Bey's servants would betray us to their neighbors, and in case of trouble we should be caged there, and probably be the cause of ruin to his family. His house is situated in the old part of the city, where the air is foul, and we should be deprived of the comforts to which we are accustomed. The result would be disastrous in every way. We would be prisoners in an old Arab house, out of spirits, out of health, and so miserable that it would soon be a mercy if the Arabs should come and cut our throats. I propose that we stay at home like brave women, and live like Christians as long as we can."

We always agree when mamma speaks, and at sunset she told the officers of her decision. They left us looking very unhappy....

July 20: The Sultan wrote to the American consul: "Your country is the only one I can rely upon for friendly services. It is the only one not asking my money; it is not waiting for a partition of my territory."

July 20th.—The boab of the Khedivial Geographical Society came to mamma this morning, and said that his uncle had been ordered to Kafr-Dowar, and would leave at noon. He said that if mamma would send a letter to papa by him, it would surely reach him, for his uncle's intention was to desert and make his way to Alexandria as soon as possible. Mamma wrote a short letter, telling papa not to be anxious, and trying to comfort him by making the best of everything. We never speak of Johnny boy to mamma....

The spy *did* understand our conversation, or at least enough of it to make trouble for us. Omar Bey was called to the War Department this morning, and told that he was reported as having talked treason in a certain house, and should it be repeated he would be put in irons in the citadel! We hear that several of the staff-officers have deserted Arabi, and arrived safely at Alexandria.

July 21: General Wolseley ordered the British army of occupation to Egypt.

July 21st. — Our cook came to mamma today and begged her to discharge Ali, Fatmah, and the boab. He said they are all traitors to us, and he is afraid we will be poisoned by one of them. "I have been your servant for eight years," said he, "and it is my pride to serve you well; but I must leave you unless those servants are sent out of the house, and forbidden to enter your doors again. You know you are safe with me, but I don't trust those three, who have access to your dining-room; and should you be poisoned it would be my ruin. I will do Ali's work, and Mohammed will attend the door." He is a good, honest man, and I know papa trusts him perfectly. Poor mamma! she looks tired to death, and I know she hardly sleeps at all, for I frequently hear her walking about her chamber, when I wake in the night. I wish the English would hasten their preparations, and attack Arabi. He is growing stronger, and the people are beginning to believe it is a *holy war*. We do not receive much political news from Europe. I believe the Turks are fooling both England and Arabi; at any rate, Arabi says he is working under the Sultan's orders, and England seems to believe that Turkey will help her to restore order in Egypt....

Every evening at about nine o'clock a band of children, led by a man, parade the streets crying, "Long live Arabi! God give him victory! Death to the Christians!" This evening they came and stood in front of our gate, crying, "Death to the Christians!" but the orderlies rushed out upon them with clubs, and frightened them well. Arabi's wife pays these children to do this, and they stand for an hour at a time before her door, shouting like so many lunatics.

Mamma paid the three faithless servants, and sent them away at sunset. The two men were very sullen, but Fatmah cried, threw herself down at mamma's feet, and begged to stay; but mamma was firm, and Fatmah left the house in tears.

July 22d. — One officer after another has been here to-day, imploring us to leave our house; but mamma positively refused to do so ... at sunset she has every door and window opening to the front thrown wide open, and lamps lit in the rooms. At night, on retiring, we see that the ground floor is well barricaded; but on the floor above we sleep with all our windows open. We sit in the vestibule opening on the front balcony until eleven o'clock, with five lamps in the chandelier, the door and windows open, and mamma has had the piano moved in there. We receive the officers there, and talk freely about the events of the day; but I think it would puzzle a spy to make much of our conversation, as we have adopted the plan of speaking four languages at once....

July 23d. — Mamma made an announcement at the breakfast-table this morning that fairly took our breath away. Our money will last only about a week longer! I don't know what she intends to do about it; but when Todas said to sister and me, "Don't fret, girls; 'mamma' will manage to have bread and beefsteaks for us every day, or I am a Dutchman, and she won't borrow the money for it either," my spirits rose, and I reproached myself for not having encouraged the dear mother, by saying we would not mind living on the stores in the magazine till the end of time. I often think of what Jo said in "Little Women," " *I wonder what girls do who have not a good mother.*"

To-night Todas saw a man perched in a tree, looking in at a window, and she gave the alarm; but he scrambled down and ran like a deer. The orderlies fired at him, but he got away through Rousseau Bey's garden.

July 24th. — Mamma sent a letter to Arabi Pacha this morning, demanding papa's pay for the month of July! The officers looked at her in perfect amazement when she told them, and said: "Madam, you will not get a centime. How could you do such an imprudent thing?" She replied: "I shall get it, but I may have to go to Kafr-Dowar before I succeed." One of them said: "If all American women are like you, I would not like to go to war against your men...."

July 25th.—The two officers are gone. They will try to escape if possible.

The moudirs (governors of provinces!) who have failed to raise troops for Arabi are being brought in and put in irons at the citadel. Among them is our acquaintance Ibrahim Bey Tewfik, who was formerly one of papa's staff-officers. He is very firm and a courageous loyalist. His beautiful little daughter is one of our schoolmates.

Mamma complained to the Prefect of Police yesterday about the band of children who parade the streets, and it has been forbidden for the future. I wonder how she dares to be so bold, but she says it is the best plan, and by the results I know she is right....

We got a letter from papa this morning. It was brought into the lines by Monsieur de Lesseps' servant. Papa and Johnny are at Ras-el-Tin palace with the Khedive. They are very anxious about us, not having heard from us since Mohammed was at Alexandria on the 12th; though they had heard that he was afterward at Kafr-Dowar, trying to get through to them. Papa thanks mamma for being so brave, as was shown by her letter by Mohammed; tells her to keep up good courage, promising to rescue us. Johnny was a week on board the flag-ship, and saw all the bombardment. We have a cousin, who took care of Johnny. He is a midshipman, and one of the officers of the flag-ship told papa that he is one of the finest young men he ever met. So our Johnny boy was in good hands.

There was a great row in the garden today. The orderlies and Mohammed called the policemen idle, lazy vagabonds, and threatened to report them to the Prefect. The policemen were insolent, and it ended in the orderlies putting on their swords and marching them off to the guard-house. One of the policemen, seeing mamma on the balcony, shouted, "I am glad to go; I don't want to protect dogs of Christians." They will be severely punished, for the Prefect of Police is an inflexible officer, and I think he deserves the approbation of the civilized world for the way in which he has preserved order in Cairo. He is untiring in his vigilance; and, although an Arabist, he will save his head, I hope, even if the English take Cairo while he is in charge. Not a Christian has been hurt here, not a house robbed, and he has even succeeded in sending all the Alexandrian ruffians out of town.

July 26th.—...Arabi has sent an order for £50 on account of papa's pay, to be given to mamma! and he sent her many compliments!!

We take our walk every morning. It is like walking through an enchanted city of the fairy tales. In the whole European quarter there is not a house open excepting our own. Even the few Arab families who have houses in this quarter have left them and gone into the heart of the city, fearing that in case of pillage they might be killed.

All the staff-officers in Cairo were here this evening, and mamma read parts of papa's letter to them.

July 27th.—Major Abdul Razak came this morning to tell us that he and Ismail-Effendi Nazim have resolved to escape to Alexandria. They will not serve Arabi, and they expect every day to be called upon to do so. They are planning to get away the day after they receive their month's pay. They implored mamma to make an effort to go with them in disguise, but she says it would be madness to attempt it.

"How could I disguise myself as an Arab peasant woman with my yellow hair and blue eyes ? And it would be almost as difficult with the girls. We would be killed before reaching Ismailia."

"Well, madam," said Abdul Razak, "you will be killed if you remain. Every hour the danger is increasing; and even if we should resolve to stay, it is more than possible that we could not reach you in time of danger. We must, for your sake, try to get to Alexandria as soon as possible, and find help for you."

"I will consult the officers before I decide," said mamma, and so the matter stands.

July 28: British Parliament recognizes preparations for war.

July 28th. — Mamma sent for all the officers this morning and held a "council of war." She told them that she was thinking of making an attempt to escape, and wanted their advice.

They were absolutely horrified at the idea, and told her that it would be impossible, that a *rat* could not escape from Cairo. Mamma did not, of course, speak of Abdul Razak's plan, as it might have compromised him; but she told them that she was determined to make every effort in her power to reach Alexandria.

While she was speaking Abdul Razak and papa's interpreter came in, and the former said that after leaving us yesterday he went to the War Department and learned there that two of mamma's letters to papa had been captured and translated, to be sent to Arabi. They were taken from two men who had promised to take them safely to papa. Fortunately they contained nothing that could be disapproved of.

Nothing was decided this morning, but mamma says she has a plan which she thinks will succeed....

We had a bad fright last night. Just about one o'clock sister heard a sharp rap at her door. She sprang out of bed and called to me. We soon roused mamma and Todas, and then we boldly demanded, "Who is there?" Then we heard Mohammed say, "I must speak to Madame." Mamma threw on her dressing-gown, and opened the door. She found Mohammed waiting to tell her that Moktar Bey had come to get a letter for papa, as Raouf Pacha had finally obtained permission to pass Kafr-Dowar and enter Alexandria, and would leave Cairo at daybreak. We girls all crept back to bed again, and mamma wrote a few lines to papa. I know now by experience that I shall be terrified almost to death if the Arabs come to attack us in the night.

July 29th. — We have been busy packing all day. Mamma has written to Arabi asking permission to leave. She stated her reasons for wishing to go, and asked that a guard might be furnished her to Ismailia. The letter was sent to the War Department yesterday, and when the officers came here this morning mamma read a copy of it to them. They said it was perfectly useless to have sent it; but mamma replied that Americans believe that what is worth having is worth asking for....

July 30th. — There was a frightful noise in the streets last night. All the population seemed to be shouting and beating tin pans. We soon heard that an English prisoner had been brought in, and the poor foolish citizens thought it was Admiral Seymour who had been captured!

To-day all papa's papers have been packed in good strong boxes. *Mamma had the iron safe, containing his diaries for twelve years, broken open, and we hope to save them even should we be unable to take them with us.* Some of the officers came to-day to tell us that when mamma's letter was read last night at the council a Pacha rose and said: "She must not be permitted to go. She is a dangerous woman to our cause. Her house has been a rendezvous for traitors, and she is kept well informed as to everything we do."

Mamma is beginning to show the strain upon her. She looked as though she were dying yesterday when she heard papa had been shot while reconnoitering the outposts from Alexandria. We did not believe it; yet such reports increase our anxiety. The officers begin to bring sorrowful faces to us. They say we will not be permitted to go, and we get almost distracted by the different counsels they offer —....

July 31 st. — No reply comes yet to mamma's letter. They evidently intend to hold on to us. Abdul Razak and Ismail Effendi are waiting to hear the decision before they attempt to escape. Their alarm for us increases day by day. They say that every evening they see men watching the house. Abdul Razak has left his own house, and sleeps at night in one nearly opposite ours, whence he could reach us quickly.

Mamma has finally decided what to do in case her demand is refused. She intends to send for the leader of that band of Greeks and ask their protection. At the first signal of danger we will go to them with Mohammed and the orderlies. Mamma was very pale when she told us of her plan, and I knew it was simple desperation that had forced her to such a decision. "We must have a fixed plan," said she. "The staff-officers may not be able to save us, as two of them are resolved to escape, and the others may be called to the seat of war any day. These Greeks are desperate men, but they are brave. I think — indeed, I believe — they would give their lives to save us, and we have Mohammed and our brave orderlies. And now, girls, I am going to give you another shock. To-night, about nine o'clock, put on your hats and wraps. I am going to reconnoiter Cairo in the open carriage." I thought she had gone mad, and felt so sick and weak that I could not stand. She quietly remarked, however, "You need fresh air, and I am going to try the effect of it on you, young lady."

True enough, after dinner she ordered the open carriage, and we all followed her to the gate. The streets were in a blaze of gaslights, and the lamps on the carriage threw their light directly on mamma's and sister's faces. The servants remonstrated, but it was useless. One of the orderlies mounted on the box beside the coachman, and away we went straight into the heart of the city, where thousands of Arabs were congregated on the sidewalks, eating, drinking, and smoking, after their day of fasting.

For once in our lives we created a sensation. Every man, woman, and child seemed petrified with astonishment on seeing four Christian ladies driving boldly through the streets at such a time.

We drove rapidly, as mamma said it would not do to leave them a moment in which to recover from their surprise, or we might be treated to a pistol-shot. We drove past nearly all the open-air cafes in Cairo, and only once heard a word spoken to us. One man cried after us, "*Affarum ya Nousranieh*," "Bravo! you Christians!"...

August 2d.—Raouf Pacha arrived here last night from Alexandria, and brought a letter and money from papa. When he passed through Kafr-Dowar, Arabi told him that we might leave, and he would furnish a guard.

It seems that *Raouf Pacha told Arabi that we were going to be demanded by the commander of the United States ship Quinnebaug, in the name of the United States Government, and that this ship would be at Ismailia on the 4th. He advised Arabi to let us go, and Arabi sent instructions to the War Department to give us notice.*

This morning His Excellency Yacoub Pacha, Under Minister of War to Arabi, came to see mamma. We girls were curious to hear what he had to say, so Todas and I hid behind a portiere, whence we could see as well as hear. He is a fine-looking man, very graceful and dignified, but there was a stern expression on his face, and I thought mamma would have trouble with him; for she had said laughingly, when his card was brought in, "Girls, I am going to get a special train for you, and select my guard, and Arabi's government will pay for it."

It was an interesting interview....

Finally he said, with a charming smile, that Arabi had ordered a special train and a guard for us. "But madam," said he, "take no care on yourself about it, whatever; I will see that you reach Port Said, and your expenses will be our affair. I have telegraphed Monsieur de Lesseps to have a steam-boat ready for you at Ismailia."

He then said she might take as much baggage as she chose, and when she asked if it would be examined, he looked horrified at the very idea. Bravo! we shall be able to get papa's papers away.

Mamma asked if she might select her own guard and take three of her servants with her. He bowed, and said nothing could give him more pleasure than to gratify any request of hers. He then told mamma that it was reported in Alexandria that the English prisoner here was treated with the greatest cruelty, and he asked her if she would be so good as to visit the gentleman and talk with him freely. He said that he had given orders that everything should be done to make him comfortable, and he hoped that mamma would be satisfied with the treatment which the gentleman received. Mamma promised to go at four o'clock....

At four o'clock Moktar Bey came to conduct mamma to the place where the prisoner is confined. I accompanied them, carrying several volumes of Dickens's,

Thackeray's, and Lever's works. Arrived there, we found that the place looked like anything else than a prison. It was the school of the young Egyptian princes, a little palace in the center of a beautiful garden near Abdin palace. We entered a pretty reception room, and a fair young English lad came forward, smiling, to meet us. He was the picture of youth and health, with all the surroundings of such luxury as can be seen in the Egyptian capital. The apartment that he occupies is that of the Khedive's eldest son, and his north country clothing had been replaced by an elegant suit of white linen, much more suitable to the climate of Cairo in August. Mamma laughingly told him that he looked to her more like a young English prince at home than a prisoner of war; and he replied that he was called the "guest of Arabi Pacha," and that he had only to express a wish for anything except liberty, and it was gratified if possible.

We remained with him an hour and a half in pleasant conversation, and mamma could find nothing in which to add to his comfort but some English books, a small addition to his wines, and a few drawing materials. Two young Egyptians who speak English remained constantly with him, and seemed to take pride in doing everything in their power to please him. These young men followed us to our carriage, and promised to serve him faithfully.

The above description of our visit to the prisoner is taken from a letter mother wrote shortly after we reached Alexandria.

The diary continues. General Stone's family made their way to Ismailia, then took a steamer via the Suez Canal to Alexandria, where they were reunited with General Stone and his son.

On August 17, Chaillé-Long submitted his resignation.[9] Simon Wolf did not return because in the interim and due to current events, Congress abolished the office of United States consul general to Egypt. Arabi was defeated at Tell el Kebir on September 13. Although accounts vary, the British losses were amazingly small (around 50) to the deaths of the Egyptians (around 2000 in the fortifications alone). On September 15 the British occupied Cairo. Arabi was put on trial and on December 3 he was condemned to exile.[10] It would take another 70-plus years before Mohammad Ali's dream of an independent Egypt would be realized.

Epilogue

In 1837, forty years before the occupation, George Robbins Gliddon, America's first consul in Cairo (see Chapter 6), made the following assessment:

> On the death of Mohammed Ali, who being now on the verge of threescore and ten may be expected to close his wonderful career within a few years, his son, Ibrahim Pasha, will succeed to the power[?] at present held by his father.... Should Ibrahim's life be also cut short, then Abbas Pasha, the grandson, or Seid [Sa'id] Bey the son of Mohammad Ali (a lad of sixteen now educating for the purpose) would follow out the Pasha's views; and if even these should fail, it is more probable the chain of events would make Egypt a province of Great Britain, and the connecting link with her Indian possessions, than she should again become a province of the Turk.[11]

13

Anna Young Thompson: Diary of a Trip on the Ibis *(Missionary, 1887)*

The Metro line from Midan Tahrir, Cairo's biggest and busiest square, travels south on its way to the once-elegant spa suburb of Helwan. One of its first stops is in Old Cairo, where around 30 B.C. the Romans built a fortress which they called Babylon and where over 600 years later the Arabs founded the city of *Il Foustat*. Here the three great religions of the world — Judaism, Christianity, and Islam — have stood side by side for centuries. The Ben Ezra Synagogue, founded in 882 and known for the *Cairo Genizah* (a collection of medieval texts), stands on the site where Moses was reputedly found in the bulrushes of the Nile. Beside it the Christian Church of the Holy Family was built over the cave believed to have housed the Holy Family on their flight into Egypt. To the north along the same street is the Mosque of Amr, the first mosque built in Egypt. Although all of these holy sites face the modern Metro line, they cannot be seen, for between the Metro and the religious buildings are some of the Christian cemeteries of Cairo. Four, the German-Swiss Cemetery, the Protestant Cemetery, the tiny American Cemetery, and the broad and spacious English Cemetery, are the closest.[1]

The loved ones of Americans who died in Egypt faced real problems. The deceased were not permitted to be buried: not in Muslim cemeteries, not in Coptic cemeteries, not in the desert. Yet they had to be buried before the second sunset, as Egyptian law dictated. In 1875 the missionaries of the United Presbyterian Church of North America, seeing the need for a resting place for the growing number of American Christians who died in Egypt, petitioned the Khedive Ismail asking for a small plot of desert land around Old Cairo to be used as a cemetery for American Christians. He agreed. The cemetery still exists today. Unfortunately, it is not well maintained. The English Cemetery next door is immaculate. So is the German Swiss cemetery. No one feels responsible for the American Cemetery where many of the missionaries are buried: not the American Embassy, nor the American University (a former president is buried there), nor the current American Protestant communities in Cairo. Neither does the United Presbyterian Church of America, which sent the missionaries to Egypt. The latter has copious records and reports from these missionaries in their archives in Philadelphia. Those are carefully maintained, but the mortal remains of the men and women who forged the path and dedicated their lives to the Presbyterian missionary system are not. This seems unforgivable. It would seem that someone should honor these dead who gave their lives in the service of the Lord.

The American Missions in Egypt

The American Board of Commissioners for Foreign Missions was established in the United States in 1810. They designated four areas in which to do their missionary work: among ancient peoples, primitive cultures, ancient Christian churches, and Muslims.[2] They sent their first missionaries off to India in 1813. Missionaries did not start coming to the Middle East until 1818–19, but when they did, sixty of them arrived in the area almost at once. Two American missionaries made the trip to Egypt to see if their efforts were needed: Levi Parsons and Pliny Fisk. The two men arrived in Egypt in January of 1822. Parsons died of dysentery on February 10, 1822, and was buried in Alexandria at the Greek Convent (the only such place Christians could be buried at the time).[3] Fisk returned to Egypt within two years with two other missionaries, the American Reverend Jonas King, and the German Jewish Christian convert Reverend Joseph Wolff. That journey was the more fruitful expedition, for the trio went south as far as Luxor, and were able to converse with Christians and Jews in various parts of the country in order to make a better assessment of the possibility of missionary work in Egypt. Within a year Parsons and company had left Egypt and no one came to officially begin the movement for three decades.

On May 21, 1853, the First United Presbyterian Church of Allegheny, Pennsylvania, "resolved that our missionaries be instructed to occupy Cairo at their earliest convenience."[4] In the meantime the Associated Reformed Church had sent the American Mission Society to the Middle East, and in 1854 sent the Rev. and Mrs. Thomas McCague to Cairo. The two churches merged in 1858–9 to create the United Presbyterian Church of North America. By 1859 they founded a Presbytery of Egypt.

This was the beginning of the American Mission in Egypt, the only American Protestant mission in Egypt from 1862 to 1882. Among the dominant missionaries in Egypt were Andrew Watson, who made many of the decisions; his son Charles Watson, who founded The American University in Cairo Press; and Julian Lansing, who served forty-five years in Egypt.

Christianity in Egypt

Through the millennia Egypt has been the center of many religious innovations. The concept of the one God was first conceived by the Pharaoh Akhenaton during the New Kingdom. When Jesus Christ was born in Bethlehem, a few hundred miles from Cairo, he and his family fled to Egypt to avoid Herod's edicts. Within forty years, Christianity, the religion with Jesus at its center, came to Egypt in the form of Saint Mark. Mark's journey bore fruit, and Christianity not only spread through the Delta and up the Nile, but also into the distant deserts. By the third century these early Christians developed the concept of monasticism. Born in the deserts of Egypt, where it is traditionally believed St. Anthony, followed by St. Paul, went into the desert to experience solitude and establish anchorites to find a pure path to God, monasticism spread throughout the Christian nations.[5]

There were issues in Christianity upon which Christians could not agree. Powerful men had theories and each believed his interpretation of Christianity was the correct one. That led to variations and schisms in the church. It gave rise to such Eastern sects as Gnosticism, Manichaeism, and Nestorianism. The Christological debate, over the simultaneous divinity and humanity of Jesus Christ, became the one issue that would divide Christians for centuries to come. Finally, in the fourth century, Eastern and Western Christians tried to come to a final decision over the human and divine nature of Jesus Christ. Three separate councils were called. Three separate creeds were established.

The Council of Nicea in 325 established the Nicean Creed: "And in one Lord Jesus Christ, the only-begotten Son of God, begotten of the Father before all worlds; God of God, Light of Light, very God of very God; begotten, not made, being of one substance with the Father, by whom all things were made." It maintained God and Jesus were one. It did not satisfy all points of view. In the end, at the Council of Chalcedon in 451, the schism became permanent. Refusing to accept the Roman doctrine, and at variance with the Eastern or Orthodox view, the Coptic Church of Egypt was born. The Copts believe, to this day: "The Lord is perfect in His divinity, and He is perfect in His humanity, but His divinity and His humanity were united in one nature called 'the nature of the incarnate word.' Which was reiterated by Saint Cyril of Alexandria. Copts, thus, believe in two natures 'human' and 'divine' that are united in one 'without mingling, without confusion, and without alteration.' These two natures 'did not separate for a moment or the twinkling of an eye'" (quotes from the declaration of faith at the end of the Coptic divine liturgy).[6]

Although most Western Christians today know little of these distinctions, the debate as to the duality of Christ continues to this day, as do religious schisms. To further complicate Christianity, the Roman church was splintered into various sects: Catholic, Protestant, Lutheran, Methodist, and more. By the nineteenth century antagonism within Christianity was just as great as antagonism between Christianity and the world's other great religions. The Moravian, as well as the European and American missionaries soon to follow (see Chapter 1), saw their role as uniting all Christians under the banner of Protestantism. The Friars de Propaganda Fide and the Padre de Terra Santa, who also established missionaries in Egypt, wanted the converts to follow the Catholic traditions. Forbidden to proselytize among the Muslims, all the missionaries did most of their work among the Copts. Needless to say, the American Protestant missionary movement did not honor or recognize the Moravian or the Catholic missionary work in Egypt.

Of course, the development of Christianity in Egypt was far more complicated than these few paragraphs suggest. All of these confusing positions would have far-reaching repercussions in developing East/West relationships.

Anna Young Thompson

Anna Young Thompson was one of dozens of women who went to Egypt as missionaries. Women brought a gift to mission work: domesticity. They were given access to the society through its women. They met them in the suks as they haggled over eggplants and tomatoes; they met them in their homes where the Americans could relate to such basic issues as submission, children, and even food; and eventually they met them in the exotic *harems* (*Zenana*) where they enjoyed leisure time feasting and playing games. They had access that was denied to most men.

Missionary work also gave the American women something else: emancipation. The missionary women had many freedoms denied to their sisters in America. They were put in charge of substantial projects, of schools, of the development of curriculum. They often traveled alone to mission locations in the Delta and Upper Egypt. They wrote articles and books and, unlike Sarah Rogers Haight, could sign their own names to their work. Their opinions counted. Anna Young Thompson stands out among American women in Egypt. In 1890 she refused to leave a mission meeting until the women were permitted to vote on important issues. The men conceded and the women won the vote — thirty years before their sisters won the right to vote in America.[7]

Thompson was born in the small town of Bavington in Washington County, Pennsylvania,

The *Ibis,* the missionary *dahabeyyiah* at Luxor Temple (in Charles R Watson's *In the Valley of the Nile*).

in 1851. Her father, Dr. David Thompson, was a minister who loaded a Conestoga wagon and took his family to Ohio and then to Oregon. Anna was sent back from Oregon to her uncle W.S. Young in Philadelphia for a while, but the family returned to Ohio and so did Anna. When she was ready to be educated she was sent back to Washington County to the Washington Seminary for Girls, which in later years would become part of Washington and Jefferson College.

When Anna was twenty years old, the mission sent her to Egypt. She was given a onetime $200 clothing allowance and a promise of $500 a year. She arrived in Alexandria aboard the ship *Hector* out of Liverpool on December 7, 1872.[8] Within a few weeks she was in the Fayoum visiting her Aunt Henrietta and Henrietta's husband Rev. Harvey. Although the Harveys wanted Anna to remain with them in the Fayoum, on her return to Cairo, Dr. Andrew Watson, the moving force behind the American Mission in Egypt, assigned her to Mansura, a village in the Delta of the Nile. He wanted to open a theological seminary there. She worked there as headmistress of the girl's school for some time, but spent most of her sixty-one years in Egypt working with women in the Bulaq and Ezybekkiah, areas of Cairo.[9] Anna either founded or took a major role in the Women's Christian Temperance Society of Egypt, the Christian Endeavor Society, and the Zanana visits. She also wrote copiously for missionary magazines.[10] Among her bountiful papers at the Presbyterian Historical Society in Philadelphia is *Diary of an Excursion aboard the Ibis.* The excursion was a month-long journey by *dahabeyyiah* along the 152-mile-long Damietta branch of the Nile between Cairo, where the Nile divided into branches, and Ras el Bar, a tiny resort village at the edge of Lake Manzala and the Mediterranean Sea. That journey is a microcosm of the routine of missionary work.

The Ibis

The *Ibis* is a story in its own right. It was an iron *dahabeyyiah* with cabins and sails, originally purchased in 1860 by three of the missionaries (McCague, Lansing, Hogg) and used to expand missionary work into Upper Egypt and the Delta. Originally built for the Viceroy Sa'id Pasha, who had intended to add steam, it had more canvas than other boats on the Nile and was the swiftest vessel in Egypt. Sa'id sold it and it was resold to the missionaries. Charles Watson reported: "The *Ibis* soon became known all along the river. The report of its movements preceded it. At many towns, it would scarce be moored before an interested crowd would be gathered, and work would begin without delay."[11] Travel on the *Ibis* was not a hardship. The missionaries spread God's word aboard a vehicle which was a home, a chapel, and a warehouse for Christian literature. Perhaps Rev. Hogg, one of the men who first bought the *Ibis*, said it best: "Life on a Nile-boat has a charm all its own. There is a subtle witchery in the river that awakens in the traveler a love for it beyond the bounds of cold reason."[12]

The Delta

Through the millennia the river Nile and the Mediterranean Sea have clashed at the Egyptian coast. The sea pushes south while the Nile pushes north. The power of the sea and its accompanying wind forces the Nile to split into channels, causing the water and the rich soil to fan out in order to find its way out of Africa. This conflict created the Delta. The ancient historian and explorer Herodotus named it a Delta because it looked to him like the Greek letter of the same name. In a country with so many amazing sites and places, the Nile Delta receives less notice than other regions of Egypt. But it is an interesting and dynamic place. At its western edge, Alexander the Great put his city. At its eastern edge is Port Said, which by Anna's day was the northern entrance to the Suez Canal. Between these two busiest ports in Egypt were and are a bevy of resorts such as Abu Qir, Baltim, and Ras el Bar. There is also a series of four lakes. They are Lake Maryut, which is not part of the Delta; Lake Idku, between Alexandria and Rosetta; Lake Burullus, containing 73 islands; and the largest, Lake Manzala, which may have been the outlet for the now-gone Tanitic distributary (branch) of the Nile. All except Lake Maryut are linked not only to the Nile but to the sea as well, so their waters are not as fresh as the Nile and not as salty as the sea. All are shallow. All are estuaries which attract birds and fish. All support a bevy of water-related industries.

As the Delta moves south it slowly narrows. About 15 miles north of Cairo the Nile becomes a single river once again. Not only did this location give the town access to Upper Egypt, but to Lower Egypt via the many distributaries. Every ruler of Egypt from the ancients to the moderns placed an important city at that location: Memphis of the Ancient Egyptians, Babylon of the Romans, Fustat of the Arabs of the seventh century, and Il Kahira of the Fatamids in the tenth century. These communities are all incorporated into the Cairo of today.

Within recorded history there were seven known distributaries of the Nile. From west to east they were the Canopic, Rosetta, Sebennitic, Damietta, Mendesian, Tanitic, and Pelusiac. Today, and probably since 900 A.D., two remain: the Rosetta, larger and more famous, which was used by early nineteenth-century travelers to reach Cairo, and the Damietta, more historic as the route of the conquering Hyksos, the site of the Fifth and Seventh Crusades, and possibly the land of Goshen of the Jews.

In August of 1887, Anna Young Thompson and a bevy of American missionaries left Cairo for a month-long journey on the *Ibis* down the Nile and through the Delta as far as the

Nile Barrage around 1899 (in Frederick C Penfield, *Present Day Egypt*).

Mediterranean Sea. She kept a diary of that journey which offers great insight into the everyday lives of the American missionaries on the Nile.

The Journey

What becomes evident as one reads Anna's diary is that the missionaries were travelers too. Most enjoyed their journey. Certainly Anna Y, as she came to be called, enjoyed it for over sixty years. Living in Cairo with its suks, bazaars, exotic foods, and visitors in native garb from all over Africa is a visual feast. Sailing on the Nile with the African landscape passing by, filled with birds and beasts and men hauling water from the Nile with exotic machines, is equally enchanting. There is no drudgery in Anna's tale. There is no superiority. The missionaries did not keep to themselves in a foreign land never tasting of its people and their customs. They imbibed. They became immersed in the life: they, too, as defined by the Middle East scholar Jason Thompson, "passed through the mirror." Thompson maintains there were two types of travelers in Egypt during the early decades of the nineteenth century: those such as Englishman Edward William Lane, who were glad to be back home and away from Egypt forever; and those who "passed through the mirror, converted to Islam, and made lives for themselves in the East." The latter, he said, "tended to be lost to the 'Other' side, rarely leaving substantial records of their adventures."[13] Francis Barthow is a likely American candidate, as, perhaps, are Khalil Aga and George Bethune English. But the missionaries, too, are late nineteenth-century candidates. At this point the mirror has evolved. The missionaries spoke Arabic, but they did not wear native clothes, and did not convert to Islam. Instead they tried to convert Islam. They did keep substantial records of their adventures, and some, like Anna, were lost to the "Other" as surely as were Thompson's candidates. Anna, fluent in Arabic, student of all things Egyptian, and patron of women's rights, wanted to die in Egypt and be buried there. She said it was her home.

On August 4, 1887, "in company with Rev W. Harvey and family (Ibrihim Girgis of the boarding school came with us.) Sufauf and Ali,"[14] they bid farewell to the Lansing and Watson families and left early morning for the *Ibis*. Setting sail by 10:30 within a few hours they sat down to a meal of "cold chicken, olives, pickles, plum jam and grapes" (1).

> Near sunset we had a fine view of what was an amazing and odd sight. The cross-
> ing of herds of buffaloes from the island to the main land. The cows were all covered
> except their faces which rose above the water, but on the shoulders several boys were
> sitting carrying their clothes on their heads like turbans. One boy said as he sailed
> past us "It is better here." About eight P.M. the wind fell and it was very pleasant sit-
> ting out on the deck in the beautiful moonlight. We thought it was delightful, every-
> thing being favourable on board and at home...[2–3].

As the *Ibis* moved north, it came to the place where the Nile splits into the Rosetta (west) and the Damietta (east) distributaries. This was a logical place to build a dam to control the flow of the river and increase agricultural production in the Delta. Mohammad Ali in the 1830s began building what was to become known as the Barrage. Building continued through the reign of Ismail and the rule of the British, and was finally finished in the first decade of the twentieth century. In Anna's day the Barrage was still unfinished, but the great gates would open to allow boats to pass. The *Ibis* arrived at the Barrrage on Friday, August 5:

> We awoke before six o'clock and found ourselves anchored near the Barrage, which
> we had reached about midnight. After a hurried breakfast we went out to see the
> dahabeeah go through the lock. As £2 had been paid as toll on the boat while passing
> through the bridge in Cairo, and three days had not passed, we were allowed free
> passage. The toll man stamping the Cairo receipt.... We walked on to the post office
> building then on past beautiful trees and shops, half hidden in the branches, over the
> swift rushing water of the canal which goes off to water the Manouf district and the
> western branch of the river is, except the sweep gates, like the bridge across the
> Damietta branch of the Nile.... The eastern bridge had seventy over arches, a very
> pretty tower and draw bridge at each end and two tall graceful towers in the middle.
> Ahmed went fishing and as the Ibis loosed from the island where we had anchored,
> before we come to it ~~and~~ the boat had to return for him. The banks of the river were
> in some places very pretty with shadoofs, water wheels, steam pumps, and not many
> villages, and as the wind was against us we did not make great progress until in a
> bend of the river near Beer [B'ir] Shams we sailed along nicely to the south east.
> When again near Aafam [Aasam, Safain?] we sent men ashore to get milk and eggs.
> Here the [river makes an S-bend.] The Captain, Rais Salim never sailed this direc-
> tion and there was an uncertainty about our movements which were both interesting
> and annoying. Most of our time was spent reading, resting, and looking at the
> scenery. At sunset it was interesting to see boatmen eat their hard bread which lay
> spread out like chips on the upper deck. They had cooked lentils to eat with it. We
> stopped at the bank to ask about milk for supper as the other men were delayed, but
> they had neither milk nor eggs at the little town. We asked them what they lived on,
> and they said on "mish." The people of Digwa, they said, were all Mohammadians
> [3–4][15].

The next morning (Saturday, August 6) they reached Banha, one of the largest cities in the Delta. Mr. Harvey went to town and got the mail, which they all were happy to receive. It was mostly news of the mission in Cairo. Some was general business. One announced the death of a mission worker's child.

> At 2:30 I was aroused by Jessie saying we were going through the RR bridge. As
> they stood looking at the boats coming up, one heavily loaded (We paid £2 for toll
> going through the bridge) with wood capsized. This gave all such a fright that we all
> went out and walked around the bridge. The boat was slow getting in place and as it

was about ready to swing into the proper current to float down through the centre of the bridge, a train was heard, and amid great shouting our Capt. was told to go back and commenced to close the bridge. The scene was exciting especially with the hull of the other boat still in sight but the train stopped, and then ours and another boat with water jars, were the last to go through. We anchored near dust piles which had been brought there on donkeys and camels to be shipped away from the old ruins beyond the bank to fields far away[16] [5–6].

The next day they were off again, this time making their way to Tanta, a major city.

The air was filled with anticipation, and hundreds and hundreds of people were seen walking beside the river. Anna described what she saw:

> Franks and scribes on the Banha side to the tribunal, which was near the old palace built by Abbas Pasha, and on the near side the country people in all styles of dress especially the women with their long narrow (compared with Christians) dark drawers sometimes with a coarse, linen, light colored garment over their black one, over their heads. Jessie and I dressed and crossed the river in the little boat and taking old Ahmed with us, went up to Annie Currie's house where we had readings and prayer, she reading the 18th of Matt. and I the 2nd [or 5th] of Romans. The house was opposite the R.R. station, a hut like place, but clean inside and they were glad to see us. Abd al Malek came in and said he had been very busy owing to the Tantah fair as sometimes he gave out 2000 or 3000 tickets a day...[7].

One hopes that in some years Anna Y also visited the Tanta Fair. It has been one of the major events throughout all of Egypt for centuries and is well described in nineteenth-century travel guides. Tanta had three fairs each year and by far the largest was the one in August. The event lasted for a week and was in honor of the birth (*mulid*) of the Saint Seyyid Badawi. Half a million people would come to sell produce and animals in the same manner as at a modern county fair in the United States. There were jugglers, food vendors, and processions: "Long processions of camels laden with chests and bales are seen converging towards the town, accompanied by crowds of men and large herds of cattle. The banks of the canal are thronged with persons washing themselves and drawing water. The streets teem with the most animated traffic, and are filled with long rows of boats in many of which the occupants are seen plying their handicrafts. There are Dervishes, cripples, idiots, pilgrims, amid the farmers."[17]

At Tafahna (Tafahna al Azab, 30 miles north of Cairo) the men ran into a bit of trouble. They needed provisions and went into town:

> Mrs. Harvey and I went to the tents and bought some things, two pigeons, two chickens, some food for them, a pumpkin, 7 eggs and some nice grapes which cost a [??] piaster a pound. The two women who sold us grapes were kind women, but we were thankful to get away from the neighborhood as we feared trouble. Our stopping was very providential however, as the two men who were sent ashore to buy chickens and eggs, came when we were there (while Mr H was up in the town) and as they got into trouble because they were carrying the chickens and would not to sell them, they were told they were thieves and got to quarreling, and screamed across for us to send the boat quickly for them. The Capt took the Ibis and we went over, and every man except Hassan whom Mrs. H would not allow to leave the boat again, left to get Ahmed. We were surprised to see them all return crest fallen but unwounded and their clothes torn and a bit of tooth being all the damage done. Mr. Harvey in the meantime had returned, surprised to see us at the other side of the river [8–9].

Now it was time for some missionary work. They had sailed on August 9 to Mit Ghamr, where the mission had established a school. At the school they performed routine tests and then tested the students to see if they were on par with other missionary students. In addition they gave special lessons. Around midnight they sailed on to near Samanoud.[18] In each of these villages they had established contacts, sometimes with Copts, sometimes with Syrians. In many they had small missions, as at Mit Ghamr. Samanoud was no exception. There they visited Mr. Thomas Knowles, who owned a factory. In addition to their work, the missionaries took the time to see the sights.

They went on to Beit el Hagar (Behbeit el Hagar). Behbeit el Hagar is named after the ancient Egyptian festival goddess Per-hebite(t), while the second part of the name refers to the actual building material: of stones. Located about four miles west of Mansura, its most important site is the temple dedicated to Isis. The Greeks called it the Iseum. Anna Y's observation about the drawings on the granite stones is exactly what is important on this site. In 2002 it was yet to be excavated. Today, a report of the British Museum says, "The site and its monument are now completely ruined." Anna called it "a beautiful ruin of a temple of Isis of the Ptolemaic time,"[19] and continued:

> The carving in Ind[??] and intaglio were very pretty in black and red granite. We were surprised to see how these immense stones were all mixed up and broken. We had a jolly ride though not a comfortable one. The donkeys were wonderfully bony and only Jennie's and mine (Mrs. H. did not go) had any kind of saddle and they had no stirrups, not one had a bridle. I asked my donkey boy what they eat in his town, he said they cook lentils, rice or beans or eat their bread with milk, cheese or mish. He was a gentlemanly boy, and I gave him a little Arabic primer when he said he would like to learn [11].

Mansura was the next stop. It is a major town in the Delta and the missionaries had their most important Delta mission there. The team aboard the *Ibis* got some mail and then got down to work:

> ... Miss Strang and her sister Lillie were there with some of the girls school having been to a friend on Monday after — a long evening owing to the absence of Miss S. waiting on Lillie in her illness in Alex. Mrs H went to the boat and brought up C. Maurietta and Lulu and we all had supper there and spent a pleasant evening. There were three men who came in to see Mr. Lansing for religious instruction as some have been doing. We rec'd letters from Dr. Watson telling of Mrs. W's illness since Labor day. A letter came from Mrs Monroe an invalid, a Presbyterian of Cleveland, containing £8 for Lareega Hanan's schooling, a letter from Saada to Mrs H. and me, and one to Mrs W. from Corpl Moore in Cairo.
>
> *Thurs. 11* Mr. H and I wrote to D and Mrs Watson. After breakfast Ms Finney brought letters from Mrs. Lansing, Miss Kyle and Afdokia, Miss McKown is now in Cairo on her way to Assiout. spending a week. Then Mr. L, Mr H. and I got a carriage and went to school, saw both boys and girls there, went on to Ms. Matta's where we tried to comfort Sitti Marta and Rosa +c a kind visit. When we returned to the Ibis, Mrs. Finney and Ethel and Lillie were there and remained until the men had returned from the market and we left after eleven o'clock. We stopped after lunch at Kafr Baramoun [Kafr el Baramon] to see Hagga Mahfouz and her family. Mrs [or Mr] H and I went up they returned with us and a Muslim Sheikh al Belid [Balad], Hagg Ahmed, and Mr. H. read a chap from Proverbs and prayed before they left. A's husband is scribe for Ibrahim Daoud, who owns the town and 700 acres of land with fine cotton +c.... About two o'clock we passed a large dahabiah flying the Union Jack and as they came along we saluted with our flags and soon saw that it was Miss Whately [a British missionary] and her family who saluted us with handkerchiefs.... Before we came to Sherebeen [Shirbin] some distance, Col Sir Colin Scott Moncrieff and Maj and Mrs Ross passed in a fine corps steamer.[20] They saluted us with their hats very kindly. They looked so nice that we felt like fellahin just out of the huts with our wrappers +c [12–13].

On August 12, at Fariskur they visited their boys' school, where a Mr. Ibrahim taught 22 boys. He had been one of Arabi's soldiers. On their way to Damietta they passed fields of Indian corn and large groves of palm trees, heavy with ripening dates:

> We moved down from the upper part of the town where the barracks, and other large buildings, and the great cisterns are down a sharp curve of the river past the market of the town and anchored, so as to do our buying and visit the town. We all went up, visited one of the silk weaving factories, one of the rice mills, with its queer giraffes looking machines pounding away. The irrigation movement of the machinery sounded like heavy horses walk over a bridge, and to look at them reminds one of a lot of blind horses grabbing madly at some thing close in front of them. We bought some crockery, or rather native pottery, pretty jars, and I got a native boy's writing board. We visited the Coptic school and church. The head teacher is a Beirut Syrian, and the boys number 140 who study Arabic, French, and Coptic, and are of many religions. The priest's father and grand father were both priests and he showed us over the church which seems new and unfinished. They had several pictures hung on the partition between the holy place and most holy, and in a niche there were silver round cases enclosing the bones of saints. The priest said one of them contained the bones of a Damietta saint who was tarred and lighted. Mr. H wished to know how his bones were preserved if they were burnt. The priest at last acknowledged that they were of no use except a remembrance. During the talk to the teacher Mr H took occasion to give a lecture on temperance, the good the English have done, the folly of infidelity +c. Every where we went we drew crowds of people around us some of whom followed us down to the boat [15–6].

That afternoon they continued their journey north to the furthest point of land: Ras el Bar. It was a small hamlet of 25 huts and a popular resort. It also had a lighthouse.

Although the first lighthouse in the world was built on Pharos Island in Alexandria, Egypt did not build another until the reign of the Khedive Ismail in the 1860s and '70s. When the American soldiers came to Egypt quite a number of them were Navy men. Some ran steamers on the Nile and to Constantinople. Others built up the coastal defenses of Egypt along the northern and eastern coasts. Charles C. Graves, a North Carolinian who taught navigation at the general staff school in Cairo, built the lighthouses along the Red Sea coast and probably built this one for Ismail as well.[21] The Egyptian Maritime Data Bank lists the lighthouse at Damietta as constructed in 1870 and renovated in 1992.[22]

> We are nearly opposite the light house, and are near two forts one on each side of the river. The town up the river a little way is called al Azbek [Ezbet el-Awaba] and is perhaps located on the pile of the old city of Damietta. Mr Hamilton's wife and a Mrs. Walker have anchored a little way above us and they called to see us after they had taken their bath. (The *Lotus* their dahabeyya). Mrs. T /Mrs H, Lulu and I went out to the sea accompanied by Ibrahim, Ahmed and Husein, some of whom took nice baths and we were invited to occupy the tent and mats of Mrs. Hamilton. The surf looks nice except that it is very dirty. We were surprised to see so many crabs running in all directions. There so many good sized sailing vessels anchored off to the left. There were many reeds +c struck into the ground in all this neighborhood to snare the quails[23] "five days" from now, when they are to be in abundant. Sufauf suffered a great deal this eve with her boil.
>
> *14th & 15th Sab and Monday*
> Yesterday we passed day quietly reading +c. In the afternoon Mr H had a Sabbath meeting taking up the special idea of the regular SS lesson in Cairo, which was about the Manna. Then I that heard Ahmed read the 2nd of Matt. and then read a psalm...[17].
> Today Mr + Mrs H. + Lulu and Sufauf went out for a bath at five. There we had

breakfast and prayers and hired a boat for five big piasters to take us over to the little islands north east from here (or a marsh) where we saw the net across a marshy canal and every little while the fish would fly clear up onto a net which lay nearly horizontally across the canal. They were of two kinds but I think the only difference in the spawn which seemed to be the most valuable part of the fish. Twenty days from now will be the fish season, where they may catch 1000–5000 a day. The government takes two thirds of the profit. We were all much interested by the cleverness of the boy who managed the boat. He pushed the boat along in the marsh for half an hour wading in sometimes to his arm pits. In the afternoon Jessie and I called on Mrs Hamilton and Mrs. Eve Walker in the next dahabieh and after giving a lesson to the Capt [18] and Hussein, we all went across to the lighthouse. It is of French make, a central iron pillar, (with a winding staircase of 236 steps) supported by three encircling pillars on tripolls. The height of the whole being 55 meters. Mrs H and Lulu did not ascent but those who went up were delighted with everything. The man in charge had been here eight years, is a Maltese who talks fair English, has a wife and five children, and every thing is much in and around the house. The light can be seen 25 miles. The lamplighter off duty, who showed them around then went with us to see our old fort near by which was commissioned by Mohammed Ali and strengthened by the Khedive Ismail. This is one ten inch gun and all four are of English make. The guide said that the black soldiers were not nice men when they were here and life was cheap with them and other people's goods... [19].

Tues 16

Very little done during the day except reading and a little writing. In the afternoon we went out along the west river bank to where the sea joined the river, perhaps a mile below where the dahabeih is tied up. The point of land which divides the two kinds of water is narrow, and very low. The shells are not brilliant and of few varieties. One great source of amusement to us down here, is the look on the Capt's face over the sea and crabs, and other things he has never seen before. The great sensation of the afternoon was the killing of a large rat which had annoyed us, and which had carried off two pairs of socks for Ibrahim from the deck where he sleeps. It took five men to kill it, poor Bistani taking the corn stalks in hand, as his weapon. Jessie sketched the light house, fort with the Ibis in the foreground. In the eve we went to see Mrs. Hamilton, and found Mrs. Walker just packing to leave as her husband is ill in Cairo. Singing some songs with her accompaniment on the piano [20].

After enjoying themselves along the seashore, the missionaries turned the *Ibis* around and began to make their way back to Cairo. They passed the time writing letters, including looking for new teachers. Pausing at Damietta again, they were visited by the English consul, Mr. Grain. Anna noted, "He had been in Egypt 21½ years and has been for years Eng. Consul here at Damietta consequently he is well informed. He was acting consul in Alex when the city was bombarded in July of 1882. He accepted an invitation to return to Damietta with us, and the Ibis moved over the distance of ten miles in less than two hours with the two smaller sails. We passed all the other boats which were going the same direction" [21]. On the way back they paused to visit a cemetery where a crusader battle took place.

In the Middle Ages, after centuries of Muslim expansion, the countries of Europe and the Roman Catholic Church decided to begin a Holy War against Islam and retake Jerusalem, where Christians, Muslims, and Jews had been living side by side for centuries. They wanted the holy shrines of Christendom to be under Christian control. They tried many times, and two of the Crusades, the Fifth and the Seventh, came to the Egyptian Delta.

The Fourth Crusade was headed for Egypt, but it never got there. The Fifth Crusade did. The Crusaders attacked Damietta in June of 1218. The siege continued for months, and the Crusaders eventually entered and pillaged the city in 1219. Then they moved on to Cairo.

They were met not only by the Egyptian army, but by the Nile flood as well. The Crusaders were caught between the two, retreated, and left Egypt. It was the last Crusade called for by a Pope. The Seventh Crusade was led by Louis IX of France. It left France in August of 1248 and headed for Egypt as the gateway to the Holy Land. Louis succeeded in capturing Damietta, but in February of 1250 he was defeated at Mansura. The king and many of his entourage were captured and held for ransom. It was paid and the men were released. Louis moved on to Acre. Louis never did reach Jerusalem during this campaign and he was back in France in 1254.

The journey continued, and once the missionaries reached Cairo it came to an end. It was one of hundreds of adventures the American missionaries enjoyed on the Nile as they went about their business in Egypt.

Epilogue

Anna Young Thompson, outspoken and with a great sense of humor, left quite a legacy in Egypt. She was known throughout the country for her wisdom and her generosity. She often used her own money to buy a student clothing or to give scholarships, and once even to pay for a wedding. She went to the hospitals to succor the patients, often sitting for hours reading to them. "One day, as she walked in the street with a young woman missionary, they caught up with a peasant woman who was having trouble balancing a large bundle of brush on her head. Miss Thompson stopped, put the load right, and then walked on without breaking the thread of her conversation."[24]

During World War I she worked tirelessly offering solace and friendship to the British soldiers, especially the wounded. When Dr. Lansing's second wife died in the 1880s, he asked Anna Y for her hand in marriage. It was an exciting time for Anna. But the mission board thought it would present a bad image to the public for Lansing to have had three wives, and the marriage was forbidden.[25]

None of the foreign missions made inroads into Islam. With conversion of Muslims being forbidden by Egyptian law, their mandate was to bring the Coptic Christians into the Protestant fold. They were not successful. What the missionaries did do was far more important. They brought education to the people. Their schools, spread throughout the country, were filled with Egyptians of all faiths eager to learn. After the turn of the twentieth century they founded The American University in Cairo Press, which thrives today with students from around the world. They also built hospitals to take care of the sick. These contributions made a difference to the average Egyptian and spread American goodwill in the Arab world.

Portrait of Anna Young Thompson (Presbyterian Historical Society, Presbyterian Church (Philadelphia, Pennsylvania).

This work did not stop with the American missionaries. Their methods were imitated and continue today. The Muslim Brotherhood, an anti-government, grassroots, religio-political group begun in 1928 by an Egyptian school teacher, followed and follows the missionary pattern.[26] They, too, were keen to have Egyptians follow their form of religion: radical, politicized Islam. They won the hearts of many Muslims because they took care of basic needs: health and education. As late as the 1980s, when the United States was building a school a day in the villages along the Nile and the Western Desert oases, wherever an American school appeared a Muslim Brotherhood school appeared nearby.

The legacy of the American missionaries reached into other areas of Egyptian life as well. In *Pioneers East*, David Finnie stated that the missionaries introduced the potato to the Middle East around 1827; the sewing machine in 1854; the camera in 1856; kerosene lighting in 1865; and probably hundreds of other incidental things of which we will never know.[27]

And what of them? Of Watson? Of Lansing? Of Anna Young Thompson? These men and women of the missions gave 40, 50, and even 65 years of their lives to working in Egypt, endured disease, and lost their children to cholera and smallpox. What happened to them? Some went home, but those who "passed through the mirror" were buried in Egypt in graves throughout the country — in Asyut, in Mansura, in Cairo, and in Alexandria. As late as the 1980s the American missionary graves dominated the small American cemetery in Old Cairo. Lying together in the northeast section of the cemetery, they were enjoying their eternal rest in the country they had come to love. The cemetery was shabby. The tombstones needed repair. Not a flower, not a handful of stones, no marker that indicated anyone was there to visit them. I took a few pictures. I cleaned a few tombstones. I wrote down their inscriptions. I wondered what stories they had to tell. These men and women inspired me to search for Americans in Egypt and were part of the genesis of this book.

In 2006 I went back to this cemetery. It seems more space was needed to bury the current American dead, and many of the missionary graves had been disrupted. The men and women who thought they would rest in peace for eternity have been dug up and thrown away. Their tombstones were destroyed. Watson is still there. His tombstone is rather ostentatious. Lansing and his wives are there too. But dozens of others are not. They deserved better. Whether one agrees with their mission or not, they were dedicated souls who gave their lives in a work in which they believed. And Anna? Anna was not so lucky. Her grave and her bones are gone. "When old age encroached on her health, she [Anna] insisted on remaining in Egypt because that was where she wanted to die and be buried — that was the place she regarded as home."[28] Anna Y was denied the eternal peace due her.

14

Walter Granger and the American Museum of Natural History's Expedition to the Fayoum (Scientist, 1907)

The American Museum of Natural History (AMNH) is a stellar American institution founded in New York City in 1869. It was the brainchild of naturalist Albert Smith Bickmore. With the assistance from a number of American financiers, the AMNH erected its first building on the upper west side of Manhattan across from Central Park in 1872. The cornerstone of the Victorian Gothic building was laid by President Ulysses S. Grant. It was the first of twenty-five buildings the museum would erect between 77th and 81st Streets.

By 1881 museum teams were in the field. In 1907[1] the museum sent a team of experts to Egypt to search for fossils in the Fayoum. It was the first time one of its teams was to venture outside the United States on an expedition the museum sponsored. It would prove to be a great success. That expedition was conceived by Henry Fairfield Osborn, curator of the Department of Vertebrate Paleontology. Osborn came from wealth and privilege. He was born in 1857, went to private schools, and graduated from Princeton. His "Uncle Pierpont" was J.P. Morgan, one of the founders of the museum. Osborn's interest in the Fayoum came after a visit to London. Paleontologist Charles Andrews of the Museum of Natural History in London showed him the many fossils he had collected in the Fayoum on his expedition in 1901. The collection included *Palaeomastodon*, which was the world's oldest known elephant fossil and the first land mammal fossil discovered in Egypt. Osborn was interested in elephants. In his article about the expedition in *The Century Magazine* he reported that the "origin of many families [of animals] was known but there remained in doubt the group of elephants."[2] Africa offered a chance to find out.

Osborn was also interested in the ancient whale *Zeuglodon* and the rhino-like mammal *Arsinoitherium*. His interest was a singularly American one, for the same ancient *Zeuglodon* had been discovered in the southern United States in 1832, long before it was found in the Fayoum. Fossil parts from Louisiana and Alabama were examined by paleontologist Dr. Richard Harlan. Most prolific in Alabama, where an entire skeleton was discovered on a plantation in 1834, *Zeuglodon* is the official state fossil and, where once its fossilized bones were used to make furniture, it is now forbidden to take any part of the giant whale out of the state. *Arsinoitherium* also had an American cousin, the four-horned *Uintatherium*.

In his role as head of the vertebrate department of the AMNH, Henry Osborn was responsible for laying the groundwork and finding the funding and support for the American

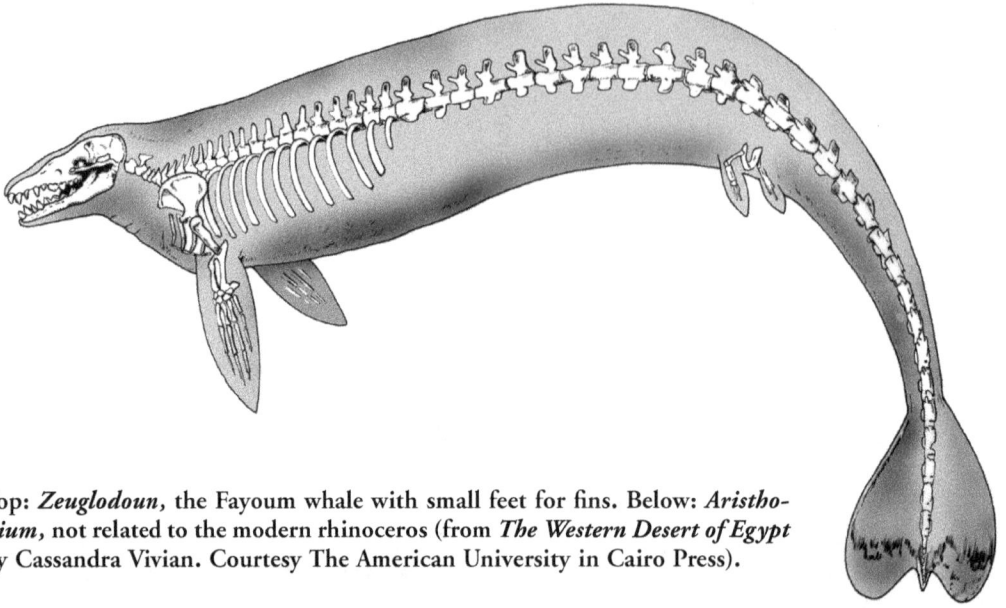

Top: *Zeuglodoun,* the Fayoum whale with small feet for fins. Below: *Aristho-nium,* not related to the modern rhinoceros (from *The Western Desert of Egypt* by Cassandra Vivian. Courtesy The American University in Cairo Press).

expedition to Egypt. He did that and more. He got the funding from his Uncle Pierpont. He selected Walter Granger to head the field work (Granger, in his field report, gave equal credit to his assistant George Olsen). He got the proper letters and necessary documents from President Theodore Roosevelt. Not to be excluded from such a journey, Osborn accompanied the expedition, and he took his family with him.

Osborn did not take command of the field work. In fact, Osborn and his family stayed only a few weeks and then went back to New York and left the field to Granger and the museum crew. But, once the expedition was over, he, as his position as head of the department and expedition permitted, published the findings not only in the museum bulletin, *New Fossil Mammals from the Fayûm Oligocene, Egypt,* but in *The Century Magazine* as well: "Hunting the Ancestral Elephant in the Fayûm Desert."[3] Because of these articles and the fact that Granger never published, Granger is often forgotten and Osborn is often credited with Granger's work.

Walter Granger

Walter Granger came from a middle-class family in Middletown Springs, Vermont. In 1890, when he was seventeen years old, he got a job at the American Museum of Natural History doing taxidermy, his first love. He went west with the museum on field expeditions in 1894 and 1895 and participated in the discovery of the Bone Cabin Quarry in Wyoming, where many dinosaurs were discovered. He was permanently appointed to the Department of Vertebrate Paleontology in 1896. He had become mesmerized by fossils and they would dominate the remainder of his professional life.

As noted, Granger published little, and, despite the fact that the AMNH would name a hall after him, like Chaillé-Long before him, Granger would become forgotten in his field. Vin Morgan, his great-grand-nephew, tried to change that by publishing Granger's diary, found in the attic of a family home in Hanover, New Hampshire. That diary forms the heart of this chapter.[4] Granger died in 1941.

The Fayoum

The expedition's mandate according to Walter Granger's *Report on the Expedition to the Fayûm, Egypt,* was to go to the fossil beds and bring home fossils of *Arsinoitherium* and the proboscideans *Moeritherium* and *Palaeomastodon.*[5] This he accomplished.

The Fayoum is an oasis to the west of the Nile just below Cairo. It is as important to Egyptians as the Nile, for from the dawn of the ancient Egyptian civilization it was the "breadbasket of Egypt." Everything still grows in the fields of the Fayoum: dates, oranges, lemons, limes, tomatoes, and even roses. The roses are sought by perfumers in Paris. The bees produce luscious honey favored by Egyptians all over the country. The fish, chickens, ducks, and turkeys are sold daily by vendors standing along the main route to and from Cairo, while small pickup trucks, loaded with the goods of the Fayoum, have replaced the donkey and his cart on the daily exodus to the Cairo markets. In addition to all this abundance, the Fayoum is a paradise for birds. Both resident and migrant birds in all varieties and sizes perch in trees, hover over their prey in the fields, or fish in the lake.

In the nineteenth century huge agricultural estates still existed in the Fayoum as they

Map of the Fayoum. Fossil beds are located north of the lake (from ***The Western Desert of Egypt*** by Cassandra Vivian, courtesy The American University in Cairo Press).

had done in antiquity. The ancient Greeks and Romans retired their soldiers to the Fayoum, giving them land to work, and from those settlements estates and smaller homesteads grew. The ruins of both rural and urban Fayoum still dot the desert edges, some say because a single lake covered almost the entire area we call Fayoum today. The papyri which kept the old records, recorded the history, kept track of the estates, noted the births and deaths, and spoke of the Roman visitors, were so profuse that in the nineteenth century they were dug up and used as fertilizer by the modern farmers. In the Christian era, the Coptic Church set up a series of monasteries in the Fayoum where black-clad monks tilled the land and gathered their people to prayer. Some were mere caves high in the northern escarpment; others sophisticated, self-contained complexes.

But life in the Fayoum began before the Romans, the Greeks, and even the ancient Egyptians. There were people in Fayoum in prehistory thousands and thousands of years ago. Only now are we beginning to realize their importance and accept that their traces will rewrite the history of ancient Egypt. The refuse of their lives is scattered along the desert floor around the edges of the Fayoum: flint arrows to kill birds, flint knives used to skin and cut their prey, grinding stones to crush grain, and sandstone hearth-stones to contain the fire, are found all through the desert surrounding the Fayoum, especially north of the current Lake Qarun.

There was life in the Fayoum before the prehistoric people, too. Millions and millions of years ago, when the earth held one giant continent, the land that is the Fayoum was at the edge of the Tethys Sea. Hundreds of land and sea animals lived in forests, savannahs, and shallow bays. As the earth moved and the continents were formed, these creatures and their habitats went through a series of evolutionary changes. The environment changed. The Fayoum became the richest bone bed in the world, filled with the fossils of trees, bushes, plants, flowers, shells, sharks, whales, sea cows, turtles, snakes, birds, elephants, primates, and trace fossils. These bone beds, which also include some of the earliest known links to modern man, are to the north of the current Lake Qarun. Beyond the lake is the desert. Nothing grows there. Throughout known history no one traveled there except along designated caravan trails.

The Fossil Hunters and the Geological Survey of Egypt

In 1845 British scientist A.B. Orlebar wrote about a petrified tree he found in the Fayoum. Although that tree and the millions of others found in the Western Desert of Egypt had been there for millions of years, no one thought them interesting until Mr. Orlebar described the one he found. A few decades later the Khedive Ismail began his expansion into the desert, sending one scientist after another into the mostly unknown area to explore and map. Among the first was Georg Schweinfurth, a German geologist and naturalist. Schweinfurth founded the Société Geographique d'Égypte, served as president of the *Institut de Égypte*, and was the single most important influence in the study of Egyptian geography and geology of the era. He discovered the first *Arsinoitherium* fossil and the first *Zeuglodon* fossil. They are probably the most exciting fossils in the entire pantheon.

The British continued the Khedive Ismail's desert exploration by establishing the Geological Survey of Egypt in 1896. They systematically began to explore and map Egypt. Two of the most prolific men of the Survey were John Ball and Hugh Beadnell. The Survey created a book and a 1:50,000 scale map for every area they surveyed, and that was quite a few. They started their work in the mythical oases, and it fell to Hugh Beadnell to map the Fayoum.[6] He began his task in 1898. Once he moved his instruments north of Lake Qarun he immediately began to find the bone beds. In 1901 he was joined by Charles Andrews, the paleontologist from the Museum of Natural History in London. As noted, Andrews's collection pulled the Americans into the exploration.

The men of the Survey began to accumulate artifacts. To accommodate their collections the Geological Museum was established in 1904. It stood beside the *Institut d'Égypte*, established by Napoleon to present scholarly papers, and near the Geographical Museum, established by the Khedive Ismail to house the maps and artifacts the American soldiers in Ismail's army created as they explored Egypt and Africa (see Chapter 10). The Survey established its headquarters to the north of Cairo, closer to the military headquarters and with easier access to the desert.

The American Museum of Natural History's Expedition to the Fayoum

In order to bring an American team of scientists to Egypt, like all the travelers before them, the AMNH had to have letters of credit, letters of introduction, and permissions from the Egyptian government. As an expedition expecting to work in Egypt, they needed official association with agencies in Egypt. Before they could acquire all those documents they needed financial backing in the United States. The expedition had the best American sponsors, including "Uncle Pierpoint," who had been to Egypt in 1871 and 1912. He spent the winter in Egypt, including joining American excavations in Kharga Oasis, and was scheduled to return to America on the maiden voyage of HMS *Titanic*. He canceled his reservations at the last minute.[7] Their second major supporter was President Theodore Roosevelt, who had also been to Egypt twice, first as a young boy in 1872–73, and a year after his presidency in 1910.[8]

Walter Granger's Diary

Walter Granger kept a diary of the expedition. Extracts were published in a number of places including Bulletin 22 of the New Mexico Museum of Natural History and Science under the title of *Notes From Dairy-Fayûm Trip, 1907*. It was excellently footnoted, explained, and transcribed by Vincent L. Morgan and Spencer G. Lucas in 2002. Up to that point, very little had appeared in print about the expedition.[9] From the abridged diary we get a day-by-day view of how a team of scientists operated in a harsh environment. We also meet a number of other scientists from different nations who were working in related fields in the Egyptian desert.

The team arrived at Alexandria about 9 o'clock on Wednesday, January 23. By 6 o'clock that evening they were ensconced at Shepheard's Hotel. The next morning Granger called on Captain Lyons of the Survey Department (S.D.) and along with Osborn the men went to the Geological Museum to view the fossils. When they were done negotiating with Cook's for outfits, they went sightseeing.

The next day, Saturday, January 26, they paid an official visit to Lord Cromer, the British Controller General in Egypt. Granger found him a "very cordial — quiet & unpretentious man." The temperature was near 40° F. But by the cool of the evening they ventured out to enjoy the Ramadan festivities. Over the next few days not only did they complete the preliminary tasks for the journey, but they met and visited other scientists working in Egypt at the time.

> **Sun. Jan. 27**[10]
> Mr. H.T. Ferrar,[11] a member of Capt. Lyon's field staff, called at hotel in forenoon. He is to go to the Fayûm with us as guide, to remain during the period of Prof. O.'s stay in the desert.

Olsen, Ferrar and I work on list of provisions and outfit needed for the working
party. Ordered these supplies from Fleurent, Flicks & Co.—to be shipped to Tamia,
Fayûm, the nearest Ry. point to the bone beds.

Plan to hire camels here and ship them to Tamia. Prof. O's party is to start from
Mena House and go up along Pyramid Field. Olsen and I are invited to join the
party. Prof. O. has failed to make arrangements with Cook's for his personal outfit, is
now dealing with one Mickawi Ali, a dragoman with a pocketful of letters of recommendation and a cunning look in his eye.

Took tea with Mr. Lucas, chief chemist of the S.D.—a fine fellow.

Mon. Jan. 28
To the Geol. Mus. in the morning with Prof. O.

Mr. Daoud Mohammed [Beadnell's worker] arrives and is placed at our disposal.
Also Talba, a sheikh, of whom we are to hire camels. We hire 12 at 75¢ per day (15
piasters). They are to proceed at once to Tamia. Daoud with the boxes of supplies
joins him there and then proceeds to the easterly bone pits to await us. Ali
Mohammed, one of the museum attendants, is loaned to us and is to be our cook.

The Survey people are most generous, and offer tents, water tanks, tools, etc. Also
a cooking outfit left in the museum by Dr. Andrews of the British Museum. This is
most convenient for us. They also offer to make our packing cases and ship out to us
as we order them. Daoud will take three or four other men out with him as laborers.
Forwarded £10 to Talba and £5 to Daoud. This advancing of money is necessary in
hiring these people, it seems.

Tues. Jan. 29
Prof. O. has completed arrangements with Mickawi Ali for an outfit.

We are to start for Mena House on the 31st. Mr. Ferrar is to have camels and tents
of his own.

Came out here to the Mena House this afternoon late. We find this hotel in some
ways more attractive than Shepherd's and more reasonable in rates.

Olsen and I spent the moonlight evening about the pyramids and Sphynx. Full
enjoyment of this though is prevented by persistent natives who try to force donkeys
and camels on us, and discourse upon the marvels of the monuments.

Our window overlooks the Nile valley with Cairo on the opposite side—a really
wonderful view.

Wed. Jan. 30
A moderate sandstorm has been on all day and this evening it has changed to a
heavy rainstorm.

Mickawi and his caravan is camped alongside the Cairo road near here and will
probably get wet. We are to start in the morning if the weather permits.

Have had a most interesting day. Spent part of the morning under the lee of
Cheops talking to the native who had plenty of leisure today because the storm kept
the tourists away.

After lunch Dr. Elliot Smith [Professor of Anatomy in Cairo medical school] came
out from town and conducted Prof. O's party to Dr. Reisner's[12] house near the 3rd
Pyramid. I was invited along. Met Dr. Buckhart at Reisner's.[13] Intensely interesting
conversation on Egyptian Antiquities and the work being done. Tea and then Dr. R.
showed us over his excavations at the eastern base of the 3rd Pyramid. Said that
probably the stone for all three pyramids came from quarry close by. Sheathing for
1st and 2nd from Mokkatam Hills. Showed us the quarry, now most filled with sand.
Is like a great inverted pyramid.

The men of the expedition were ready to make their way to Fayoum and then north to
the bone beds. There were no paved highways to the Fayoum in 1907. One could travel south
along the Nile and follow the railway to the railhead at Tamia; or one could move south

through the desert to Karanis. The expedition chose to take the route to Tamia along the Nile. It was best because they were able to visit the various antiquities and meet more of the men who were working at the various sites.

Thurs. Jan. 31
Camp tonight on the edge of the Nile bottom at Sakkara. Mr. Ferrar's caravan has just joined us.

Rain ceased before day light this morning. I was up early and climbed Cheops before breakfast, without assistance. One young Arab went part way up and a second one insisted on going all the way up with me. Couldn't fight him off— no baksheesh though.

Started from Mena House at 10 o'clock with caravan —13 camels and 5 donkeys. Very imposing! Photographed at the Sphynx by a professional from Cairo. Two other caravans waiting to pose also — quite the thing. Trail from the Sphynx leads along the edge of Nile valley to Abusir Pyramids where we took luncheon. Met Herr Muller [a German Egyptologist] who is excavating at Abusir under Dr. Buckhart's direction. Reached here at Sundown. Camp ready. Have 5 round sleeping tents, a large green mess tent, rugs on the floor and interior of the tent decorated with Koran verses in colored cloth. Regular course dinner, with two waiters.

Ferrar has 8 camels and three tents.

Tomorrow we are to go over the Sakkara ruins with Mr. Quibell.[14]

Fri. Feb. 1
Camp about a mile beyond Dashur Pyramids tonight. Spent entire forenoon at Sakkara where Mr. Quibell met us and accompanied us over part of his excavations. Visited all of the important tombs and an enormous excavation made by Quibell where several cultures are shown in strata graphic form. Also an interesting Coptic temple or place of worship.

Mr. Quibell is to furnish us with ten men for our excavation work. These men are skilled and will be of great service. They are to come out after we are settled in camp.

Lunch at Sakkara and a rapid ride on to camp, mostly along the Nile bottom.

Weird music by our camel men at Sakkara this morning.

Sat. Feb. 2
Awakened before sunrise this morning by wailing of women up in a cemetery near our camp — professional mourners, so Ferrar says, from the village back of camp.

Start early and reach Lisht Pyramids (northern one) for lunch. Mr. Lythgoe[15] of Metropolitan Museum who is conducting explorations here joins us after lunch. Invited to his house and are shown over the pyramid. Work just begun. Work done by French excavation previously careless & not very successful. Tomb chamber very low and filled with water.

We camped near Lythgoe's house. He and his wife and two assists. invited to dinner.

Tomorrow we strike across the narrow strip of desert and enter the Fayûm.

Weather comfortable in daytime but too cool at night.

Sun. Feb. 3
Camped tonight just on the outskirts of Tamia.

Lythgoe photographed caravan this morning just as we started.

Saw Meidum Pyramid to the south as we crossed the desert.

Lunch in desert about half way to Tamia and in sight of the Fayûm.

Tried the camels for the first time — don't think I had a good one.

A party of "Cedric" people camped near us tonight — paid us a visit.[16]

They were now in the Fayoum, at least in the fertile portion of the oasis. They would still have to make their way north, across Lake Qarun, into the desert. Granger was not the only one keeping a diary of their journey; Osborn had also recorded some interesting insights into their journey into the Fayoum. He published them in *The Century Magazine*.[17]

On Monday, February 4, the journey into the desert began. This was not an easy journey. First they had to skirt the eastern shore of the lake, which was no problem. Then they had to ascend to the shelf that held the Middle Kingdom Qasr el Sagha Temple. That wasn't hard either. But the cliffs of the escarpment lay beyond and they had to be climbed. They were almost vertical and some of the animals, packed with equipment, needed to be pushed and pulled up. Atop the cliff the team found a variety of shells making it clear they were standing on the site of an ancient sea. As they moved further along, seashells disappeared and freshwater fossils began to appear. Then came the fossilized tree trunks, some seventy feet long.

Osborn and his family, and Granger and his men, settled into respective camps and the work of the expedition began. The working team originally broke their excavation into two areas: Quarry A at the base of Gebel Quatrani, and Quarry B, a little to the southeast (see map). The very next day a palate of *Saghatherium*, a mammal similar to the small rat-like Hyrax, was found.

As with any expedition into the desert there were logistical problems. There was not enough water in the camp. The workers tried to extort more money from the team. Osborn commented:

> The entire force was cheerfully working under Olsen, wielding their mattocks, dumping the loose sand from their baskets, and singing their refrains. They were quickly impressed with due reverence for the supreme value and delicate character of a fossilized bone. As soon as one was exposed, they folded up like jack-knives, and with their faces between their knees in the attitude of the Mussulman at prayer, and gently blew away the sand. Then it was a delight to see the enthusiasm over a discovery.... The labor problem was solved....[18]

And there were fleas. Thousands of them, making the work uncomfortable. As for the work itself, the shellac to hold fragmented bones together was not working and new glue had to be ordered from Cairo (as well as powder for the fleas). The animal bones were not completely fossilized, which made them difficult to join together. On February 12 the jaw of a young *Arsinoitherium* "with good teeth" was found.

The team grew accustomed to their environment. Osborn and Ferrar made a three-day journey to Wadi Zeuglodon. Osborn recorded:

> The absence of all the modern families of carnivore on land is no more striking than the entire absence of seals, dolphins, or whales in the seas bordering Eocene Libya. Their place was filled by the archaic whales, or zeuglodonts, of the marine inlets, seashores, and open ancestral Mediterranean. Since Schweinfurth's discovery, in 1879, zeuglodonts have been found in every part of the Fayûm region, as well as farther north in the Mokattam hills overlooking Cairo. The most famous fossil locality in the Fayûm is known as Zeuglodon Valley. With a very light outfit I made a forced three days' journey with Mr. Ferrar to the southwest of our camp, in order personally to observe this most interesting deposit. Directing our course toward the Gar el Gehannem, a geographical point which, being translated into Western phrase, would be known as "Hell Butte," we climbed over some high sand-dunes which the camels with difficulty crossed and finally reached the famous valley. We found it strewn with the remains of monster zeuglodonts including heads, ribs and long series of vertebrae, most tempting to the fossil-hunter, yet too large and difficult of removal from this very remote and arid point. This expedition was specially impressive as forcing upon our minds the enormous abundance of these zeuglodonts, the height of their evolution, as well as their wide geographical distribution to the Southern United States region.[19]

The use of the term Wadi Zeuglodon or Zeuglodon Valley in Granger's diary and Osborn's articles is an example of the continuing problem of mapping and consulting sources (see Chapter 10). On the maps of the scientists published with articles about the whales of the Western Desert, the valley was called Wadi Zeuglodon. When I used that name in my book *The Western Desert of Egypt,* my British editor questioned it and consulted a modern-day British naturalist in Cairo. He had never heard of it either. But my evidence allowed it to stand. On the official maps of the Geological Survey done decades later, the area was not called Wadi Zeuglodon. It was called Wadi el Hitan, Valley of the Devil. That is the name locals had given it because it was a dangerous area inhabited by thieves and robbers. Hitan has been carried forward in the modern day protected area. As for the name *Zeuglodon,* that too has changed in Egypt. Never mind that the name *Zeuglodon* was given to this fossil in Alabama where it was first found decades before it was found in the Fayoum. Never mind that Schweinfurth correctly named it *Zeuglodon,* after the American name. The Wadi Rayyan Protected Area calls this animal *Basilosaurus,* king of reptiles. Obviously *Basilosaurus* is the name of a reptile. *Zeuglodon* is not a reptile. It is a whale. A whale is a mammal. But *Basilosaurus* is now the name of this mammal in Egypt. This confusion is endemic throughout areas where more than one nation was involved.

Richard Markgraf

Then Richard Markgraf came into camp. Markgraf was a German who came to Egypt for his health. He moved to the Fayoum and began dabbling in fossils. He aligned himself with almost every scientific expedition working in the Fayoum at one time or another. Eventually he was commissioned by scientists in Stuttgart, Germany, and the AMNH to find specific fossils. Granger earned a great deal of respect for his work.

Sat. Feb. 16

Prof. O's party back from Zeuglodon Valley this evening.

Mrs. O. & Josephine visited Quarry C before lunch. Someone camped in the wady East of quarry attracted attention and Mrs. O. became worried and we all returned to camp with her. Mickawi rode over to find out who he was—returned saying he was a German prospector.

Lunch at upper camp. Returned to Q. C in afternoon. Saw the German who had just uncovered a good *Arsinoitherium* jaw.—he knew the name of it. Is apparently a prospector of some experience. Up to Osborn's camp in the evening. The Keating's Powder has arrived.

Sun. Feb. 17

The German prospector called on Osborn today. He is a Mr. Markgraf—has done considerable work here for Prof. Fraas.[20] Says he has a quarry of creodonts in an upper level. Prof. O. mentioned employment to him but he says he is under agreement with Fraas.

Prof. O. has decided to send the three Helouan men back. They are worse than useless. The two old men from Tamia are better workers and much more careful. Talba and camels in tonight.

Mon. Feb. 18

Tonight we are lonesome. Prof. O. and party got off about 10: o'clock—took photographs of our entire working party—including camel men.

Still at Quarry C which appears to be pretty well worked out. A few bones in the upper end.

Herr Markgraf called over to camp this evening. Expressed a willingness to work for us. Shall try and get Prof. O. to make arrangements. I am to see his collection tomorrow.

Ferrar has left his tent with us also a drawing table, which was much needed. The three Helouan men have been paid off and leave tomorrow morning for home. They are Abas Abdulla, Abdulla Mohammed & Mohammed Mohammed,— the two latter are brothers of Daoud and Ali.

Tues. Feb. 19
Went with Daoud to Markgraf's camp and then under Markgraf's guidance to the westerly bone pits of Beadnell.

Herr M. pointed out location of all of his important finds which I plotted. Some of his finest skulls were broken in transit.

Saw his collection from the upper level; they are not creodonts but *Ancodon, Megalohyrax* & *Geniohyus* — well-preserved white bone — apparently from gypsum layers. Find him very agreeable. Have written Prof. O., hoping to make arrangement for his employment. Herr M. lives in a tiny tent with bare necessities; has two camels and two men. Speaks Arabic well.

Olsen has begun to find good bones in Quarry B. Weather beautiful today. Helouan men returned with camels this morning.

Thurs. Feb. 21
This afternoon Markgraf's native came over to camp saying that he had found a "ras." I went over the found he had a fine skull of *Palaeomastodon*— incisors and arcus gone but otherwise excellent.

Markgraf uses hot glue for hardening bones. Has the Arab collect dead brush and boil the glue and applies while hot & thin. Seems to penetrate and harden well. The skull was an isolated specimen — just north of his tent in the bottom of the wady.

Olsen at stripping in Q. B today.

Sun. Feb. 24
Herr Markgraf over to dinner this evening. he has found nothing new since the skull. Olsen and I have a great time talking with him, have to use English, German, Arabic and sign language but manage to get along. We find him very agreeable. He is a native of Austria, his wife is dead and a small daughter is being brought up in Italy. He was a violinist and came to Egypt on account of his health — has some lung or throat affection, possibly t'b. Makes his headquarters in Cairo but has recently purchased land in Sinnoures and will set out date & orange trees this spring. His camels go to Sinnoures instead of Tamia.

Eventually Markgraf moved his tent near the Americans. Osborn agreed to hire him with generous terms: $60 per month salary—$4.00 per day expenses and $20.00 for initial expense for the outfit. By March 7, he was on his way further west with a mandate to open up new quarries where he had found skulls before.

Two days later Granger went to Cairo. On his way he had a shave by a native barber and called it a "terrible experience." This time he stayed at the Eden Palace Hotel just north of Ezbekiyyah. He got supplies, revisited the Geological Museum collection, saw H.G. Lyons and invited Mr. Converse[21] to visit the camp.

They reached camp on March 13. The weather was changing and so were the vermin. Camel flies, a spring and summer pest, began to attack the camels. They were particularly ferocious and could kill a camel. When the season of this fly arrives in the desert all camels are removed from the oases, where the vegetation attracts the flies, and taken into the desert, where the air is dry and there are no flies, until the season ends. As for the men, the fleas continued; but the bane of the oases, the house fly, was about to hatch. The flies of Egypt are a true pestilence. They bite. They number in the thousands, if not the millions. They are particularly cruel to babies. Constantly in need of water, they attack the eyes, the nose, and any place there is moisture. Hands must constantly be free to tend them. That makes work almost impossible.

The consolation for the AMNH expedition was that the bone beds were beginning to yield great treasures. Olson found a palate of *Palaeomastodon*. Markgraf had a good skull of *Moeritherium* and a large skull of *Tomistoma*, an ancient crocodile. As of March 15 the team had accumulated about 200 specimens. By the 23rd the hot desert winds were affecting the work. Markgraf was working a mile east of the trail from Qasr Qarun to Alexandria. Qasr Qarun was a Roman complex erected at the edge of the Fayoum to guard its western flank against invaders. It was on an ancient caravan trail that began in Baharia Oasis and made its way through the desert northeast to the Fayoum, skirting the Fayoum to the west, and continuing north to Wadi Natrun and the coast. The wine of Baharia and the grain of the Fayoum were transported to Rome via this road. There were desert outposts and water stations along the route. Granger called this the Alexandria Trail.

Things fell into a routine. It was occasionally broken, like the time the cook tent caught fire. The desert itself brought entertainment. Granger was pleased to see so much life in the desert. He saw lizards, storks on migration, quail, raptors, antelope, beetles, and, alas, more "millions of house flies." April came and with it came not only the heat, but the sandstorms as well.

Sun. Apr. 7
Fine day — cool north breeze. Last night occurred our worst sandstorm, a regular corker. Blew down the Quft mens' tent, tore up the cook tent and would have taken our own if we had not been up every half hour to strengthen the ropes and keep the walls tied up. The men came out twice and readjusted the chunks of fossil wood on the guy ropes. It was impossible to face the wind and everything was black as pitch. This morning the beds and everything in the tents were covered with a thick layer of fine sand. Camels should have been in yesterday and we had only one fanitas of water left — too close a margin in this weather. Camels have just arrived, 9: P.M.

Our heavy sandstorms are all from the north and all come at night. The day winds are mostly So-West. Last night's storm lasted from about 9 until 4.

Yesterday Olsen and I spent the forenoon in the Middle Eocene collecting invertebrates but finding no good vertebrates. Took only ½ bottle water and came home very dry.

Fri. Apr. 12
Uncomfortable between 10: & 4: a cool breeze occasionally but mostly dead calm.
Got up at 5 and packed two more cases — sent four in by camels.
Finished up work in quarry B; nothing more being found.
Remained in camp all day packing boxes & labeling.
The flies are getting to be the greatest nuisance, the heat would not be so bad without them; they are particularly bad when pasting bones. The paste draws the flies and with both hands engaged they have a free swing at one's face. The weather is not excessively hot yet but still uncomfortable — about like a hot day in Wyoming.

Wed. Apr. 17
Camels in with Amer. Mail. Weather cool and comfortable. There has been a very noticeable decrease in the number and the energy of the flies since the Khamsine [sandstorm] of Sunday.

Are planning now to break this camp on the 21st and go to Qasr-el-Sagha for a few days before going in to Tamia.

Both Olsen and I worked in upper beds today. Took photographs of gebel. Daoud and men prospecting found half of a *Moeritherium* skull.

Fri. Apr. 19
The only *hot* day I have ever seen! Weather conditions were not unusual in the morning. After breakfast I went with Daoud and Ibrahim to the west to collect the

small turtle skull and the *Ars.*— humerus of Markgraf's — took the camera. Atmosphere began to be hazy about 10: o'clock, preventing good photographs, growing hotter and with strong So-west wind. By noon the air was full of dust and the wind strong and hot. I realized a Khamsine was on and packed up the turtle and started for camp. The hot sand was moving freely by this time but the wind was fortunately at our backs. Reached camp at 1: o'clock about used up. Olsen had returned earlier from upper beds. Spent afternoon lying in bottom of tent — suffocated with sand and scorched with heat. Natives wrapped our water bottles in wet burlap which afforded some relief. At 6: P.M. the wind died down suddenly and after a few moments of calm a cool north breeze sprung up causing hundreds of tiny whirlwinds as it came in contact with the So.-west wind. It is now (9: P.M.) very comfortable again.

On April 21 the Americans were camped just below the Middle Kingdom temple of Qasr al Sagha, the Golden Fortress. Only now did they have an attempt to really look it over because it was near the temple that the Middle Eocene strata of rock and fossils are exposed. The temple had been discovered by Georg Schweinfurth in 1884. It is totally enclosed, which is unusual; is made of large limestone slabs, which is also unusual; and has a hidden room with no entrance or exit, most unusual of all. To make it even more perplexing nothing holds the temple together. There is no mortar. The pressure of the slabs upon one another have kept it standing for nearly 5,000 years. When it was built it stood at the northeastern edge of Lake Qarun, but when Granger was there it was a good distance away because the lake has shrunk in size (and is still shrinking). However, the location both then and now is not only majestic, but strategic. The temple overlooks the lake like an outpost. It is close to the Old Kingdom basalt road to the quarries at Widan al-Faras (Ears of the Horse). The quarries, eight in number, contained black basalt, which was used to decorate temples and make statues for the Old Kingdom pharaohs. The six-mile-long road leading from Qasr al-Sagha to the quarries at Widan al-Faras was built of the same basalt slabs. It can still be seen today. Perhaps the men of the quarries built the temple.

Another reason the temple is strategic is that it was just to the northeast of the ancient port that we now call Dimeh. Granger visited that as well. Dimeh is the Roman name of the outpost. Soknopaiou Nesos is the Greek name. In both instances it was a town built at the beginning (or the end) of the caravan trail on the northern edge of Lake Qarun. There is also evidence that it was important in prehistory too. Wine, grain, and other items from Fayoum were ferried across the lake to the port, unloaded at the quay, given a tax at the customs, repacked on mules (no camels in Egypt at that time) and shipped north along the caravan trail to Alexandria. From there the goods were sent to Rome, which expected one-third of its yearly grain from Egypt. Granger and his men had a lot to see at Dimeh: houses, temples, cemeteries, and the quay had all withstood the centuries because of the dry climate of the desert. Although ruins, they were (and are) still impressive.

Granger took the time to visit the ruins because the AMNH team was beginning to pack up and end their expedition to the Fayoum. They were well on their way to breaking camp and sending boxes of fossils to Cairo when Granger received a cable from Osborn for the team to continue excavating. It was an extension not necessarily wanted by Granger, but to this point they had not found a good skull of *Arsinoitherium*. In fact, as late as April 22 they still did not have one. Osborn wrote a letter to Richard Markraf in April:

> Up to the present time we have not secured a fine skull of *Arsinoitherium*. This seems to me a gap in our collections which must be filled sooner or later. Messers. Granger and Olsen are now prospecting diligently and will probably remain in the field some time longer and they may find one. If not, I hope you may come across one in your prospecting which you will dispose of to us. I should be willing to pay a

handsome price for it, say $60 or 240 marks, provided it reached us in good condition.... I also desire especially to secure a skull of *Moeritherium* showing the anterior portion with the teeth preserved. For a complete skull of *Moeritherium* with teeth preserved I would be willing to pay $50. or $200. marks. I desire also the anterior portion of the skull of *Palaeomastodon* with the upper tusks preserved.[22]

The team continued to search the various strata of the escarpment north of Lake Qarun.

Mon. Apr. 22
Today with Daoud, Ibrahim & Machmud we walked to the Birket, stopping on the way at Dime to look on the ruins and take photographs.

At the lake we found native fishermen and engaged them to run in their nets for us. The fish come up into the shallow water along the shore in great numbers. The method of capture is to select a small bay and creep up with great caution and suddenly rush across the entrance of the bay with one end of the long gill net. Two or three naked natives they enter from the shore side and by great splashing & commotion drive the fish into the net in their attempt to reach the open lake. Several fish jumped over the net and escaped. 84 fish about 8 inches long were caught. Cost us 6 piasters. Most of the fish caught here are shipped daily to Cairo.

Saw Markgraf's trail near camp today where he had passed recently with his outfit. Apparently he is in the field again. Collected invertebrates from the Lake Moeris sediment. Ali informs us that the grub is about exhausted — the fish will help out though.

Tues. Apr. 23
Camels in late this afternoon with American mail. We are to go in to Tamia tomorrow.

Collected *Moeritherium* jaws and weathered skulls of *Tomistomi* and *Zeuglodon*, and Olsen got good turtle — all from 1 mile west of Temple [between Qasr al-Sagha and Dimeh].

Very hot during middle of day. Food almost entirely gone this evening — barely enough for breakfast. Our leaving is now a necessity.

Thurs. Apr. 25
Cairo. Got our fossil cases out of storage at Abdulla's this morning and had them weighed & shipped as luggage on our train — Daoud and Ali sitting on them all the way and watching after their transfer. Our camp outfit was loaded on the camels and ready to start for Cairo and Olsen and I were ready to take the train when I was handed a cable-gram from Prof. O. saying to continue work in Fayûm. We decided it would be necessary to go into Cairo as our working clothes had all been given away to the natives and we needed new tents since the old ones are all seriously damaged by sandstorms. We also need hot weather clothing — helmets, etc.

Left Tamia at 10: A.M. Lunch and transfer at Medinet-el-Fayûm with time enough to look about the place a trifle and Cairo at 8:20 this evening. Quartered at Mrs. Scott's Pension [English Pension located at Sharia el-Genaineh] opposite Eshekeih [Ezybekkiah] Gardens. Daoud and Ali are to hire truck men and deliver the cases at the Geol. Museum tonight.

Granger continued with his work in Cairo. More boxes came in from the desert and he stored the fossils at the Geological Museum. The team had to buy new clothes because most of what they had was winter wear. Then they did a bit more sightseeing around Heliopolis, where they visited the famous Obelisk and the Virgin Tree. Then they went to an ostrich farm which had 1400 ostrich. The next day Granger was invited to dinner at Dr. Ferrar's and found that the apartment along the Shubra Road was shared with "eight other Oxford and Cambridge men."

By May 1, Granger was back in the Fayoum working in the various bone beds. Like nomads, the AMNH team began moving to different locations in the region during the last part of their exploration. They were also running out of supplies, specifically "St. Galmier," an imported French bottled water. Although they had not been successful before, Granger and his workers moved west of the Alexandria Trail one more time. Then Granger fell ill to desert dangers. He had a sore ankle caused by flea bites which had become infected. Although he was injured he continued to work, finding a "good turtle." By the 27th his ankle had not improved. They arrived in Cairo on May 30. The next few days, Granger was hospitalized as they were packing up to make their departure. They left via Port Said.

The diary ended on June 15.

Home at Last

It took fourteen days for the expedition and all its baggage to reach New York from Naples. This is a far cry from earlier travelers who took up to three months. Once they arrived in New York they began the work of unpacking and working on the material. In his report, Granger assessed his fossils as follows:

> Twenty-seven cases containing the fossils collected by the expedition were shipped from Cairo. The number of specimens of vertebrates recorded in the field book approximate 500, of which about 25 are reptiles, the balance mammals. A small collection of invertebrate fossils was made from the Qasr-el-Sagha Beds, and collections of Formicidae and Coeloptera were made for Professor Wheeler and Mr. Beutenmüller. About fifty 5 × 7 photographs illustrating the geology, topography, and methods of collecting, camping, etc., were taken; and in addition a series of Kodak film negatives was made by Professor Osborn, illustrating chiefly the work in the quarries. Data was collected for a new geological section of the region north of Lake Qurun, and also for a map showing the location of all important finds of fossils made by the various parties. Charts showing the development of the two principal quarries "A" and "B" were prepared.
>
> Among the more noteworthy fossils collected were the skull of a young *Arsinoitherium*, missing horns; skull of *Moeritherium* from the Qasr-el-Sagha beds; skull of a *Palaeomastodon*; skull of *Tomistoma*; skull of *Crocodilus*; shells of three types of turtles.[23]

According to Vin Morgan, the AMNH's expedition to the Fayoum was the most important scientific expedition of the decade.[24] Henry Osborn, as head of the expedition, published the findings in a number of magazines and journals. Granger did not publish. So for many years it was believed that the work in the Fayoum belonged to Osborn. According to Morgan, *The Century Magazine's* 1907 article, "Hunting the Ancestral Elephant in the Fayûm Desert," as well as the *Illustrated London News Supplement* article of March 1908, "Hunting the Two Million Year Old Elephant," were highly dependent on Granger's notes and never mention his name. That is not true. There is a lot of background information in Osborn's article. He introduces the subject, he presents background, and in the *Century* article he clearly states, "As head assistant I selected Mr. Walter Granger.... As second assistant I chose Mr. George Olsen."[25] In Osborn's "New Fossil Mammals from the Fayûm Oligocen" for the bulletin of the AMNH, he stated: "Mr. Walter Granger, assisted by Mr. George Olsen, both of the American Museum of Natural History staff, remained in charge until June 14, and displayed energy and skill in the work of collection." He continued a little later by crediting Granger with cataloging the 550 pieces in the collection.[26] The article continues by describing the fossils and is completed by drawings, photographs, and maps. The material was surely the product of the vertebrate section of the AMNH and its director certainly made good use of the work.

15

Theodore M. Davis: America's Man in the Valley of the Kings (Scientist, 1889–1915)

Theodore M. Davis represented both sides of the "Gilded Age." From humble beginnings he raised himself into a life of privilege at the time when an agrarian America was developing into an industrial America. He did this, as did many of the men of the Gilded Age, through dishonesty, fraud, and outright thievery. Davis took his ill-gotten gains, and after he satiated his own outrageous wants, became a philanthropist. The difference is that he took his fortune abroad and spent it unraveling the mysteries of another culture across an ocean and thousands of miles away from his life in America. In Egypt, not only did he fund his own archaeological digs and those of other scholars, but he also built schools and dig houses, and supported any number of philanthropic projects. In fact, he drew other Americans to Egyptian shores. Theodore Davis, it must be said, was not a scientist; he was a patron. He fulfilled that role with gusto and, it appears, with a newly acquired honesty and integrity.

The grateful Egyptians rewarded Davis by naming a hall in the Egyptian museum the *Salle Theodore Davis*. Egyptologists and archaeologists rewarded him by calling him difficult and by denigrating his work. John M. Adams, who has been researching Davis's life, believes that the negative attitude toward Davis is not deserved. Adams believes the origin of this reputation is "hard to determine" and the stance is "seriously skewed."[1] He points out that Lord Carnarvon, in fact, "argued with archaeologists, alienated the world press, left his collection to be sold to the highest bidder and his agreement with the government, unlike Davis's, called for him to receive a share of any finds."[2] I believe this is one more instance of an American in Egypt being denied the honors due him. It follows in the path of the missionary John Antes, the American soldier-explorers George Bethune English, Charles Chaillé-Long, and Alexander Mason, and scientists like Frederick Cope Whitehouse (who wanted to create a lake and irrigation system in Wadi Raiyan — in the 1800s).

Theodore M. Davis (1837–1915) was born in Springfield, New York to minister Richard Montgomery Davis and Catherine Hubble Davis. When the minister died, Theodore's mother remarried and moved to Detroit, where her new husband served as a warden of the state prison in Jackson, Michigan. Theodore was but fifteen when he left home and headed into the wilderness to seek his fortune. The young Theodore studied and practiced law at Iowa City, Iowa, from 1855 to 1865.[3]

After leaving his law practice and enduring a lawsuit with his former partner, Davis moved to New York City. There he worked his way into the favors of Boss Tweed. William Tweed was one of the most corrupt officials that ever served New York. Preying on the fears of recent immigrants, he used them to gain power. With the backing of a group of men dubbed the Ring, Tweed and his Tammany Hall cronies manipulated banks, controlled media, and pirated city projects for their own gain. Tweed could elevate someone to power or bring him to his knees. Under his leadership every project in the city suddenly cost more as Tweed and his associates amassed a fortune from kickbacks. In 1871, tired of the corruption in the city, George Jones, Republican editor of the *New York Times*, began a systematic attack on Tweed and Tammany Hall. By 1873 Tweed was in prison, where he died in 1878.[4]

Davis's role in the Ring included a receivership for the Ocean Bank at the corner of Greenwich and Fulton Streets in Manhattan. The liquidation of the assets was a drawn-out affair and it was alleged that Davis, like Tweed, served himself first and the patrons of the bank last. From 1871 to 1879 the bank was being liquidated under Davis. The trail ended without an indictment against Davis because, it was alleged, Davis's kickbacks stopped witnesses from testifying against him.[5] John M. Adams concluded: "An astute attorney, Davis was guilty of perjury, bribery and fraud during his career in New York and became fabulously wealthy...."[6]

The Gilded Age

Mark Twain and Charles Dudley Warner, in their book *The Gilded Age: A Tale of Today*, dubbed the period between the American Civil War and the end of the nineteenth century the "Gilded Age." It was a period of superficial values, ostentatious displays of wealth, and a lack of morality. In other words, what you saw was not the reality: just like gold leaf laid over any ordinary object made that object look like something that it was not.

It was a time of the industrial revolution, unfettered capitalism, and no regulations, and the men who took the power were dubbed "robber barons" because of their ruthless abuse of competition and their lack of moral responsibility in their business practices. Men like John D. Rockefeller, Cornelius Vanderbilt, and the Astor family forged a new America and a new class of people: the 400. Once they were well sated, had built their palaces and filled them with exotic items from around the world, they turned their wealth and their power to the world of philanthropy, where their names would live forever. It was a demi-god type of existence where they alone decided who received their bounty and who did not. In keeping with this type of philanthropy, Theodore Davis (and Charles Wilbour) turned their ill-gotten gains to philanthropy in Egypt.

The First Nile Tour and the City of Luxor

In the winter of 1889, Theodore M. Davis was on the Nile. That journey and sixteen others were recorded by his wife's cousin Emma B. Andrews, who eventually became Davis's lover. Emma's journal, written almost daily for seventeen winters, was compiled into a type-written manuscript of over 800 pages and presented to the Metropolitan Museum of Art by Albert M. Lythgoe in 1919. Lythgoe left instructions that, as per Emma's wishes, it should never be published. A carbon copy can be found at the American Philosophical Society in Philadelphia.[7]

By December 12, 1889, the Davis party was ensconced in Shepheard's Hotel making plans for their first trip up the Nile. They viewed the steamers, but settled on a *dahabeyyiah*, the *Nubia*, an iron sailboat belonging to a Prince Achmed.[8] It appears to have been an unusual winter, with too many squalls and rainstorms, for the Davis party was always fleeing the weather. They leisurely made their way south along the Nile until they reached Luxor in Upper Egypt. Luxor at the time of Theodore Davis was not the Luxor of today; nor was it the city of 5000 years ago. Then it had a different name, and by the time of the New Kingdom, when the first tomb was built in what we call the Valley of the Kings, the town was already a thousand years old. It was also at the apex of its power and its beauty. Hundred-gated Thebes had a population of hundreds of thousands. It was the seat of power in Egypt and foreign dignitaries came to the city in Upper Egypt to pay homage.

> Yet, New Kingdom Thebes was a queen of the ancient world. It was the time of Hatshepsut, the female pharaoh who is best remembered for her supposed feud with Thutmose III, her fabulous expedition to Punt, and her elegant mortuary temple tucked against the Theban Hills on the West Bank; Thutmose III, the great warrior pharaoh, who expanded the ancient empire in all directions and began the building frenzy that made Karnak the greatest religious center in the country; Akhenaten, who wearied of the power of the priests of Amun, picked another god, and moved his religious center elsewhere; Tutankhamen, who returned to the city the glory of the past; and the Ramesside Dynasty, dominated by the power and personality of Ramses II, who built more monuments than any other pharaoh.[9]

These were the pharaohs who would be buried in the hills on the west bank of Thebes. Their final resting places would be among the tombs Davis was hoping to find when he excavated there. But Thebes was not called Thebes at the turn of the nineteenth century when Davis moored his *dahabeyyiah* below Amenhetep III's temple.[10] It was called Luxor, and it got

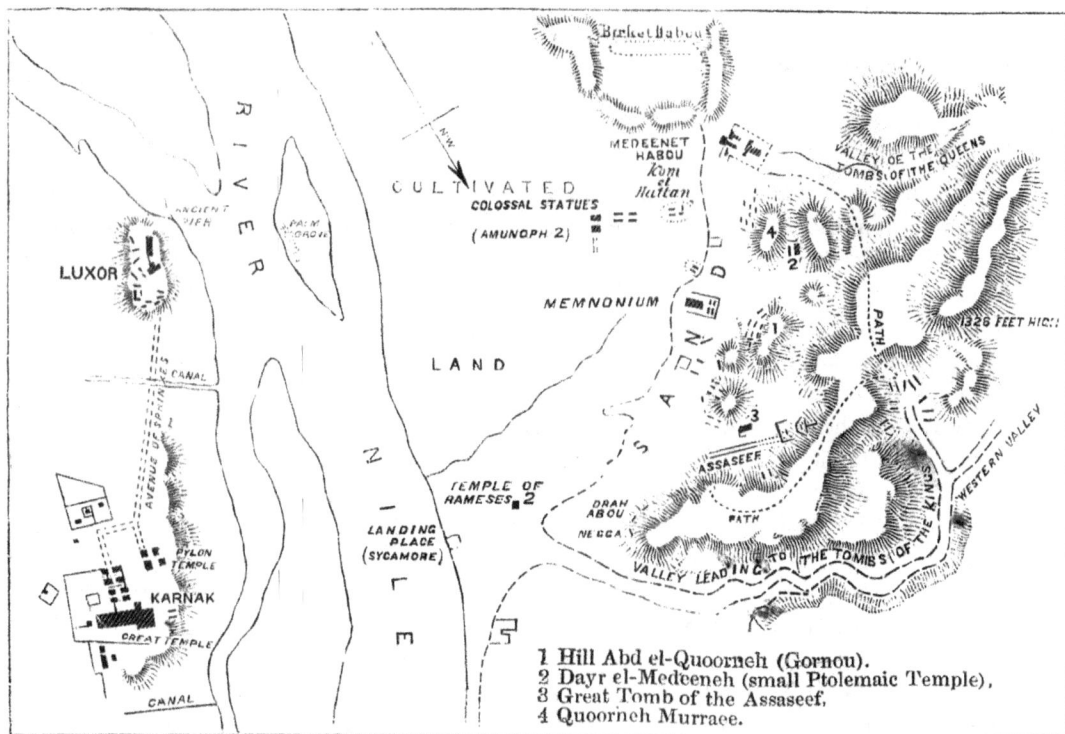

Map of Thebes as seen in 1857 (from *Photographic Views of Egypt, Past and Present* by Joseph P. Thompson).

that name after the Arab invasion of the seventh century. Luxor, or *al-Uqsur*, means the palaces, and is aptly named, for the palaces of hundred-gated Thebes of the ancient civilization still stood in the hot, dry climate that was Upper Egypt. Luxor did not have the importance of Thebes. It was not the seat of government. It no longer built temples in honor of ancient gods. It was a rural Arab town where people did not honor the palaces but built their hovels in their courtyards.

In Davis's days the modern tourists had been coming to see the ancient wonders for some time. The modern town ran from just north of Karnak to just south of Luxor Temple. The Luxor Hotel, opened in 1878, and the Winter Palace, built in 1886, were the best of the few accommodations available. The hotels were equipped with electric lights, steam laundries, billiard rooms, and exquisite tropical gardens. There was no sound and light, such as today's tourists can experience, and few shops for souvenirs, but the *dahabeyyiahs* of travelers like Davis were moored directly in front of Luxor Temple. The temple itself had been cleared from the debris of centuries by Maspero in the early 1880s. He also removed the squatters from within the temples. Ramses II's statues were buried up to their breasts. That was the Luxor that Theodore Davis entered in 1889. He continued to return year after year. In 1897, sure that his destiny was to be found on the Nile, Davis bought a *dahabeyyiah* and named it the *Beduin*. It would become a focal point for archaeologists in Egypt for the next thirteen years.

The Service des Antiquités, the Valley of the Kings, and the Theban Mapping Project (TMP)

The *Service des Antiquités*, or the Antiquities Service, was founded in 1858 by Sa'id Pasha in order to control the ebb and flow of artifacts from the ancient civilization. Sa'id appointed the French scholar Auguste Mariette (1858–1881) director and mandated that the *Service* excavate antiquities, supervise digs, and approve foreigners who had come to Egypt to dig for antiquities. By 1863 Mariette had established the Bulaq Museum in an old City Transit Authority building in Cairo. Mariette was followed by Gaston Maspero (1881–1886 and 1899–1914). The French dominated the Service until the 1950s, when Egypt finally won its independence.[11] It was men from the *Service* who wooed and won Davis's dollars to the purpose of exploring in the Valley of the Kings. His first venture into Egyptology was to fund English archaeologist Percy Newberry's work in the chapel of vizier Rekhmire (Valley of the Nobles) of the Eighteenth Dynasty in 1900.[12] That began Theodore Davis's philanthropy in Egypt. Next he would turn to the Valley of the Kings and spend the better part of a decade and a half looking for the lost tombs of the pharaohs of the New Kingdom.

Why were the tombs cut into the mountains of western Thebes? When the pharaohs of ancient Egypt found that their tombs were being vandalized, they tried to find some way to protect them from the tomb robbers. It was important since the ancient Egyptians believed in an afterlife, and in order to have the comforts enjoyed on earth the pharaoh had to take his wealth with him. So the tombs were filled with gold statues, chariots, jewelry, and many of the objects that surrounded the pharaoh in life. Thutmose I was the first to dig deep into the Theban hills to hide his tomb. Others followed.

But Thutmose's dream of hiding his tomb did not work. None of the tombs were safe from plunder. Robbers found the tombs in ancient times and pillaged them, leaving items scattered about. Although some of the tombs were lost through the ages, some were never lost. The Greek geographer Strabo knew and wrote about the tombs. Hermits lived in the tombs during Christian times. They left their graffiti on the walls and scratched out some of the "pagan" murals that were offensive to their religious views. In 1737 Richard Pococke saw fourteen open tombs. James Bruce discovered the tomb of Ramses III in 1769. Savants of the French army (maybe) discovered the tombs of Ramses VI and Amunhotep III. Giovanni Belzoni found and lived in the tomb of Seti I and Rameses I and Ay. Then came the German explorer Riachard Lepsius and his expedition. Lepsius surveyed the valley from 1843 to 1845. By 1858, when Francis Frith photographed Thebes, twenty-seven tombs were known to exist. In 1898 Victor Loret cleared the tombs of Amunhotep II and Thutmose III.[13] Then came Theodore Davis, who would change our knowledge of the Valley of the Kings forever.

Theodore Davis in the Valley of the Kings

It was Inspector of Antiquities for Upper-Egypt, Howard Carter, who enticed Theodore Davis to invest in the excavations in the Valley of the Kings. First he intrigued Davis with the idea and then he convinced Gaston Maspero, head of the Antiquities Service, to grant Davis permission to finance excavations. Carter wrote in his unpublished autobiography: "Davis often told me that he would like to have some active interest during his sojourns in Upper Egypt. Thus ... I put the following proposition to him. The Egyptian Government would be willing, when my duties permitted, for me to carry out the researches in the Valley of the tombs of the Kings on his behalf, if he would cover the costs thereof, that the Egyptian Government in return for his generosity would be pleased, whenever it was possible, to give him duplicate antiquities resulting from these researches...."[14] The Antiquities Service granted the concession, which permitted Davis to fund excavations for a number of years. The agreement also stated that everything he found would belong to Egypt. He surrounded himself with a bevy of archaeologists, and although he did not originally become hands-on, he is credited with the discovery of many tombs.

Out of the years of effort came seven well-illustrated books retelling the story of the excavations of some of the most important tombs found in the Valley of the Kings. In his own words, Theodore Davis described his work this way:

> It was the custom of the kings to excavate their tombs in the mountains or the foot-hills, in such site as promised the greatest concealment: the doors of the tombs were hidden with tons of rocks, great and small, thereby giving the appearance of a natural deposit. It is known that the Priests of Ammon were aware of the location of every tomb in the valley, and that this knowledge was handed down to the priests from generation to generation; that they made, at stated times, the examinations of the outward conditions of the sites of the tombs, and reported the results. For some years before November, 1905, I sought to find tombs in "The Valley of the Kings" by exploring hither and thither where I supposed the greatest probability existed. This manner of exploring yielded several tombs, but it was not satisfactory work, inasmuch as it neglected the intervening locations which might bear fruits. For this reason I established in November, 1905, the policy of exhausting every mountain and foot-hill in the valley.
>
> In execution of my "policy," I commenced at the south end of the "valley," which is a "cul-de-sac," and cleared every foot of the mountains and foot-hills of all the deposits of stone and debris, and continued this manner of search by following the rock down as long as it was vertical, and until it flatted, by which it must be understood that the inhabitants of Thebes knew that the space between the rocks and foot-hills on either side was a great water-course, consequently they rarely or never made a tomb in the horizontal course.[15]

When it was all over, Theodore M. Davis would have worked in the Valley of the Kings for twelve years and found or explored around thirty tombs, more than any other excavator then and now. He would publish seven major publications describing what he considered his most important finds: the tomb of Thutmes (Thutmoses) IV, the tomb of Hatshepsut, the tomb of Yuya and Thuyu, the tomb of Siptah, the tomb of Queen Tiye (the Amarna Cache), the tomb of Horemheb, and the embalming cache of Tutankhamen. What is so wonderful about the books is that we have an account of the discovery of each tomb as described by Davis. Four will be explored below: tomb of Thutmes (Thutmoses) IV, the tomb of Hatshepsut, the tomb of Yuya and Thuyu, and the tomb of Queen Tiye (the Amarna Cache).

As noted, the first archaeologist to work with Davis was Howard Carter. Carter was an English artist and archaeologist who arrived in Egypt in 1891 when he was only seventeen years old. His mission for the Egypt Exploration Fund was to join and assist British Egyptologist Percy Newberry at the Middle Kingdom tombs at Beni Hasan in Middle Egypt. By 1892 he was working with another British Egyptologist, Flinders Petrie, at Amarna. He arrived in Luxor in 1894, where for five years he recorded reliefs in the temple of Hatshepsut. In 1899 he was appointed the very first Inspector of Antiquities in Luxor. This led to Theodore Davis's Valley of the Kings adventure. Just after working with Davis, Carter was sent to Lower Egypt, mostly the Delta area, as inspector there. Carter, of course, would go on to discover one of the most famous discoveries in all of ancient Egyptian history: the tomb of Tutankhamen. He did this after Davis had proclaimed nearly ten years earlier that there was nothing new to discover in the Valley of the Kings. When Davis left the valley he was only a few meters away from Tut's tomb. In all, Carter would excavate or discover eleven tombs in the Valley of the Kings while working with Davis.

Tomb of Thutmes IV (KV-43)[16]

In 1903 Carter discovered a tomb high on the cliff side of the Theban hills. It was the tomb of Thutmes IV, KV-43. Carter wrote the introduction to Theodore Davis's book about the exploration of this tomb explaining how they found it and what they found in the tomb.

> After consulting with M. Maspero, the Director-General, and Mr. Davis, it was decided to carry out excavations in such a manner as to thoroughly exhaust the small valley running west from Tomb No. 3, continuing the work right up to the sheer cliff. These excavations were commenced in January, 1902, and resulted in minor discoveries, already chronicled in the Service's "Annales." In the first part of the excavations there was found in the debris, some way up the valley, a small fragment of an alabaster vase, bearing the cartouche of Thoutmosis IV, which led me to believe I was in the near neighbourhood of the tomb of that king. In January, 1903, the work had reached the base of the cliff, where there were distinct signs of artificial working, and eventually the opening of a tomb was found.... Here, in the debris, many fragments of antiquities turned up, and, among others, the end of a wooden axe-handle, bearing the name of Thoutmosis IV. This at once led me to believe that the tomb discovered belonged to this Monarch, and, in clearing down to the surface of the rock, I came upon two small holes which contained complete, undisturbed sets of foundation deposits bearing the name of the king.
> On the 18th January, 1903, the door of the tomb was sufficiently cleared to permit entrance. Unfortunately Mr. Davis had sailed for Assuan, and being unable to reach him by telegraph, I concluded to enter the tomb and make an examination of its contents. I invited Mr. Robb. de P. Tytus to accompany me in my inspection.
> ... We then entered, accompanied by the head Reis, finding a passage partially filled with rubbish and strewn with broken antiquities. This immediately indicated to us that the tomb had been anciently plundered. Sliding down the passage over the rubbish for about 30 metres, we found ourselves over a gaping well obstructing further progress. Here we were obliged to wait until our eyes became accustomed to the

dim light of our candles before we could see the further side or bottom. Gradually there loomed before us the opposite wall, in which we saw an opening had been cut, and, on finding that the well was very deep, we sent for ladders and ropes. Looking around us we saw that the upper part of the walls of this well were painted with scenes in which the cartouche of Thoutmosis IV figured prominently. Here was, at last, final evidence of the true ownership of the tomb. Ropes and ladders having been procured, we with difficulty descended on the one side of the well and ascended on the other (the well having but little rubbish in it), and succeeded then in entering through the hole into a rectangular hall with two columns. Fastened round the nearest column to this opening was an ancient cable rope made of palm fibre, knotted at intervals, and with its end hanging down and reaching to the bottom of the well. Here was further evidence of plunderers. This chamber was practically clean and contained but few antiquities, save some unimportant pieces and an inscribed paddle of a boat. In the lefthand corner of this chamber we found a staircase leading into a sloping passage about 20 metres in length, which gave access to a small square chamber. This passage was partially filled with rubbish, which made our descent difficult, stones rolling down at every step.[17]

This was an important find. Yes, it had been robbed in antiquity, but when the modern workers entered the tomb they found the drawings and painting as fresh as they were when they were first painted over 2000 years before. There were also many amazing artifacts, including a chariot and the king's quartzite sarcophagus.

Tomb of Hatshepsut (KV-20)

In 1903–04, Howard Carter excavated and cleared the known tomb of Hatshepsut. The tomb originally belonged to Thutmes I, but when his daughter Hatshepsut died she was also buried there. In 1906 Theodore Davis published *The Tomb of Hâtshopsîtû*. In the introduction he describes just how the tomb was finally identified as belonging to the ancient queen. But first he provided a history of the excavation of the tomb, which reached far back to 900 B.C. Strabo also visited the tomb in 24 B.C. Napoleon's soldiers examined it and cleared a portion of it in 1799. More modern visitors were Charles H. Gordon in 1804, Belzoni in 1817, and Lepsius in 1844. Davis concluded: "Beyond these explorations no work was done in or about it until I undertook its thorough exploration in March, 1903."[18]

In addition to the history of exploration, Davis's introduction to his publication also describes how they entered the tomb, what they found inside, and how they concluded the tomb belonged to Hatshepsut.

Long before we reached this chamber the air had become so bad, and the heat so great, that the candles carried by the workmen melted, and would not give enough light to enable them to continue their work; consequently we were compelled to install electric lights, in the shape of hand wires, which could be extended to any length, with lamps attached as needed. For a time this enabled the work to progress, but as soon as we got down about 50 metres, the air became so foul that the men could not work. In addition to this, the bats of centuries had built innumerable nests on the ceilings of the corridors and chambers, and their excrement had become so dry that the least stir of the air filled the corridors with a fluffy black stuff, which choked the noses and mouths of the men, rendering it most difficult for them to breathe. To overcome these difficulties, we installed an air suction pump at the mouth of the tomb, to which was attached a zinc pipe, which before the burial chamber was reached extended about 213 metres....

Therefore, with some timidity, I trespass in the field of Egyptology to the extent of expressing my convictions that Hâtshopsîtû's body was moved with that of Thoutmosis from her tomb to the "cachette," and that the logic of the situation justifies the conclusion that one of the two unidentified female bodies is that of the great Queen Hâtshopsîtû. "Sic transit gloria mundi."[19]

The mummy of the queen was not in this tomb. But two mummies were found in an undecorated tomb that the TMP would identify as the tomb of Sit-Ra, KV-60. That tomb was discovered by Howard Carter for Davis in 1903 too. Edward R. Ayrton went back to the undecorated Tomb KV-60 in 1906. It proved to have been ransacked, but some items including two mummies, tools from the workers, jewelry, scarabs, seals, and some vessels were still within the tomb. It also created identity problems because there were two female mummies in the tomb and a coffin with the inscription "royal nurse." Ayrton reopened the tomb and took that coffin and its mummy (KV-60B) to the Egyptian Museum. Little work was done at the time and eventually the tomb was lost. In 1990 the tomb was found again. The drama continued without any conclusion.[20] In 2007, once again the tomb was reopened. This time the remaining mummy, called KV-60A, was removed. The head of the Supreme Council of Antiquities, as the Antiquities Service was now called, determined that this female mummy was indeed Hatshepsut.[21] Not everyone agrees.

Soon after, the Service removed Carter from Luxor and there was a period of flux. During that time British Egyptologist James E. Quibell took over the inspectorship at Thebes. He only worked with Davis for a short time, but in that interim he discovered the tomb of Yuya and Thuyu, KV-46. Quibell, a protégé of Flinders Petrie, arrived in Egypt around 1893. By 1899 he was chief inspector of antiquities in the Delta; in 1904 he moved to Sakkara and served as chief inspector there. In 1914 he was the Keeper of the Cairo Museum. In addition to discovering this tomb, he found the Narmer Palette, a slab with the earliest known hieroglyphics (at the time). That was after his association with Davis.

Tomb of Yuya and Thuyu KV-46

The Tomb of Yuya and Thuyu, KV-46, has been called "the richest and best preserved tomb found in the valley, and the first to be found with major items in situ." It was exactly that, and its discovery surely was an exciting moment for the excavators. Quibell did find the tomb intact, despite the fact that it had been robbed at least three times through the ages. It still contained most of the items that the entombed couple felt they needed in antiquity. In addition to the two mummies, the tomb contained clothing, furniture, jewelry, musical instruments, scarabs and seals, a full-size chariot, warfare and hunting equipment, and more.[22]

Davis published *The Tomb of Iouiya and Touiyou*, which is how, in 1907, he translated their names from hieroglyphics. In the introduction he wrote the interesting story of its discovery:

> From the 25th of January, 1905, until the 5th of February, the work progressed without sign of promise. My daily visits were most discouraging, but on my arrival at the work on the 6th February, I was greeted by my Reis (Captain) and workmen with great acclamation. I quickly made my way to the spot, where I saw a few inches of the top of a well-cut stone step, which promised steps below and the possible existence of a tomb.
>
> From the 6th of February until the 11th my workmen were hard at work removing the overhanging *debris* which concealed the door; but before the night of the 11th a small portion of the doorway was disclosed, and from that moment the doorway was guarded day and night by policemen and valley guards. At the close of the twelfth day the door was entirely cleared — a most satisfactory sight! It was cut in the solid rock, and was 4.02 meters high and 1.35 wide, with a decorated lintel. The doorway

was closed within eighteen inches of the top with flat stones, about twelve inches by four, laid in Nile mud plaster. This opening indicated that, at some early date, the tomb had been entered and probably robbed — a most unwelcome indication! Although it was nearly dark, I concluded to have a look through the opening. Mr. Arthur Weigall, the appointed but not formally confirmed Chief Inspector in succession to Mr. Quibell, had ridden out to the valley with me, and was invited to join me in the first sight of the corridor of the tomb. The opening was chin high, but we could dimly see a few yards of the corridor, which seemed to be about five feet wide and high, with a steep decline. As soon as my eyes became used to the semi-darkness, I saw what I thought to be a cane, or small club, lying on the floor a few feet from the doorway. Neither of us could get up to the opening, nor through it, without a ladder — which did not exist in the valley — so I selected a small native boy and had him lifted up to the opening, through which he entered. We watched the boy closely and saw him pick up the cane; then he came towards us, picked up two other objects and passed them to me. They proved to be a wooden staff of office, a neck yoke, and a large stone scarab, covered more or less with gold foil, which made it seem, at first glance, to be solid gold.[23]

Davis believed that this was an important find. He left the tomb and went to the Nile to find someone from the antiquities department to join him before he opened the tomb. There were a number of archaeologists in Luxor at the time, including Maspero; Archibald Sayce, a British scholar who first distinguished himself in Assyriology; and Arthur Weigall, who was to replace Quibell as inspector at Thebes.

> Consequently, next morning, Monsieur Maspero and Mr. Weigall joined me at the tomb, and I at once set the men to work taking down the wall which barred the

View of interior of a tomb in 1857 (from *Photographic Views of Egypt, Past and Present* by Joseph P. Thompson).

outer door. It was very slow work, as every stone had to be examined for hieroglyphs and signs, and every basket of sand and *debris* sifted and examined for objects of interest which might be concealed in the deposit. However, nothing was found, and, in the course of an hour or so, the doorway was cleared.

The electric wire had been installed at the outer doorway, but as the introduction down the corridor would have required the services of electricians, we concluded that it would be safer to use candles for our entry and examinations. Monsieur Maspero and I and, at my invitation, Mr. Weigall, each with a candle, started down the corridor, which proved to be 1.75 meters wide and 2.05 meters high, cut out of the solid rock and descending so sharply as to require care not to fall. It was neither painted nor inscribed. After descending about twenty feet, we found a shelf cut into one side of the wall and on it a large ceremonial wig made of flax and dyed black, also an armful of dried flowers which doubtless were offerings to the dead (as is done in our day and generation). Passing on some 9 meters, we came to another flight of stone steps descending almost perpendicularly, at the bottom of which we found a doorway 2.10 meters high and 1.20 meters wide, closed with stones set in Nile mud plaster, with an opening at the top of about the same size as was found in the first doorway, confirming our fears of a robbery. The face of the wall was plastered with mud and stamped from top to bottom with seals.

On either side of this doorway, carefully placed to escape injury, stood a reddish pottery bowl about twelve inches wide, showing the finger marks of the man who with his hands gathered the mud and plastered it on the doorway wall. In each bowl was a wide wooden stick, evidently used to scrape the mud from his hands. Having copied the seals, we investigated the possibility of entry without taking down the wall. We found that the opening which the robber had made was too high and too small to allow of Monsieur Maspero getting through without injury. Though we had nothing but our bare hands, we managed to take down the upper layer of stones, and then Monsieur Maspero and I put our heads and candles into the chamber, which enabled us to get a glimpse of shining gold covering some kind of furniture, though we could not identify it. This stimulated us to make the entry without further enlarging the opening. I managed to get over the wall and found myself in the sepulchral chamber. With considerable difficulty we helped Monsieur Maspero safely to scale the obstruction, and then Mr. Weigall made his entry. The chamber was as dark as dark could be and extremely hot. Our first quest was the name of the owner of the tomb, as to which we had not the slightest knowledge or suspicion. We held up our candles, but they gave so little light and so dazzled our eyes that we could see nothing except the glitter of gold. In a moment or two, however, I made out a very large wooden coffin, known as a funeral sled, which was used to contain all the coffins of the dead person and his mummy and to convey them to his tomb. It was about six feet high and eight feet long, made of wood covered with bitumen, which was as bright as the day it was put on. Around the upper part of the coffin was a stripe of gold-foil, about six inches wide, covered with hieroglyphs. On calling Monsieur Maspero's attention to it, he immediately handed me his candle, which, together with my own, I held before my eyes, close to the inscriptions so that he could read them. In an instant he said, "Iouiya."[24]

Yuya and Thuyu were the parents of Queen Tiy, the wife of Pharaoh Amenhotep III, and the mother of Amenhetep IV, whom we call Akhenaten. Akhenaton was the first known ruler to believe in the concept of the one God. So finding the grandparents of the "heretic king" was exciting in itself. The contents of the tomb would be equally exciting. As they walked deeper into the tomb they began to find objects: a chariot, alabaster vases, and the coffin of the royal pair.

The mummies of Iouiya and Touiyou were lying in their coffins. Originally each mummy was enclosed in three coffins; the inner one holding the body. Evidently the robber had taken the inner coffins out and then had taken off their lids, though he did not take the bodies out of their coffins, but contented himself with stripping off the mummy-cloth in which they were wrapped. The stripping was done by scratching off the cloth with his nails, seeking only the gold ornaments or jewels. At least that seems to have been the manner of robbing the bodies, as we found in both coffins, on either side of the bodies, great quantities of mummy-cloth torn into small bits. Among the shreds were found numerous valuable religious symbols, several scarabs, and various objects of interest and beauty. In lifting the body of Iouiya from his coffin, we found a necklace of large beads made of gold and of lapis lazuli, strung on a strong thread, which the robber had evidently broken when scratching off the mummy-cloth, causing the beads to fall behind the mummy's neck....

When I first saw the mummy of Iouiyou she was lying in her coffin, covered from her chin to her feet with very fine mummy-cloth arranged with care. Why this was done no one can positively state, but I am disposed to think that the robber was impressed by the dignity of the dead woman whose body he had desecrated. I had occasion to sit by her in the tomb for nearly an hour, and having nothing else to do or see, I studied her face and indulged in speculations germane to the situation, until her dignity and character so impressed me that I almost found it necessary to apologize for my presence.

From all the evidence furnished by the acts of the robber, it seems reasonable to conclude that the entry into the tomb was made within the lifetime of some person who had exact knowledge of its location. Evidently the robber had tunnelled through the overlying *debris* which concealed the door of the tomb; otherwise he would have been compelled to remove a mass of rock and soil which would have required many days, and would also have exposed the robbery to the first passer-by. When the robber found the outer doorway barred by a wall, he took off enough of it to enable him to crawl through; and when he reached the second and last doorway, he found a corresponding wall, which he treated in the same manner. He seems to have had either a very dim light or none at all, for when he was in the burial chamber he selected a large stone scarab, the neck-yoke of the chariot, and a wooden staff of office, all of which were covered with thick gold foil, which evidently he thought to be solid gold: he carried them up the corridor until he came to a gleam of daylight, when he discovered his error and left them on the floor of the corridor, where I found them.

When the robber got out of the tomb, he carefully concealed the doorway and his tunnel with stones and *debris*, and did it so effectively, that it was not disturbed until its discovery three thousand years later.[25]

The Tomb of Queen Meie (Tiye), or the Armana Cache (KV 55)

In 1905 Davis had a new excavator: Edward R. Ayrton. Ayrton was also an English Egyptologist. He was twenty years old when he arrived in Egypt to work with Flinders Petrie in Abydos, where he remained from 1902 to 1904, just before joining Davis in the Valley of the Kings. He remained with Davis until 1908. In all he explored and/or discovered seventeen tombs for Davis. He left Egypt for Ceylon in 1911, where he drowned in 1914.

On January 6, 1907, Edward Ayrton explored the tomb of an Egyptian queen that he and Theodore Davis originally called Meie. By the time Davis published his book on the discovery in 1910, the team used the name Tiye. By that time the archaeologists had been able to ascertain more details about the discovery. In the introduction Davis once again described how the excavators entered the tomb and the problems they encountered.

On the 1st of January, 1907, having exhausted the surrounding sites, I had to face a space of about forty feet oblong and at least fifty feet high, covered with limestone chippings, evidently the dumping of the surrounding tombs. Within a few feet was the open tomb of Rameses IX. and on the east and south sides were the open tombs of Seti I, and Rameses I, II, and III, all of which had contributed to the hill. There was no sign of the probability of a tomb. On the contrary, it seemed to be a hopeless excavation, resulting in a waste of time and money. Nevertheless, it had to be cleared, whatever the result. Possibly it may interest the reader to know that the most difficult, delaying, and expensive work is the finding of a place where the debris can be dumped. Generally, it has to be moved two or three times, as the first dumping-ground may probably cover some tomb, therefore the debris must be returned to the original spot, in case no tomb is found.

With a large gang of men, we commenced clearing on the apex of the hill, within a few feet of the tomb of Rameses IX. In the course of a few days we reached the level of the door of his tomb, finding nothing but the chippings of the surrounding tombs. But down we went some thirty feet, when we found stone steps evidently leading to a tomb. Finally, we discovered the lintel of a door which proved to be about eight feet high and six feet wide. It had been closed with large and small stones, held in place with cement or plaster, but, with the exception of a wall about three feet high, these had been pulled down. The clearing of the door, so that we could enter, was soon done, when we found that within a few feet of the door, the mouth of the tomb was filled with stones to within four feet of the roof. On this pile of stones were lying two wooden doors, on each of which copper hinges were fixed. The upper faces of the doors were covered with gold foil marked with *the name and titles of Queen Tiyi.* It is quite impossible to describe the surprise and joy of finding the tomb of the great queen and her household gods, which for these 3,000 years had never been discovered.[26]

But the task of identifying the occupant of the tomb proved to be very complex. The men continued to examine the artifacts in the tomb. The wooden coffin (covered in gold foil) was quite visible. It must have been dropped because the side was broken and the upper torso of the mummy was visible.

> The mouth was partly open, showing a perfect set of upper and lower teeth. The body was enclosed in mummy-cloth of fine texture, but all of the cloth covering the body was of a very dark colour. Naturally it ought to be a much brighter colour. Rather suspecting injury from the evident dampness, I gently touched one of the front teeth (3,000 years old), and alas! it fell into dust, thereby showing that the mummy could not be preserved. We then cleared the entire mummy, and found that from the clasped hands to the feet, the body was covered with pure gold sheets, called gold foil, but nearly all so thick that when taken in the hands, they would stand alone without bending. These sheets covered the body from side to side. When we had taken off the gold on the front of the mummy, we lifted it so as to get the gold underneath, which was plainly in sight....
>
> Subsequently the wrappings of the mummy were entirely removed, exposing the bones. Thereupon, I concluded to have them examined and reported upon by two surgeons who happened to be in the "Valley of the Kings." They kindly made the examination and reported that the pelvis was evidently that of a woman. Therefore, everyone interested in the question accepted the sex, and supposed that the body was doubtless that of Queen Tiyi. Some time thereafter, the bones were sent to Dr. G. Elliot Smith, Professor of Anatomy in the Egyptian Government School of Medicine, Cairo, for his inspection and decision. Alas! Dr. Smith declared the sex to be male. It is only fair to state that the surgeons were deceived by the abnormal pelvis and the conditions of the examination....[27]

The problem with the tomb now known as KV-55 was and is the fact that it was more than the burial site of a single person. In fact, it has been called by a number of names, including the Armana cache. As Davis noted in his book which was published a few years after his discovery, the mummy proved to be a man and not a woman. It also had all the equipage of a pharaoh. So, it was hoped that Akhenaton himself was buried in this tomb. Current consensus is that it is Akhenaten. Today it is believed that the remains of the dead from Amarna were brought to Thebes and placed in this tomb.

Theodore M. Davis was America's most important Egyptologist in the Valley of the Kings. His efforts did much for Egyptomania in America, as did those of George Robbins Gliddon nearly a hundred years before. His work remains the most prolific and, arguably, the most important ever carried out in the Valley of the Kings. Who among the Egyptologists of the world discovered or cleared thirty tombs in twelve years?

Notes

Chapter 1

1. John Antes, *Observations on the Manners and Customs of the Egyptians, The overflowing of the Nile and its effects; with remarks on the plague, and other subjects written during a residence of twelve years in Cairo and its vicinity* (London: John Stockdale, 1800), 9. Print.

2. Johann Friedrich Peter, "String Chamber Music in the Moravian Musical Heritage," October 24, 2005, New World Records 80507. http://www.newworld records.org/linernotes/80507.pdf. Web.

3. John Antes, "Letter from Grand Cairo to Benjamin Franklin. July 10, 1779," in Isaac Minis Hayes, ed. *Calendar of the Franklin Papers in the Library of the American Philosophical Society.* 5 Volumes. No. XV, 31 (Philadelphia: American Philosophical Society, 1908). Microfilm.

4. Portions of this chapter were first presented as *John Antes: Dilettante Americano or What?* Travel and Travellers in Egypt and the Nile Valley. Conference on Travellers in Egypt and the Near East. ASTENE. Pollock Halls, Edinburgh University (Scotland). July 11–15, 2001. Conference.

5. Rufus A. Grinder, *Music in Bethlehem, Pennsylvania from 1741 to 1871* (Philadelphia: J. Hill Martin, 1873), 5. Print. Only a few of these instruments have survived: a violin can be found at the Moravian Music Foundation in Winston-Salem, North Carolina; a signed viola is with the Moravian Historical Society in Nazareth, Pennsylvania; and a viola cello is with a Moravian church in Bethlehem, Pennsylvania.

6. John W. Livingston, "Ali Bey Al-Kabir and the Jews," *Middle Eastern Studies* 7, No. 2 (May 1971): 221–228. Print.

7. John Antes, *Excerpts from Narrative of the Life of our Late Dear and Venerable Brother John Antes, Written by Himself in Periodical Accounts Relating to the Mission of the Church of the United Brethren Established Among the Heathen,* Volume 5 (London: E. Baker for Bristol Society for Promoting Religious Knowledge, 1815), 447. Print.

8. For an in-depth account of the establishment of the Moravians in Cairo see John Beck Holmes, *Historical Sketches of the Missions of the United Brethren for Propagating the Gospel Among the Heathen, from their commencement to the year 1817* (London: 1827), 448. Print.

9. John Antes, Letter from Cairo. (in German) to Rev. Benjamin LaTrobe. December 22, 1773. AB 140, Moravian Archives London (MAL). Translated by Gabriele Hallof. 1–2. Print.

10. The Moravian daily diary of events in Cairo is found in the archives of the Moravian center in Herrnhut, Germany. It includes 44 letters to Herrnhut, listing all interesting events day by day including the work of the Moravians, their journeys to Middle and Upper Egypt, political affairs, news, and gossip. The 19 × 23 cm sheets are handwritten on both sides in the archaic German called Deutscher Kurrentschrift, with 50 and more lines on one side. The diary begins on March 13, 1769, and ends on February 16, 1783, with the arrival of the last Moravians in Barby (Germany). It contains 401 pages on 201 sheets. It has never been translated into English.

11. Jochen Hallof, Email to Cassandra Vivian, Tuesday, March 11, 2003. Email.

12. John Antes, Letter from Cairo (in German) to Rev. Benjamin LaTrobe. April 23, 1773. AB 140, Moravian Archives London (MAL). Translated by Gabriele Hallof. 1–2. Print.

13. John Antes, Letter from Cairo. (in German) to Br. Wollin (in London), September 28, 1778. AB 140, Moravian Archives London (MAL). Translated by Gabriele Hallof. Print.

14. John Antes, Letter of John Antes to Brother Benjamin Latrobe from Cairo (in German), September 8, 1770. AB 140, Moravian Archives London (MAL). Translated by Gabriele Hallof. Print.

15. He was buried in a vault in Old Cairo's Church of Saint George.

16. John Antes, Letter from Cairo (in German) to Rev. Benjamin LaTrobe. September 3, 1780. AB 140, Moravian Archives London (MAL). Translated by Gabriele Hallof. 4p. Print.

17. John Antes, Extract of a Letter from Grand Cairo (in English) to Rev. Benjamin LaTrobe. August 15, 1771. AB 140, Moravian Archives London (MAL). 4p. Print.

18. Antes is referring here to a number of famous travelers. The Englishman Richard Pococke (1704–

1765), who eventually emigrated to the United States, visited Egypt from September 1737 to March of 1738. He traveled along the Nile as far as Philae and later wrote *A Description of the East.* Frederik Ludwig Norden (1708–1742) was a Danish sea captain who explored Egypt for Christian VI in 1738. He stayed for a year and traveled extensively in Egypt. He published his *Travels in Egypt and Nubia* in 1751. Carsten Niebuhr (1733–1815), a German geographer and astronomer, accompanied the Royal Danish Expedition, a scientific expedition of Frederick V of Denmark, to Egypt, September 26, 1761 to October 8, 1762. Niebuhr visited Lower Egypt only, and as the only survivor of his ill-fated expedition, he returned to Germany. He measured the pyramids and determined they were aligned along the cardinal points (NSEW). He published *Reisenbeschreibung nach Arabien und andern umliegenden Ländern in* 2 Volumeumes in 1774–8 and edited *Flora Aegyptiaco-Arabica,* a botany book compiled by Pehr Forskål, a member of the expedition who died in Yemen in 1763. Claude Etienne Savary (1750–1788) was a French traveler who was in Egypt from 1776 to 1779. Constantin François Chasseboeuf Volney (1757–1820) was a French savant and traveler. He visited Egypt and Syria in 1785 and published *Voyage en Egypte et en Syrie* in 1787, a book that influenced Napoleon.

19. Antes to LaTrobe, September 8, 1770.

20. Antes to LaTrobe, August 15, 1771.

21. John Antes, Extract of a Letter from Cairo (in English) to Rev. Benjamin LaTrobe, London, April 22, 1772, AB 140, Moravian Archives London (MAL). 2p. Print.

22. Antes to LaTrobe, April 23, 1773.

23. Salt's story is well told in Deborah Manley and Peta Ree, *Henry Salt: Artist, Traveller, Diplomat, Egyptologist* (London: Libri, 2001). Print. His papers are archived at the British Museum Department of Egyptian Antiquities, Central Archives, and British Library.

24. John Antes, "Considerations on the Opinions expressed on Mr. Bruce, by Lord Valentia, and Mr. Salt," *Select Reviews and Spirit of the Foreign Magazines 1809–1811* 4, No. 20 (August 1810): 130–134. Print.

25. Antes, "Considerations," 131.

26. Antes, "Considerations," 133.

27. For interesting biographical information on Italians in Egypt see L.A. Balboni, *Gli' Italiani nella Civilta Egizian del Secolo XIX. Sotto gli auspice del comitato alessandrino della Societa Dante Alighieri,* (Alessandria D'Egitto, 1906). ebook.

28. Peter, "String Chamber Music." Web.

29. John Antes to Benjamin Franklin, July 10, 1779.

30. The Bristol Moravian Church's archives are located at the University of Bristol, special collections. See Jonathan Barry and Kenneth Morgan, *The Moravians in Revival and Reformation in 18th century Bristol* (Bristol: Bristol Record Society, 1994), 110. Print.

Chapter 2

1. Jared Sparks, *The Life of John Ledyard, the American Traveller* (Cambridge, MA: Hilliard and Brown, 1828), 281. Print.

2. Sparks, 288.

3. Sparks, 288–9.

4. Ledyard wrote the book *A Journal of Captain Cook's Last Voyage to the Pacific Ocean, and in quest of a North-West Passage between Asia and America; performed in the years 1776, 1777, 1778 and 1779,* published in 1783, heavily reliant on other sources. It made him famous. It also made him America's first copyright owner. For the text of his book and comments on the plagiarism issues, see James Zug, ed., *Last Voyage of Captain Cook: The Collected Writings of John Ledyard* (Margate, FL: National Geographic Adventure Classics, 2005). Print. Zug offers fresh transcription of Ledyard's letters and journals.

5. Thomas Jefferson, *Autobiography.* Washington ed. University of Virginia Catalog (Virgo) March 9, 2011. "4559 Ledyard" 68 and Ford ed., i, 94. 1821. At The Jeffersonian Cyclopedia. http://etext.lib.virginia.edu/etcbin/foleyx-browse?id=Ledyard. Web.

6. Jefferson, *Autobiography,* 4559.

7. Joseph Banks has been described as "the Father of Research, the laborious advocate of enquiry, and the friend of the adventurous traveler." Some 10,000 pages of his papers are found at the Mitchell and Dixson collections of the State Library of New South Wales, in Sydney, Australia. The African Association's archives rest with the Royal Geographical Society. References can be viewed online at http://www.aim25. ac.uk/cgi-bin/frames/fulldesc?inst_id=10&coll_id=2748 Reference code: GB 0402 AAS. Web.

8. Robin Hallett, *Records of the African Association 1788–1831* (London: Thomas Nelson and Sons for The Royal Geographical Society, 1964), 53. Print.

9. Sparks, 391. For an outstanding account of the African Association see Anthony Sattin, *The Gates of Africa: Death, Discovery, and the Search for Timbuktu* (New York: St. Martin's Press, 2005). Print.

10. See Albert Adu Boahen, *Britain, the Sahara, and the Western Sudan 1788–1861* (Oxford: Clarendon, 1964). Print.

11. Hallett, 51.

12. Sparks, 291–292.

13. In 1806 Lord Valentia described Rossetti's home as "very large, with lofty rooms, and well furnished; a part of the end of the state apartment is raised from the floor, and covered with rich carpet, around which are couches composed of cushions, in the Eastern style, which is called a Divan. The whole room is covered either with a mat or a carpet, and in the middle are chairs and tables: the windows are large and glazed." See George, Viscount Valentia, *Voyages and Travels to India, Ceylon, the Red Sea, Abyssinia, and Egypt,* vol. 3 (London: F.C. and J. Rivington, 1811), 357. ebook.

14. Sparks, 297.

15. Sparks, 321.

16. Sparks, 312.

17. Sparks, 314.

18. Sparks, 313.

19. For this and more information about trade see Terence Walz, *Trade Between Egypt and Bilan as-Sudan 1700–1820* (Institut Français D'Archéologie Orientale du Caire, 1978), 66. Print. It is usually assumed that there was but one Inn of the Traveling Merchants. Walz

disagrees: "The first was located on Hutt al-Harratin, also called as-Sanadiqiyya (under which name the street continues to be known).... opposite the great Wakalat al-Gallaba or at least on the same street was another building called Wakjalat al-Gallaba as-Sugra, the small.... Finally, there was another small Wakalat al-Gallaba situated around the corner from these two structures on the ancient Qasaba Street ... [the] quarter was known in the eighteenth century as Bab az-Zuhuma...."

20. Nafisa al-Bayda, "Nafisa the white one," was a very interesting, emancipated woman who lived in Cairo when Antes and Ledyard were there. She was a slave who married Ali Bey al-Kabir, and when he died she married another Mamluk ruler, Murad Bey. It was Murad who fought against Napoleon at the Battle of the Pyramids. When Murad fell from power, Nafisa managed to befriend the French and continued her enterprises, which she organized from this *wakala*. It still stands near the Bab Zuwayla and has recently been restored. It still sells candles. For more on buildings in Cairo see Caroline Williams, *Islamic Monuments of Cairo: A Practical Guide* (Cairo: The American University in Cairo Press, 2002). Print.

21. Sparks, 301.

22. Sparks, 417.

23. For a discussion of the various trade routes, including an in-depth report of the *Darb al Arbain,* see Cassandra Vivian, *The Western Desert of Egypt* (Cairo: The American University in Cairo Press, 2000, 2003, and 2nd edition 2008).

24. Hallett, 58.

25. Hallett, 58–59.

26. Hallett, 60.

27. Sparks, 419.

28. Hallett, 59.

29. Nelly Hanna, *Making Big Money in 1600: The Life and Times of Isma'il Abu Taqiyya, Egyptian Merchant* (Cairo: The American University in Cairo Press, 1998), 44. Print.

30. Hanna, 44, xxii. See also Walz.

31. The country of Sudan did not exist at this time, but the word was being used to define the land south of Egypt, also called Nubia. In a letter to Thomas Appleton dated July 1824, the American Luther Bradish stated, "Almost the whole of the Soudan has already acknowledged his [Mohammed Ali's] power." Letter from Luther Bradish to Thomas Appleton, July 1, 1824, Luther Bradish Papers, MS 71, New York Historical Society Archives. Print.

32. Jefferson did not receive this letter until May 21, 1789, as noted in Julian Boyd, *The Papers of Thomas Jefferson,* vol. 15, 1788–89 and 1804–6 (Princeton, NJ: Princeton University Press, 1950), 137. Print.

33. Boyd, 181.

34. Boyd, 182.

35. Boyd, 137.

36. Boyd, 197–98. This Mr. Hunter does not appear to be John Hunter of the African Association. Ledyard met the man on his journey from Rosetta to Cairo and seems to have remained in contact.

37. Jefferson to Rev. James Madison, 1789.

38. Elliott Coues, *History of the Expedition under the command of Lewis and Clark,* vol. 1 (New York: Francis P. Harper, 1893), xix. Print.

39. George Robbins Gliddon, *Appendix to The American in Egypt* (Philadelphia: Merrihew and Thompson, 1842), 7. Print.

40. Correspondence, the Freneau ms., Ledyard's journal of his Russia expedition, and other documents are to be found in the Rauner Library Special Collections at Dartmouth College. Jared Sparks's papers are at Houghton Library at Harvard University. For the most recent and highly detailed account of John Ledyard's life see James Zug, *American Traveler: The Life and Adventures of John Ledyard, the Man Who Dreamed of Walking the World* (New York: Basic Books, 2005). Print.

41. William C. Prime, "The Grave of John Ledyard," *New York Daily Times* (July 29, 1857): 2. Print. Prime continued his comments on Ledyard in two other sources: *Among the Northern Hills* features a chapter on Ledyard's journey from Dartmouth and *I Go A-Fishing* provides a chapter similar to the *New York Times* article. See bib.

42. Prime, 2.

43. Pliny Fisk, Letter from Mr. Fisk to the Corresponding Secretary, respecting the sickness and death of Mr. Parsons. Alexandria Feb 10, 1822 in *Washington Theological Repertory* 3, No. 12 (July 1822): 383. Print.

44. Prime, 2.

45. Prime, 2.

46. Prime, 2. Bigelow was a 26-year-old American attorney, a graduate of Harvard University who died in Cairo April 9, 1854.

47. Prime, 2.

48. The author is indebted to Richard Lobban of Rhode Island College for bringing Robert Adams to her attention.

49. George Bethune English, *A Narrative of the Expedition to Dongola and Senaar, under the command of His Excellence Ismael Pasha, undertaken by order of His Highness Mehemmed Ali Pasha, Viceroy of Egypt. By an American in the service of the Viceroy* (Boston: Wells and Lilly, 1823). Appendix, no page number. Print.

50. Sparks, 322.

Chapter 3

1. Portions of this chapter were first presented at the ASTENE Conference *Travel and Travellers in Egypt and the Near East.* Newnham College, Cambridge University (England), July 15–18, 1999 as *William Eaton: A Forgotten American Voice,* and later appeared in both Janet Starkey and Okasha El-Daly, eds. *Travellers in the Deserts of the Orient. William Eaton: A Forgotten American Voice* (London: ASTENE, 2000) and Cassandra Vivian, *The Western Desert of Egypt* (Cairo: The American University in Cairo Press, 2000).

2. Article 11 of this treaty defined the separation of church and state as seen by the formers of the American constitution: "As the government of the United States of America is not in any sense founded on the Christian Religion, — as it has in itself no character of enmity against the laws, religion or tranquility of Musselmen, — and as the said States never have entered into

any war or act of hostility against any Mehomitan nation, it is declared by the parties that no pretext arising from religious opinions shall ever produce an interruption of the harmony existing between the two countries." "Treaty of Peace and Friendship, Signed at Tripoli November 4, 1796," *The Barbary Treaties 1786–1816,* The Avalon Project. Yale Law School. http://avalon.law.yale.edu/18th_century/bar1796t.asp. Web.

3. Claude A. Swanson, *Naval Documents related to the Quasi-War between the United States and France: From February 1797 to October 1798,* vol. 1 (Washington, D.C.: United States Government Printing Office, 1935), 20–34. Print.

4. Edgar Stanton Maclay, *A History of the United States Navy from 1775 to 1893,* vol. 1 (New York: D. Appleton, 1893), 163–64. Print.

5. Maclay, 217–218.

6. Ralph D. Paine, *The Old Merchant Marine: A Chronicle of American Ships and Sailors* (New Haven: Yale University Press, 1919), 68. Print.

7. "The United States and the Barbary States," *Atlantic Monthly* 6, No. 38 (December 1860): 641–657, 643.

8. Andrew A. Lipscomb, ed. *The Writings of Thomas Jefferson,* vol. 11 (Washington, D.C.: The Thomas Jefferson Memorial Association, 1905), 70. Print.

9. For a full and interesting account of events related to the Americans and the Barbary Coast see Richard Zacks, *The Pirate Coast: Thomas Jefferson, the First Marines, and the Secret Mission of 1805* (New York: Hyperion, 2005). For a firsthand account of life on board the *Philadelphia* and as a prisoner in Tripoli see William Ray, *Horrors of Slavery, or The American Tars in Tripoli* (New York: Troy, 1808).

10. Charles Prentiss, *Life of William Eaton: compiled from his correspondence and MSS* (Brookfield, MA: E. Merriam, 1816) 15. Print.

11. For a list of names see: A.B.C. Whipple, *To the Shores of Tripoli: The Birth of the U. S. Navy and Marines* (New York: William Morrow, 1991), 329–331. Print.

12. "Extract of a letter from Mr. Pascal Paoli Peck (son of Col. William Peck, of this town) an officer on board the United States brig *Argus,* commanded by Isaac Hull, Esq, Malta. July 4, 1805," *Gettysburg Sentinel* (Wednesday, October 30, 1805): 172–73. Print.

13. The final midshipman was not Eli E. Danielson, William Eaton's stepson. Danielson was with the party at Rosetta, but is not mentioned at all on the desert journey, because he returned to the *Argus.* Samuel Edwards, in a horrifically flawed biography, placed Danielson on the desert journey. This and other errors created authenticity problems for scholars.

14. Dudley W. Knox, *Naval Documents Related to the U.S. Wars with the Barbary Powers,* volume 5: *Naval Operations Including Diplomatic Background from September 7, 1804 through April 1805* (Washington, D.C.: Government Printing Office, 1944), 142. Print.

15. Dudley W. Knox, *Naval Documents Related to the U.S. Wars with the Barbary Powers,* volume 6: *Naval Operations Including Diplomatic Background from May 1805 through 1807* (Washington, D.C.: Government Printing Office, 1944) 29. Print.

16. Knox, vol. 5, 395.

17. Knox, vol. 5, 518. Samuel Barron was commander of the American Mediterranean fleet during Eaton's expedition. His letterbook of August 17–30, 1804, containing letters about the Tripoli blockade, is found at the American Antiquarian Society, Tripolitan War Collection, 1804–1805. http://www.yale.edu/lawweb/avalon/diplomacy/barbary/bar1805t.htm#art1

18. Knox, vol. 5, 512–13.

19. Samuel Edwards, in his nearly fictitious biography, placed Richard Farquhar on the desert journey.

20. Knox, vol. 5, 186.

21. Knox, vol. 5, 185–88.

22. Knox, vol. 5, 206.

23. "Claim of Colonel Leitensdorfer," in *A Century of Lawmaking for a New Nation:* U.S. Congressional Documents and Debates, 1774–1875. 23rd Congress, No 589, 1834, 455. American Memory Collection in Library of Congress Online. lcweb2.loc.gov/cgi-bin//ampage?collId=llsp&... March 3, 2003. Web.

24. The cannoniers are listed in Knox, 6, 4, and include 28 names.

25. Prentiss, 303.

26. On this journey they stopped to view the battlefield at Abu Qir, where several battles had taken place a few years earlier. They found it "yet covered with human skeletons." Knox, 5, 169.

27. Knox, vol. 5, 171.

28. Knox, vol. 5, 174, Prentiss, 275.

29. Knox, vol. 5, 301–02.

30. Knox, vol. 5, 193.

31. Knox, vol. 5, 254.

32. Mendes Cohen, *Journal from Cairo on to Wady Halfa or Second Cataract Copied from Notes in Pencil in M.I.C's Guide Book.* MS-251.3, Mendes I. Cohen Correspondence, 1829–1835. Box 4, Journal, 1832. Maryland Historical Society, 3. Print.

33. Knox, vol. 5, 545.

34. Prentiss, 289.

35. Samuel Edwards, *Barbary General: the Life of William H. Eaton* (Englewood Cliffs, NJ: Prentice-Hall, 1968), 162–63. Print.

36. Knox, vol. 5, 304; Prentiss, 290–91.

37. Edwards, 163. This is one of several instances where Edwards makes such a claim.

38. Leitensdorfer, 456.

39. Knox, vol. 5, 184, 189.

40. Prentiss, 309.

41. Knox, vol. 5, 472.

42. Edwards, 160.

43. Edwards, 176.

44. Edwards, 161.

45. Prentiss, 208; Knox, vol. 5, 444.

46. Prentiss, 313, Knox, vol. 5, 472.

47. Ray, 256. I owe this source to Richard Zacks, author of *The Pirate Coast,* who concurs with my views of Samuel Edwards's book.

48. Unfortunately this myth was reinforced in 2004. The History Channel's depiction of the Battle of Tripoli, although aware of the false representations, followed Edwards's fallacies concerning language, dress, and the Lawrence of Arabia comparisons.

49. The English Cut is the place where the British

cut through the Alexandria fresh water canal in 1801 to allow the salt waters of Abu Qir Bay to flood into the freshwater Lake Mareotis.

50. Knox, vol. 5, 304–5.

51. Knox, vol. 5, 349.

52. Knox, vol. 5, 339–40.

53. Knox, vol. 5, 367–69.

54. Orin Bates, "Excavations at Marsa Matruh," *Harvard African Studies* 8 (1927): 125–36.

55. Peck, 172.

56. Knox, vol. 5, 305–08; Prentiss, 305.

57. Peck, 172.

58. Peck, 172–3; Knox, vol. 5, 262–63.

59. Prentiss, 305–6.

60. Knox, vol. 5, 433.

61. Knox, vol. 5, 490–92.

62. Knox, vol. 5, 20.

63. Knox, vol. 5, 268.

64. Knox, vol. 5, 353.

Chapter 4

1. On the various monuments in Egypt where we find Barthow's name carved, including the kiosk of Qertassi, Amada, Dendur, El-Kab, Gebel el-Silsila, and the Temple of Medinet Habu, it is spelled Barthow. See: Roger O. De Keersmaecker, *Travellers' Graffiti from Egypt and the Sudan,* Volume 1: *The Kiosk of Qertassi* (Antwerp: Graffito Graffiti, 2001), 3. Print. Portions of this chapter were presented at the ASTENE conference as *Francis Barthow: American Dragoman in Egypt.* Conference on Travellers in Egypt and the Near East. ASTENE. Worcester College, Oxford University (England). July 11–14, 2003.

2. Giovanni Finati, *Narrative of the Life and Adventures of Giovanni Finati,* Volume 2 (London: J. Murray, 1830), 72. ebook.

3. Letter from Victor Barthow to John Gliddon, Alexandria, April 15, 1844, *Despatches from the United States Consuls in Alexandria 1835–1873,* Roll 1, Volume 1, T-45, August 28, 1835, to January 10 1849, National Archives, Washington, D.C., 1955. Microfilm.

4. Butler to Fish, July 14, 1870, No. 10, *Despatches from the United States Consuls in Alexandria 1835–1873,* Roll 6, Volume 6, March 28, 1870, to December 8, 1872. National Archives, Washington, D.C., 1955. Microfilm. American Consul to Egypt Charles Hale, in an article for the *Atlantic Monthly* in 1877, also stated that Francis Barthow was a naval officer and credited Victor Barthow as the source. See: Charles Hale, "Consular Service in Egypt," *Atlantic Monthly* 150, No. 229 (September 1877): 280–290. Print.

5. George, Viscount Valentia, *Voyages and Travels to India, Ceylon, the Red Sea, Abyssinia, and Egypt,* 4 volumes (London: F.C. and J. Rivington, 1811), 371. Print. Thanks to Peta Ree for this reference.

6. Bank of the Manhattan Company, *Ships and Shipping of Old New York: A Brief Account of the Interesting Phases of the Commerce of New York from the Foundation of the City to the Beginning of the Civil War* (New York, 1915), 20, ebook. For additional information on the Red Sea Trade of the 17th century see Thomas Jan-

vier, "The Sea-Robbers of New York," *Harper's New Monthly Magazine* 89 (November 1894): 814–827. Print.

7. Bank of Manhattan, 24.

8. Congress authorized the construction of six frigates. The 44-gun, 1,576-ton ships were the *Constitution,* the *President,* and the *United States.* The 36-gun frigates were the *Chesapeake* at 1,244 tons, the *Congress* at 1,268 tons, and the *Constellation* at 1,265 tons. Edgar Stanton Maclay, *A History of the United States Navy from 1775 to 1894,* Volume 1 (New York: D. Appleton, 1895), 158. Print.

9. Knox, vol. 5, 264–65.

10. I am grateful to Peta Ree for discovering Barthow in Lord Valentia's book.

11. Valentia, vol. 2, 349.

12. Valentia, vol. 2, 590–91.

13. Valentia, vol. 2, 403.

14. Valentia, vol. 2, 405.

15. Valentia, vol. 3, 329–30.

16. Valentia, vol. 3, 331–333.

17. Finati, 77.

18. Thomas Legh, *Narrative of a Journey in Egypt and the Country Beyond the Cataracts,* 2nd Edition (London: John Murray, 1817), 78. Print.

19. Legh, 82.

20. Legh, 75–76.

21. John Lewis Burckhardt, *Travels in Nubia,* 2nd ed. (London: John Murray, 1822), 15. Print.

22. Most of these temples were affected by the creation of the High Dam Lake in the 1960s. Called the Nubian Salvage, it was an extraordinary archaeological and engineering feat that involved 54 nations and required moving 23 of the monuments. Some were dismantled and removed to foreign lands, such as Dender, which in now in the Metropolitan Museum in New York City, but others were dismantled and rebuilt on higher ground. Among the latter were Abu Simbel, Derr, Amada, Dakka, Seboua, Kertassi, Beit el Wali, Kalabsha, and, of course, Philae on the other side of the dam. Ibrim was high enough to be protected from the flood and is now a small island in the lake.

23. Roger De Keersmaecker, *Travellers' Graffiti from Egypt and the Sudan,* Volume 8: *Elkab–The Temple of Amenophis III* (2010). Print.

24. Legh, 221–228.

25. Legh, 235.

26. Legh, 121–23e.

27. Patricia Usick, *Adventures in Egypt and Nubia: The Travels of William John Bankes (1786–1855)* (London: British Museum Press, 2002). Print. Also Patricia Usick, "William John Bankes' Collection of Drawings of Egypt and Nubia," in *Travellers in Egypt,* Paul and Janet Starkey, eds. (New York: I.B. Taurus, 1998), 51–60. Print.

28. Richard Burton, *Personal Narrative of a Pilgrimage to Al-Madinah and Meccah,* Volume 2 (London: George Bell and Sons, 1906), 392. Print.

29. Finati, 71–72.

30. Finati, 73.

31. Finati, 76.

32. Finati, 87–89.

33. Finati, 89–99.

34. Ruurd B. Halbertsma, *Scholars, Travellers, and Trade: The Pioneer Years of the National Museum of Antiquities in Leiden, 1818–1840* (London: Routledge, 2003), 97. Print.

35. Sylvie Guichard, *Lettres de Bernardino Drovetti consul de France a Alexandrie 1803–1830* (Paris: Maisonneuve and Larose, 2003), 294: Letter from Drovetti to Pierre Balthalon, May 3, 1818. MS 508 (1, 16) 11 a 12, Print.

36. Guichard. MS 508 (1, 16) 18 a 23, 80 6 juillet 1818 a Pierre Balthalon, Alexandrie, le 6 juillet 1818. Print.

37. Silvio Curio and Laura Donatelli, *Bernardino Drovetti Epistolario (1800–1851)* (Milano: Istituto Editoriale Cisalpino — La Goliardica, 1985) letter 341, 456. Print.

38. Giovanni Marro, *Il Corpo Epistolare di Bernadino Drovertti* (Roma, Stampate nell'Istituto poligrafico dello Stato per la Reale Societa_ di geografia d'Egitto, 1940), 454. Print.

39. A good description of life at Mahon can be found in Francis Schroeder, *Shores of the Mediterranean with Sketches of Travel,* Volume 1 (London: John Murray, 1846). Print.

40. Victor Barthow to John Gliddon, Alexandria, April 15, 1844.

41. http://lhpc.arts.kuleuven.ac.be/collections_folder/leiden_museum.html. Web.

42. Francis Barthow and Tossiza, Letter to Guiseppe Terreni in Livorno, Italy (in French), August 30, 1827, National Museum of Antiquities, Leiden, The Netherlands. Print.

43. Scholars, 98–99.

44. Halbertsma, 99.

45. Halbertsma, 100.

46. Halbertsma, 102.

47. Halbertsma, 102–3.

48. Halbertsma, 106.

49. Halbertsma, 102–3.

50. Mendes Cohen, *Journal of Mendes Cohen* (unpublished). MS-251.3, Mendes I. Cohen Correspondence, 1829–1835, Box 4, Journal, 1832. Baltimore: Maryland Historical Society, 1832. 38–39. Print.

51. Cohen, 68.

52. For a description of the battle, list of ships, and more details see *Battle of Navarino.* http://www.mlahanas.de/Greece/History/BattleOfNavarino.html. Web.

53. McCauley to the Egyptian Government, Alexandria, December 15, 1851. *Despatches from the United States Consuls in Alexandria,* Roll 2, Volume 1–2, T45–1, 1835–1873, National Archives, Washington, D.C., 1955. Microfilm.

54. Barthow to John Gliddon, Alexandria, April 15, 1844.

55. "McCauley to Daniel Webster, Alexandria, March 16, 1850." No. 15. *Despatches from the United States Consuls in Alexandria 1835–1873,* Roll 2, Volume 1–2, T45–2 March 28, 1870, to December 8, 1872. National Archives, Washington, D.C., 1955. Microfilm.

56. "McCauley to Daniel Webster, Alexandria, February 21, 1852." No. 33. *Despatches from the United States Consuls in Alexandria, 1835–1873,* Roll 2, Volume 1–2, T45–2, March 28, 1870, to December 8, 1872. National Archives, Washington, D.C., 1955. Microfilm.

57. "McCauley to the Minister of Foreign Affairs," Roll 2, Volume 1–2, T45–2.

58. "McCauley to Daniel Webster March 16, 1852," No 35. *Despatches from the United States Consuls in Alexandria 1835–1873,* Roll 2, Volume 1–2, T45–2, March 28, 1870 to December 8, 1872. National Archives, Washington 1955. Microfilm.

59. "Egypt." *New York Daily Times* (1851–1857) April 19, 1852. ProQuest Historical Newspapers. The New York Times, p 1. Web.

60. "Letter from Victor Barthow to George H. Butler, Alexandria, July 14, 1870." No. 10. *Despatches from the United States Consuls in Alexandria 1835–1873,* Roll 6, Volume 6, March 28, 1870, to December 8, 1872. National Archives, Washington, D.C., 1955. Microfilm.

61. "Butler to Fish, July 14, 1870." No 10. *Despatches from the United States Consuls in Alexandria 1835–1873,* Roll 6, Volume 6, March 28, 1870, to December 8, 1872. National Archives, Washington, D.C., 1955. Microfilm.

62. "Beardsley to Fish August 31, 1872." No 7. *Despatches from the United States Consuls in Alexandria 1835–1873,* Roll 6, Volume 6, March 28, 1870, to December 8, 1872. National Archives, Washington, D.C., 1955. Microfilm.

Chapter 5

1. Felix Mengin, *Histoire de l'Égypte sous le gouvernement de Mohammed-Aly,* Volume 2 (Paris: Chez Arthus Bertrand, 1823), 194. Print.

2. Robinson, 47, 164.

3. George Bethune English, *A Narrative of the Expedition to Dongola and Senaar, under the command of His Excellence Ismail Pasha, undertaken by order of His Highness Mehemmed Ali Pasha, Viceroy of Egypt by an American in the service of the Viceroy* (London: J. Murray, 1822), B. Print. In-text citations are for this 1822 edition.

4. Not one of the Arabic-language accounts of this expedition has been translated into English, including one account by a Sudanese historian. It was published for the first time, in Arabic, in Cairo in 1903: *Na'um Shuqayr. Ta'rikh al-Sudan al-qadim wa l'hadith wa-djughrafiyyatuhu.* 3 volumes. Print.

5. For a discussion of the Jewish polemics see: Richard H. Popkin, *The Third Force in Seventeenth-Century Thought* (Leiden: E.J. Brill, 1992). Print. Also Richard H. Popkin, *Disputing Christianity: The 400-Year-Old Debate over Rabbi Isaac ben Abraham of Troki's Classic Arguments* (Amherst: Humanity Books, 2007). Print.

6. Stephen Paschall Sharples, *Records of the Church of Christ at Cambridge in New England 1632–1830* (Boston: Eben Putnam, 1906), 393–4. Print.

7. "George Bethune English," Senate Executive Journal, February 27, 1815. *A Century of Lawmaking for a New Nation: U.S. Congressional Documents and Debates, 1774–1875.* American Memory. Library of Congress Online. Naval Records give the date of March 1, 1815. Web.

8. Count Gallatin, *The Diary of James Gallatin, Secretary to Albert Gallatin, a Great Peace Maker 1813–1827* (New York: Charles Scribner's Sons, 1916), 85. Print.

9. Edward William Callihan, et al., *List of Officers*

of the Navy of the United States and the Marine Corps from 1775 to 1900 (New York: L.R. Hamersly), 184. Print.

10. *Register of the Commissioned and Warrant officers of the navy of the United States* (Washington, D.C.: Wade and Company, 1819). Print.

11. For a discussion of Adams and his beliefs in foreign trade and American noninvolvement in foreign matters, see David Mayers, *Dissenting Voices in America's Rise to Power* (Cambridge: Cambridge University Press, 2007). ebook. For Adams and English and the Greek War of Independence, see Samuel J. Raphalides, *United States Policy Toward the Greek War of Independence,* Ph.D. thesis, New School for Social Research, 1974. Print.

12. James Ellsworth De Kay, *Sketches of Turkey in 1831 and 1832* (New York: J. and J. Harper, 1833), f488. ebook.

13. George Bethune English, *Five Pebbles from the Brook: A Reply to 'A Defence of Christianity' written by Edward Everett* (Philadelphia, 1824). ebook.

14. George Waddington and Barnard Hanbury, *Journal of a Visit to Some Parts of Ethiopia* (London: John Murray, 1822), 114–17. ebook.

15. *U.S. Naval Ships Visiting Egypt.* National Archives and Records Administration. Old Military and Civil Records. According to the USS *Constitution* Museum, the *Constitution* did not depart for the Mediterranean until May 13, 1821, too late for this expedition.

16. De Kay, f488.

17. Finati, 382–3.

18. M.L. Bierbrier, *Who Was Who in Egyptology* (London: The Egypt Exploration Society, 1995), 356. Print.

19. Finati, 381.

20. Identifying Abdin Kashief, 368; describing Dongola horses, 370; identifying Korti, 374; use of cannon, 375; speaking of Malek of Shendy's horsemen, 384; crossing Bahr el Abiat, 392; building in Sennar, 408; and on Shouus, 419.

21. Finati, 356.

22. Waddington, 155.

23. Waddington, 88–89.

24. A version of this section was first presented as "Khalil Aga: A Lost American in the Sudan." Conference on Travellers in Egypt and the Near East. ASTENE. Southampton University (England) July 12–16, 2007. To see text, go to www.cassandravivian.com. It was further published as "Khalil Aga: A Lost American in the Sudan," in *Saddling the Dogs,* Diane Fortenberry, ed. (London: ASTENE, 2009). Print. In-text notes to the journal will be made by date, not page number.

25. *Journal of an Englishman Who traveled to Sennar with Ismail Pasha's Expedition to subdue the Eastern Sudan, 26 Aug. 1820 to 23 Aug. 1821* (British Library Add 54195 ff.46–76. Henry Salt papers FRS d 1827). Print. To see transcription with notes, titled "The Lost Journal of the American Khalil Aga," go to www.cassandravivian.com.

26. George Bethune English, *A Narrative of the Expedition to Dongola and Senaar, under the command of His Excellence Ismail Pasha, undertaken by order of His* Highness Mehemmed Ali Pasha, Viceroy of Egypt by an American in the service of the Viceroy (Boston: Wells and Lilly, 1823), 16. ebook.

27. Waddington, 115–117.

28. Frederic Cailliaud, *Voyage à Meroë, au Fleuve Blanc, au-delà de Fazgol dans le midi du Royaume de Sennar, à Syouah et dans cinq autres oases,* Volume 2 (Paris: L'Imprimerie Royale, 1826), 320–21. "Ibrahym perdit son premier medecin, qui mourut d'une fievre inflammatoire; el etait Genois, et se nommait Scot. Le pharmacien de ce prince eut plus tard le meme sort. Un Americain avait precedemment succombe. La morte semblait vouloir tout moissonner autour de moi. Deja six Europeens n'existaient plus." Thanks to Cheryl Hanson for this translation.

29. "Letter from Luther Bradish to Thomas Appleton, July 1, 1824," Luther Bradish Papers, MS 71, New York Historical Society Archives. Print.

30. English, 1923, B.

31. Waddington, 2.

32. E.A. Wallis Budge, *Cook's Handbook for Egypt and the Sudan,* Volume 2 (London: Thomas Cook and Son, 1906), 753. Print.

33. Finati, 360–1.

34. Budge, 753.

35. Budge, 755.

36. Khalil, 5.

37. Budge, 756.

38. Waddington, 114; Khalil, December 12.

39. "Mr. George Bethune English, whose eccentric..." *The Religious Intelligencer* (December 28, 1822): 81. APS Online, 496. Web.

40. Budge, 757.

41. In 2003 the archaeological remains in this region were the first Sudanese sites named to the World Heritage List by UNESCO.

42. Although mentioned by Roman and Greek texts, the first modern explorer to identify the site was James Bruce, the Scottish explorer in 1772. Part of the myth of Meroë is that Alexander the Great brought his army up the Nile to conquer the kingdom, but when met by the forces of the ruler, turned around. Modern scholars maintain this never happened.

43. Finati, 392.

44. Ward, 72.

45. For Khalil Aga's adventurers on the Fourth and Fifth Cataracts, see my essay "Khalil Aga: A Lost American in the Sudan" in Fortenberry's *Saddling the Dogs,* as well as "The Lost Journal of the American Explorer Khalil Aga" at www.cassandravivian.com.

46. James Bruce, *Travels in Abyssinia and Nubia in 1768–1773 to Discover the Source of the Nile* (Edinburgh: Adam and Charles Black, 1873), 348. ebook.

47. Some historians believe that Ismail was burned alive because of his father's constant demands for slaves. Ismail had none to send and began to demand too many from his new subjects. They killed him. For that and more, see William Y. Adams's *Nubia: Corridor to Africa* (Princeton: Princeton University Press, 1984). Print.

48. Silvio Curio and Laura Donatelli, *Bernardino Drovetti Epistolario (1800–1851)* (Milano: Istituto Editoriale Cisalpino—La Goliardica, 1985), letter 186, 242. Print.

49. Letter from Henry Salt, dated May 2, 1821 (but internal evidence proves it was 1822). Thanks to Peta Ree for this reference.

50. Joseph Wolff, "Extracts from the Journal of Mr. Wolff," *The Religious Intelligencer* 2, No. 12 (October 10, 1823): 165, 177–181. Print.

51. Wolff, 175–76.

52. Charles Francis Adams, *Memoirs of John Quincy Adams 1874–1877* (Philadelphia: J.B. Lippincott, 1875), 62. Print.

Chapter 6

1. The Levant Company was a joint venture company formed by English merchants in the late Elizabethan period. It had the monopoly on trade in the eastern edge of the Mediterranean, so that other countries wanting to trade with the Ottoman Empire had to do so through the Company. Consisting mostly of spices brought to the Mediterranean via the Red Sea, the volume of trade made the Levant Company extremely successful. For example, pepper, the stellar commodity in the Levant warehouses, was an exclusive license.

2. Charles Oscar Paullin, *Diplomatic Negotiations of American Naval Officers, 1778–1883, The Albert Shaw Lectures on Diplomatic History, 1911* (Baltimore: Johns Hopkins Press, 1912), 125. Print.

3. "Treaty with the Sublime Porte." Message from the President of the United States, Serial 221, Doc. 250, Bradish to Adams, December 20, 1820. 4–5. Web.

4. After leaving Constantinople, Bradish visited Egypt in 1821 and took a trip up the Nile. He stayed for five months, traveling as far south as Wadi Halfa in Nubia. As reported in the previous chapter, Bradish was not on the Egyptian Expedition to Sudan with George Bethune English. He complained about the French taking the zodiac from the temple at Dendera. After his visit to Egypt he corresponded for some time with Mohammad Ali.

5. "Treaty with the Sublime Porte," Message from the President of the United States, Serial 221, Doc. 250, Adams to English, April 2, 1823, 13. ebook.

6. "Treaty with the Sublime Porte," Message from the President of the United States. Serial 221, Doc. 250, English to Adams, December 27, 1823, 13–14. ebook.

7. English to Adams, "Treaty with the Sublime Porte," December 27, 1823, 12–13.

8. English to Adams, "Treaty with the Sublime Porte," December 27, 1823, 14.

9. "Treaty with the Sublime Porte," Message from the President of the United States. Serial 221, Doc. 250, English to Adams, February 8, 1824, 15. ebook.

10. Journal of the executive proceedings of the Senate of the United States of America, 1829–1837 Tuesday, February 1, 1831, *A Century of Lawmaking for a New Nation: U.S. Congressional Documents and Debates, 1774–1875.* http://memory.loc.gov/cgi-bin/query. Web.

11. Journal of the Senate of the United States of America, 1789–1873 Wednesday, December 7, 1831. *A Century of Lawmaking for a New Nation: U.S. Congressional Documents and Debates, 1774–1875.* http://memory.loc.gov/cgi-bin/query. Web.

12. George Rapelje, *A Narrative of Excursions, Voyages, and Travels performed at different periods in America, Europe, Asia, and Africa* (New York: privately printed, 1834). Print. A New York City ship-owning merchant, Rapelje was a gentleman traveler, a person who made his way through Europe and the Middle East for the joy of it all and to complete his education in the manner of the Grand Tour. The Egypt section of Rapelje's 416-page book is merely 60 pages. He arrived at Alexandria on Tuesday, April 9, 1822.

13. George Gliddon made it clear that the Gliddon family was not paid: "...my Father for 12, myself for 8, my brother William for 2, my brother-in-law Alexander Tod for 6, and all of us during 17 years that we upheld gratuitously the honor of the flag in Egypt, ever received compensation, personally, in a single United States' 'red cent.' We have severally been the mere channels of payment...." J.C. Nott and George R. Giddon, *Indigenous Races of the Earth* (Philadelphia: J.B. Lippincott, 1868), 1. Print.

14. Wendy Norman, *The Gliddons in London 1760–1850, Including a Family Record by Anne Gliddon* (New Zealand: Steele Roberts. 2000), 27. Print.

15. *Biography of George Gliddon.* Academy of Natural Sciences, Philadelphia. ANS 128 ANSP ms 239. Print.

16. "George R. Gliddon to Hon. John Forsyth," Consular Records: Letter, September 11, 1833, *Despatches from the United States Consuls in Constantinople 1835–1873* (Microfilm Publications T-194, Roll T-I) December 20, 1820–September 1, 1837, No. 17. National Archives, Washington, D.C., 1955. Microfilm.

17. "Mendes Cohen to Hon. John Forsyth." Consular Records: Baltimore August 13, 1837. No. 17. *Despatches from the United States Consuls in Alexandria 1835–1873* (Microfilm Publications T-45, Roll 6, Volume 1), August 28, 1835–January 10, 1849. National Archives, Washington, D.C., 1955. Microfilm. Cohen's journals of his journey in Egypt can be found at the Maryland Historical Society. (Cohen, Mendes. *Journal of Mendes Cohen* (unpublished). MS-251.3, Mendes I. Cohen Correspondence, 1829–1835. Box 4, Journal, 1832. Baltimore: Maryland Historical Society, 1932.)

18. William Hauptman, *Charles Gleyre, 1806–1874,* 2 volumes (Princeton: Princeton University Press; Basel, Switzerland: Swiss Institute for Art Research, 1996), 78–79. Print. Lowell's journals (as of 2010 still owned by the Lowell family and Lowell Institute) are in the Boston Museum of Fine Art archives. The museum has denied access to the journals because they are considered too fragile to use, to photocopy, or to digitize.

19. "F.C. Lowell, Esq. Brother to the late John Lowell Esq. of Boston for George R. Gliddon to John Forsyth at the Department of State," Boston, July 24, 1837. Record Group 59 (General Records of the Department of State), Records of Application and Recommendation During the Administrations of Martin Van Buren, William Henry Harrison, and John Tyler, 1837–1845, folder for George Gliddon. Microfilm.

20. "John L. Stephens of New York for George R. Gliddon to John Forsyth at the Department of State." June 27, 1837. Record Group 59 (General Records of the Department of State), Records of Application and

Recommendation during the Administrations of Martin Van Buren, William Henry Harrison and John Tyler, 1837–1845, folder for George Gliddon. Microfilm.

21. "John L. Hammersley in New York for George R. Gliddon to John Forsyth at the Department of State." July 4, 1837. Submitted August 10, 1837, Record Group 59 (General Records of the Department of State), Records of Application and Recommendation during the Administrations of Martin Van Buren, William Henry Harrison, and John Tyler, 1837–1845, folder for George Gliddon. Microfilm.

22. Sarah Rogers Haight, *Letters from the Old World,* 2 volumes (New York: Harper and Brothers, 1840). ebook.

23. "Richard Haight of Philadelphia for George R. Gliddon to John Forsyth at the Department of State." July 29, 1837. Record Group 59 (General Records of the Department of State), Records of Application and Recommendation During the Administrations of Martin Van Buren, William Henry Harrison, and John Tyler, 1837–1845, folder for George Gliddon. Microfilm.

24. "Richard Randolph of Philadelphia for George R. Gliddon to John Forsyth at the Department of State." August 5, 1837. Record Group 59 (General Records of the Department of State), Records of Application and Recommendation During the Administrations of Martin Van Buren, William Henry Harrison, and John Tyler, 1837–1845, folder for George Gliddon. Microfilm.

25. George Gliddon in New York to John Forsythe in Washington, D.C. Consular Records: Letter April 15, 1837. *Despatches from the United States Consuls in Alexandria 1835–1873* (Microfilm Publication T-45, Roll 6, Volume1), National Archives, Washington, D.C., 1955. Microfilm.

26. George Gliddon in New York to John Forsythe in Washington D.C. Consular Records: Report April 17, 1837. No. 17. *Despatches from the United States Consuls in Alexandria, 1835–1873* (Microfilm Publication T-45, Roll 6, Volume1), August 28, 1835–January 10, 1849. National Archives, Washington, D.C., 1955, 16. Microfilm.

27. When the Porte sought assistance in rebuilding its fleet, the American government would not help. But Charles Rhind, one of the treaty negotiators, contacted Henry Eckford, a noted American shipbuilder, and Eckford arrived in Constantinople in the ship *United States* in August of 1831. A contract was negotiated and Eckford sent home for the workers who were to build the schooners and battleships, in all around 22 ships. Eckford died during the process and the ships were finished by his foreman Foster Rhodes. See Lester D. Langley, "Jacksonian America and the Ottoman Empire," *The Muslim World* 68, no. 1 (January 1978): 46–56.Valentine Mott, the American physician, and his traveling companion Henry McVickar, who both visited Egypt in 1838, saw the fleet of American- built ships lying at Alexandria's harbor. See Valentine Mott, *Travels in Europe and the East Embracing Observations made during a Tour through Great Britain in 1834, 34, 36, 37, 38, 39, 40, and 41 ...* (New York: Harper and Brothers, 1842).

28. John Gliddon in Alexandria to Francis Griffin,

John L. Stephens, Frederick Bronson and W Hamersley in New York. July 11, 1838. J.L. Stephens Papers Z-Z 116. The Bancroft Library, University of Cal Berkeley. 4p. Print.

29. L. Lent Letter from New York to George Gliddon in Cairo. William J. Clements Library, University of Michigan. Benjamin Brown Collection, No. 37. Nov 19, 1838. 4p.

30. George Gliddon in Wadi Halfa to Benjamin Brown in Dongola. J. Clements Library, University of Michigan. Benjamin Brown Collection, Dec 28, 1839. 3p.

31. Interview with B. Brown and 1880 obit of Brown, "The Oldest of Showman: Aged Benjamin Brown's Recollections of Pioneer Circus Life," *Croton Falls News,* July 17, 1879; reprint in *New York Sun,* Clements Library, University of Michigan. Benjamin Brown Collection.

32. Abbott did go to America and he took his artifacts with him. He set them up in New York, but, as with so many of these ventures, it did not make money. He returned to Egypt. The artifacts were eventually purchased by the New York Historical Society and are now part of their collection.

33. George Gliddon in Alexandria to Samuel George Morton in Philadelphia. May 21–24, 1840. Samuel George Morton Papers, 1838–1844, American Philosophical Society Series I Correspondence M843 ALS 3p and enc of 10p. Print.

34. George Gliddon in Cairo to John Forsythe in Washington D.C. Consular Records: Letter, May 20, 1840. No. 17. *Despatches from the United States Consuls in Alexandria 1835–1873,* Roll 6, Volume1, August 28, 1835–January 10, 1849. National Archives, Washington, D.C., 1955. The Zoological Institute was an organization created in 1835 in Somers, New York. One of their missions was to bring exotic animals from Africa for the circuses of America. In 1835 it would merge with the Boston Zoological Association. See Richard W. Flint. "Rufus Welch: America's Pioneer Circus Showman" *Bandwagon* 14, No. 5 (September–October 1970): 4–11. www.circushistory.org/Bandwagon/bw-1970Sep. htm.

35. George Gliddon in Cairo to John Forsythe in Washington D.C. Consular Records: Letter June 30, 1839. No. 17. Dispatches from the United States consuls in Alexandria 1835–1873, Roll 6, Volume1, August 28, 1835–January 10, 1849. National Archives, Washington, D.C., 1955.

36. Stebb June in Alexandria to Benjamin Brown in Cairo, April 19, 1840. J. Clements Library, University of Michigan. Benjamin Brown Collection. 4p. Print.

37. George Gliddon in Alexandria to Samuel George Morton in Philadelphia. May 21–24, 1840.

38. "The U.S. Naval Lyceum," *Brooklyn Eagle,* Saturday, November 4, 1871. NewspaperArchives.com. Web.

39. George Gliddon in New York at Globe Hotel to Samuel George Morton in Philadelphia, January 22, 1842. Samuel George Morton Papers, 1838–1844, American Philosophical Society Series IV Microfilm 1838–44, No 41. Microfilm.

40. George Gliddon in Cairo to Francis Griffin in

New York, July 16, 1840, J.L. Stephens Papers Z-Z 116. The Bancroft Library, University of Cal Berkeley. 4p. Print.

41. Flint, 4–11.

42. H. Abbott in Cairo to Benjamin Brown in London, April 18 1841. Benjamin Brown Collection, William J. Clements Library, University of Michigan. Print.

43. Warren R. Dawson, *Who Was Who in Egyptology: A Biographical Index of Egyptologists; of Travellers, Explorers and Excavators in Egypt; of Collectors of and Dealers in Egyptian Antiquities; of Consuls, Officials, Authors, Benefactors, and Others Whose Names Occur in the Literature of Egyptology, from the Year 1500 to the Present Day, but Excluding Persons Now Living*, 3rd ed., revised by M.L. Bierbrier (London: Egyptian Exploration Services, 1995), 169. Print.

44. George R. Gliddon, *An Appeal to the Antiquaries of Europe and the Destruction of the Monuments of Egypt* (London: 1841), 34. Print.

45. George Gliddon in New York at Globe Hotel to Samuel George Morton in Philadelphia, January 18, 1842. Samuel George Morton Papers, 1838–1844, American Philosophical Society Series IV Microfilm 1838–44, No 40. Print.

46. George Gliddon in New York to Samuel George Morton in Philadelphia, February 17, 1842, Samuel George Morton Papers, 1838–1844, American Philosophical Society Series IV Microfilm 1838–44, No 42. Microfilm. Ippolito Rosellini of Pisa was the father of Egyptology in Italy. A friend of Jean François Champollion, he wrote an impressive and comprehensive multi-volume account of the monuments, *Monumenti de l'Egypte et Nubie*, which took many years to produce and included many illustrations and an atlas.

47. Caroline Ransom Williams, "A Surprising Sales Record," *Bulletin of the Metropolitan Museum of Art*, 1920, 88–89. ebook. Those books, as well as the remainder of Richard Haight's collection, are in the library of the New York Historical Society.

48. George Gliddon in Boston to Samuel George Morton in Philadelphia, January 4, 1843. Samuel George Morton Papers, 1838–1844, American Philosophical Society Series IV Microfilm 1838–44, No 48. Microfilm.

49. George Gliddon in New York to Samuel George Morton in Philadelphia, February 14, 1843. Samuel George Morton Papers, 1838–1844, American Philosophical Society Series IV Microfilm 1838–44, No 51. Microfilm.

50. George Gliddon in New York to Samuel George Morton in Philadelphia, February 20, 1843. Samuel George Morton Papers, 1838–1844, American Philosophical Society Series IV Microfilm 1838–44, No 52. Microfilm.

51. Dawson, 169.

52. Cohen, 22.

53. George Gliddon to Joseph Bonomi, Philadelphia 1844. Yvonne Neville-Rolfe Collection (Private Collection), 1. Print.

54. Joseph Bonomi was an English artist who accompanied the famous Robert Hay expedition to Egypt in 1824 and illustrated a number of publications by various travelers.

55. "Brooklyn Institute Lecturers," *Brooklyn Daily Eagle*, October 21, 1846, newspaperarchive.com, 2. Web.

56. Gliddon to Squier, Pittsburgh, March 15, and Cincinnati, April 23, 1847, Ephraim George Squier Papers, Library of Congress, Washington, D.C. Web.

57. Terry A. Barnhart, "Toward a Science of Man: European Influences on the Archaeologist Ephraim George Squier," in *New Perspectives on the Origins of Americanist Archaeology*, David L. Browman and Stephen Williams, eds. (Tuscaloosa: University of Alabama Press, 2002), 91. Print.

58. Gliddon to Squier, Philadelphia, September 21, and Charleston, November 21, 1847, Ephraim George Squier Papers, Library of Congress, Washington, D.C. Web.

59. George Gliddon, *Hand-book to the American Panorama of the Nile: being the original transparent picture exhibited in London, at Egyptian Hall, Piccadilly, purchased from its painters and proprietors, Messrs. H. Warren, J. Bonomi, and J. Fahey* (London 1849), 17. Print.

60. "Panorama of the Nile," *Saturday Evening Post*, 30, No. 1521 (September 21, 1850). APS Online 0–002. Web.

61. "Panorama of the Nile," *Brooklyn Daily Eagle* 9, No. 33 (February 8 1850). NewspaperArchive.com, p 2.

62. "Opening the Mummy," *Defiance Democrat* 6, No. 44 (June 29 1850). NewspaperArchive.com, 1.

63. Caroline Ransom Williams, "The Place of the New York Historical Society in the Growth of American Interest in Egyptology." *New York Historical Society Quarterly Bulletin* 4 (April 1920–January 1921): Index, 2–20. ebook.

64. George Gliddon to Sirs (Bonomi and company), London and New York, January 22, 1850. Yvonne Neville-Rolfe Collection.

65. Gliddon's Panorama of the Nile, *Graham's American Monthly Magazine of Literature, Art and Fashion* 36 (May 1850): 344. NewspaperArchive.com. Web.

66. "Amusements." *Saturday Evening Post* 30, No. 1532 (December 7, 1850). NewspaperArchive.com. Web.

67. "1851," *Gettysburg (Pennsylvania) Star and Banner*, Friday, January 24, 1851. NewspaperArchive.com. Web.

68. Marc Rothenberg, *The Papers of Joseph Henry*, Volume 8: *January 1850–December 1853, The Smithsonian Years* (Washington and London: Smithsonian Institution Press), 173–76. Print.

69. Ned Kern in Philadelphia to George Gliddon in Pittsburgh, October 27, 1851. Gilcrease Museum Library Collection, reel 3281, frames 642–45. Microfilm.

70. "The Mummy Again," *Daily Picayune*, Thursday, March 4, 1852. NewspaperArchive.com. Web.

71. *A Guide for Visitors to the National Gallery, Revised in Accordance with the Instructions of the Commissioner of Patents*. January 1857. http://www.myoutbox.net/poguide.htm. Web.

72. Robert S. Leopold, *A Guide to Early African Collections in the Smithsonian Institution*, "George Robins Gliddon (1809–1857)," Catalog Numbers E-4797, E-5454, Received 1867, http://anthropology.si.edu/leopold/pubs/early_african_collections.pdf. Web.

73. Ephraim G. Squier is considered the father of American anthropology.

74. John Trautwine, Letter to E. Geo. Squier from Omoa May 12, 1857. Papers of E.G. Squier 1841–1888 (bulk 1846–1874). Manuscript Division, Library of Congress Honduras Interoceanic Railway File, 1853–1870. Box 5, Reel 8. Correspondence, 1853–1870. Reports, George R. Gliddon No. 1, May 16, 1857. Web.

75. George Gliddon from Comayagua to H.S. Stanford, October 10, 1857. Papers of E.G. Squier 1841–1888 (bulk 1846–1874). Manuscript Division, Library of Congress Honduras Interoceanic Railway File, 1853–1870. Box 5, Reel 8. Correspondence, 1853–1870. Reports, George R. Gliddon No. 1, May 16, 1857. Web.

76. Henry Shelton Stanford in Panama to E.G. Squier. Papers of E.G. Squier, 1841–1888 (bulk 1846–1874). Manuscript Division, Library of Congress Honduras Interoceanic Railway File, 1853–1870. Box 5, Reel 8. Correspondence, 1853–1870. Reports, George R. Gliddon No. 1, May 16, 1857. Web.

77. Henry Shelton Stanford to E.G. Squier, Panama, November 17, 1857 (2nd letter). Papers of E.G. Squier 1841–1888 (bulk 1846–1874). Manuscript Division, Library of Congress, Honduras Interoceanic Railway File, 1853–1870. Box 5, Reel 8. Correspondence, 1853–1870. Reports, George R. Gliddon No. 2, May 22, 1857. Web.

78. Ephraim George Squier, *Peru: Incidents of Travel and Exploration in the Land of the Incas* (New York: Henry Holt, 1877), 18–19. ebook.

Chapter 7

1. H.P. Spratt, *Outline History of Transatlantic Steam Navigation.* Ministry of Education. Science Museum (London: His Majesty's Stationery Office, 1950), 7–8. Print.

2. David H. Finnie, *Pioneers East: The Early American Experience in the Middle East* (Cambridge: Harvard University Press, 1967), 165–66. Print.

3. Walter Barrett, *The Old Merchants of New York City* (New York: John W. Lovell, c. 1885), 199. ebook.

4. Two American travelers, Dr. John Thornton Kirkland, president of Harvard University, and his wife, Elizabeth Cabot Kirkland, traveled to Egypt aboard the naval vessel *Concord* in 1832. He was a Unitarian minister and she was a member of the shipping merchant Cabot family. The only records we have of the Kirklands' adventures in Egypt are a number of letters Elizabeth wrote home to her sister and an unpublished diary John kept of the journey. The Kirkland papers are in the archives of the Massachusetts Historical Society.

5. John Lloyd Stephens was also in Egypt in 1836, and his book *Incidents of Travel in Egypt, Arabia Petraea and the Holy Land,* published in 1837, makes him the first known American travel writer in Egypt. John Lloyd Stephens, *Incidents of Travel in Egypt, Arabia Petraea and the Holy Land,* 2 volumes (New York: Harper and Bros., 1838; reprint, Norman, OK: University of Oklahoma Press, 1967). Print.

6. Sarah Rogers Haight, *Letters from the Old World,* 2 volumes (New York: Harper and Brothers, 1840), ebook.

7. LaVerne Kuhnke, *Lives at Risk: Public Health in Nineteenth Century Egypt* (Berkeley: University of California Press, 1990), 94. Print.

8. Kuhnke, 3–4.

9. Kuhnke, 50–51.

10. Kuhnke, 86.

11. Sir Gardner Wilkinson, *Modern Egypt and Thebes,* volume 1 of 2 (London: John Murray, 1843), 202. ebook.

12. Richard William Howard Vyse and John Shae Perring, *Operations Carried on at the Pyramids of Gizeh in 1837,* volume 1 of 3 (London: John Weale, 1840), 3. ebook.

13. Thanks to Andrew Humphreys for some of this information. Further, the Alfi Palace was headquarters for the French Expedition in Egypt. For an excellent description of *Ezbekiyyiah* through the centuries, see Doris Behrens-Abouseif, *Azbakiyya and its Environs from Azbak to Ismail 1476–1879. Supplement Aux Annals Islamologiques,* Cahier No. 6 (Cairo: Institut Francais D'Archeologie Orientale, 1985). Print.

14. Elizabeth Kirkland, "Letter to My Dear Sister," April 18, 1832, Henry Cabot Lodge Collection, Box 87, Massachusetts Historical Society, 2. Print.

Chapter 8

1. Bayard Taylor, *A Journey to Central Africa: or, Life and landscapes from Egypt to the Negro Kingdoms of the White Nile,* 10th ed. (New York: G.P. Putnam, 1859), 2–4. ebook.

2. Marie Hansen-Taylor and Horace E. Scudder, *Life and Letters of Bayard Taylor,* 2 volumes (Boston: Houghton Mifflin, 1884), f224. Print.

3. This person could be Elbert H. Champlin, member of the American Oriental Society.

4. Edward Lane, *Manners and Customs of the Modern Egyptians* (Society for the Diffusion of Useful Knowledge, 1836). ebook.

5. George William Curtis, *Nile Notes of a Howadji* (New York: Harper & Brothers, 1851). ebook.

6. William C. Prime, *Boat Life in Egypt and Nubia* (New York, Harper & Brothers, 1857). ebook.

7. Charles Dudley Warner, *My Winter on the Nile* (Hartford: American Publishing Co., 1876). ebook.

8. Francis Steegmuller, *Flaubert in Egypt, A Sensibility on Tour: A Narrative Drawn from Gustave Flaubert's Travel Notes & Letters* (Chicago: Academy Chicago, 1979). Print.

9. William Hauptman, *Charles Gleyre, 1806–1874,* 2 volumes (Princeton, NJ: Princeton University Press; Basel, Switzerland: Swiss Institute for Art Research, 1996). Print. Both Lowell and Gleyre wrote journals. Lowell's is at the Boston Museum of Art, where the curators feel it is too fragile to view. Hauptman somehow got to view it and wrote this fantastic book, complete with both journal entries and many of Gleyre's images.

10. Bayard Taylor, *Egypt and Iceland in the Year 1874* (New York: Putnam and Sons, 1874), 31. ebook.

Chapter 9

1. Charles Hale, "Alpha Delta Phi, College Secret

Society in Convention," *Boston Globe,* June 4, 1875. ProQuest Historical Newspapers *Boston Globe,* 1. Web.

2. Papers of William Sydney Thayer, 1835–1895, Accession #3445, M-546, Reels 1, 6, 8. Copy of Thayer's journal for part of 1861, made by his sister Sarah. Special Collections SC-STKS, MSS3445, University of Virginia Library, University of Virginia, Charlottesville, Va. OCLC 647967494. 141. Microfilm.

3. Thayer, reel 8, 153.

4. Thayer, reel 8, 191.

5. George William Curtis of New York was asked to replace Thayer, but refused. See Thayer, reels 1 and 6. Undated letters for this period and several clippings on Thayer's immediate successors in Egypt. Unnamed newspaper clipping. Special Collections, University of Virginia Library, University of Virginia, Charlottesville, Va. OCLC 647967494. Microfilm.

6. Lucie Duff Gordon, *Letters from Egypt,* revised edition (London: R. Brimley Johnson, 1902), 76. ebook.

7. "The National Capital, Action of the House on the Appropriation Bill," *New York Times,* January 25, 1872. http://query.nytimes.com/gst/abstract.html?res=FA0E10FC3C5D1A7493C7AB178AD85F468784F9. Web.

8. Francis Dainese, *The History of Mr. Seward's Pet in Egypt: His Acts Denounced and His Usurpations Condemned by the Courts* (self-published, 1866), 66. Print.

9. "Obituary The Hon. Charles Hale," *New York Times,* March 3, 1882. http://query.nytimes.com/mem/archivefree/pdf?res=F20C14FB3D5910738DDDAA08 94DB405B8284F0D3. Web.

10. James Grant Wilson and John Fiske, *Appleton's Cyclopedia of American Biography,* volume 3 (New York: D. Appleton, 1887), 33. Print.

11. "Biographical Note," Hale Family Papers, 1787–1988, Sophia Smith Collection, Smith College. http://asteria.fivecolleges.edu/findaids/sophiasmith/mnsss90_bioghist.html. Web.

12. Charles Hale, "The Khedive and his Court," *Atlantic Monthly* 37, No. 223 (May 1876): 513–520. ebook.

13. Hale, "Khedive," 513.

14. Hale, "Khedive," 516.

15. Elbert E. Farman, *Egypt and Its Betrayal* (New York: Grafton Press, 1908), 247. ebook.

16. Farman, 275–77.

17. "Alpha Delta Phi," 1.

18. Hale, "Consular Service in Egypt," 283.

19. Hale, "Consular Service in Egypt," 283–84.

20. Hale, "Consular Service in Egypt," 285–86.

21. "Mr. Thayer to Mr. Seward," November 12, 1862, No. 24. *Papers Relating to Foreign Affairs, accompanying the Annual Message of the President to the First Session Thirty-Eighth Congress,* Part 2 (Washington, D.C.: Government Printing Office, 1864), 1104. ebook.

22. Edward Everett Hale, *Memories of a Hundred Years,* revised edition (New York: Macmillan, 1904), 63. ebook.

23. "Charles Hale to William Seward," June 13, 1867, No. 91 and attachment, *Rules for the Consular Courts in Egypt of the United States of America* (Alexandrie:

Imp. Francaise Mounds ,1867). Microfilm Publications T-45, Roll 4, August 26, 1865–December 16, 1867. National Archives, Washington, D.C., 1955. Microfilm.

24. Zouaves were French soldiers. In this instance, reference is to the Papal Zouaves, created to protect the Vatican.

25. The Hon. John F. Doyle, "The Case of John Harrison Surratt, Jr." Condensed from a speech before the Surratt Society, September 25, 1999. Printed in the *Surratt Courier,* March 2000. Print.

26. Document 25, John H. Surratt, "Mr. Swann in Naples to Mr. Seward," November 21, 1866, No. 4. *United States Department of State, Executive documents printed by order of the House of Representatives, during the first session of the thirty-ninth Congress, 1865–66 Part 3,* 2–3. ebook.

27. Document 25, John H. Surratt, "Winthrop to Legh," November 19, 1866, *Executive Documents,* 1866–67, 3. ebook.

28. Document 25, John H. Surratt, "Legh to Winthrope," November 19, 1866, No. 4593. *Executive Documents,* 1866–67, 5–6. ebook.

29. Document 25, John H. Surratt, "Legh to Winthrope," November 20, 1866, No: 4600. *Executive Documents,* 1866–67, 6. ebook.

30. Document 25, John H. Surratt, "Winthrope to Hale," November 19, 1866, *Executive Documents,* 1866–67, 8. ebook.

31. Document 25, John H. Surratt, "Winthrope to Hale," November 21, 1866, *Executive Documents,* 1866–67, 10. ebook.

32. Document 25, John H. Surratt, "Hale to Seward," No. 66, November 27, 1866, *Executive Documents,* 1866–67, 12–14. ebook.

33. Document 25, John H. Surratt, "Hale to Seward," No. 68, December 4, 1866, *Executive Documents,* 1866–67, 17. ebook.

34. Dainese, i.

35. The Evangelides family were Greek merchants in Cairo. Christo Evangelides found a wife for Henry Stanley on the island of Siro in 1866. See James L. Newman, *Imperial Footprints: Henry Morton Stanley's African Journeys* (Dulles, VA: Brassey's, 2004), 26–27. Microfilm.

36. Papers of William Sydney Thayer, Special Collections SC-STKS, MSS3445, Reel 2, May 4, 1863, 398.

37. "Mr. Thayer to Mr. Seward," January 23, 1864, No. 44, *Papers Relating to Foreign Affairs, accompanying the Annual message of the President to the Second Session Thirty-Eighth Congress,* Part 4 (Washington, D.C.: Government Printing Office, 1865), 405. ebook.

38. "Mr. Thayer to Mr. Seward," January 21, 1864, No. 54, 47–48.

39. "The Difficulty at Alexandria," *New York Times,* August 17, 1864. http://www.nytimes.com/1864/08/17/news/the-difficulty-at-alexandria.html. Alexandria, Saturday, July 23. Web.

40. Dainese, 46.

41. Another American operating a newspaper in Alexandria in 1865 was E.P. Mirzan. His *Bulletin*

Financier dealt with financial and commercial news. For a review of foreign newspapers operating in Egypt at this time see Philip Sadgrove, "The European Press in Khedive Isma'il's Egypt (1863–66): A Neglected Field," a paper presented at the 2nd International Symposium History of Printing and Publishing in the Languages and Countries of the Middle East, November 2–4, 2005. Bibliotheque nationale de France, Paris. Print.

42. Dainese, 72.
43. Dainese, 82–83.
44. Dainese, v–vi.
45. Dainese, 69.
46. Dainese, viii–ix.
47. Dainese, 71.
48. Dainese, 75–76.
49. "Personal," *Chicago Tribune*, May 6, 1872, Google News Archives, ProQuest Historical Newspapers *Chicago Tribune*, 4. Web.
50. U.S. 13 *Dainese v. Hale*, October Term, 1875. http://openjurist.org/print/15999 12/13/2010. Web.

Chapter 10

1. 1. David W. Icenogle, "The Expedition of Chaillé-Long," *Saudia Aramco World* (November–December 1978): 2–7. http://www.saudiaramcoworld.com/issue/197806/the.expeditions.of.Chaillé-long.htm. Web.
2. Charles Chaillé-Long, *My Life in Four Continents* (London: Hutchinson, 1912), 82. Print. Samuel Baker explored the Nile, discovered Lake Albert, and served as Governor-General in the Sudan before Gordon.
3. Charles Chaillé-Long, *Central Africa: Naked Truths of Naked People, An Account of Expeditions to the Lake Victoria Nyanza and Makraka Niam-Niam, West of the Bahr el Ab'ad* (New York: Harper Bros., 1876), 101. ebook.
4. "Charles Chaillé-Long, Captain, United States Army." http://www.arlingtoncemetery.net/charles-Chaillé-long.htm. Posted: 12 November 2005. Updated: 4 March 2006. Web.
5. Lynn R. Meekins, *Men of Mark in Maryland: Johnson's Makers of America Series Biographies of Leading Men of the State*, volume 2 (Baltimore: B.F. Johnson, 1910), 81–82. ebook.
6. Edwin Swift Balch, "American Explorers of Africa," *The Geographical Review* 5 (January–June 1918): 274–80. http://www.jstor.org/pss/207420. Web.
7. The opera *Aida* was commissioned from Giuseppe Verdi by the Khedive Ismail to inaugurate the opening of the Cairo Opera House in 1869. It was an expensive and opulent production with real gold and rare gems in the costumes and sets. The opera was not completed in time for the opening and it was first performed in 1871. All of the costumes and sets were burned in the great Cairo fire one hundred years later in 1971.
8. Meekins, 82.
9. Sadgrove, 4.
10. "Summary of Letters and Reports of his Excellency the Governor-General," in *Provinces of the Equator,* Publications of the Egyptian General Staff. Part 1:

Year 1874. (Cairo, London: Printing Office of the General Staff, 1877), 5. ebook.
11. Chaillé-Long, *Life*, 67–68.
12. Pierre Crabites, *Americans in the Egyptian Army* (London: George Routledge and Sons, 1938). Print.
13. Charles Chaillé-Long, "England in Egypt and the Soudan by Colonel Charles Chaillé-Long, Formerly Chief of Staff to the Late General Gordon, Governor-General of the Soudan," *North American Review:* 168, No. 510 (May 1899): 570–80. APS Online. Web.
14. For a further assessment of these events see Elbert E. Farman's *Egypt and Its Betrayal* and the quote by Farman in the chapter on Charles Hale (note 16).
15. In later years it would be told again and again in letters, journal reports and public speaking engagements as Chaillé-Long attempted to vindicate himself.
16. Charles Chaillé-Long, "Expedition from Gondokoro to Lake Victoria and discovery of Lake Ibrahim," in *Provinces of the Equator.* Publications of the Egyptian General Staff, Part 1: Year 1874, (Cairo, London: Printing Office of the General Staff, 1877). ebook.
17. Chaillé-Long, *Provinces*, 45.
18. Chaillé-Long, *Central Africa*, 73–75.
19. Chaillé-Long, *Central Africa*, 90.
20. Chaillé-Long, *Central Africa*, 97–100.
21. Chaillé-Long, *Provinces*, 56.
22. Chaillé-Long, *Central Africa*, 106–08.
23. Chaillé-Long, *Provinces*, 62.
24. Chaillé-Long, *Provinces*, ff62.
25. Charles Chaillé-Long, "The Uganda Protectorate and the Nile Quest," *Bulletin of the American Geographical Society* 36, No. 1 (1904): 52–54. ebook. While returning from his assignment, Ernest was killed.
26. "To the Mountains of the Moon: Mapping African Exploration, 1541–1880." http://libweb 5.princeton.edu/visual_materials/maps/websites/africa/contents.html. Web. Drawing from the cartographic and rare book resources of the Department of Rare Books and Special Collections of Princeton University Library, this exhibition documents the evolution of the map of Africa, 1541–1880. It is a story told in the expedition maps, illustrations, and words of those explorers.
27. *Encyclopaedia Britannica* calls Stanley "a British Explorer," while American sources vary from an "Anglo-American explorer" to a "Welsh-American explorer."
28. Alan Moorehead, *The White Nile* (New York: HarperCollins, 2000), 191–94. Print.
29. "The Nile," *Wikipedia.* http://en.wikipedia.org/wiki/Nile#The_search_for_the_source_of_the_Nile. Web. The same line appears in all of them: "It was ultimately Welsh-American explorer Henry Morton Stanley who confirmed Speke's discovery, circumnavigating Lake Victoria and reporting the great outflow at Ripon Falls on the Lake's northern shore." See www.wordiq.com/definition/Lake_Victoria; www.answers.com/topic/lake-victoria; and www.newworldencyclopedia.org/entry/Lake_Victoria.
30. Chaillé-Long, *Central Africa*, 137–38.
31. Chaillé-Long, *Provinces*, 63.
32. Chaillé-Long, *Provinces*, 64.
33. Chaillé-Long, *Central Africa*, 157–60.
34. Chaillé-Long, *Provinces*, 68–69.

35. Chaillé-Long, *Provinces,* 69–70.

36. Laurence Oliphant, "African Explorers," *North American Review* 124, No. 256 (May–June 1877). APS Online. Web.

37. Sir Harry Johnston, *The Nile Quest* (London: Lawrence and Bullen, 1903), 239. ebook.

38. Sir Harry Johnston, *The Uganda Protectorate* (New York: Dodd, Mead, 1902), 221. ebook.

39. Charles Chaillé-Long, "The Part of the Nile that Colonel Chaillé-Long Discovered," *American Geographical Society Bulletin* 41 (1904): Correspondence, 222. ebook.

40. Sir William Garstin, "Fifty Years of Nile Exploration, and some of its Results," *The Geographical Journal* 33, No. 2 (February 1909): 127–128. ebook.

41. Garstin, 150.

42. Chaillé-Long, "Part of the Nile," 203.

43. Google Maps. http://maps.google.com/maps?hl=en&tab=wl. Web.

44. Chaillé-Long, *Central Africa,* 306.

45. For a modern-day assessment see John P. Dunn, *Khedive Ismail's Army* (London and New York: Routledge, 2005).

Chapter 11

1. Elbert E. Farman, *Along the Nile: An Account of the Visit to Egypt of General Ulysses S. Grant and his Tour Through that Country* (New York: Grafton Press. 1904), 3–4. ebook.

2. Farman; Jesse Root Grant, with Henry Francis Granger, *In the Days of My Father General Grant* (New York and London: Harper and Brothers, 1925). Grant's son also sent letters to newspapers while on the journey; John Y. Simon, ed., *The Personal Memoirs of Julia Dent Grant* (Carbondale: Southern Illinois University Press, 1975). Grant's wife; William H. Hicks, *General Grant's Tour Around the World* (Chicago: Rand McNally, 1879). Single chapter on Egypt; John M. Keating, *With General Grant in the East* (Philadelphia and London: J.B. Lippincott, 1879). Keating sent letters to the *Philadelphia Evening Telegraph.* The book skims over Egypt; James Dabney McCabe, *A Tour Around the World by General Grant* (Philadelphia National, 1879); J.F. Packard, *Grant's Tour Around the World* (Cincinnati: Forshee and McMakin, 1880); Loomis T. Remlap, *General U.S. Grant's Tour Around the World* (Chicago: J. Fairbanks, 1880). Remlap is Palmer backward; John Russell Young, *Around the World with General Grant,* volume 1 (New York: American News, 1879).

3. American Express, although it invented the traveler's check in 1881, did not come to Egypt until well after our timeframe.

4. Farman, *Nile,* 4–5.

5. Young, 233–34.

6. Julia Grant, 221–222.

7. Young, 234–236.

8. Farman, *Nile,* 42–3.

9. Farman, *Egypt,* 66f.

10. That palace was built entirely of wood, a precious commodity in Egypt, where there were too few trees, but several fires over the decades that followed forced a new design and a new stone façade created by architect Antoine Lasciac along a neoclassical style. That was in 1900, long after the American soldiers left Cairo. It remained the seat of government until the coup of 1952 and is used as such today.

11. Valentine Mott, *Travels in Europe and the East* (New York: Harper and Brothers, 1842). ebook.

12. John P. Dunn, *Khedive Ismail's Army* (London and New York: Routledge, 2005). Print.

13. Young, 238–243.

14. Young, 244–46.

15. Farman, *Nile,* 268–70.

16. Young, 255- 59.

17. Julia Grant, 223.

18. Julia Grant, 223.

19. Young, 259–64.

20. Farman, *Nile,* 178. The General wears his pith helmet, swathed in silk. Mrs. Grant sits near him. Jesse Grant holds an Arab child close to him. Crouching close to the ground is the face of our ever-kindly leader, that good Moslem Sami Bey, his head enveloped in a silk cloth of orange and green, that was brought to him from Mecca. There is Brugsch, with the cane in his hand. The bearded face is that of Dr. Cooke. Hadden sits in the corner with his legs crossed. The consul general looks like a clergyman about to open service, and the young mustached face near him is that of Ensign Wilner. On the extreme left is Hassan, with his saber. Next to Hassan is the Marquis.

21. Young, 298–99.

22. Julia Grant, 231.

23. Julia Grant, 231–32.

24. Young, 159–160.

Chapter 12

1. In 1882, Alexander Macomb Mason, inspector in the cadastral survey on the Fayoum, was in Egypt but not in the army. Chaillé-Long would become interim American consul general during the crucial summer months of 1882. Erastus S. Purdy had died in Egypt in 1881.

2. Battle of Abu Kir, 1798; Battle of Abu Kir, 1801.

3. Wolf (correctly spelled without the e) had an interesting insight into Arabi: "When I was leaving Egypt on a vacation in April, 1882, Arabi Pacha was the Chief Executive and had assumed supreme authority, although the Khedive was still reigning. In making my farewell visit, I said to him, 'Your Excellency, I hope when I return I will find you well, and Egypt happy.' Arabi Pacha, who had a great deal of the native humor of Abraham Lincoln, promptly replied, 'That reminds me of a Sheik speaking in the Mosque, who said, 'All of you who are afraid of your wives stand up.' All except one man stood up. At the close of the service the Sheik went up to this man and said, 'Evidently you are not afraid of your wife,' and the man in a plaintive tone said, 'She gave me such a beating this morning that I am not able to stand up.' So, my dear Consul-General, when you return you may find me well, but you will also find that England has given us such a drubbing that we can't stand up.' His prophecy was fulfilled." Simon Wolf, *The Presidents I have Known from 1860–1918* (Washington, D.C.: Byron S. Adams, 1918), 452. ebook.

4. Charles Chaillé-Long, *Three Prophets: Chinese Gordon, Mohammed Ahmed, Arabi Pasha Events before and after the Bombardment of Alexandria* (New York: D. Appleton, 1884), 130–61. ebook.

5. Fanny Stone, "Diary of an American Girl in Cairo during the War of 1882," *The Century Magazine* 28, No. 2 (June 1884): 288–302. ebook. Stone never wrote a book or published her views on events in Egypt. He did write a letter to Alfred Mordecai, his friend from West Point, which was found and partially published by Frederick Cox as "Arabi and Stone: Egypt's First Military Rebellion, 1882," in *Cahiers d'histoire égyptienne* 2–3 (1956): 155–75. Print.

6. Long, *Three Prophets*, 166.

7. The tradition of putting or throwing sand or mud over the head and wailing is an ancient Egyptian custom of mourning. Although the custom is not specifically Islamic or Christian, one still sees women of both religions in the countryside, especially in Upper Egypt, perform this ritual. It simply reflects being covered with sand, just like the one who died and has been buried.

8. Long, *Three Prophets*, 166.

9. Chaillé-Long was awarded the cross of Commander of the Osmanieh by the Egyptian government for his service during this time.

10. Chaillé-Long, *Three Prophets*, 201–205. While returning from Korea in 1889, Chaillé-Long stopped in Ceylon and visited Arabi. He recorded, "He was much changed since I had seen him in 1882.... It was not until I stepped forward and announced my name, as well as that of my companion, that he recognized me. Arabi was polite, but not cordial. I had published a book (in 1884), in fact, in which I had treated him as an automaton. Arabi, however, quickly relaxed, and graciously sent for kowah (coffee) and cigarettes. I said that it was my purpose to stay in Egypt for a few days and would meet many of our mutual friends. Ibn el Belad (Son of the country) as he was, I could not pass him by in exile without visiting him.... Arabi was visibly affected. He seized me by the hand when we arose to go and accompanied us to the door, thanking us for the visit and bidding us God-speed." Colonel Chaillé-Long, *My Life in Four Continents*, volume 2, 392. Print.

11. "Gliddon, George, in New York to John Forsythe in Washington D.C." Consular Records: Report April 15, 1837. *Despatches from the United States Consuls in Alexandria 1835–1873*. Microfilm Publication T-45, Roll 6, Volume 1, National Archives, Washington, D.C., 1955, 8–10. Microfilm. The Kirkland papers are in the archives of the Massachusetts Historical Society.

Chapter 13

1. There are other foreign cemeteries in the area, including the French Cemetery, where a few French soldiers from the Napoleon invasion can be found. The British Cemetery nearby was in existence as early as 1859; the American Irving N. Hall, who went to Egypt for his health and died in Cairo of consumption, was buried there in May of that year. See Joseph Anderson et al., *The Town and City of Waterbury, Connecticut* (New Haven, CT: Price and Lee, 1896), 967. ebook.

2. History of American Missionary, Online catalog.

American Board of Commissioners for Foreign Missions Records, ca. 1810–1985 RG 4352/RG 1200 http://www.14beacon.org/fguides/abcfm1.htm. Web.

3. Pliny Fisk, "Letter from Mr. Fisk to the Corresponding Secretary, respecting the sickness and death of Mr. Parsons, Alexandria, February 10, 1822," in *Washington Theological Repertory* 3, No. 12 (July 1822): 383. Print.

4. Charles R. Watson, *Egypt and the Christian Crusade* (New York: Young People's Missionary Movement, 1907), 152. ebook.

5. William Harmless, *Desert Christians: An Introduction to Early Christian Monasticism* (New York: Oxford University Press, 2004). Print. The early Christian literature is examined and new ideas are proposed, including one that maintains neither Anthony nor Paul were the first of the desert fathers.

6. *Encyclopedia Coptica*. www.coptic.net/EncyclopediaCoptica/3of 8) 8/30/2007. Web.

7. Heather J. Sharkey, *American Evangelicals in Egypt* (Princeton, NJ: Princeton University Press, 2008), 89. Print.

8. Elizabeth Kelsey Kinnear, *She Sat Where They Sat: A Memoir of Anna Young Thompson of Egypt* (Grand Rapids, MI: Christian World Mission Books, William B. Erdmans, 1971), 15, 21. Print.

9. By 1898 there were 204 pupils in the school at Mansura: 9 Protestant, 67 Copts, 76 Moslems, 29 Catholics, and 23 Jews. Arthur T. Pierson, *The Missionary Review of the World*, volume 22 (New York: Funk and Wagnalls, 1899), 479. ebook.

10. Anna Young Thompson, "The Zar in Egypt," *Moslem World* (July 1913): 275–89; also in *The Influence of Animism on Islam: An Account of Popular Superstitions*, Samuel Marinus Zwemer, ed. (New York: Macmillan, 1930), 229–233. ebook. Also "The Woman Question in Egypt," *The Moslem World* 4, No. 2 (1914): 266–72. Print. These are among the most famous.

11. Watson, *Crusade*, 218–221.

12. Rena L. Hogg, *A Masterbuilder on the Nile: being a record of the life and aims of John Hogg* (Pittsburgh: United Presbyterian Board of Publication, 1914), 90. ebook.

13. Jason Thompson, "Osman Effendi: A Scottish Convert to Islam in Early 19th Century Egypt," in *Historians in Cairo: Essays in Honor of George Scanlon*, Jill Edwards, ed. (Cairo: The American University in Cairo Press, 2002), 81–105. Print.

14. Anna Young Thompson, "Diary of a Trip on the *Ibis*," Anna Young Thompson (1851–1932) Papers 1868–1931, Presbyterian Historical Society, RG 58, Box 1, Folder 12, Microfilm, MF. POS 1009. Microfilm.

15. Mish is a poor man's cheese. As other cheeses are consumed, the remnants are added to a crock and allowed to ferment in a milky liquid.

16. Athribis, the capital of the 10th Nome of Lower Egypt in the 2nd millennium, is located just north of Banha.

17. *Egypt: Handbook for Travelers: Part First: Lower Egypt, with the Fayum and the Peninsula of Sinai* (Leipzig: Karl Baedeker, 1885), 226. ebook.

18. The town of Samannud was known as Djebnetjer in ancient Egypt and Sebennytos to the Greeks. It is the home of Manetho, the historian who wrote *Aegyp-*

tiaca. It is believed to be a resting place for the Holy Family on their journey into Egypt.

19. See Christine Favard-Meeks, "The Present State of the Site of Behbeit el-Hagar." http://www.british-museum.org/pdf/3b%20The%20present%20state%20of%20the%20site.pdf. Web.

20. Anna is referring here to the British Corps of Engineers, who were in charge of the Nile and its irrigation. Col. Sir Colin Scott Moncrieff restored the Nile Barrage and other works in the Delta. He went on to become Undersecretary of State Public Works. Ross, his assistant, eventually assumed a leadership role.

21. Charles C. Graves's letters to his wife from Egypt are in University of North Carolina at Chapel Hill sp. coll. Called papers, 1831–1962. His papers from 1838 to 1896 include 1500 items. They include several hundred letters about Egypt.

22. Egyptian Maritime Data Bank. http://www.emdb.gov.eg/english/inside_e.aspx?main=eafms&level1=lighthouses. Web.

23. Egypt sits on the great flyway for birds as they migrate north and south with the turn of the seasons. The fishermen along the coast often have pet pelicans who accompany them fishing in their small boats. For centuries along the northern coast, Bedouins have set up fabric fences to catch the small quail. Worn out by their journey across the Mediterranean Sea, the small birds are easy prey to the fences. They get tangled in the mesh.

24. Kinnear, 96.

25. Kinnear, 93–109.

26. For an excellent account of this and other thoughts, see Heather J. Sharkey, *American Evangelicals in Egypt* (Princeton: Princeton University Press, 2008). Print.

27. David H. Finnie, *Pioneers East: The Early American Experience in the Middle East* (Cambridge: Harvard University Press, 1967), 133. Print.

28. Sharkey, 88.

Chapter 14

1. Dates are a problem when working with the American Museum expedition. Some sources say Osborn became president in 1906, others in 1908. Likewise the American expedition to Egypt is listed as having occurred in 1907 and in 1908. I have used the first date in both instances.

2. Henry Fairfield Osborn, "Hunting the Ancestral Elephant in the Fayûm Desert: Discoveries of the Recent African Expedition of the American Museum of Natural History," *The Century Magazine* 74, No. 6 (1907): 815–835. ebook.

3. Henry Fairfield Osborn, "New Fossil Mammals from the Fayûm Oligocene, Egypt," Article 16, *Bulletin of the American Museum of Natural History* 24 (1908): 265–72. ebook.

4. Vincent L. Morgan and Spencer G. Lucas, "Walter Granger, 1872–1941, Paleontologist," *Bulletin of the New Mexico Museum of Natural History and Science,* Bulletin 19 (Albuquerque: New Mexico Museum of Natural History and Science, 2002), 1. ebook.

5. Walter Granger, "Report on the Expedition To The Fayûm, Egypt 1907," in *Notes From Dairy-Fayûm Trip, 1907,* Vincent L. Morgan and Spencer G. Lucas, eds. (Albuquerque: New Mexico Museum of Natural History and Science, 2002), Appendix B, 142–144. ebook.

6. H.J.L. Beadnell, *The Topography and Geology of the Fayûm Province of Egypt* (Cairo: National Printing Department, 1905). ebook.

7. "J.P. Morgan Sails; is Going to Egypt," *New York Times,* Sunday, December 31, 1911. http://query.nytimes.com/mem/archivefree/pdf?res=F50B15FD395E13738DDDA80B94DA415B818DF1D3. Web.

8. *Theodore Roosevelt: An Autobiography.* "Boyhood and Youth, 1913." *http://www.bartleby.com/55/1.html.* Web.

9. AMNH mounted a website called The Granger Papers Project with many excellent photos and some entries from Granger's diary. http://users.rcn.com/granger.nh.ultranet/. Web.

10. The diary is not documented by page number, but by date.

11. Henry Ferrar was an Irishman who lived as a child in South Africa and returned to England to attend Cambridge University. He accompanied Capt. Scott's first expedition to the Antarctic in 1901–04. The great Ferrar Glacier was named in his honor. He worked with the Geological Survey until the First World War and then went to New Zealand.

12. George Andrew Reisner was an American archaeologist, who from 1899 to 1905 led the Hearst Expedition to Quif. In 1907, during the time of the AMNH expedition, he was to conduct an archaeological survey of Nubia for the Egyptian government.

13. This could be Dr. Ludwig Borchardt, who founded the German Archaeological Institute in Cairo in 1907. It was Borchardt who discovered the beautiful and now contentious bust of Nefertiti at Tell el Armana in 1912. Egypt has asked for its return and Germany has refused.

14. Quibell was a British Egyptologist who worked in many places in Egypt under Sir Flinders Petrie and on his own. He wrote a number of books about the sites. Inspector of Antiquities for the Delta in 1898, he team found the Narmer Palette in 1898, discovered the tomb of Yuya and Tjuya (Thuya) in Valley of the Kings in 1905, was director of the Egyptian Museum 1914–23, and was Secretary General of Antiquities until 1925.

15. Dr. Albert Morton Lythgoe (1868–1934), was the curator of the Egyptian Department at the Metropolitan Museum of Art in New York City. He worked at Lisht.

16. The AMNH crossed the Atlantic on the *Cedric.* One assumes this party in the desert also crossed on the *Cedric.*

17. Osborn, *Century,* 823.

18. Osborn, *Century,* 826–7.

19. Osborn, *Century,* 830.

20. Dr. Eberhard Fraas was the chairman of the Natural History Museum in Stuttgart, Germany. He met Markgraf exploring in the Eastern Desert around the Mokattam Hills south of Cairo behind the spa community of Helwan and hired him to collect fossils for his museum. In 1906 they went to the Fayoum on a

German expedition and found *Arisnoitherium* and *Zeu-glodon,* which they called *Basilosaurus.*

21. Mr. Converse could be the American Morton E. Converse of Morton E. Converse and Company, manufacturers of children's wooden toys. He was in Egypt around that time. Joe Mitchell Chapple, "Where Santa Claus Gets his Toys," *National Magazine* 27 (October 1907–March 1908): 342–46. ebook.

22. Morgan, *Diary,* 44.

23. W. Granger, *Report on the Expedition To The Fayûm, Egypt, 1907,* Archives, Department of Vertebrate Paleontology, American Museum of Natural History. ebook. Also in Morgan, *Diary,* 143.

24. Morgan, *Diary,* 40.

25. Osborn, *Century,* 820.

26. Osborn, "Bulletin," 265.

Chapter 15

1. John M. Adams, "Generous Benefactor or Arrogant Ignoramus? Theodore Davis and his Excavators, 1900–1914." *Kmt, A Modern Journal of Ancient Egypt* 22, No. 2 (Summer 2011). Print. I am heavily indebted to John Adams for his views on Davis and his willingness to share his information with me.

2. John M. Adams, *Doubtless The Sky Will be Brighter: Theodore Davis and his Excavators, 1900–1914,* Unpublished draft, 1. Title changed to "Generous Benefactor or Arrogant Ignoramus?," etc.

3. John M. Adams to Cassandra Vivian, April 11, 2011. email.

4. See Mark D. Hirsch, "More Light on Boss Tweed," *Political Science Quarterly,* 1945. Print. Also David Wiles, "Boss Tweed and the Tammany Hall Machine," *EAPS* 760. http://www.albany.edu/~dkw42/tweed.html. Web.

5. "Mr. Frost Boiling Over," *New York Times,* November 8, 1879. http://query.nytimes.com/gst/abstract.html?res=F70816F73B5A127B93CAA9178AD95F4D8784F9. Web.

6. John M. Adams, 2. Print. Adams maintains that Charles Wilbour, another American Egyptologist, also earned his fortune under Tweed. See John M. Adams, "Wilbour in Egypt: The Maiden Voyage of *The Seven Hathors.*" Brooklyn Museum, Community: bloggers@brooklynmuseum, April 15–16 2010, http://www.brooklynmuseum.org/community/blogosphere/2010/04/14/wilbour-in-egypt-the-maiden-voyage-of-the-seven-hathors/. Web.

7. Emma B. Andrews, *A Journal on the Bedwin 1889–1913: A Diary kept on board the dahabeyeh of Theodore M. Davis during seventeen trips up the Nile,* volumes 1 and 2. Mss.916.2.An2. Philadelphia: American Philosophical Society. Microfilm.

8. Andrews, 5.

9. Cassandra Vivian, et al., *Father of Rivers: A Travelers Companion to the Nile Valley* (Cairo: Trade Routes Enterprises, 1989), 91–96. Print.

10. Spellings are always a problem when dealing with names. For the names from the ancient kingdom of Egypt I have followed the Theban Mapping Project spellings. Quoted text names have remained the same.

11. "A Brief History of the Supreme Council of Antiquities (SCA): 1858 to present." Supreme Council of Antiquities. http://www.sca-egypt.org/eng/SCA_History.htm. Web.

12. P.E. Newberry, *Scarabs: An Introduction to the Study of Egyptian Seals and Signet Rings* (London: Archibald Constable, 1906). Print.

13. Vivian, 128.

14. "Theodore Davis," Ancient Egyptian Website, Egyptology through images. http://www.ancientegypt.co.uk/people/pages/theodore_davis.htm. Updated on August 16, 2009. Web.

15. Theodore M. Davis, "The Finding of the Tomb of Siphtah, the Unnamed Gold Tomb, and the Animal Pit Tombs," in *The Tomb of Siphtah* (London: Archibald Constable, 1908), 1. ebook.

16. Kent Weeks founded the Theban Mapping Project (TMP), now housed at the American University in Cairo, and digitized his information. Each site now has not only an identifying number (as seen above), but general information, architectural plans, a list of noteworthy features, and a GPS location. All this information and more is now available at www.thebanmappingproject.com.

17. Theodore M. Davis, *Mr. Theodore M. Davis Excavations: Bibân el Molûk: The Tomb of Thoutmosis IV* (Westminster: Archibald Constable, 1904), vii–xii. ebook. Prior to Davis, Robb dePeyster Tytus (1875–1913 was a wealthy American working in Luxor excavating the ancient civilization. Born in North Carolina and educated at Yale, in Luxor he worked with Percy Newbury and was later granted a concession to dig. It seems he found eight bathrooms belonging to Amenhotep. Robb de Peyster Tytus, "The Palace of Amenhotep III, Husband of Queen Thiy," *New Century Magazine* 78, No. 2 (June 1909): 738. ebook.

18. Edouard Naville, et al. *Theodore M. Davis's Excavations: Biban el Molûk: The Tomb of Hâtshopsîtû* (London: Archibald Constable, 1906), xii–xv. ebook.

19. Naville, xii–xv.

20. "KV-60 SIT-RA, Atlas of the Valley of the Kings," Theban Mapping Project. http://www.theban-mappingproject.com/atlas/index_kv.asp. Web.

21. "Press Release: Identifying Hatshepsut's Mummy," Zahi Hawass, http://www.drhawass.com/blog/press-release-identifying-hatshepsuts-mummy. Web.

22. "KV-46 (Yuya and Thuyu), Atlas of the Valley of the Kings," Theban Mapping Project. http://www.thebanmappingproject.com/sites/browse_tomb_860.html. Web.

23. Theodore M. Davis, "The Finding of the Tomb of Iouiya and Touiyou," in *The Tomb of Iouiya and Touiyou* (London: Archibald Constable, 1907), xxv–xxviii. ebook.

24. Davis, *Iouiya and Touiyou,* xxvii–xviii.

25. Davis, *Iouiya and Touiyou,* xxxiii–xxx.

26. Theodore M. Davis, "The Finding of the Tomb of Queen Tiyi," *The Tomb of Queen Tiyi* (London: Archibald Constable, 1910), 1–2. Print.

27. Davis, *Tiyi,* 2–4.

Works Cited

John Antes

Antes, John. "Considerations on the Opinions expressed on Mr. Bruce, by Lord Valentia, and Mr. Salt." *Select Reviews and Spirit of the Foreign Magazines 1809–1811* 4, No. 20 (August 1810): 130–134, 131. Print.

_____. Letter from Grand Cairo to Benjamin Franklin, July 10, 1779. In Isaac Minis Hayes, ed. *Calendar of the Franklin Papers in the Library of the American Philosophical Society.* 5 vols. No. XV, 31. Philadelphia: American Philosophical Society, 1908. Microfilm.

_____. Letter to Rev. Benjamin LaTrobe (in German), Cairo, September 8, 1770. AB 140, Moravian Archives London (MAL). 4. Print.

_____. *Excerpts from Narrative of the Life of our Late Dear and Venerable Brother John Antes, Written by Himself in Periodical Accounts Relating to the Mission of the Church of the United Brethren Established Among the Heathen.* Volume 5. London: E. Baker for Bristol Society for Promoting Religious Knowledge, 1815. Print.

_____. Extract of a Letter from Grand Cairo (in English) to Rev. Benjamin LaTrobe, August 15, 1771. AB 140, Moravian Archives London (MAL). 4p. Print.

_____. Extract of a Letter from Cairo (in English) to Rev. Benjamin La Trobe, London. April 22, 1772. AB 140, Moravian Archives London (MAL). 2p. Print.

_____. Letter from Cairo (in German) to Rev. Benjamin LaTrobe, April 23, 1773. AB 140, Moravian Archives London (MAL). Translated by Gabriele Hallof. Print. 2p. Print.

_____. Letter from Cairo (in German) to Rev. Benjamin LaTrobe, December 22, 1773. AB 140, Moravian Archives London (MAL). Translated by Gabriele Hallof. 1–2. Print.

_____. Letter from Cairo (in German) to Dr. Wollin (in London), September 28, 1778. AB 140, Moravian Archives London (MAL). Translated by Gabriele Hallof. 8p. Print.

_____. Letter from Cairo (in German) to Rev. Benjamin LaTrobe, September 3, 1780, AB 140, Moravian Archives London (MAL). Translated by Gabriele Hallof. 4p. Print.

_____. *Observations on the Manners and Customs of the Egyptians, The overflowing of the Nile and its effects; with remarks on the plague, and other subjects written during a residence of twelve years in Cairo and its vicinity.* London: John Stockdale, 1800. Print.

Balboni, L.A. *Gli' Italiani nella Civilta Egizian del Secolo XIX.* Sotto gli auspice del comitato alessandrino della Societa Dante Alighieri. Alessandria D'Egitto, 1906. ebook.

Barry, Jonathan, and Kenneth Morgan. *The Moravians in Revival and Reformation in 18th-Century Bristol.* Bristol: Bristol Record Society, 1994. Print.

Grinder, Rufus A. *Music in Bethlehem, Pennsylvania from 1741 to 1871.* Philadelphia: J. Hill Martin, 1873. Print.

Hamilton, John Taylor, and Kenneth G. Hamilton. *History of the Moravian Church: The Renewed Unitas Fratrum 1722–1957.* Moravian Church of America. 1967. Print.

Holmes, John Beck. *Historical Sketches of the Missions of the United Brethren for Propagating the Gospel Among the Heathen, from their commencement to the year 1817.* London, 1827. Print.

Livingston, John W. "Ali Bey Al-Kabir and the Jews." *Middle Eastern Studies* 7, No. 2 (May 1971): 221–228, 221. Print.

Manley, Deborah, and Peta Ree. *Henry Salt: Artist, Traveller, Diplomat, Egyptologist.* London: Libri, 2001. Print.

Peter, Johann Friedrich. "String Chamber Music in the Moravian Musical Heritage." October 24, 2005. New World Records 80507. http://www.newworldrecords.org/linernotes/80507.pdf. Web.

Vivian, Cassandra. "John Antes: Dilettante Americano or What?" *Travel and Travellers in Egypt and the Nile Valley.* Conference on Travellers in Egypt and the Near East. ASTENE. Pollock Halls, Edinburgh University (Scotland). July 11–15, 2001. Print.

Wilson, John A. *Signs and Signs and Wonders Upon Pharaoh.* Chicago: University of Chicago Press, 1964. Print.

John Ledyard

Adu Boahen, Albert. *Britain, the Sahara, and the Western Sudan 1788–1861.* Oxford, UK: Clarendon, 1964. Print.

Boyd, Julian. *The Papers of Thomas Jefferson.* Volumes 14, 15, 16, 17, 18: 1788–89 and 1804–6. Princeton, NJ: Princeton University Press, 1950. Print.

Bradish, Luther. Letter from Luther Bradish to Thomas Appleton, July 1, 1824. Luther Bradish Papers, MS 71. New York Historical Society Archives. Print.

Coues, Elliott. *History of the Expedition under the Command of Lewis and Clark.* Volume 1. New York: Francis P. Harper, 1893. Print.

English, George Bethune. *A Narrative of the Expedition to Dongola and Senaar, under the command of His Excellence Ismael Pasha, undertaken by order of His Highness Mehemmed Ali Pasha, Viceroy of Egypt. By an American in the service of the Viceroy.* Boston: Wells and Lilly, 1823. Print.

Fisk, Pliny. "Letter from Mr. Fisk to the Corresponding Secretary, respecting the sickness and death of Mr. Parsons, Alexandria, February 10, 1822." In *Washington Theological Repertory* 3 (July 1822): 12. Print.

George, Viscount Valentia. *Voyages and Travels to India, Ceylon, the Red Sea, Abyssinia, and Egypt.* Volume 3. London: F.C. and J. Rivington, 1811. ebook.

Gliddon, George Robbins. *Appendix to "The American in Egypt."* Philadelphia: Merrihew and Thompson, 1842. Print.

Hallett, Robin. *Records of the African Association 1788–1831.* London: Thomas Nelson and Sons, for the Royal Geographical Society, 1964. Print.

Hanna, Nelly. *Making Big Money in 1600: The Life and Times of Isma'il Abu Taqiyya, Egyptian Merchant.* Cairo: The American University in Cairo Press, 1998. Print.

Jefferson, Thomas. *Autobiography.* Washington ed. University of Virginia Catalog (Virgo), March 9, 2011. "4559 Ledyard" i. 68 and Ford ed., i, 94. 1821. At the Jeffersonian Cyclopedia. http://etext.lib.virginia.edu/etcbin/foleyx-browse?id=Ledyard. Web.

Prime, William. "The Grave of John Ledyard." *New York Daily Times* (July 29, 1857): 2. ProQuest Historical Newspapers. Web.

Sparks, Jared. *The Life of John Ledyard, the American Traveller.* Cambridge, MA: Hilliard and Brown, 1828. Print.

Vivian, Cassandra. *The Western Desert of Egypt.* Cairo: The American University in Cairo Press, 2000, 2003, and 2nd ed. 2008. Print.

Walz, Terence. *Trade Between Egypt and Bilan as-Sudan 1700–1820.* Cairo: Institut Français D'Archéologie Orientale du Caire, 1978. Print.

Zug, James. *American Traveler: The Life and Adventures of John Ledyard, the Man Who Dreamed of Walking the World.* New York: Basic Books, 2005.

———, ed. *The Last Voyage of Captain Cook: The Collected Writings of John Ledyard.* Margate, FL: National Geographic Adventure Classics, 2005. Print.

William Eaton

Bates, Orin. "Excavations at Marsa Matruh." *Harvard African Studies* 8 (1927): 125–36. Print.

"Claim of Colonel Leitensdorfer." In *A Century of Lawmaking for a New Nation*: U.S. Congressional Documents and Debates, 1774–1875. 23rd Congress, No 589, 1834, 455. American Memory Collection in Library of Congress Online. lcweb2.loc.gov/cgi-bin//ampage?collId=llsp&... March 3, 2003. Web.

Cohen, Mendes. *Journal from Cairo on to Wady Halfa or Second Cataract Copied from Notes in Pencil in M.I.C's Guide Book.* MS-251.3, Mendes I. Cohen Correspondence, 1829–1835. Box 4, Journal, 1832, 3. Maryland Historical Society. Print.

Edwards, Samuel. *Barbary General: The Life of William H. Eaton.* Englewood Cliffs, NJ: Prentice-Hall, 1968. Print.

"Extract of a letter from Mr. Pascal Paoli Peck (son of Col. William Peck, of this town) an officer on board the United States brig *Argus*, commanded by Isaac Hull, Esq.," Malta, July 4, 1805." *Gettysburg Sentinel*, Wednesday, October 30, 1805, 172–73. Print.

Knox, Dudley W. *Naval Documents Related to the U.S. Wars with the Barbary Powers.* Vol. 4: *Naval Operations Including Diplomatic Background from April to September 6 1804.* Washington, D.C.: Government Printing Office, 1942. Print.

———. *Naval Documents Related to the U.S. Wars with the Barbary Powers.* Vol. 5: *Naval Operations Including Diplomatic Background from September 7, 1804 through April 1805.* Washington, D.C.: Government Printing Office, 1944. Print.

———. *Naval Documents Related to the U.S. Wars with the Barbary Powers.* Vol. 6: *Naval Operations Including Diplomatic Background from May 1805 through 1807.* Washington, D.C.: Government Printing Office, 1944. Print.

Lipscomb, Andrew A., ed. *The Writings of Thomas Jefferson.* Vol. 11. Washington D.C.: The Thomas Jefferson Memorial Association, 1905. Print.

Maclay, Edgar Stanton. *A History of the United States Navy from 1775 to 1893.* Vol. 1. New York: D. Appleton, 1893. Print.

Paine, Ralph D. *The Old Merchant Marine: A Chronicle of American Ships and Sailors.* New Haven: Yale University Press, 1919. ebook.

Prentiss, Charles. *The Life of the Late General William Eaton.* Brookfield, MA: E. Merriam, 1813. University Micro 1980. ebook.

Ray, William. *Horrors of Slavery, or The American Tars in Tripoli.* New York: Troy, 1808. ebook.

Starkey, Janet, and Okasha El-Daly, eds. *Travellers in the Deserts of the Orient. William Eaton: A Forgotten American Voice.* London: ASTENE, 2000. Print.

Swanson, Claude A. *Naval Documents related to the Quasi-War between the United States and France: From February 1797 to October 1798.* Vol. 1. Washington, D.C.: United States Government Printing Office, 1935. Print.

"The United States and the Barbary States." *Atlantic Monthly* 6, No. 38 (December 1860): 641–657. Print.

Vivian, Cassandra. "William Eaton: A Forgotten American Voice." *Travel and Travellers in Egypt and the Near East.* ASTENE Conference. Newnham College, Cambridge University (England), July 15–18, 1999. Conference.

Whipple, A.B.C. *To the Shores of Tripoli: The Birth of the U.S. Navy and Marines.* New York: William Morrow, 1991. Print.

Zacks, Richard. *The Pirate Coast: Thomas Jefferson, the First Marines, and the Secret Mission of 1805.* New York: Hyperion, 2005. Print.

Francis Barthow

Barthow, Victor, to John Gliddon, Alexandria, April 15, 1844. *Despatches from the United States Consuls in Alexandria 1835–1873*, Roll 1, vol. 1, T-45, August 28, 1835, to January 10, 1849. National Archives, Washington, D.C., 1955. Microfilm.

_____, to George H. Butler, Alexandria, July 14, 1870. No. 10. *Despatches from the United States Consuls in Alexandria 1835–1873*, Roll 6, vol. 6, March 28, 1870, to December 8, 1872. National Archives, Washington, D.C., 1955. Microfilm.

"Battle of Navarino." http://www.mlahanas.de/Greece/History/BattleOfNavarino.html. Web.

Beardsley to Fish, August 31, 1872. No 7. *Despatches from the United States Consuls in Alexandria 1835–1873*, Roll 6, vol. 6, March 28, 1870, to December 8, 1872. National Archives, Washington, D.C., 1955. Microfilm.

Burckhardt, John Lewis. *Travels in Nubia.* 2nd ed. London: John Murray, 1822. Print.

Butler to Fish, July 14, 1870, No 10. *Despatches from the United States Consuls in Alexandria 1835–1873*, Roll 6, vol. 6, March 28, 1870, to December 8, 1872. National Archives, Washington, D.C. 1955. Microfilm.

Cohen, Mendes. *Journal of Mendes Cohen* (unpublished). MS-251.3, Mendes I. Cohen Correspondence, 1829–1835. Box 4, Journal, 1832. Baltimore: Maryland Historical Society, 1932. Print.

Curio, Silvio, and Laura Donatelli. *Bernardino Drovetti Epistolario (1800–1851).* Milano: Istituto Editoriale Cisalpino — La Goliardica, 1985. Print.

De Keersmaecker, Roger. *Travellers' Graffiti from Egypt and the Sudan.* Vol. 8: *Elkab: The Temple of Amenophis III.* 2010. Print.

_____. *Travellers' Graffiti from Egypt and the Sudan: The Kiosk of Qertassi.* Berchem, Antwerp: Graffito Graffiti, 2001. Print.

Finati, Giovanni. *Narrative of the Life and Adventures of Giovanni Finati.* Vol. 2. London: J. Murray, 1830. ebook.

George, Viscount Valentia. *Voyages and Travels to India, Ceylon, the Red Sea, Abyssinia, and Egypt.* Vols. 2 and 3. London: F.C. and J. Rivington, 1811. ebook.

Guichard, Sylvie. *Lettres de Bernardino Drovetti consul de France a Alexandrie 1803–1830.* Paris: Maisonneuve and Larose, 1830. Print.

Halbertsma, Ruurd B. *Scholars, Travellers, and Trade: The Pioneer Years of the National Museum of Antiquities in Leiden, 1818–1840.* London: Routledge, 2003. Print.

Hale, Charles. "Consular Service in Egypt." *Atlantic Monthly* 150, No. 229 (September 1877): 280–290.

Janvier, Thomas. "The Sea-Robbers of New York." *Harper's New Monthly Magazine* 89 (November 1894): 814–827. Print.

Knox, Dudley W. *Naval Documents Related to the U.S. Wars with the Barbary Powers.* Vol. 4: *Naval Operations Including Diplomatic Background from April to September 6 1804.* Washington, D.C.: Government Printing Office, 1944. Print.

_____. *Naval Documents Related to the U.S. Wars with the Barbary Powers.* Vol. 5: *Naval Operations Including Diplomatic Background from September 7, 1804 through April 1805.* Washington, D.C.: Government Printing Office, 1944. Print.

_____. *Naval Documents Related to the U.S. Wars with the Barbary Powers.* Vol. 6: *Naval Operations Including Diplomatic Background from May 1805 through 1807.* Washington, D.C.: Government Printing Office, 1944. Print.

Legh, T. *Narrative of a Journey in Egypt and the Country Beyond the Cataracts,* 2nd ed. London: John Murray, 1817. Print.

Maclay, Edgar Stanton, *A History of the United States Navy from 1775 to 1894.* Vol. 1: New York: D. Appleton, 1895. Print.

"McCauley to Daniel Webster. Alexandria, March 16, 1850." No 15. *Despatches from the United States Consuls in Alexandria 1835–1873.* Roll 2, Volume 1–2, T45–2, March 28, 1870, to December 8, 1872. National Archives, Washington, D.C. 1955. Microfilm.

"McCauley to Daniel Webster. Alexandria, February 21, 1852." No 33. *Despatches from the United States Consuls in Alexandria 1835–1873.* Roll 2, Volume 1–2, T45–2, March 28, 1870, to December 8, 1872. National Archives, Washington, D.C. 1955. Microfilm.

"McCauley to Daniel Webster. March 16, 1852." No 35. *Despatches from the United States Consuls in Alexandria 1835–1873.* Roll 2, Volume 1–2, T45–2. March 28, 1870, to December 8, 1872. National Archives, Washington, D.C. 1955. Microfilm.

"McCauley to the Egyptian Government. Alexandria, December 15, 1851." *Despatches from the United States Consuls in Alexandria.* Roll 2, Volume 1–2, T45–2, 1835–1873. National Archives, Washington, D.C. 1955. Microfilm.

Marro, Giovanni. *Il Corpo Espisolare di Bernadino Drovertti.* Roma. Stampate nell'Istituto poligrafico dello Stato per la Reale Società di geografia d'Egitto, 1940. Print.

Schroeder, Francis. *Shores of the Mediterranean with Sketches of Travel.* Vol. 1. London: John Murray, 1846. Print.

Ships and Shipping of Old New York: A Brief Account of the Interesting Phases of the Commerce of New York from the Foundation of the city to the Beginning of the Civil War. New York: Bank of the Manhattan Company, 1915. ebook.

Usick, Patricia. *Adventures in Egypt and Nubia: The Travels of William John Bankes (1786–1855).* London: British Museum Press, 2002. Print.

_____. "William John Bankes' Collection of Drawings of Egypt and Nubia." In *Travellers in Egypt.* Paul and Janet Starkey, eds. New York: IB Taurus, 1998. 51–60. Print.

George Bethune English

Adams, D.V., ed. *Memoirs of John Quincy Adams 1874–1877.* Vol. 8. Philadelphia: J.B. Lippincott, 1875. Print.

Adams, William Y. *Nubia: Corridor to Africa.* Princeton: Princeton University Press, 1984. Print.

Aga, Khalil. *Journal of an Englishman who traveled to Sennar with Ismail Pasha Expedition to subdue the Eastern Sudan.* 26 August 1820 to 23 August 1821. Add 54195 ff.46–76 Henry Salt papers FRS d 1827. Print.

Bierbrier, M.L. *Who Was Who in Egyptology.* London: The Egypt Exploration Society, 1995. Print.

Bradish, Luther. Letter from Luther Bradish to Thomas Appleton, July 1, 1824. Luther Bradish Papers, MS 71. New York Historical Society Archives. Print.

Bruce, James. *Travels in Abyssinia and Nubia in 1768–1773 to Discover the Source of the Nile.* Edinburgh: Adam and Charles Black, 1873. ebook.

Budge, E.A. Wallis. *Cook's Handbook for Egypt and the Sudan.* Vol. 2. London: Thomas Cook and Son, 1906. Print.

Cailliaud, Frederic. *Voyage à Meroë, au Fleuve Blanc, au-delà de Fazgol dans le midi du Royaume de Sennar, à Syouah et dans cinq autres oases.* Paris: L'Imprimerie Royale, 1826. Print.

Callihan, Edward William, *List of Officers of the Navy of the United States and the Marine Corps from 1775 to 1900.* New York: L.R. Hamersly. Print.

Curio, Silvio, and Laura Donatelli. *Bernardino Drovetti Epistolario (1800–1851)* Milano: Istituto Editoriale Cisalpino — La Goliardica, 1985. Print.

De Kay, James Ellsworth. *Sketches of Turkey in 1831 and 1832.* New York: J. and J. Harper, 1833. ebook.

English, George Bethune. *Five Pebbles from the Brook: A Reply to 'A Defence of Christianity' written by Edward Everett.* Philadelphia, 1824. ebook.

_____. *A Narrative of the Expedition to Dongola and Senaar, under the command of His Excellence Ismail Pasha, undertaken by order of His Highness Mehemmed Ali Pasha, Viceroy of Egypt by an American in the service of the Viceroy.* London: J. Murray, 1822. Print.

_____. *A Narrative of the Expedition to Dongola and Senaar, under the command of His Excellence Ismail Pasha, undertaken by order of His Highness Mehemmed Ali Pasha, Viceroy of Egypt by an American in the service of the Viceroy.* Boston: Wells and Lilly, 1823. ebook.

Finati, Giovanni. *Narrative of the Life and Adventures of Giovanni Finati.* Volume 2. London: J. Murray, 1830. ebook.

Gallatin, Count. *The Diary of James Gallatin, Secretary to Albert Gallatin, a Great Peace Maker 1813–1827.* New York: Charles Scribner's Sons, 1916. Print.

"George Bethune English," *Senate Executive Journal, February 27, 1815.* A Century of Lawmaking for a New Nation: U.S. Congressional Documents and Debates, 1774–1875. American Memory. Library of Congress Online. Naval Records give the date of March 1, 1815. Web.

Mayers, David. *Dissenting Voices in America's Rise to Power.* Cambridge: Cambridge University Press. 2007. ebook.

Mengin, Felix. *Histoire de l'Egypte.* Vol. 2. Paris: Chez Arthus Bertrand, 1823. ebook.

"Mr. George Bethune English." *The Religious Intelligencer.* December 28, 1822 81. APS Online, 496. Web.

Popkin, Richard M. *The Third Force in Seventeenth-Century Thought.* Leiden: E.J. Brill, 1992. Print.

Raphalides, Samuel J. *United States Policy Toward the Greek War of Independence.* Ph.D. thesis, New School for Social Research, 1974. Print.

Register of the Commissioned and Warrant Officers of the Navy of the United States. Washington, D.C.: Wade and Company, 1819. Print.

Salt, Henry. Letter, dated May 2, 1821 (but internal evidence proves it was 1822). Print.

Sharples, Stephen Paschall. *Records of the Church of Christ at Cambridge in New England 1632–1830.* Boston: Eben Putnam, 1906. Print.

U.S. Naval Ships Visiting Egypt. National Archives and Records Administration. Old Military and Civil Records. Print.

Vivian, Cassandra. *Khalil Aga: A Lost American in the Sudan.* Conference on Travellers in Egypt and the Near East. ASTENE. Southampton University, England, July 12–16, 2007. Conference.

_____. "Khalil Aga: A Lost American in the Sudan." In *Saddling the Dogs.* Diane Fortenberry, ed. London: ASTENE, 2009. Print.

Waddington, George, and Barnard Hanbury. *Journal of a Visit to Some Parts of Ethiopia.* London: John Murray, 1822. Print.

Wolff, Joseph. "Extracts from the Journal of Mr. Wolff." *The Religious Intelligencer* 2, No. 12 (October 10, 1823): 177–181, 165. Print.

George Gliddon

"1851." *Gettysburg (Pennsylvania) Star and Banner*, Friday, January 24, 1851. NewspaperArchive.com. Web.

"Abbott, H. in Cairo to Benjamin Brown in London." April 18, 1841. Benjamin Brown Collection. William J. Clements Library, University of Michigan. Print.

"Amusements." *Saturday Evening Post* 30, No. 1532 (December 7, 1850). NewspaperArchive.com. Web.

Barnhart, Terry A. "Toward a Science of Man: European Influences on the Archaeologist Ephraim George Squier." In *New Perspectives on the Origins of Americanist Archaeology*, David L. Browman and Stephen Williams, ed. Tuscaloosa: University of Alabama Press, 2002. Print.

Biography of George Gliddon. Academy of Natural Sciences, Philadelphia. ANSP Coll. 128, ANSP ms 239. Print.

"Brooklyn Institute Lecturers." *Brooklyn Daily Eagle*, October 21, 1846, 2. Newspaper Archives.com. Web.

Cohen, Mendes, to Hon. John Forsyth. Consular Records: Baltimore. August 13, 1837. No. 17. *Despatches from the United States Consuls in Alexandria 1835–1873.* Microfilm Publications T-45, Roll 6, Volume 1, August 28, 1835–January 10, 1849. National Archives, Washington, D.C. 1955. Microfilm.

Dawson, Warren R. *Who Was Who in Egyptology: A Biographical Index of Egyptologists; of Travellers, Explorers and Excavators in Egypt; of Collectors of and Dealers in Egyptian Antiquities; of Consuls, Officials, Authors, Benefactors, and Others Whose Names Occur in the Literature of Egyptology, from the Year 1500 to the Present Day, but Excluding Persons Now Living.* 3rd ed., revised by M.L. Bierbrier. London: Egyptian Exploration Services, 1995. Print.

Flint, Richard W. "Rufus Welch: America's Pioneer Circus Showman." *Bandwagon* 14, No. 5 (September-October 1970): 4–11. www.circushistory.org/Bandwagon/bw-1970Sep.htm. Web.

Gliddon, George R. *An Appeal to the Antiquaries of Europe and the Destruction of the Monuments of Egypt.* London: 1841. Print.

_____. *Hand-book to the American Panorama of the Nile: being the original transparent picture exhibited in London, at Egyptian Hall, Piccadilly, purchased from its painters and proprietors, Messrs. H. Warren, J. Bonomi, and J. Fahey.* London, 1849. Print.

_____, in Alexandria to Samuel George Morton in Philadelphia. May 21–24, 1840. *Samuel George Morton Papers, 1838–1844.* American Philosophical Society Series I Correspondence M843 ALS 3p and enc of 10p. Print.

_____, in Boston to Samuel George Morton in Philadelphia. January 4, 1843. *Samuel George Morton Papers, 1838–1844.* American Philosophical Society Series IV Microfilm 1838–44, No 48. Microfilm.

_____, in Cairo to John Forsythe in Washington, D.C. Consular Records: Letter June 30, 1839. No. 17. *Despatches from the United States Consuls in Alexandria* 1835–1873. Roll 6, Volume 1, August 28, 1835–January 10, 1849. National Archives, Washington, D.C. 1955. Microfilm.

_____, in Cairo to John Forsythe in Washington, D.C. Consular Records: Letter May 20, 1840. No. 17. *Despatches from the United States Consuls in Alexandria 1835–1873.* Roll 6, Volume 1, August 28, 1835–January 10, 1849. National Archives, Washington 1955. Microfilm.

_____, in New York to Samuel George Morton in Philadelphia, February 17, 1842. *Samuel George Morton Papers, 1838–1844.* American Philosophical Society Series IV Microfilm 1838–44, No 42. Microfilm.

_____, in New York to Samuel George Morton in Philadelphia. February 14, 1843. *Samuel George Morton Papers, 1838–1844.* American Philosophical Society Series IV Microfilm 1838–44, No 51. Microfilm.

_____, in New York to Samuel George Morton in Philadelphia. February 20, 1843. *Samuel George Morton Papers, 1838–1844.* American Philosophical Society Series IV Microfilm 1838–44, No 52. Microfilm.

_____, in New York to Samuel George Morton in Philadelphia. January 22, 1842. *Samuel George Morton Papers, 1838–1844.* American Philosophical Society Series IV Microfilm 1838–44, No 41. Microfilm.

_____, in New York to John Forsythe in Washington, D.C. Consular Records: Letter April 17, 1837. No. 17. *Despatches from the United States Consuls in Alexandria 1835–1873,* (Microfilm Publication T-45, Roll 6, Volume 1), August 28, 1835–January 10, 1849. National Archives, Washington, D.C. 1955. Microfilm.

_____, from Comayagua to H.S. Stanford, October 10, 1857. Papers of E.G. Squier 1841–1888 (bulk 1846–

1874), Manuscript Division. Library of Congress. Honduras Interoceanic Railway File, 1853–1870 Box 5 Reel 8 Correspondence, 1853–1870 Reports, George R. Gliddon No. 1, May 16, 1857. Web.

_____, to Joseph Bonomi, Philadelphia 1844. Yvonne Neville-Rolfe Collection (Private Collection), 1. Print.

_____, to Sirs. (Bonomi and company.) London, New York. January 22, 1850. Yvonne Neville-Rolfe Collection. (Private Collection).

_____, to Squier, Philadelphia, September 21, 1847, and Charleston, November 21, 1847. Ephraim George Squier Papers. Library of Congress, Washington, D.C. Web.

_____, to Squier, Pittsburgh, March 15, 1847, and Cincinnati, April 23, 1847. Ephraim George Squier Papers, Library of Congress, Washington, D.C. Web.

_____, in Wadi Halfa to Benjamin Brown in Dongola. J. Clements Library, University of Michigan. Benjamin Brown Collection, December 28, 1839. 3p. Print.

_____, to Hon. John Forsyth. Letter, September 11, 1833. *Despatches from the United States Consuls in Constantinople 1835–1873.* (Microfilm Publications T-194, Roll T-1), December 20, 1820–Sept 1, 1837, No. 17. National Archives, Washington, D.C. 1955. Microfilm.

Gliddon, John, in Alexandria to Francis Griffin, John L. Stephens, Frederick Bronson and W. Hamersley in New York. July 11, 1838. J.L. Stephens Papers BANC MSS Z-Z 116. The Bancroft Library, University of California at Berkeley. 4p. Print.

_____, in Alexandria to John Forsythe in Washington, D.C. Consular Records: Letter October 31, 1836. No. 17. *Despatches from the United States Consuls in Alexandria 1835–1873.* (Microfilm Publication T-45, Roll 6, Volume 1), August 28, 1835–January 10, 1849. National Archives, Washington, D.C. 1955. Microfilm.

"Gliddon's Panorama of the Nile." *Graham's American Monthly Magazine of Literature, Art and Fashion* 36 (May 1850). NewspaperArchive.com. 344. Web.

A Guide for Visitors to the National Gallery, Revised in Accordance with the Instructions of the Commissioner of Patents. January 1857. http://www.myoutbox.net/poguide.htm. Web.

Haight, Richard, of Philadelphia for George R Gliddon to John Forsythe at the Department of State. July 29, 1837. Record Group 59 (General Records of the Department of State), Records of Application and Recommendation During the Administrations of Martin Van Buren, William Henry Harrison, and John Tyler, 1837–1845, folder for George Gliddon. Microfilm.

Haight, Sarah Rogers. *Letters from the Old World.* 2 vols. New York: Harper and Brothers, 1840. ebook.

Hammersley, John L., in New York for George R. Gliddon to John Forsyth at the Department of State. July 4, 1837. Submitted August 10, 1837, Record Group 59 (General Records of the Department of State), Records of Application and Recommendation during the Administrations of Martin Van Buren, William Henry Harrison, and John Tyler, 1837–1845, folder for George Gliddon. Microfilm.

Hauptman, William. *Charles Gleyre, 1806–1874*. 2 vols. Princeton, N.J.: Princeton University Press. Basel, Switzerland: Swiss Institute for Art Research, 1996. Print.

Interview with B. Brown and 1880 obit of Brown. *The Oldest of Showman: Aged Benjamin Brown's Recollections of Pioneer Circus Life. Croton Falls News*, July 17, 1879; reprint in *New York Sun*. J. Clements Library, University of Michigan. Print.

Journal of the executive proceedings of the Senate of the United States of America, 1829–1837. Tuesday, February 1, 1831. A Century of Lawmaking for a New Nation: U.S. Congressional Documents and Debates, 1774–1875. http://memory.loc.gov/cgi-bin/query. Web.

Journal of the Senate of the United States of America, 1789–1873. Wednesday, December 7, 1831. A Century of Lawmaking for a New Nation: U.S. Congressional Documents and Debates, 1774–1875. http://memory.loc.gov/cgi-bin/query. Web.

June, Stebb, in Alexandria to Benjamin Brown in Cairo, July 17, 1879; includes obituary of 1880. J. Clements Library, University of Michigan. Benjamin Brown Collection, April 19, 1840. University of Michigan. Benjamin Brown Collection. Print.

Kern, Ned, in Philadelphia to George Gliddon in Pittsburgh, October 27, 1851. Gilcrease Museum Library collection, reel 3281, frames 642–45. Microfilm.

Lent, L. Letter from New York to George Gliddon in Cairo, November 19, 1838. William J. Clements Library, University of Michigan. Benjamin Brown Collection, No. 37. Print.

Leopold, Robert S. *A Guide to Early African Collections in the Smithsonian Institution.* "George Robins Gliddon (1809–1857)." Catalog Numbers E-4797, E-5454. Received 1867. Print. http://anthropology.si.edu/leopold/pubs/early_african_collections.pdf. Web.

Lowell, F.C., Esq. Brother to the late John Lowell Esq. of Boston for George R. Gliddon to John Forsyth at the Department of State. Boston, July 24, 1837. Record Group 59 (General Records of the Department of State), Records of Application and Recommendation During the Administrations of Martin Van Buren, William Henry Harrison, and John Tyler, 1837–1845, folder for George Gliddon. Microfilm.

Mott, Valentine. *Travels in Europe and the East Embracing Observations made during a Tour Through Great Britain in 1834, 34, 36, 37, 38, 39, 40, and 41 ...* New York: Harper and Brothers, 1842. Print.

"The Mummy Again." *Daily Picayune*. Thursday, March 4, 1852. NewspaperArchive.com. Web.

Norman, Wendy. *The Gliddons in London 1760–1850, Including a Family Record by Anne Gliddon.* New Zealand: Steele Roberts, 2000. Print.

Nott, J.C., and George R Gliddon. *Indigenous Races of the Earth.* Philadelphia: J.B. Lippincott, 1868. Print.

"Opening the Mummy." *Defiance Democrat* 6, No. 44 (June 29, 1850): 1. NewspaperArchive.com. Web.

"Panorama of the Nile." *Brooklyn Daily Eagle* 9, No. 33 (February 8, 1850): 2. NewspaperArchive.com, Web.

"Panorama of the Nile." *Saturday Evening Post* 30, No. 1521 (September 21, 1850). APS Online 0–002. Web.

Paullin, Charles Oscar. *Diplomatic Negotiations of American Naval Officers, 1778–1883.* The Albert Shaw Lecturers on Diplomatic History, 1911. Baltimore: Johns Hopkins Press, 1912. Print.

Randolph, Richard, of Philadelphia for George R. Gliddon to John Forsyth at the Department of State, August 5, 1837. Record Group 59 (General Records of the Department of State). Records of Application and Recommendation During the Administrations of Martin Van Buren, William Henry Harrison, and John Tyler, 1837–1845, folder for George Gliddon. Microfilm.

Rapelje, George. *A Narrative of Excursions, Voyages, and Travels performed at different periods in America, Europe, Asia, and Africa.* New York: privately printed. 1834. ebook.

Rothenberg, Marc. *The Papers of Joseph Henry.* Vol. 8: *January 1850–December 1853. The Smithsonian Years.* Washington and London: Smithsonian Institution Press. Print.

Squier, Ephraim George. *Peru: Incidents of Travel and Exploration in the Land of the Incas.* New York: Henry Holt, 1877. Print.

Stanford, Henry Shelton, in Panama to E.G. Squier. Papers of E.G. Squier 1841–1888 (bulk 1846–1874). Manuscript Division, Library of Congress Honduras Interoceanic Railway File, 1853–1870, Box 5, Reel 8: Correspondence, 1853–1870 Reports, George R. Gliddon No. 1, May 16, 1857. Web.

_____, to E.G. Squier Panama, November 17, 1857 (2nd letter). Papers of E.G. Squier 1841–1888 (bulk 1846–1874). Manuscript Division, Library of Congress. Honduras Interoceanic Railway File 1853–1870, Box 5, Reel 8: Correspondence, 1853–1870 Reports, George R. Gliddon No. 2, May 22, 1857. Web.

Stephens, John Lloyd. *Incidents of Travel in Egypt, Arabia Petraea and the Holy Land.* 2 vols. New York: Harper and Bros, 1838; reprint, Norman, OK: University of Oklahoma Press, 1967. Print.

_____, of New York for George R. Gliddon to John Forsyth at the Department of State. June 27, 1837. Record Group 59 (General Records of the Department of State), Records of Application and Recommendation during the Administrations of Martin Van Buren, William Henry Harrison and John Tyler, 1837–1845, folder for George Gliddon. Microfilm.

Trautwine, John. "Letter to E. Geo. Squier from Omoa," May 12, 1857. Papers of E.G. Squier, 1841–1888 (bulk 1846–1874). Manuscript Division, Library of Congress Honduras Interoceanic Railway File, 1853–1870. Box 5, Reel 8. Correspondence, 1853–1870. Reports, George R. Gliddon No. 1, May 16, 1857. Web.

"Treaty with the Sublime Porte." *Message from the President of the United States.* Serial 221, Doc. 250, Adams to English, April 2, 1823, 13. ebook.

"Treaty with the Sublime Porte." *Message from the President of the United States.* Serial 221, Doc. 250, Bradish to Adams, December 20, 1820. 4–5. ebook.

"Treaty with the Sublime Porte." *Message from the President of the United States.* Serial 221, Doc. 250, English to Adams, December 27, 1823. ebook.

"Treaty with the Sublime Porte," *Message from the Pres-*

ident of the United States. Serial 221, Doc. 250, English to Adams, February 8, 1824, 15. ebook.

"The U.S. Naval Lyceum." *Brooklyn Eagle*, Saturday, November 4, 1871. NewspaperArchives.com. Web.

Williams, Caroline Ransom. "The Place of the New York Historical Society in the Growth of American Interest in Egyptology." Index, *New York Historical Society Quarterly Bulletin* 4 (April, 1920–January 1921): 2–20. ebook.

_____. "A Surprising Sales Record." *Bulletin of the Metropolitan Museum of Art*. 1920. 88–89. ebook.

Sarah Haight

Barrett, Walter. *The Old Merchants of New York City*. New York: John W. Lovell, c. 1885. ebook.

Behrens-Abouseif, Doris. *Azbakiyya and its Environs from Azbak to Ismail 1476–1879. Supplement Aux Annals Islamologiques*. Cahier No. 6. Cairo: Institut Francais D'Archeologie Orientale, 1985. Print.

Cooley, James Ewing. *The American in Egypt with Rambles Through Arabia Petraea and The Holy Land during The Year 1839 and 1840*. Elibron Classics Replica Edition. Adamant Media Corporation, 2003. Print.

Finnie, David H. *Pioneers East: The Early American Experience in the Middle East*. Cambridge: Harvard University Press, 1967. Print.

Haight, Sarah Rogers. *Letters from the Old World*. 2 vols. New York: Harper and Brothers, 1840. ebook.

Kirkland, Elizabeth. "Letter to My Dear Sister," April 18, 1832. Henry Cabot Lodge Collection, Box 87, Massachusetts Historical Society, 2. Print.

Kuhnke, LaVerne. *Lives at Risk: Public Health in Nineteenth Century Egypt*. Berkeley: University of California Press, 1990. Print.

Spratt, H.P. *Outline History of Transatlantic Steam Navigation*. Ministry of Education. Science Museum. London: His Majesty's Stationery Office, 1950. Print.

Stephens, John Lloyd. *Incidents of Travel in Egypt, Arabia Petraea and the Holy Land*. 2 vols. New York: Harper and Bros, 1838; reprint, Norman, OK: University of Oklahoma Press, 1967. Print.

Wilkinson, Sir Gardner. *Modern Egypt and Thebes*. 2 vols. London: John Murray, 1843. ebook.

Bayard Taylor

Curtis, George William. *Nile Notes of a Howadji*. New York: Harper & Brothers, 1851. ebook.

Hansen-Taylor, Marie, and Horace E. Scudder. *Life and Letters of Bayard Taylor*. 2 vols. Boston: Houghton Mifflin, 1884. Print.

Hauptman, William. *Charles Gleyre, 1806–1874*. 2 vols. Princeton, NJ: Princeton University Press; Basel, Switzerland: Swiss Institute for Art Research, 1996. Print.

Lane, Edward. *Manners and Customs of the Modern Egyptians*. Society for the Diffusion of Useful Knowledge, 1836. ebook.

Prime, William C. *Boat Life in Egypt and Nubia*. New York: Harper & Brothers, 1857. ebook.

Steegmuller, Francis. *Flaubert in Egypt, A Sensibility on Tour: A Narrative Drawn from Gustave Flaubert's Travel Notes & Letters*. Chicago: Academy Chicago Limited, 1979. Print.

Taylor, Bayard. *Egypt and Iceland in the Year 1874*. New York: Putnam and Sons, 1874. ebook.

_____. *A Journey to Central Africa: or, Life and landscapes from Egypt to the Negro Kingdoms of the White Nile*. 10th ed. New York: G.P. Putnam, 1859. ebook.

Warner, Charles Dudley. *My Winter on the Nile*. Hartford, CT: American Publishing, 1876. ebook.

Charles Hale

91 US 13 Dainese v. Hale. October Term, 1875. http://openjurist.org/print/15999 12/13/2010. Web.

Alpha Delta Phi. Special Despatch to the *Boston Globe*. Boston: June 4, 1875: ProQuest Historical Newspapers *Boston Globe* (1872–1927), 1. Web.

"Biographical Note." Hale Family Papers, 1787–1988. Sophia Smith Collection. Smith College. http://asteria.fivecolleges.edu/findaids/sophiasmith/mnsss90_bioghist.html. Web.

"Charles Hale to William Seward." June 13, 1867, No. 91 and attachment. *Rules for the Consular Courts in Egypt of the United States of America*. Alexandrie: Imp. Francaise Mounds, 1867). Microfilm Publications T-45, Roll 4, August 26, 1865–December 16, 1867. National Archives. Washington, D.C. 1955. Microfilm.

Dainese, Francis. *The History of Mr. Seward's Pet in Egypt: His Acts Denounced and His Usurpations Condemned by the Courts*. Self-published, 1866. Print.

"The Difficulty at Alexandria." *New York Times*. August 17, 1864. http://www.nytimes.com/1864/08/17/news/the-difficulty-at-alexandria.html. Alexandria, Saturday, July 23. Web.

Document 25, John H. Surratt. "Mr. Swann in Naples to Mr. Seward." November 21, 1866. No. 4. United States Department of State/ Executive documents printed by order of the House of Representatives, during the first session of the thirty-ninth Congress, 1865–66. Part 3, 2–3. ebook.

Doyle, The Hon. John F. *The Case of John Harrison Surratt, Jr.* Condensed from a speech before the Surratt Society, September 25, 1999. Printed in the *Surratt Courier*, March 2000. Print.

Farman, Elbert E. *Egypt and Its Betrayal*. New York: Grafton Press. 1908. ebook.

Gordon, Lucie Duff. *Letters from Egypt*. Revised Edition. London: R. Brimley Johnson, 1902. ebook.

Hale, Charles. "The Khedive and his Court." *Atlantic Monthly* 37, No. 223 (May 1876): 513–520. ebook.

Hale, Edward Everett. *Memories of a Hundred Years*. New York: Macmillan, 1904. ebook.

"Mr. Thayer to Mr. Seward." November 12, 1862, No. 24. *Papers Relating to Foreign Affairs, accompanying the Annual Message of the President to the First Session Thirty-Eighth Congress*, Part 2. Washington, D.C.: Government Printing Office, 1864. ebook.

"Mr. Thayer to Mr. Seward." January 23, 1864, No. 44. *Papers Relating to Foreign Affairs, accompanying the Annual message of the President to the Second Session Thirty-Eighth Congress.* Part 4. Washington, D.C.: Government Printing Office, 1865. ebook.

"The National Capital, Action of the House on the Appropriation Bill." *New York Times.* January 25, 1872. http://query.nytimes.com/gst/abstract.html?res= FA0E10FC3C5D1A7493C7AB178AD85F468784F9 . Web.

Newman, James L. *Imperial Footprints: Henry Morton Stanley's African Journeys.* Dulles, VA: Brassey's, 2004. Microfilm.

"Obituary: The Hon. Charles Hale." *New York Times.* March 3, 1882. http://query.nytimes.com/mem/ archive-free/pdf?res=F20C14FB3D5910738DDD AA0894DB405B8284F0D3. Web.

Papers of William Sydney Thayer covering his varied activities, 1835–1895, Accession #3445, M-546, Reels 1, 6, 8. Copy of Thayer's journal for part of 1861, made by his sister Sarah. Special Collections SC-STKS, MSS3445, University of Virginia Library, University of Virginia, Charlottesville, Va. OCLC 647967494. 141. Microfilm.

"Personal." *Chicago Tribune.* May 6, 1872, Google News Archives, ProQuest Historical Newspapers *Chicago Tribune,* 4. Web.

Sadgrove, Philip. "The European Press in Khedive Ismail's Egypt (1863–66): A Neglected Field." Paper presented at 2nd International Symposium History of Printing and Publishing in the languages and Countries of the Middle East, November 2–4, 2005. Bibliotheque nationale de France, Paris. Print.

Wilson, James Grant, and John Fiske. *Appleton's Cyclopedia of American Biography.* Vol. 3. New York: D. Appleton, 1887. Print.

Chaillé-Long

Balch, Edwin Swift. "American Explorers of Africa." *Geographical Review* 5 (January–June 1918): 274–80. ebook.

"Chaillé-Long, Charles. Captain, United States Army." http://www.arlingtoncemetery.net/charles-Chaillé-long.htm Posted: November 12, 2005. Updated: March 4, 2006. Web.

Chaillé-Long, Charles. *Central Africa: Naked Truths of Naked People, An Account of Expeditions to the Lake Victoria Nyanza and Makraka Niam-Niam, West of the Bahr el Ab'ad.* New York: Harper Bros., 1876. ebook.

_____. "England in Egypt and the Soudan by Colonel Charles Chaillé-Long, Formerly Chief of Staff to the Late General Gordon, Governor-General of the Soudan." *North American Review* 168, No. 510 (May 1899): 570–80. Web.

_____. "Expedition from Gondokoro to Lake Victoria and Discovery of Lake Ibrahim." In *Provinces of the Equator.* Publications of the Egyptian General Staff. Part 1: Year 1874. Cairo, London: Printing Office of the General Staff, 1877. ebook.

_____. *My Life in Four Continents.* London: Hutchinson, 1912. Print.

_____. "The Part of the Nile that Colonel Chaillé-Long Discovered." *American Geographical Society Bulletin* 41 (1904): 222, Correspondence. ebook.

_____. *Three Prophets: Chinese Gordon, Mohammed Ahmed, Arabi Pasha. Events before and after the Bombardment of Alexandria.* New York: D. Appleton, 1884. ebook.

_____. "The Uganda Protectorate and the Nile Quest." *Bulletin of the American Geographical Society* 36, No.1 (1904): 52–54. ebook.

Crabites, Pierre. *Americans in the Egyptian Army.* London: George Routledge and Sons, 1938. Print.

Farman, Elbert E. *Egypt and Its Betrayal.* New York: Grafton Press, 1908. ebook.

Garstin, Sir William. "Fifty Years of Nile Exploration, and some of its Results." *Geographical Journal* 33, No. 2 (February 1909): 127–128. ebook.

Google Maps. http://maps.google.com/maps?hl=en& tab=wl. Web.

Icenogle, David W. "The Expedition of Chaillé-Long." *Saudia Aramco World* (November–December 1978): 2– 7. http://www.saudiaramcoworld.com/issue/197806/ the.expeditions.of.Chaillé-long.htm. Web.

Johnston, Sir Harry. *The Nile Quest.* London: Lawrence and Bullen, 1903. ebook.

_____. *The Uganda Protectorate.* New York: Dodd, Mead, 1902. ebook.

Meekins, Lynn R. *Men of Mark in Maryland: Johnson's Makers of America Series, Biographies of Leading Men of the State.* Vol. 11. Baltimore: B.F. Johnson, 1910. ebook.

Moorehead, Alan. *The White Nile.* New York: Harper-Collins, 2000. Print.

"To the Mountains of the Moon: Mapping African Exploration, 1541–1880." http://libweb5.princeton.edu/ visual_materials/maps/websites/africa/contents.html. Web.

"The Nile." Wikipedia. http://en.wikipedia.org/wiki/ Nile#The_search_for_the_source_of_the_Nile. See www.wordiq.com/definition/Lake_Victoria; www. answers.com/topic/lake-victoria; and www.new worldencyclopedia.org/entry/Lake_Victoria. Web.

Oliphant, Laurence. "African Explorers." *North American Review* 124, No. 256 (May–June 1877), APS Online.

Sadgrove, Philip. "The European Press in Khedive Ismail's Egypt (1863–66): A Neglected Field." Paper presented at 2nd International Symposium History of Printing and Publishing in the languages and Countries of the Middle East, November 2–4, 2005. Bibliotheque nationale de France, Paris. Print.

"Summary of Letters and Reports of his Excellency the Governor-General." *Provinces of the Equator.* Publications of the Egyptian General Staff., Part 1: Year 1874. Cairo, London: Printing Office of the General Staff, 1877. ebook.

General Grant

Dunn, John P. *Khedive Ismail's Army.* London and New York: Routledge, 2005. Print.

Farman, Elbert E. *Along the Nile: An Account of The Visit to Egypt of General Ulysses S. Grant and his Tour Through That Country.* New York: Grafton Press, 1904. ebook.

Grant, Jesse Root. *In the Days of My Father General Grant*. With Henry Francis Granger. New York and London: Harper and Brothers, 1925. Print.

Hicks, William H. *General Grant's Tour Around the World*. Chicago: Rand McNally, 1879. Print.

Keating, John M. *With General Grant in the East*. Philadelphia and London: J.B. Lippincott, 1879. Print.

McCabe, James Dabney. *A Tour Around the World by General Grant*. Philadelphia: National, 1879. Print.

Mott, Valentine. *Travels in Europe and the East*. New York: Harper and Brothers, 1842. ebook.

Packard, J.F. *Grant's Tour Around the World*. Cincinnati: Forshee and McMakin, 1880. Print.

Remlap (Palmer), Loomis T. *General U.S. Grant's Tour Around the World*. Chicago: W.M. Farrar. 1880. Print.

Simon, John Y., ed. *The Personal Memoirs of Julia Dent Grant* Carbondale, IL: Southern Illinois University Press, 1975. Print.

Young, John Russell. *Around the World with General Grant*. Vol. 1. New York: American News, 1879. ebook.

Fanny Stone

Chaillé-Long, Colonel. *My Life in Four Continents*. Vol. 2. London: Hutchinson, 1912. Print.

_____. *Three Prophets: Chinese Gordon, Mohammed Ahmed, Arabi Pasha. Events before and after the Bombardment of Alexandria*. New York: D. Appleton, 1884. ebook.

Stone, Fanny. "Diary of an American Girl in Cairo during the War of 1882." *The Century Magazine* 28, No. 2 (June 1884): 288–302. ebook.

Wolf, Simon. *The Presidents I have Known from 1860–1918*. Washington, D.C.: Byron S. Adams. 1918. ebook.

Anna Young Thompson

Anderson, Joseph Anderson, et al. *The Town and City of Waterbury Connecticut*. New Haven: Price and Lee, 1896.

Baedeker, Karl. *Egypt: Handbook for Travelers: Part First: Lower Egypt, with the Fayum and the Peninsula of Sinai*. Leipsic: Karl Baedeker, 1885. ebook.

Encyclopedia Coptica. www.coptic.net/EncyclopediaCoptica/3of 8) 8/30/2007. Web.

Egyptian Maritime Data Bank. http://www.emdb.gov.eg/english/inside_e.aspx?main=eafms&level1=lighthouses. Web.

Favard-Meeks, Christine. "The Present State of the Site of Behbeit el-Hagar." http://www.britishmuseum.org/pdf/3b%20The%20present%20state%20of%20the%20site.pdf. Web.

Finnie, David H. *Pioneers East: The Early American Experience in the Middle East*. Cambridge: Harvard University Press, 1967. 133. Print.

Fisk, Pliny. "Letter from Mr. Fisk to the Corresponding Secretary, respecting the sickness and death of Mr. Parsons. Alexandria February 10, 1822." *Washington Theological Repertory* 3, No. 12 (July 1822): 383. Print.

Harmless, William. *Desert Christians: An Introduction to Early Christian Monasticism*. New York: Oxford University Press, 2004. Print.

"History of American Missionary." Online catalog. *American Board of Commissioners for Foreign Missions Records*, ca. 1810–1985 RG 4352/RG 1200. http://www.14beacon.org/fguides/abcfm1.htm. Web.

Hogg, Rena L. *A Masterbuilder on the Nile: being a record of the life and aims of John Hogg*. Pittsburgh: United Presbyterian Board of Publication, 1914. ebook.

Kinnear, Elizabeth Kelsey. *She Sat Where They Sat: A Memoir of Anna Young Thompson of Egypt*. Grant Rapids, MI: Christian World Mission Books, William B. Erdmans, 1971. Print.

Pierson, Arthur T. *The Missionary Review of the World*. Vol. 22. New York: Funk and Wagnalls, 1899. ebook.

Sharkey, Heather J. *American Evangelicals in Egypt*. Princeton: Princeton University Press, 2008. Print.

Thompson, Anna Young. "Diary of a Trip on the *Ibis*." Anna Young Thompson (1851–1932) Papers 1868–1931, Presbyterian Historical Society, RG 58, Box 1, Folder 12, Microfilm, MF. POS 1009. Microfilm.

_____. "The Zar in Egypt." In *The Influence of Animism on Islam: An Account of Popular Superstitions*, Samuel Marinus Zwemer, ed. New York: Macmillan, 1930. ebook.

Thompson, Jason. "Osman Effendi: A Scottish Convert to Islam in Early 19th Century Egypt." In *Historians in Cairo: Essays in Honor of George Scanlon*, Jill Edwards, ed. Cairo: AUC Press, 2002. Print.

Watson, Charles R. *Egypt and the Christian Crusade*. New York: Young People's Missionary Movement, 1907. ebook.

Walter Granger

Beadnell, H.J.L. *The Topography and Geology of the Fayûm Province of Egypt*. Cairo: National Printing Department, 1905. ebook.

Granger, Walter. "Report on the Expedition To The Fayûm, Egypt 1907." In *Notes from Diary-Fayûm Trip, 1907*, Vincent L. Morgan and Spencer G. Lucas, eds. Albuquerque: New Mexico Museum of Natural History and Science, 2002. ebook.

_____. *Report on the Expedition to the Fayûm, Egypt, 1907*. Archives, Department of Vertebrate Paleontology, American Museum of Natural History. ebook.

The Granger Papers Project. http://users.rcn.com/granger.nh.ultranet/. Web.

"J.P. Morgan Sails; is Going to Egypt." *New York Times*. Sunday, December 31, 1911. http://query.nytimes.com/mem/archivefree/pdf?res=F50B15FD395E13738DDDA80B94DA415B818DF1D3. Web.

Morgan, Vincent L., and Spencer G. Lucas. "Walter Granger, 1872–1941, Paleontologist." *Bulletin of the New Mexico Museum of Natural History and Science*. Bulletin 19. Albuquerque: New Mexico Museum of Natural History and Science, 2002. ebook.

Osborn, Henry Fairfield. "Hunting the Ancestral Elephant in the Fayûm Desert: Discoveries of the Recent African Expedition of the American Museum of

Natural History." *The Century Magazine* 74, No. 6 (1907). ebook.

_____. "New Fossil Mammals from the Fayûm Oligocene, Egypt." Article 16, *Bulletin of the American Museum of Natural History* 24 (1908): 265–72. ebook.

Theodore Roosevelt: An Autobiography. "Boyhood and Youth, 1913." http://www.bartleby.com/55/1.html. Web.

Theodore M. Davis

Adams, John M. *Doubtless the Sky Will be Brighter: Theodore Davis and his Excavators, 1900–1914*. Unpublished draft, 1. Print.

_____. "Generous Benefactor or Arrogant Ignoramus? Theodore Davis and his Excavators, 1900–1914." *Kmt: A Modern Journal of Ancient Egypt* 22, No. 2 (Summer 2011). Print.

Andrews, Emma B. *A Journal on the Bedwin 1889–1913: A Diary kept on board the dahabeyeh of Theodore M. Davis during seventeen trips up the Nile*. Vols.1 and 2. Mss.916.2.An2. Philadelphia: American Philosophical Society. Microfilm.

"A Brief History of the Supreme Council of Antiquities (SCA): 1858 to present." Supreme Council of Antiquities. http://www.sca-egypt.org/eng/SCA_History.htm. Web.

Davis, Theodore M. "The Finding of the Tomb of Iouiya and Touiyou." In *The Tomb of Iouiya and Touiyou*. London: Archibald Constable, 1907. ebook.

_____. "The Finding of the Tomb of Queen Tiyi." In *The Tomb of Queen Tiyi*. London: Constable, 1910. Print.

_____. "The Finding of the Tomb of Siphtah, the Unnamed Gold Tomb, and the Animal Pit Tombs." In *The Tomb of Siphtah*. London: Archibald Constable, 1908. ebook.

_____. *Mr. Theodore M. Davis Excavations: Bibân el Molûk: The Tomb of Thoutmosis IV*. Westminster: Archibald Constable, 1904. ebook.

Hirsch, Mark D. "More Light on Boss Tweed." *Political Science Quarterly* (The Academy of Political Science), 1945. Print.

"KV-46 (Yuya and Thuyu). Atlas of the Valley of the Kings." Theban Mapping Project. http://www.thebanmappingproject.com/sites/browse_tomb_860.html. Web.

"KV-60 SIT-RA, Atlas of the Valley of the Kings," Theban Mapping Project. http://www.thebanmappingproject.com/atlas/index_kv.asp. Web.

"Mr. Frost Boiling Over." *New York Times*. November 8, 1879. http://query.nytimes.com/gst/abstract.html?res=F70816F73B5A127B93CAA9178AD95F4D8784F9. Web.

Naville, Edouard, et al. *Theodore M. Davis's Excavations: Biban el Molûk: The Tomb of Hâtshopsîtû*. London: Archibald Constable, 1906. ebook.

Newberry, P.E. *Scarabs: An Introduction to the Study of Egyptian Seals and Signet Rings*. London: Archibald Constable, 1906. Print.

"Newport Mansions: The Reefs." The Preservation Society of Newport County. http://www.newportmansions.org/page9647.cfm. Web.

"Theft Centuries Old at Last Revealed." *New York Times*. May 17, 1908. http://query.nytimes.com/gst/abstract.html?res=FA0A10FB3F5A17738DDDAE0994DD405B888CF1D3. Web.

"Theodore Davis." Ancient Egyptian Website, Egyptology through images. http://www.ancient-egypt.co.uk/people/pages/theodore_davis.htm. Updated on August 16, 2009. Web.

Tytus, Robb de Peyster. "The Palace of Amenhotep III, Husband of Queen Thiy." *New Century Magazine* 78, No. 2 (June 1909): 738–38. ebook.

Vivian, Cassandra, et al. *Father of Rivers: A Travelers Companion to the Nile Valley*. Cairo: Trade Routes Enterprises, 1989. Print.

Weigall, Arthur E.P. "A New Egyptian Discovery: The Tomb of Horemheb." *New Century Magazine* 78, No. 2 (June 1909): 289–293. ebook.

Wiles, David. "Boss Tweed and the Tammany Hall Machine." EAPS 760. http://www.albany.edu/~dkw42/tweed.html. Web.

Index

Page numbers in **bold italics** indicate illustrations

www.ingramcontent.com/pod-product-compliance
Lightning Source LLC
Chambersburg PA
CBHW080550270326
41929CB00019B/3255